EUROPEAN BOOKDEALERS

LIBRAIRIES D'OCCASION EUROPÉENNES

EUROPÄISCHE ANTIQUARIATE

Uniform with this volume are:

Pareil à ce tome sont:
Diesem Bande gleich sind:

DEALERS IN BOOKS

A directory of dealers in secondhand
and antiquarian books in the
British Isles

BOOKDEALERS IN NORTH AMERICA

A directory of dealers in secondhand
and antiquarian books in Canada and
the United States of America

EUROPEAN BOOKDEALERS

A DIRECTORY OF DEALERS IN SECONDHAND AND
ANTIQUARIAN BOOKS ON THE CONTINENT OF EUROPE

LIBRAIRIES D'OCCASION EUROPÉENNES

UN RÉPERTOIRE DE MARCHANDS DE LIVRES ANCIENS
ET D'OCCASION DE L'EUROPE CONTINENTALE

EUROPÄISCHE ANTIQUARIATE

EIN ADRESSBUCH DER ANTIQUARIATSBUCHHÄNDLER
IN DEN EUROPÄISCHEN LÄNDERN

1976–78

THIRD EDITION: TROISIÈME ÉDITION: DRITTE AUSGABE

LONDON : SHEPPARD PRESS

First published: Première édition: Erste Auflage
(1967–9) August 1967

Second edition: Deuxième édition: Zweite Ausgabe
(1970–72) March 1971

Third edition: Troisième édition: Dritte Ausgabe
(1976–78) October 1975

ISBN 0 900661 12 7

Printed by : Imprimeur : Druck :

W & J Mackay Limited
Chatham, Kent, England

CONTENTS

PREFACE ix

TELEGRAPHIC ADDRESSES xiii

REFERENCE BOOKS xix

PERIODICALS.. xxi

LIST OF COUNTRIES xxii

EXPLANATORY NOTE xxiii

GEOGRAPHICAL SECTION xxix
    Principal list of dealers arranged
    according to their country

ALPHABETICAL INDEX 145
    List of dealers arranged alphabetically

SPECIALITY INDEX.. 175
    List of dealers arranged according
    to their speciality

LIST OF ADVERTISERS 215

TABLE DE MATIÈRE

PRÉFACE x

ADRESSES TÉLÉGRAPHIQUES xiii

BIBLIOGRAPHIE xix

JOURNAUX xxi

LISTE DE PAYS xxii

EXPLICATIONS xxiv

SECTION GÉOGRAPHIQUE xxix
    Liste principale de marchands selon leurs pays

INDEX ALPHABÉTIQUE 145
    Liste de marchands en ordre alphabétique

INDEX DE SPÉCIALITÉS 175
    Liste de marchands selon leurs domaines
    de spécialisation

LISTE DES ANNONCES 215

INHALTSANGABE

VORWORT xi

TELEGRAMMADRESSEN xiii

NACHSCHLAGEBÜCHER xix

ZEITSCHRIFTEN xxi

VERZEICHNIS DER LÄNDER xxii

ERLÄUTERUNGEN xxv

GEOGRAPHISCHER ABSCHNITT xxix
    Hauptverzeichnis der Händler nach Ländern

ALPHABETISCHES VERZEICHNIS 145
    Händler in alphabetischer Reihenfolge

SPEZIALGEBIETE 175
    Verzeichnis spezialisierter Händler

VERZEICHNIS DER INSERENTEN 215

WARNING

ADVERTISSEMENT

ZUR BEACHTUNG!

PREFACE

This is the third edition of a comprehensive directory of dealers in second-hand and antiquarian books on the continent of Europe and is a companion volume to the well-known directories for the British Isles and North America, which are now in their eighth and sixth editions respectively.

In compiling it the editors encountered a number of problems, mostly arising from the use of so many different languages. After much experimenting it was decided that the entries for French and German-speaking countries should be in their own languages and all the rest in English. It was thought that most dealers, librarians, and collectors would have a working knowledge of one of these languages, and that by supplying a simple translation card that served also as a bookmark all entries could be easily understood.

In solving orthographical problems and those caused by the amalgamation of several alphabets into one index, due regard was paid to accuracy and convention, but where they seemed to conflict with common sense the latter was allowed to triumph.

Names are usually given in the form used by the person or country to which they belong, so one will find MÜLLER and MUELLER, HELSINKI and HELSINGFORS. Accents and umlauts have been printed, but in indexing they have been ignored, Ø and Ö being included among the O, and LL with L, because it was thought that most people would look for them there.

The publishers would be glad to receive information about any dealers who have not been included, or any alterations or additions that should be made in the next edition.

PRÉFACE

Cette troisième édition d'un répertoire qui comprend les marchands de livres d'occasion et anciens dans toute l'Europe continentale, se joint à celles, pour les Iles Britanniques et l'Amérique du Nord dont respectivement la huitième et la sixième éditions ont paru.

En composant de répertoire les éditeurs avaient rencontré de nombreux problèmes provenant pour la plupart de l'emploi de tant de langues différentes. Après des tentatives diverses on décida de donner les reseignements pour les pays où on parle français ou allemand dans ces langues-ci, tandis que tout le reste serait en anglais, puisqu'on pouvait supposer que la plupart des marchands, bibliothécaires et amateurs de livres auraient au moins une connaissance élémentaire d'une de ces trois langues. En outre, pour faciliter la comprehension, une simple carte de traduction fut ajouté qui peut servir en même temps de signet.

Lorsqu'il s'agissait de résoudre des difficultés d'orthographe ou des problèmes crées par l'amalgamation de différents alphabets en un seul index, le plus grand régard fut accordé à la précision ainsi qu'à la tradition orthographique, et ces deux principes ne furent abandonnés que dans le cas ou ils étaient en criant désaccord avec le sens commun.

En général les noms propres sont indiqués dans la forme habituelle dans le pays d'origine. Ainsi on trouvera MÜLLER et MUELLER, HELSINKI et HELSINGFORS. Les accents et les umlauts, bienqu'imprimés sont ignorés dans l'index lui-même, on trouvera alors Ø et Ö parmi O, et LL parmi L, puisque sans doute la plupart des gens seront naturellement portés a les y rechercher.

Les éditeurs seraient très reconnaissants de recevoir des renseignements sur des marchands omis dans cette édition, ou sur les changements ou addition qu'il faudrait faire dans la quatrième édition.

VORWORT

Dies ist die dritte Ausgabe eines umfassenden Adressbuches von Antiquaren in Kontinentaleuropa. Sie folgt den bereits wohlbekannten Bänden für die britischen Inseln und Nordamerika, deren achte, bzw. sechste Auflage bereits erschienen sind.

Bei ihrer Zusammenstellung stiessen die Herausgeber auf mehrere Schwierigkeiten, die hauptsächlich vom Gebrauch so vieler verschiedener Sprachen herrührten. Nach einigem Hin- und Herexperimentieren wurde beschlossen, Angaben in Bezug auf deutsche und französisch sprechende Länder in der Originalsprache und alles übrige auf englisch abzufassen. Es wurde angenommen, dass die meisten Händler, Bibliothekare und Sammler ausreichende Kenntnisse einer dieser drei Sprachen besitzen, und dass durch Beifügung einer einfachen Übersetzungskarte, die auch als Lesezeichen dienen kann, alle Angaben leicht verständlich sind.

Wenn es sich darum handelte, orthographische Probleme zu lösen oder verschiedene Alphabete in einem Index zu vereinen, wurde mit grösster Genauigkeit und im Sinne der Übereinkunft verfahren, ausgenommen dort, wo dies dem gesunden Menschenverstand widersprochen hätte.

Eigennamen sind gewöhnlich in der in dem Herkunftslande üblichen Form eingetragen: so findet man z.B. MÜLLER und MUELLER, HELSINKI und HELSINGFORS. Akzente und Umlaute wurden gedruckt, aber beim Aufstellen der Verzeichnisse nicht beachtet, Ø und Ö sind unter O, und LL unter L zu finden, da man annehmen konnte, dass die meisten Benutzer sie dort nachschlagen würden.

Die Verleger wären dankbar, von Händlern, die in dieser Ausgabe nicht enthalten sind, in Kenntnis gesetzt und über Vorschläge für Änderungen und Addenda für die vierte Auflage unterrichtet zu werden.

TELEGRAPHIC ADDRESSES
ADRESSES TÉLÉGRAPHIQUES
TELEGRAMMADRESSEN

ANTIQVA, GOTEBORG	Thulin & Ohlson
ARDLOWY, PARIS	Edouard Loewy
ARTANCIEN, ZURICH	L'Art Ancien, S.A.
ARTBOOKS, 's-GRAVENHAGE	Martin Veeneman
ARTBRUG, AMSTERDAM	Antiquariaat Broekema
ARTUS, BERN	Kornfeld & Klipstein
ATHBOOKS, AMSTERDAM	Athenaeum Antiquarian Booksellers
BAERLIN, PARIS	Alexandre Baer
BENPER, AMSTERDAM	John Benjamins
BERGBOOKS, AMSTERDAM	Van Berg Antiquariaat
BIBLIOCRAMER, GENÈVE	Galerie Gérald Cramer
BOERNERKUNST, DÜSSELDORF	C. G. Boerner
BOGKUNST, KØBENHAVN	Rosenkilde & Bagger
BOKBOR, OSLO	Børsums Forlag
BOKBORJE, STOCKHOLM	Björck & Börjesson, A.B.
BOKFRITZE, STOCKHOLM	Fritzes Kungl Hovbokhandel
BOOKBUSCK, KØBENHAVN	Arnold Busck
BOOKS, REYKJAVIK	Snaebjorn, Jonnson & Co.
BOOKS, 's-GRAVENHAGE	Martinus Nijhoff
BOOKBEE, UTRECHT	J. L. Beijers, N.V.

xiii

BUCHKRIEG, WIEN	Walter Krieg
BUCHLAUBE, ZÜRICH	August Laube & Sohn
BUCHSAGNER, MÜNCHEN	Kubon & Sagner
BUCHTENNER, HEIDELBERG ..	Helmut Tenner
BUCHWASMUTH, BERLIN	Wasmuth Buchhandlung
BUCHWENNER, OSNABRUCK ..	H. Th. Wenner
BUECHERHAUS, FRANKFURT ..	Peter Naacher
BUCHERSTUBE, KONSTANZ ..	S. & P. Neser (Bücherstube am See)
BURCHARD, WUPPERTAL	Friedrich Burchard
CANTABILE, GENÈVE	E. Engelberts, S.A.
CHARAUTOGRAPHE, PARIS	Maison Charavay
CURIOBOOK, BRUXELLES	Louis Moorthamers
DAMMANFIKK, OSLO	Damm's Antikvariat
DEGRAAF, NIEUWKOOP	Antiquariaat de Graaf
DENOBELEF, PARIS	F. de Nobele
DESIDERATA, ZÜRICH	Büchersuchdienst Pinkus & Co.
DOERLINGANT, HAMBURG	F. Dörling
DOMSCH, FIRENZE	Domsch & Cie.
ELWERT, MARBURG	N. G. Elwert'sche Universitäts Buchhandlung
ENNIBOOK, AMSTERDAM	N. Israel
ERASMUS, TORINO	Bottega d'Erasmus
ESMO, ATHENS	Les Amis du Livre
EUROACADEMIC, BRUXELLES ..	Presses Academiques Europeén, S.A.
FAB, STUTTGART	F. A. Brockhaus

GALBAS, BERLIN	Galerie Gerda Bassenge
GARISENDA, BOLOGNA	Garisenda Libri
GEROLDBUCH, WIEN	Gerold & Co.
GILBURG, WIEN	Gilhofers Buch und Kunst Antiquariat
GILHAG, LUZERN	Giohofer & Ranschburg, GmbH.
GSELLIUS, BERLIN	Gsellius'sche Buchhandlung
GUMPERTS, GÖTEBORG	Gumperts Bokhandel
HACHTER, PARIS	Hachette
HAFNIABOOKS, KØBENHAVN ..	Grønholt Pedersens Boghus
HECKBOOKS, WIEN	V. A. Heck
HEITZEDITION, STRASBOURG ..	Paul H. Heitz
HERBERTBOOK, BERN	Herbert Lang & Cie
HYCBOOKS, AMSTERDAM	Halcyon Antiquariaat
IFFCASS, LONDON-WC2	Sheppard Press
INGOBOOKS, WIEN	Ingo Nebehay
ISRAELBOOK, AMSTERDAM	B. M. Israel
KLEMANTIK, STOCKHOLM	H. Klemmings Antikvariat
KREBSERCO, THUN	W. Krebser & Co.
LAURIARTH, PARIS	Arthur Lauria
LIBLAGET, Paris	Léonce Laget
LIBRANNICA, KØBENHAVN ..	Branners Bibliofile Antikvariat
LIBHANKARD, BRUXELLES	Hankard Librairie, S.P.R.L.
LIBORIENT, PARIS	Paul Geuthner
LIBRATUL, BRUXELLES	Fl. Tulkens

LIBREMON, NEUCHATEL	Mme. Eugene Reymond
LIBRI, NAPOLI	Libreria di lo Schiavo
LIBRIKA, ATHENS	Libraire Kauffmann
LIBRIRE, MILANO	Renzo Rizzi
LIBRISACK, GENÈVE	H. Sack
LIBRISANTIK, STOCKHOLM	Libris Antikvariatet
LIBRORUM, BUREN	Frits A. M. Knuf
LIBROSC, FIRENZE	Leo Olschki
LIVRANCIEN, LAUSANNE	Maurice Bridel
LUBARDON, MADRID	Louis Bardon
LUDROS, HILVERSUM	Ludwig Rosenthals Antiquariaat
MADLIGERSCHWAB, ZÜRICH	Hilde & Rud. Madligerschwab
MEDIAEVIST, BONN	Emil Semmel
MEDIZINBUCH, FREIBURG	Hans Ferdinand Schulz
MILLBOOKS, SOEST	Antiquariaat van Coevorden
MOBIN, AMSTERDAM	C. P. J. van der Peet
MOLINSUR, MADRID	Gabriel Molina
MUSICANT, BILTHOVEN	A. B. Creyghton
MUSIKANTIQUAR, TUTZING	Hans Schneider
MUSIKDOB, WIEN	Ludwig, Doblinger
NATURA, BERLIN	R. Friendländer & Sohn
NORDANTIQUARIAT, ROSTOCK	Norddeutsches Antiquariat
NUMISMATIQUE, AMSTERDAM	Jacques Schuman
OFLIBRI, BRUXELLES	Office International de Librairie, S.P.R.L.

PIBY, PARIS	Pierre Berès
PINCBOOKS, TEL-AVIV	F. Pinczower
POLIFILO, MILANO	Il Polifilo
PRELIBER, TORINO	Arturo Pregliasco
RIGHTBOOK, AMSTERDAM	Menno Hertzberger
ROENNELLBOK, STOCKHOLM	G. Rönnell
ROOSBOOKS, PARIS	Jean Rousseau-Girard
ROTHACBUCH, BERLIN	Oscar Rothacker
SANBABILA, MILANO	Peppi Battaglini
SANDIQUAR, WIESBADEN	Dr. Martin Sändig
SCHUMANNBUCH, ZÜRICH	Helmut Schumann
STATLIVRE, GENÈVE	M. Slatkine & Fils
SWEZEIT, AMSTERDAM	Swets & Zeitlinger
THOMLIB, PARIS	Lucien Scheler
THULANTIK, STOCKHOLM	Thulin's Antikvariat
THULIMAGO, LINDINGO	P. Thulin
UPSALABOK, UPSALA	A. Cederbergs Eftr., A.B.
VIRIDITAS, AMSTERDAM	B. R. Grüner
VITRUV, BERLIN	Bruno Hessling
WALEDIT, PARIS	Editart
WEGA, LUGARNO	Fuchs & Reposo
WIDAWAKE, PARIS	Dawson-France, S.A.
WUENDISCH, HEIDELBERG	Hans Wündisch

REFERENCE BOOKS
BIBLIOGRAPHIE   NACHSCHLAGEBÜCHER

AFRICAN BOOKS IN PRINT. Part I, 6,000 titles, ed. Hans H. Zell. £15.50 (Mansell, 3 Bloomsbury Place, London WCIA 2QA)

AMERICAN BOOK PRICES CURRENT. ed. Edward Lazare (509 Fifth Avenue, New York, N.Y. 10017)

AMERICAN BOOK TRADE DIRECTORY, (R. R. Bowker Company, 1180 Avenue of the Americas, New York 10036. U.S.A.)

AMERICAN LIBRARY DIRECTORY (Bowker, New York) ed. Helaine MacKeigan

AUSTRALIAN AND PACIFIC BOOK PRICES CURRENT. ed. Jennifer Alison & Barbara Palmer. (O.P. Books Pty. Ltd., P.O. Box 591, Brookvale, N.S.W. 2100, Australia)

BOOK-AUCTION RECORDS (Dawsons of Pall Mall, Cannon House, Folkestone, Kent, England)

BOOKDEALERS IN NORTH AMERICA, a directory of dealers in secondhand and antiquarian books in Canada and the U.S.A. (Sheppard Press, P.O. Box 42, 15 James Street, London WC2E 8BX)

BOOKMANS PRICE INDEX (Gale Research Company, Book Tower, Detroit, Michigan 48226, U.S.A.)

BOOKS IN PRINT (U.S.A.) lists 435,000 titles. (Bowker, New York)

BRITISH NATIONAL BIBLIOGRAPHY. New British books published for the year. (B.N.B., 7 Rathbone Street, London W1P 2AL)

CANADIAN BOOK PRICES CURRENT. ed. Robert M. Hamilton. (McClelland and Stewart, 25 Hollinger Road, Toronto 16, Canada)

CUMULATIVE BOOK INDEX, world index of books in the English language (H. W. Wilson Company, 950 University Avenue, New York 10452 N.Y. USA)

DEALERS IN BOOKS. A directory of dealers in secondhand and antiquarian books in the British Isles (Sheppard Press, P.O. Box 42, 15 James Street, London WC2E 8BX)

INTERNATIONAL DIRECTORY OF ANTIQUARIAN BOOK-SELLERS. Published by I.L.A.B.

INTERNATIONAL MAPS AND ATLASES IN PRINT. ed. Kenneth Winch (Bowker, New York)

INTERNATIONAL GUIDE TO THE ACADEMIC MARKET PLACE, (Bowker, New York)

INTERNATIONAL BIBLIOGRAPHY OF REPRINTS/INTER-NATIONALES VERZEICHNIS DER REPRINTS. ed. Christa

Gnirss. Band I, Books and Serials; Band II, Annuals and Periodicals. (Verlag Dokumentation, München)

INTERNATIONAL DIRECTORY OF ARTS. ed. Helmut Rauschenbusch. (Deutsche Zentraldruckerei, 1 Berlin 61, Dessauerstrasse 6–7)

INTERNATIONAL LITERARY MARKET PLACE. ed. J. A. Neal (Bowker, New York)

JAHRBUCH DER AUKTIONSPREISE. Buchauktionen in Deutschland, Österreich, Niederland und Schweiz. (Hauswedell, Pöseldorferweg 1 2 Hamburg 13. Deutschland)

LIBROS EN VENTA. Lists 120,000 Spanish language books available. ed. Mary Turner. (Bowker, New York)

SUBJECT GUIDE TO BOOKS IN PRINT. Classified list of books from American publishers (Bowker, New York)

ULRICH'S INTERNATIONAL PERIODICALS DIRECTORY (Bowker, New York)

PERIODICALS

JOURNAUX ZEITSCHRIFTEN

ANTIQUARIAN BOOKMAN'S WEEKLY, books for sale and wanted in U.S.A. (AB Weekly P.O. Box 1100, Newark, N.J. 17101, U.S.A.)

THE BOOKDEALER, trade weekly for books wanted and for sale. Subscription £5·50/$14.00 (Fudge & Co., Sardinia House, Sardinia Street, London WC2A 3NW)

THE BOOKSELLER, weekly journal of the new book trade in Britain. Subscription £8·50. (J. Whitaker and Sons, 13 Bedford Square, London WC1B 3JE)

THE CLIQUE, antiquarian booksellers weekly. (The Clique, 109 Wembley Park Drive, Wembley HA 8HG, England)

EDITION, Book advertiser, Buch-Anzeiger, Indicateur du Livre. 4 pro Jahr. (Stauffacher Verlag, Birmensdorferstrasse 318, 8055 Zürich, Schweiz)

GAZZETTINO LIBRARIO, Richieste ed offerte di libri antichi e moderni. Pubblicazione mensile (Gazzettino Librario, Via J. Nardi 6, 50132 Firenze, Italia)

PUBLISHERS WEEKLY (U.S.A.), weekly record of new books published etc. (Publishers Weekly, 1180 Avenue of the Americas, New York, N.Y. 10036, U.S.A.)

TAAB WEEKLY, the Library Bookseller. (TAAB Weekly, P.O. Box 7791, Philadelphia 1, Pa. U.S.A.)

LIST OF COUNTRIES
LISTE DES PAYS
VERZEICHNIS DER LÄNDER

	English	*Français*	*Deutsch*
BELGIE/BELGIQUE	BELGIUM	BELGIQUE	BELGIEN
BULGARIYA	BULGARIA	BULGARIE	BULGARIEN
CESKOSLOVENSKO	CZECHO-SLOVAKIA	TCHECO-SLOVAQUIE	TSCHECHO-SLOWAKEI
DANMARK	DENMARK	DANEMARK	DANEMARK
DEUTSCHLAND	GERMANY	ALLEMAGNE	DEUTSCHLAND
ELLAS	GREECE	GRÈCE	GRIECHENLAND
ESPAÑA	SPAIN	ESPAGNE	SPANIEN
FRANCE	FRANCE	FRANCE	FRANKREICH
ISLAND	ICELAND	ISLANDE	ISLAND
ISRAEL	ISRAEL	ISRAEL	ISRAEL
ITALIA	ITALY	ITALIE	ITALIEN
JUGOSLAVIJA	YUGOSLAVIA	YOUGOSLAVIE	JUGOSLAWIEN
KYPRIAKI DIMOKRATIA KIBRIS CUMHURIYETI	CYPRUS	CHYPRE	ZYPERN
LIECHTENSTEIN	LIECHTENSTEIN	LIECHTENSTEIN	LIECHTENSTEIN
LUXEMBOURG	LUXEMBOURG	LUXEMBOURG	LUXEMBURG
MAGYARORSZAG	HUNGARY	HONGRIE	UNGARN
MALTA	MALTA	MALTE	MALTA
NEDERLAND	NETHERLANDS/HOLLAND	PAYS-BAS	NIEDERLANDE
NORGE	NORWAY	NORVÈGE	NORWEGEN
ÖSTERREICH	AUSTRIA	AUTRICHE	ÖSTERREICH
POLSKA	POLAND	POLOGNE	POLEN
PORTUGAL	PORTUGAL	PORTUGAL	PORTUGAL
ROMINA	ROUMANIA	ROUMANIE	RUMANIEN
SCHWEIZ/SUISSE/SVIZZERA	SWITZERLAND	SUISSE	SCHWEIZ
SOYUZ SOVYETSKIKH SOTSIALISTICHESKIKH RESPUBLIK (C.C.C.P.)	U.S.S.R.	U.R.S.S.	U.D.S.S.R.
SUOMI	FINLAND	FINLANDE	FINNLAND
SVERIGE	SWEDEN	SUÈDE	SCHWEDEN

EXPLANATORY NOTE

The information given, if available, for each entry is:

Name and address of business.

Name of proprietor if different from business name.

Telephone number and telegraphic address.

Date of establishment.

Type of premises occupied. If they are described as a shop or store they are, unless otherwise stated, open to the public and members of the trade without appointment during normal business hours. If described as a storeroom or private premises, information as to whether an appointment is necessary or not is added.

Type and size of the business. Whether the firm deals in new books also and the size of the normal stock of secondhand and antiquarian books.

Under 2,000 volumes = very small stock.

2,000–5,000 volumes = small stock.

5,000–10,000 volumes = medium stock.

10,000–20,000 volumes = large stock

20,000 + volumes = very large stock.

In what subjects, if any, the business specialises and if catalogues are issued.

Language in which correspondence can be conducted in addition to the local language.

Bank and account number.

Membership of any trade associations.

EXPLICATIONS

Dans chaque cas les détails suivant ont, si possible, été fournis:

Nom et adresse de la maison.

Nom du propriétaire s'il diffère du nom de la maison.

Numéro de téléphone et adresse télégraphique.

Date de la fondation.

Genre de local occupé. S'il est décrit comme boutique il est ouvert au public et aux commerçants négociants pendant les heures normales d'ouverture sans qu'il soit nécessaire de prendre préablement un rendez-vous. Si, par contre, il est dècrit comme dèpôt ou domicile il est indiqué si un rendez-vous est nécessaire ou non.

Type et grandeur de la maison. Si elle fait aussi le commerce de livres neufs et l'étendue du stock en livres anciens et d'occasion.

Moins que 2,000 volumes = assez restreint stock.

2,000–5,000 volumes = restreint stock.

5,000–10,000 volumes = moyen stock.

10,000–20,000 volumes = important stock.

20,000 + volumes = très important stock.

Si la maison se spécialise dans un certain domaine, si oui, lequel, et si des catalogues sont issus.

Langues, autres que celle du pays, dans lesquelles une correspondence est possible.

La Banque et le numéro du compte.

Si le marchand est membre d'une association de négociants.

ERLÄUTERUNGEN

Jede Eintragung enthält wo möglich folgende Angaben:

Name und Adresse der Firma.

Names des Besitzers, falls anders als der Firmenname.

Telefon- und Telegrammadresse.

Datum der Gründung.

Art des Lokals. Wo es als Laden beschrieben ist, ist es, wenn nicht speziell erwähnt, für das Publikum und Branchen-mitglieder während der normalen Geschäftszeit ohne vorherige Anmeldung geöffnet. Wo es als Lagerraum oder Wohnung bezeichnet ist, wird angegeben, ob vorherige Anmeldung erwünscht wird oder nicht.

Art und Grösse des Geschäfts. Ob die Firma auch mit neuen Büchern handelt, und die Grösse des Vorrat an antiquarischen Büchern.

Weniger als 2,000 Bände = sehr kleiner Vorrat.

2,000–5,000 Bände = kleiner Vorrat.

5,000–10,000 Bände = mittelgrosser Vorrat.

10,000–20,000 Bände = grosser Vorrat.

20,000 + Bände = sehr grosser Vorrat.

Auf welchem Gebiet die Firma spezialisiert, wenn überhaupt, und ob Kataloge enthältlich sind.

In welcher Sprache, abgesehen von der Landesprache, korrespondiert werden kann.

Bank und Kontonummer.

Mitgliedschaft von Geschäftsverbänden.

TRANSLATION
TRADUCTION
ÜBERSETZUNG

English	Français	Deutsch
P. O. Box	BOITE POSTALE	POSTFACH
PROPRIETOR	PROPRIÉTAIRE	INHABER
TELEPHONE	TÉLÉPHONE	TELEFON
TELEGRAPHIC ADDRESS	ADRESSE TÉLÉGRAPHIQUE	TELEGRAMM-ADRESSE
ESTABLISHED	FONDÈE	GEGRÜNDET
PREMISES	LOCAUX	GESCHÄFTSRÄUME
Shop	Boutique	Laden
Storeroom	Dépôt	Lagerräume
Private House	Domicile	Wohnung
BY APPOINTMENT	SUR RENDEZ-VOUS	NACH VEREINBARUNG
CLOSED	FERMÉ	GESCHLOSSEN
Monday	Lundi	Montag
Tuesday	Mardi	Dienstag
Wednesday	Mecredi	Mitwoch
Thursday	Jeudi	Donnerstag
Friday	Vendredi	Freitag
Saturday	Samedi	Samstag
Morning	Martın	Morgen
Afternoon	Aprésmidi	Nachmittag
VERY SMALL STOCK	ASSEZ RESTREINT STOCK	SEHR KLEINER VORRAT
SMALL STOCK	RESTREINT STOCK	KLEINER VORRAT
MEDIUM STOCK	MOYEN STOCK	MITTELGROSSER VORRAT
LARGE STOCK	IMPORTANT STOCK	GROSSER VORRAT
VERY LARGE STOCK	TRÈS IMPORTANT STOCK	SEHR GROSSER VORRAT
SPECIALITIES	SPECIALITÉS	SPECIALGEBIETE
CATALOGUES ON REQUEST	CATALOGUES SUR DEMANDE	KATALOGE AUF WUNSCH
CORRESPONDENCE	CORRESPONDANCE	KORRESPONDENZ
BANK	BANQUE	BANK
POST CHEQUE ACCOUNTS	COMPTES DE CHÈQUES POSTAUX	POSTSCHECK-KONTEN
MEMBER	MEMBRE	MITGLIED

Prop.: PROPRIETOR
T.: TELEPHONE
T.A.: TELEGRAPHIC ADDRESS
Spec.: SPECIALITIES
Cat.: CATALOGUES ON REQUEST
Corresp.: CORRESPONDENCE
B: BANK
C.P.: POST CHEQUE ACCOUNTS
M: MEMBER

English	*Français*	*Deutsch*
SPECIALITIES	**SPÉCIALITÉS**	**SPEZIALGEBIETE**
Agriculture	Agriculture	Landwirtschaft
Auctioneers	Ventes aux enchères	Auktionen
Autographs and Manuscripts	Autographes et manuscrits	Autographen und Handschriften
Bibliography	Bibliographie	Buchwesen
Biography	Biographies	Biographie
Collecting	Livres pour collectionneurs	Bücher für Sammler
Crafts and useful arts, food and drink	Arts et métiers, gastronomie	Kunstgewerbe Speise und Getränk
Entertainments	Théatre et cinéma	Theater und Kino
Eroticism and curious	Curiosités	Erotik
Fiction	Fiction, romans	Prosadichtung
Fine and rare editions	Beaux livres	Schöne und seltene Bücher
Foreign	Livres etrangères	Ausländisch
History	Histoire	Geschichte
Juvenile	Livres d'Enfants	Kinderbücher
Law and criminology	Droit et criminologie	Recht
Medicine	Médecine	Medizin
Music	Musique	Musik und Noten
Natural history	Sciences naturelles	Naturwissenschaften
Pictorial art	Beaux arts	Kunst und Graphik
Poetry	Poésie	Dichtkunst
Religion and philosophy	Religions et philosophie	Theologie und Philosophie
Periodicals	Périodiques	Zeitschriften
Remainders and overstocks	Soldes	Restauflage
Science	Sciences exactes	Wissenschaften
Sociology	Sociologie	Soziologie
Sport and games	Sports et jeux	Sport und Spiele
Technical and educational	Technique et érudition	Technik
Topography and travel	Regionalism et voyages	Topographie und Reisen

GEOGRAPHICAL SECTION
SECTION GÉOGRAPHIQUE
GEOGRAPHISCHER ABSCHNITT

Autograph letters, Manuscripts, Ephemera, bought and sold. Catalogues issued

Henry Bristow Ltd, 105 Southampton Road, Ringwood, Hants. BH24 1HR.
England (Tel: 042-54 3388)

BELGIE BELGIQUE

BELGIUM   BELGIEN

Associations: Verbände

S.B.L.A.M.   =Syndicat Belge de la Librairie Ancienne et Moderne, 112 rue de Trèves, Bruxelles 4.

C.B.L.   = Cercle Belge de la Librairie.

Public Holidays: Jours de Fête: Feiertage

Jan. 1: Easter Monday: May 1: Ascension Day: Whitmonday: July 21: Aug. 15: Nov. 1 and 11: Dec. 25.

Jan. 1: Lundi de Pâques: May 1: Ascension: Lundi de Pentecôte: Juillet 21: Août 15: Nov. 1 et 11: Dec. 25.

Jan. 1: Ostermontag: Mai 1: Himmelfahrt: Pfingstmontag: Juli 21: Aug. 15: Nov. 1 und 11: Weihnachtstag.

ANVERS / ANTWERPEN (Antwerp): BRUXELLES / BRUSSEL (Brussels): BRUGGE/BRUGES: GENT/GAND (Ghent): HOVE; LIÈGE/LUIK (Lüttich): MARKE LEZ COURTRAI.

LES AMIS DE LA MUSIQUE S.P.R.L., RUE DAUTZENBERG 58, 1050 BRUXELLES. TN: 47 81 18. Established 1945. Private premises, open only mornings 9–12. Medium stock. Spec: music. Cata: 10 a year. Corresp: English, Deutsch, Italiano. B: Banque de la Société Générale de Belgique (Agence Louise) 915304. CP: Bruxelles 3346 26. Cercle Belge de la librarie. International Association of Music Libraries.

LOUIS CHEVALIER, 176A, RUE BLAES, 1000 BRUXELLES. TN: (02) 131677. S.B.L.A.M.

MADAME DELPLACE, 23 BOULEVARD DE WATERLOO, BRUXELLES 1. TN: 511 13 92. Spec: prints, drawings, paintings, topography. B: Société Générale de Belgique, 44 rue de Namur, Bruxelles. CP: 69998. S.B.L.A.M.

GEORGES A. DENY, RUE DU CHÊNE 5, 1000 BRUXELLES. TN: (02) 11 71 45. Established 1943. Shop, closed Saturday afternoon. Small stock.

Spec: early science and technology, old and rare books. Cata. Corresp: English, Français. B: Banque de Bruxelles, No. A.07. 68525. CP: Bruxelles 7539.51. S.B.L.A.M. S.L.A.M.

LIBRAIRIE ENCYCLOPEDIQUE, RUE DU LUXEMBOURG 40, 1040 BRUXELLES. Prop: M. Leyenberger. TN: 511 35 51. Established 1939. Shop. Very large stock. Spec: history, art, philosophy, religion, economics, sociology, law, science, philology. Cata: occasionally. Corresp: English, Français, Deutsch. B: Banque Nagelmackers, No. 635 1281110 82. CP: Bruxelles 0708707 25., and Frankfurt 3005 76 609.

LIBRAIRIE DE L'EUROPE, 1 VAL DES ROSES, 1000 BRUXELLES. Prop: Ch.-D. Macoir. TN: (02) 512 44 95. Moyen stock, aussi livres neufs. Spec: histoire contemporaine, topographie, généalogie. CP: Bruxelles 003 08 02–53. S.B.L.A.M.

FERNAND GOTHIER, LIBRAIRIE UNIVERSITAIRE, PLACE DU 20 AOÛT 11, 4000 LIÈGE. TN: (041) 232 776 and 230 594. Established 1828. Shop. Medium stock, also new books. Spec: history, documentation. Cata: 4 a year. Corresp: English, Français, Deutsch. B: Banque Nagelmackers, No. 634 8243803 39. CP: Bruxelles 0117340 67. S.B.L.A.M., C.B.L.

LIBRAIRIE ANCIENNE ET MODERNE PAUL GOTHIER, RUE BONNE FORTUNE 3 et 5, LIÈGE. TN: (041) 32 24 19. Established 1828. Two Shops. Very large stock, also new books. Spec: Belgicana, erudition, XV and XVI centuries, old and rare. Cata: 6 a year. Corresp: Français. B: Nagelmackers, 4000 Liège. CP: Liège 51604–97. S.B.L.A.M. Cercle Belge de la Librarie. I.L.A.B.

LIBRAIRIE DES GALERIES, GALERIE DU ROI, 2, 1000 BRUXELLES. TN: (02) 511 24 12. Prop: J. Boloukhère. Established 1941. Shop. Medium stock, also new books. Spec: art, architecture, antiquarian. Corresp: Français. B: Soc. Gén. Banque, 210 0281 186 35. CP: Bruxelles 0064515 70. C.B.L.

LE GRENIER DU COLLECTIONNEUR, AVENUE ORBAN 238, 1150 BRUXELLES. Prop: Jean-Léo. Established 1967. Postal business only. Spec: toys, children's books, performing arts, tobacco, Napoléon, books for collectors, curiosities, printed ephemera. Corresp: English, Français. B: Société Générale de Banque, No. 210 0155242 94. CP: Bruxelles 0075057 76. S.B.L.A.M., L.I.L.A.

HALBART, WAHLE & CIE, RUE DES CARMES 11, 4000 LIÈGE. Prop: E. Wahle. TN: (041) 232125 and 235 428. Established 1952. Shop.

Medium stock, also new books. Spec: local history, topography, prints. Cata: 4 a year. Corresp: English, Français, Deutsch. CP: Bruxelles 0021557 23. S.B.L.A.M., S.L.A.M.

JEAN-JACQUES HANKARD, 25 RUE DE LA PAIX, 1050 BRUXELLES. TN: 512 36 42. Established 1910. Shop. Very large stock. Spec: philosophy, history, arts, fine editions; occult (also new books). Corresp: English, Français. B: Société Générale de Banque, No. 837007. CP: Bruxelles 0031602 77. S.B.L.A.M.

VICTOR HANKARD LIBRAIRIE S.P.R.L., 27 RUE DE LA MADELEINE, BRUXELLES 1. TN: 1281 94. TA: Libhankard Bruxelles. Spec: philology, history. B: Banque de la Société Générale de Belgique, compte 16337. CP: Bruxelles 66274. S.B.L.A.M.

FRÉDÉRIC VAN HOETER, 61 RUE SAINT-QUENTIN, BRUXELLES 4. TN: (02) 34 66 47. Spec: periodicals, science, topography, folklore, old and rare. CP: Bruxelles 276970. S.B.L.A.M.

IN DEN BRUGSCHEN EENHOORN, GENTHOF 16, BRUGGE. Prop: J. Meijer. TN: (050) 34246. Established 1954. Shop, open every day 8 to 21 hours. Medium stock, also new books. Cata: 4–6 a year. Corresp: English, Deutsch. B: Kredietbank Brugge, 2200/13/4527. CP: J. Meijer, Brugge 4836 23.

BOEKHANDEL LESCRAUFWAET, OUDE BURG, 31, BRUGGE. Prop: Vos. Maréchal. TN: (050) 313 05. Established 1844. Shop. Small stock, also new books. Spec: Flanders, illustrated books. B: Gen. Bank, 220.362. CP: Brugge 415.18. C.B.L.

A. VAN LOOCK, RUE SAINT JEAN 51, 1000 BRUXELLES. TN: (02) 512 74 65. Established 1945. Shop and storeroom. Very large stock. Spec: old and rare, science, travel, old engravings. B: Banque de Bruxelles, No. 310 0076328 75. CP: Bruxelles 0098837 91. S.B.L.A.M., S.L.A.M., L.I.L.A.

3

LIBRAIRIE "LE LOTUS", RUE MALIBRAN 53, 1050 BRUXELLES. Prop: E. Vandenbroeck. TN: 648 70 74. Established 1912. Shop on second floor, closed Wednesday. Medium stock, also new books. Spec: occult, psychology, Orientalia. Cata. Corresp: English, Deutsch, Dutch. CP: Bruxelles 0063270 26. S.B.L.A.M.

ROMAIN LOUIS, 31–33 RUE ST. JEAN, 1000 BRUXELLES. TN: (02) 121200· S.B.L.A.M.

LIBRAIRIE LOUIS MOORTHAMERS, RUE LESBROUSSART 124, 1050 BRUXELLES. TN: 47 85 48. TA: Curiobook Bruxelles. Shop. Very large stock. Spec: documentation, catalogues, periodicals. Cata: regularly. Corresp: English, Français, Deutsch. B: Banque de Bruxelles, A/38/2. CP: Bruxelles 776596. S.B.L.A.M., C.B.L.

FÉLIX NICOLAS, LELIESTRAAT 61, HOVE. TN: 55 30 03. Spec: history, theology, topography. S.B.L.A.M.

OFFICE INTERNATIONAL DE LIBRAIRIE S.P.R.L., 30 AVENUE MARNIX, 1050 BRUXELLES. TN: 13 66 75. TA: Oflibri Bruxelles. B: Société Générale de Banque. CP: Bruxelles 2260.33. S.B.L.A.M.

ANTIQUARIAAT H. K. OVERDIEP, KORTE GASTHUISSTRAAT 45, 2000 ANTWERPEN. TN: (031) 31 13 28. Established 1938. Shop. Very large stock. Spec: languages, folklore, history, Belgium. Cata: about 4 a year. Corresp: English, Français, Deutsch, Dutch. B: Kredietbank, Antwerpen, 410 0339191 05. CP: Bruxelles 0475981 02. S.B.L.A.M.

FRANCINE VAN DER PERRE, RUE DE LA MADELEINE 23, 1000 BRUXELLES. TN: (02) 511 75 59. Established 1954. Shop. Medium stock, also new books. Spec: genealogy, heraldry, topography. Corresp: English, Français. B: Société Générale de Banque, Agence Agora, 210 0280 304 26. CP: Bruxelles 0205771 34. S.B.L.A.M., I.L.A.B.

PAUL VAN DER PERRE, RUE DE LA RÉGENCE 21, 1000 BRUXELLES. TN: 11 82 45. Established 1934. Shop, early closing Saturday, closed during August. Medium stock, also new books. Spec: fine arts, bibliography, prints, engravings, drawings, first editions and auction sales. Cata: auction catalogues. Corresp: English, Dutch. B: Société Générale de Belgique, Nr. 12392. CP: Bruxelles 285 793. S.B.L.A.M. Cercle Belge de la librairie.

JEAN-MARIE VAN DE PLAS, 10 RUE DES EPERONNIERS, 1000 BRUXELLES. TN: (02) 122 296. S.B.L.A.M.

PRESSES ACADÉMIQUES EUROPÉENES, S.C., 98 CHAUSSÉE DE CHARLEROI, BRUXELLES; 6. Prop: Ch. B. Trocki. TN: 38 32 43 and 38 36 97. TA: Euroacademic Bruxelles. Spec: mathematics, medicine, scientific periodicals. CP: Bruxelles 16737. S.B.L.A.M.

LA PROUE, 6 RUE DES EPERONNIERS, 1000 BRUXELLES. Prop: H. Mercier. TN: 513 03 09. Established 1945. Magasin. Large stock, also new books. Spec: modern art, Belgian literature, poetry, surrealism. Cata: 4–5 a year. Corresp: English, Deutsch, Flemish. B: Banque de Bruxelles, 310–0675–121. CP: Bruxelles 000–0770913–54. S.B.L.A.M.

EMILE RELECOM, RUE DES CHARDONS 19, 1030 BRUXELLES. TN: (02) 241 58 01. Established 1958. Shop and storeroom, appointment necessary. Very large stock, also new books. Spec: modern books after 1900. Cata: monthly. Corresp: English, Français, Español, Italiano, Deutsch. CP: 6061097 84. S.B.L.A.M., C.B.L., S.L.A.M.

DE RENAISSANCE VAN HET BOEK, WALPOORTSTRAAT 7, 9000 GENT. Prop: Mme. Derryx dit Derks. TN: (91) 254808. Established 1970. Shop. Medium stock. Spec: gravures et cartes anciennes; livres épuisés. Corresp: English, Français, Niederlandse. B: Crédit Lyonnais, Koophandelplein 4, Gent, No. 694 45 10475 48. S.B.L.A.M.

LIBRAIRIE A. ROMBAUT, LIEVESTRAAT 14, 9000 Gent. Prop. Charles Lammens. TN: (091) 235646. Established 1923. Shop. Medium stock, also new books. Spec: fine arts, music; genealogy; topography. Corresp: English, Français, Deutsch, Dutch. B: Gemeentekrediet van Belgie, No. 062 1154650 18. CP: 0156937 88. S.B.L.A.M.

LIBRAIRIE SIMONSON, 20 AVENUE DES ARTS, 1040 BRUXELLES. TN: (02) 114530. S.B.L.A.M.

W. H. SMITH & SON, BOULEVARD ADOLPHE MAX 71–75, 1000 BRUXELLES. TN: 17 67 22, 19 27 07 and 19 27 08. Shop. C.B.L.

LIBRAIRIE-EDITIONS THANH-LONG, 34 RUE DEKENS, 1040 BRUXELLES. TN: (02) 733 16 18. Established 1963. Shop, open Monday, Wednesday and Saturday 14 to 21.30 hours. Large stock, also new books. Spec: Far East, books in Vietnamese language. Cata: 3 a year. Corresp: English, Français. B: National Westminster, External Account, London, No. 04561635. CP: Bruxelles 006867091. S.B.L.A.M., L.I.L.A.

L. TULKENS, 21 RUE DU CHÊNE, BRUXELLES 1. TN: (02) 13 05 25. TA: Libratul Bruxelles. Spec: old and rare, old bindings, fine arts. B:

Banque de Bruxelles, Agence Lombard. CP: Bruxelles 77268. S.B.L.A.M.

A. W. VANDEVELDE, DWEERSTRAAT 6, 8000 BRUGES. Established 1967. Shop and storeroom. Medium stock, also new books. Spec: Dutch literature, Flandrica, the Far East. Corresp: English, Français, Deutsch. B: Banque de Bruxelles, Bruges, No. 380 0009456 21. CP: Bruxelles: 000 1012181 83.

LA VIE RUSTIQUE, S.P.R.L., AVENUE WINSTON CHURCHILL 40, 1180 BRUXELLES. Prop: Mme. Cécile de Wyngaert. TN: (02) 375 50 15 Established 1955. Shop, closed Saturday. Very large stock, also new books. Spec: natural history, geology, travels, hunting; history; exact sciences. Cata: 10–12 a year. Corresp: English, Français, Deutsch Italiano. B: Continental Bank, No. 590 0012844–66. CP: 00 221 81 65 S.B.L.A.M., C.B.L.

ROGER WASTIAU, RUE DE L'INDUSTRIE 9, 1040 BRUXELLES. TN: 513 02 36. Spec: first editions, literature, history, bindings. Cata. S.B.L.A.M

BULGARIYA

BULGARIA   BULGARIE   BULGARIEN

SOFIA.

ANTIKVARNI KNIGI, 19 ULITSA GRAF IGNATIEV, SOFIA. Shop, open 9–13
and 14–18 hours, Saturdays 8–14 hours. Large stock Bulgarian and
foreign, also new books. Corresp: Deutsch, Français.

"HEMUS", 11 SLAVEIKOV SQUARE, SOFIA. State Export-Import Enterprise
for all books.

ČESKOSLOVENSKO

CZECHOSLOVAKIA
TCHEKOSLOVAKIE
DIE TSCHECHOSLOWAKEI

BRATISLAVA: BRNO (Brünn): ČESKÉ BUDĚJOVICE (Budweis): DVUR KRÁLOVÉ: GOTTWALDOV: HRADEC KRÁLOVÉ: HODONÍN: JABLONEC (Gablonz): JIHLAVA (Iglau): KARLOVY VARY (Karlsbad): KOLÍN: KOŠICE: KROMĚŘIŽ: LIBEREC (Reichenberg): LOUNY: MOST: NÁCHOD: NITRA: OLOMOUC: OPAVA: OSTRAVA: PARDUBICE: PLZEŇ (Pilsen): PRAHA (Prag, Prague): TABOR: TEPLICE LAZNE V. CECHACH: TRNAVA: ÚSTÍ: ZILINA: ZNOJMO.

KNIHA, MALÉ NÁMĚSTI No. 11, PRAHA 1. Shop. TN: 23 39 18. Large stock. Spec: foreign literature (English, French, German); topography

KNIHA, ULICE RADNICE, PRAHA 1. Shop. Small stock. Spec: fine and rare also some prints, etc.

KNIHA, KARLOVA ULICE 16. PRAHA 1. TN: 240275. Shop. Large stock of prints, drawings, manuscripts, and autographs.

KNIHA n.p., ULICE 28, ŘÍJNA 13, PRAHA 1. TN: 23 72 57/8. Shop. Very large stock of Czech and foreign literature. Spec: poetry and drama Corresp: English, Deutsch, Français, Russian.

KNIHA, n.p., 2 SKOŘEPKA, PRAHA 1. TN: 24 77 08.

KNIHA n.p., KARLOVA ULICE, 2 PRAHA 1. TN: 23 42 82. Shop. Medium stock, also prints and drawings. Corresp: English, Deutsch, Français Russian.

KNIHA n.p., 36 JEČNÁ, PRAHA 2. TN: 22 22 26.

KNIHA n.p., 5 DLAŽDENÁ, PRAHA 2. TN: 22 18 61.

KNIHA n.p., 10 MYSLÍKOVA, PRAHA 2. TN: 23 44 02. Secondhand musical literature. Medium stock. Corresp: Deutsch.

KNIHA n.p., 42 NÁMĚSTÍ REPUBLIKY, PLZEŇ. TN: 354 93.

KNIHA n.p., 12. CS. ARMADY, KARLOVY VARY. TN: 34 13.

KNIHA n.p., 12 PAŘÍŽSKA, USTÍ n/L. TN: 28 70.

KNIHA n.p., 4 PRAŽSKÁ, LIBEREC. TN: 42 04.

KNIHA n.p., 169 V. KOPEČKY, HRADEC KRÁLOVÉ. TN: 53 25.

KNIHA n.p., 2 NAMESTI OSVOBOZENÍ, PARDUBICE. TN: 20270.

KNIHA n.p., 28 ČESKÁ UL., BRNO. TN: 22501.

KNIHA n.p., 9 OSTRUZNICKÁ, OLOMOUC. TN: 55 79.

KNIHA n.p., 15 LENINOVA 212, GOTTWALDOV. TN: 27 12.

KNIHA n.p., 4 ZÁMECKÁ UL., OSTRAVA. TN: 218 71.

KNIHA n.p., 2 KOMENSKÉMO JABLONEC n/Nis TN: 43 70.

KNIHA n.p., RIEGROVO NÁMĚSTÍ 10, KROMĚŘÍŽ. TN: 30 00.

KNIHA n.p., 13 KOLLÁROVA, ZNOJMO. TN: 32 07.

KNIHA n.p., 109 LENINOVA, LOUNY. TN: 263.

KNIHA n.p., NÁMĚSTÍ 9 KVĚTNA 30, PROSTĚJOV. TN: 3812.

KNIHA n.p., 1 BEZRUČOVA, MOST. TN: 21 26.

KNIHA n.p., LENNINOVA UL. 15, TEPLICE LÁZNĚ V ČECHÁCH. TN: 48 13.

KNIHA n.p., 6 PALACKÉHO, TÁBOR. TN: 4219. Est. 1953. Shop. Large Stock. Corresp: German.

KNIHA n.p., 4 STALINGRADSKÁ, HODONÍN. TN: 2195.

KNIHA n.p., ULICE 9 KVĚTNA 1, BRNO. TN: 24863.

KNIHA n.p., 32 KIROVOVA, PRAHA 5-SMÍCHOV. TN: 53 35 60.

KNIHA n.p., 25 OSTRONZNÁ, OPAVA. TN: 26 35.

KNIHA n.p., ŽIŽKOVO n. 31, Č. BUDEJOVICE. TN: 27 91.

KNIHA n.p., 37 GOTTWALDOVO NÁMĚSTÍ, DVUR KRÁLOVÉ n/L. TN: 2513.

KNIHA n.p., 58 NÁMĚSTÍ ŘÍJNOVÉ REVOLUCE, NÁCHOD. TN: 34 43.

KNIHA n.p., 20 VINOHRADSKÁ, PRAHA 2—VINOHRADY. TN: 24 42 26.

KNIHA n.p., 29 PALACKÉHO, JIHLAVA. TN: 22003.

KNIŽNÍ VELKOOBCHOD n.p., Ústřední nákup antikvariátu, 5⁵ SPÁLENA, PRAHA 2. TN: 23 23 23.

KNIŽNÍ VELKOOBCHOD n.p., Exportní stredisko antikvariátu, 6⁵ STEPÁNSKÁ, PRAHA 2. TN: 24 65 61.

SLOVENSKÁ KNIHA n.p., SEDLIÁRSKÁ 9, BRATISLAVA. TN: 30117.

SLOVENSKÁ KNIHA n.p., 10 MICKIEWICZOVA, BRATISLAVA. TN: 501 64 Very large stock. Corresp. Deutsch.

SLOVENSKÁ KNIHA n.p., 45 LENINOVA, NITRA. TN: 22 04.

SLOVENSKÁ KNIHA n.p., 2 HVIEZDOSLAVOVA, TRNAVA. TN: 24 23.

SLOVENSKÁ KNIHA n.p., 4 MARX ENGELSA, ZILINÁ. TN: 20067. Est 1918. Corresp: English, Deutch, Français, Italian.

SLOVENSKÁ KNIHA n.p., 29 LENINOVA, KOŠICE. TN: 24 27.

SLOVENSKÝ KNIŽNÝ VELKOOBCHOD n.p. (odor antikvariát), 2 DUNAJSKÁ, BRATISLAVA. TN: 512 64.

DANMARK

DENMARK   DANEMARK
DÄNEMARK

Associations: Verbände

A.B.F. = Den danske Antikvarboghandlerforening,
Kron-Prinsens-Gade 3
1114 København-K

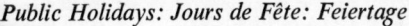

D.B.F. = Den danske Boghandlerforening.

D.F.F. = Den danske Forlaeggerforening.

K.D.F. = Københavns Detailhandlerforening.

Public Holidays: Jours de Fête: Feiertage

Jan. 1: Easter: Whitmonday: Ascension Day: Day of Prayer: Jun. 5: Dec. 25 and 26.

Jan. 1: Pâques: Lundi de Pentecôte: Ascension: Jour de Prière: Juin 5: Dec. 25 et 26.

Jan. 1: Ostermontag: Pfingstmontag: Himmelfahrt: Busstag: Juni 5: Dez. 25 und 26.

AALBORG: AARHUS: ESBJERG: KØBENHAVN (Copenhagen): SORØ.

CARL ANDERSEN, ABOULEVARDEN 60, 2200 KØBENHAVN-N. Prop: Peter Andersen. TN: 39 62 71. CP: København 5094461. A.B.F.

S. C. ANDERSENS ANTIKVARIAT, ALHAMBRAVEJ 22, 1826, KØBEN-HAVN-V. TN: Ve 8833. Established 1944. Shop, early closing Saturday. Large stock. Spec: science-fiction, detective fiction, pocket-books, also stamps for collectors. Cata: 1 a year. Corresp: English, Français, Deutsch. B: Daurmandsbanken, Gl. Kongevej 107, København-V. CP: København 58248. A.B.F.

K. V. BLOCH, FIOLSTRAEDE 34, 1171 KØBENHAVN-K. TN: (01) 14 24 62. A.B.F.

BØCKMANN'S ANTIKVARIAT, Rosensgade 11, DK-8000 Aarhus-C. Prop: A. Aabenhus. TN: (06) 120278. Established 1942. Shop, early closing Saturday. Very large stock. Spec: art, first editions, old, prints. Cata: occasionally. Corresp: English, Deutsch. B: Sparekassen SDS, 980-01-02092. CP: 4 18 74 23.

BOG-BORSEN, Studiestraede 10, 1455 København-k. Prop: Kristian Andersen. TN: 0113 2580. Established 1935. Shop. Large stock, also new books. CP: København 10 56 379.

BOGHALLENS ANTIKVARIAT, Raadhuspladsen 37, DK 1585 København-V. Prop: Ole Dam. TN: (01) 118511, extension 397. Spec: fine and old, manuscripts, finely bound English sets, art books. A.B.F.

BOG-MESSEN, Gammel Kongevej 19, 1610 København-V. Prop: Jørgen Andersen. TN: (01) 24 09 00. Established 1940. Shop, early closing Saturday. Large stock. Spec: fine arts, literature, music and ballet. Cata: 4 a year. Corresp: English, Deutsch. B: Den danske Landmandsbank. CP: København 26228. A.B.F.

BRANNERS BIBLIOFILE ANTIKVARIAT, Bredgade 10, 1260 København-K. Prop: Mrs. Maria Bloch. TN: 13 91 07. TA: Librannica København. Established 1946. Shop, early closing Saturday. Very small stock. Spec: old and rare, illustrated books, decorative prints, maps, views, etc. Corresp: English, Français, Deutsch, Italiano. B: Københavns Handelsbank, Store Kongensgade. CP: København 6489559. LILA. A.B.A.

ARNOLD BUSCK, Fiolstraede 24, 1171 København-K. Prop: C. F. Simonsen. TN: (01) 12 24 53. TA: Bookbusck København. Spec: art. architecture, bibliography topography. CP: København 3457. A.B.F.

BYENS ANTIKVARIAT, Studiestraede 25, 1455 København-K. Prop: Richard Sørensen. TN: BYen 6250. Established 1930. Shop, early closing Saturday. Medium stock. Cata. Corresp: Deutsch. B: Københavns Handelsbank, account 117633. CP: København 88099. A.B.F.

J. E. CHRISTENSENS ANTIKVARIAT, L. Hammerichsvej 5, 8200 Aarhus-N. TN: (061) 64894. Appointment necessary. Library Service. A.B.F.

DAN FOG MUSIKANTIKVARIAT, Graabrødre torv 7, 1154 København-K. A.B.F.

H. DIRCKINCK-HOLMFELD, Aabenraa 29, 1124 Københaven-K. TN BYen 785. A.B.F.

GERTRUDE DREWSEN, Fredensgade 16, 2200 København-N. TN: NOra 5347. Spec: music. A.B.F.

FREDE ENGHOLST, Studiesstraede 35, 1455 København-K. TN: (01) 13 48 51. CP: 9 12 66 94. A.B.F.

FREDERIKSBERG ANTIKVARIAT, Gammel Kongevej 120, 1850 København-V. Prop: Leif Nørballe. TN: (01) EVa 9708. Spec: arts and crafts, Scandinavian literature, periodicals. CP: København 84635. A.B.F.

GAMMELTORVS ANTIKVARIAT, Gammel Torv 8, 1457 København-K. TN: PAlae 5487. A.B.F.

J. GRUBB'S ANTIKVARIAT, Nørregade 47, Dk-1165 København-K. TN: (01) 15 9402. Shop. Very large stock. Spec: theology, philosophy, philology, history, art, fiction. Corresp: English, Deutsch. CP: København 700 1398. A.B.F.

J. GUSTAFSSON, Volden 12, 8000 Aarhus-C. TN: (061) 26806. Established 1926. Shop, early closing Saturday. Large stock. Corresp: English, Deutsch. B: Aarhus Privatbank. CP: Aarhus 35156. A.B.F.

HARCKS ANTIKVARIAT, Fiolstraede 33, 1171 København-K. TN: (01) 129148. A.B.F.

ANDR. FRED. HØST & SØN, Bredgade 35, 1260 København-K. TN: 15 50 51. Spec: art; applied art; history; philology; freemasonry; zoology; botany. A.B.F.

KAABERS ANTIKVARIAT, Skindergade 34, 1159 København-K. TN: BYen 4177. Spec: fine arts; maps and prints. A.B.F.

KNAGSTEDS ANTIKVARIAT, Kompagnistraede 8, 1208 København-K. A.B.F.

RICHARD LEVIN, Dannebrogsgade i/iv, 1660 København-V. TN: (01) 310594. Established 1945. Private premises, appointment necessary. Very large stock. Spec: old and rare books; Judaica; early science; maps. Cata. Corresp: English, Deutsch. B: Den Danske Landmandsbank, Holmens Kanal, København-K., account 2928–5. A.B.F.

LYNGE & SON, Løvstraede 8–10, 1152 København-K. TN: (01) 15 53 35. Spec: Arctic (Greenland); linguistics; natural science; rare books; periodicals. A.B.F.

MADSEN-LINDS ANTIKVARIAT, Klosterstraede 24, 1157 København-K. Prop: Mrs. Aly Lind. TN: PAlae 6402. Spec: art and folk art. A.B.F.

H. C. NØRGART, Fiolstraede 15, 1171 København-K. TN: BYen 1052y. Spec: pictorial art. A.B.F.

MARINUS OLSEN, Studiestraede 41. 1455 København-K. TN: PAlae 7624. A.B.F.

ERIK PALUDAN — INTERNATIONAL BOOKSELLER, Fiolstraede 10, 1171 København-K. TN: 15 06 75. Established 1947. Shop, early closing Saturday. Very large stock, also new books. Spec: humanities. Cata: 5–6 a year. Corresp: English, Deutsch. B: Københavns Handelsbank. CP: København 1921.

GRØNHOLT PEDERSENS BOGHUS, Fiolstraede 19, 1171 København-K. Prop: Einar Grønholt Pedersen. TN: 12 13 44. TA: Hafniabooks København. Established 1878. Shop. Very large stock, also new books. Spec: old and rare; maps. Cata: 5 a year. Corresp: English, Français, Deutsch. B: Den Danske Provinsbank A/S., Nygade 1, København-K. CP: København 28428. A.B.F.

GUNNAR PILEGAARD, Algade 65, Aalborg. Prop: G. Pilegaard. TN: (08) 139221. Established 1963. Shop. Medium stock. Corresp: English, Deutsch. B: Nørresundby Bank, Aalborg, Account 20 00 37–1. CP: 5 10 85 19. A.B.F.

RANCH'S ANTIKVARIAT, Vesterbrogade 110, 1620 København-V. Prop: Finn Ranch. TN: (01) 21 10 35. A.B.F.

ROSENKILDE OG BAGGER, 3 Kron-Prinsens-Gade, 1114 København. Prop: Hans Bagger and V. Rosenkilde. TN: (01) 15 70 44. TA: Bogkunst. Est: 1941. Shop. Very large stock, also new books. Spec: Old and rare. Cata: 12 to 15 a year. Corresp: English, Deutsch. B: Den danske Landmansbank, Nytorv afdeling, København, Account No. 14089–1. CP: København 700 1146. A.B.F., Den Danske Boghandlerforening.

YOUNG SCHMIDT, Osloplads 2A, 2100 København-Ø. TN: PAlae 5252. A.B.F.

SKAKHUSET (THE CHESS HOUSE), 24 Studiesstraede, 1455 København-K. Prop. Stellan Persson and Sven Klerstam. TN: (01)-14 62 91. Est: 1947. Shop. Small stock, also new books. Spec: chess books. Cata: every 18 months. Corresp: English, Deutsch, Svenska. B: Den Danske Landmansbank, Vesterbro afd. København. Account 12075-6. CP: 20 58 715.

SORØ ANTIKVARIAT, Frederiksbergvej 8, 4180, Sorø. Prop: Bjarne Zukunft. TN: (03) 63 35 85. Est: 1900. Storeroom; by appointment only. Very large stock. Cata: 15 a year. Corresp: English, Deutsch. B: Sjallandske Bank.

ANTIKVARIAT GUSTAV STRAND, Sankt Pedersstraede 47, 1453 København-K. TN: PAlae 1151. Established 1935. Shop, closed Saturday. Medium stock. Corresp: English, Français, Deutsch. B: Landmandsbanken, Vesterbro afd., 2941-4. CP: København 26607. A.B.F.

THORNAMS ANTIKVARIAT, Kompagniestraede 16, 1208 København-K. Prop: Mrs. B. Samuelsson. TN: BYen 2878. Spec: fine arts; French and Scandinavian literature. CP: København 46670. A.B.F.

THUESENS ANTIKVARIAT, Fiolstraede 23, 1171 København-K. Prop: Hans. Chr. Thuesen. TN: (01) 119962. Established 1933. Shop. Medium stock. Cata: 2 a year. Corresp: English, Deutsch. B: Bikuben, No. 725-900054. CP: København 20 31566. A.B.F., I.L.A.B.

PREBEN WITT, Hestemøllestraede 3, 1464 København-K. TN: (01) 14 50 90. (Private TN: He 4827). Established 1945. Shop and storeroom. Medium stock. Spec: old books: Hans Christian Andersen, auction commissions. B: Den danske Landmandsbank, Nytorv afdeling, København CP: København 63999. A.B.F.

BUNDESREPUBLIK DEUTSCHLAND

FEDERAL GERMANY
ALLEMAGNE FÉDERALE

Associations: Verbände

V.D.A. = Verband Deutscher Antiquare, E.V.,
Die Vereinigung von Buchantiquaren,
Autographen- und Graphikhandlern,
7570 Baden-Baden, Iberststrasse 36.
TN: (07221) 22423

B.V.D.B. = Borsenverein des Deutscher Büch.
handels.

Public Holidays: Jours de Fête: Feiertage

Jan. 1: Good Friday: Easter Monday: May 1: Ascension Day: Whitmonday: Jun. 17: Nov. 17: Dec. 25 and 26.

Jan. 1: Vendredi-Saint: lundi de Pâques: Mai 1: Ascension: Lundi de Pentecôte: Jun. 17: Nov. 17: Déc. 25 et 26.

Jan. 1: Karfreitag: Ostermontag: Mai 1: Himmelfahrt: Pfingstmontag: Jun. 17: Nov. 17: Dez. 25 und 26.

Section Teil	Postcode Postleitzahl	
I	1	BERLIN (WEST)
II	2 & 3	NORDDEUTSCHLAND, ALLEMAGNE (NORD) NORTHERN GERMANY
III	4 & 5	NORDRHEIN & RUHR
IV	6	MAIN & TAUNUS
V	7	SUDWESTDEUTSCHLAND, ALLEMAGNE (SUDOUEST) SOUTHWEST GERMANY
VI	8	BAYERN, BAVIERE, BAVARIA

I

BERLIN (West)   **Postcode 1. Postleitzahl 1.**

GALERIE GERDA BASSENGE, Erdenerstrasse 5 a, 1 Berlin 33. TN:
(0311) 886 1932. V.D.A.

DAS BIBLIOGRAPHIKON, Carmerstrasse 19, 1 Berlin-Charlottenberg 2. Prop: Frau Hilly Boerner. TN: 32 20 72. Spec: Alte Graphik;
Farbstiche; Stadtansichten. CP: Berlin-West 65494. V.D.A.

BICKHARDT'SCHE BUCHHANDLUNG, Karl-Marx-Strasse 168, 1
Berlin-Neukölln. Prop: Peter Severin. TN: 62 13 44. Gegründet 1879.
Laden, Samstag Nachmittag geschlossen. Cata: B: Berliner Bank,
Depka 8, Konto 237. CP: Berlin-West 3924. V.D.A.

DAS BÜCHERFASS ANTIQUARIAT, Muskauerstrasse 35, 1 Berlin
36. Prop: Edgar A. Ruff.

DER BÜCHERWURM, Motzstrasse 24, 1 Berlin 30. TN: 24 63 23. TA:
Bücherwurm Berlin. Gegründet 1923. Prop: Heinz Hannmann. Laden,
Samstag Nachmittag geschlossen. Sehr grosser Vorrat. Spec: Humani-
ties. Cata: 2–3 pro Jahr. Corresp: English. B: Berliner Bank A.G.,
Depka 41, Konto 71311000. CP: Berlin-West 124 36 V.D.A.

ANTIQUARIAT CHRISTOPHÉ UND GROTHE, Uhlandstrasse 50,
1 Berlin 15. Prop: Regina Grothe. TN: (030) 881 99 18. Gegründet
1946. Laden und Lagerräume; Geschäftszeit 14.00 bis 18.30. Mittelgrosser Vorrat. Cata. Corresp: English, Français. B: Berliner Commerzbank, Konto 502 750 300. CP: Berlin-West 136 507-104.

ROBERTE FRICKE, VERSAND- UND ANTIQUARIATS-BUCH-
HANDLUNG, G.m.b.H., Hardenbergplatz 13, 1 Berlin 12. TN:
31 62 70. Gegründet 1946. Laden und Lagerräume, Samstag geschlossen.
Nach Vereinbarung. Grosser Vorrat, auch neue Bücher. Spec: Ge-
schichte; Philologie; Philosophie; Politik. Cata: 6 pro Jahr. Corresp:
English. B: Bank für Handel und Industrie AG, Berlin, Konto 19 3019,
und Dresdner Bank, Stuttgart, Konto 101 284. CP: Stuttgart 9221.
V.D.A.

R. FRIEDLÄNDER UND SOHN, Nonnendammallee 92f, 1 Berlin 13.
Direktor: Harri Kreuschner. TN; (030) 382 60 91. TA: Natura Berlin.
Gegründet 1828. Lagerräume; Besuch nach Vereinbarung, Lager nicht
zugänglich. Sehr grosser Vorrat. Spec: Naturwissenschaften (Botanik,
Zoologie, Geologie u.s.w.) Cata: 4 pro Jahr. Corresp: English. B:
Berliner Disconto Bank, Konto 524-5550. CP: Berlin-West 91 12-100.
V.D.A.

GSELLIUS'SCHE BUCH-, ANTIQUAR- UND GLOBENHANDLUNG G.m.b.H. HERTASTRASSE 16, 1 BERLIN 37. Prop: Georg Scheringer. TN: (0301) 813 3027. TA: Gsellius, Berlin. Gegründet 1737. Lagerräume und Büro. Grosser Vorrat. Spec: Bücher des 15. bis 20. Jahrhunderts; Bibliophilie; Geisteswissenschaften und alte Naturwissenschaften; Geschichte; Philosophie; Berlin; Goetheana; Literatur und Kunst; alte Stadtansichten und Lankarten. Cata: 10 pro Jahr. Corresp: English, Français. B: Berliner Commerzbank, Konto 12 399 20 00. CP: Berlinwest 5049-109. V.D.A., B.V.D.B., Berliner Verleger und Buchhändler Vereinigung.

MAX GÜNTHER, CHARLOTTENBRUNNERSTRASSE 5a, 1 BERLIN 33. Prop: Gertrud Knapps. TN: 823 29 50. Gegründet 1894. Wohnung, nur nach Vereinbarung. Grosser Vorrat. Spec: Seltenheiten; Sammlerstücke, Luxusdrucke, Moderne Bibliophilie, Deutsche Literatur, Gesamtausgaben, Kulturgeschichte; Baedeker. Cata: in unregelmässiger Folge. Corresp: English, Français. B: Berliner Disconto Bank, Konto 141-0174. CP: Berlin-West 713 68-104. B.V.D.B., V.D.A.

GEORGE C. HAMEL, BREGENZERSTRASSE 7, 1 BERLIN 15 TN: 881 2707. Gegründet New York 1948. Sehr Grosser Vorrat. Spec: Geschichte; Politik; Zeitgeschichte; Judaica; Zeitschriften. Cata. Corresp: English, Français. B: Berliner Disconto Bank, Dep.-K. R. CP: Berlin-West 178960. V.D.A., B.V.D.B.

HANS HARTINGER Nachf., XANTENER STRASSE 14, 1 BERLIN 15. Prop: Marlene Wittkowski. TN: 883 24 04. Gegründet 1933. Lagerräume im 1. Stock, Montag, Dienstag, Donnerstag und Freitag 9–14, Mittwoch 9–18.30., und nach Vereinbarung. Grosser Vorrat, auch neue Bücher. Spec: Linguistik; Slavica; Orientalia. Cata: 2 pro Jahr. Corresp: Français, Español. B: Berliner Bank AG, Konto 99-71991 und National Westminster Bank Ltd., London, Account No. 04545564. CP: Berlin-West 6712. V.D.A., B.V.D.B.

HEINRICH HEINE, IM BAHNHOF ZOO, 1 BERLIN 2. Prop: Paul Schulz. TN: 312 54 84. Gegründet 1945. Spec: Politik und Staatswissenschaften; Zeitschriften; Sozialismus. CP: Berlin-West 22244. V.D.A.

BRUNO HESSLING, RANKESTRASSE 31-32, 1 BERLIN 30. Prop: Ernst Zahn. TN: 24 34 69 und 24 59 82. TA: Vitruv Berlin-West. Gegründet 1871. Laden, Samstag Nachmittag geschlossen. Mittelgrosser Vorrat, auch neue Bücher. Spec: Archäologie; Altertumswissenschaft; Buch- und Bibliothekswesen; Kunst. Corresp: English, Français. B: Bank für Handel und Industrie, 1 Berlin 12, Kantstrasse 17. Konto-Nr. 9230117. CP: Berlin-West 10357/103. V.D.A.

KIEPERT K.G., HARDENBERGSTRASSE 4–5, 1 BERLIN 12. Prop: Robert Kiepert. TN: (030) 31 07 11. Gegründet 1897. Laden. Kleiner Vorrat, auch neue Bücher. Spec: Naturwissenschaften; Technik. Corresp: English. B: Berliner Diskonto Bank, Konto 460 4120; First National City Bank, London, Konto 013 37 4; First National City Bank, New York, Konto 0275 9109. CP: Berlinwest 1800-100. B.V.D.B., L.I.A., S.B.L.A.M. (Belgien). Berliner Verleger- und Buchhändlervereinigung.

HANS HORST KOCH, HAUPTSTRASSE 7–8, 1 BERLIN 62. TN: 781 72 87. TA: Buchkoch Berlin-West. Gegründet 1950. Lagerräume, Montag—Freitag 10–17 Uhr. Sehr grosser Vorrat. Spec: Alte und Schöne Bücher; Bibliographie. Cata: 2 pro Jahr. Corresp: English, Français. B: Berliner Bank, Konto-Nr. 2407890 500. CP: Berlin-West 7199. V.D.A.

ALBERT KOHLS, WINTERFELDSTRASSE 44, 1 BERLIN 30. TN: 261 45 28. Gegründet 1932. Laden und Lagerräume, Samstag geschlossen. Kleiner Vorrat. Spec: Literatur; Geschichte; Berolinensia. Cata. B: Bank für Handel und Industrie, 1 Berlin 30, Konto 38 52 20. CP: Berlin-West 10161. V.D.A.

GÜNTHER KUBIAK, MARTIN-LUTHER-STRASSE 127. 1 BERLIN 62. TN: (030) 782 28 43. Gegründet 1947. Laden. Grosser Vorrat, auch neue Bücher. Spec: Geschichte. Cata: 2 pro Jahr. B.V.D.B.

LANGE UND SPRINGER, HEIDELBERGERPLATZ 3, 1 BERLIN 33. TN: 822 001. Gegründet 1816. Spec: Naturwissenschaften; Medizin: Technik; Zeitschriften. B: Berliner Disconto Bank, Berlin Konto 021-0716. V.D.A.

GALERIE MATTHIESEN, MEINEKESTRASSE 11, 1 BERLIN 15. Prop: Dr. M. Neolle. TN: 8817166. Spec: Alte und moderne Graphik; Gemälde; Skulpturen. V.D.A.

GALERIE NIERENDORF, HARDENBERGSTRASSE 19, 1 BERLIN 12. Prop: Florian Karsch. TN: 66 03 94. Spec: Kunst; Gemälde; Skulptur; Graphik, Deutsche Expressionisten. V.D.A.

GÜNTER RICHTER, BREITE STRASSE 29, 1 BERLIN 33. TN: 89 80 79. Gegründet 1945. Laden, Samstag Nachmittag geschlossen. Spec: Militaria; Geschichte; Politik; alte Landkarten und Städteansichten (Merian). Auch neue Bücher. Cata. B: Bank für Handel und Industrie, Depka 12, 1 Berlin 45, Baselerstrasse, Konto 127786. V.D.A., B.V.D.B.

OSCAR ROTHACKER, HARDENBERGSTRASSE 11, 1 BERLIN 12. Prop: Dr Heinz Urban, Ernst Urban und Michael Urban. TN: 313 70 15. Telex:

185 409 (urbln d). TA: Rothacbuch, Berlin. Gegründet 1872. Laden und Lagerräume, Samstag Nachmittag geschlossen. Grosser Vorrat. Spec: Medizin; Naturwissenschaften; Technik. Cata: periodische. Corresp: English, Français. B: Berliner Disconto Bank, 1 Berlin 30. CP: Berlin-West 9339-106.

WALTER SEUFFER, STEGLITZER DAMM 57, 1 BERLIN 41. TN: (0311) 796 3848. V.D.A.

RUDOLF J. SPRINGER, FASENENSTRASSE 13, 1 BERLIN 12. TN: (0311) 313 9088. Spec: 20 Jahrhunderts (Luxusdrucke—Mappenwerke). V.D.A

WOLFGANG STASCHEN, BULOWSTRASSE 11, 1 BERLIN 30. TN: 215 55 44. Gegründet 1958. Laden, Mittwoch Morgen geschlossen. Mittelgrosser Vorrat. Spec: Stahlstich Ansichten. 1 pro Jahr. Corresp: English, Français. B: Sparkasse der Stadt Berlin West. Konto 11 500 1650. CP: Berlin-West 11 27 27. B.V.D.B.

HUGO STREISAND, EISLEBENER STRASSE 4, 1 BERLIN 30. TN: 24 23 14. Laden. Spec: Politik und Staatswissenschaften; Soziologie; Pädagogik. B: Berliner Bank, Konto 417296. CP: Berlin-West 7518. V.D.A.

STRUPPE UND WINKLER, POTSDAMERSTRASSE 103, 1 BERLIN 30. Prop: Helmut Hildebrandt. TN: (030) 261 10 89. Gegründet 1890. Spec: Recht, Wirtschsft. Cata. B: Berliner Bank, Konto 32 07689 400. CP: Berlin-West 207-101. V.D.A.

WASMUTH BUCHHANDLUNG & ANTIQUARIAT KG., HARDENBERG-STRASSE 9a, 1 BERLIN 12. TN: 31 69 20 und 313 82 93. TA: Buchwasmuth Berlin. Gegründet 1872. Laden, Samstag Nachmittag geschlossen. Mittelgrosser Vorrat, auch neue Bücher. Spec: Kunst; Architektur; Archäologie. Cata: 4 pro Jahr. Corresp: English, Français. B: Bank für Handel und Industrie, Uhlandstrasse 9–11, 1 Berlin 12, Konto 694 390. CP: Berlin-West 100 39. V.D.A., B.V.D.B.

CARL WEGNER, MARTIN-LUTHER-STRASSE 113, 1 BERLIN 62. Prop: Carlos Kühn. TN: 782 2491. Gegründet 1953. Laden. Grosser Vorrat. Spec: Literatur; Philosophie, Sozialwissenschaften; Berlinensia; Theater; Städteansichten und Landkarten. Cata: 1 oder 2 pro Jahr. Corresp: English. B: Berliner Disconto Bank Konto 391-1302. B.V.D.B.

HEINZ WÜNSCHMANN, PFALZ BURGER STRASSE 9, 1 BERLIN 15. TN: 881 57 89. Laden. Spec: Militaria; Deutsche Literatur; Kunst und Kunstgewerbe; Geisteswissenschaften. B: Bank für Handel und Industrie, Berlin, Konton 695924. CP: Berlin-West 92072. V.D.A.

II

NORTHERN GERMANY: NORDDEUTSCHLAND: ALLEMAGNE (NORD)

Postcodes: Postleitzahlen 2+ & 3+

2202 BARMSTEDT	3522 KARLSHAFEN
33 BRAUNSCHWEIG	35 KASSEL
28 BREMEN	23 KIEL
3011 GEHRDEN	24 LÜBECK
338 GOSLAR	
34 GÖTTINGEN	355 MARBURG
2 HAMBURG	29 OLDENBURG
3 HANNOVER	3360 OSTERODE

ARNO ADLER, HÜXSTRASSE 55, 24 LÜBECK. (Postfach 2048). TN: 7 44 66. Gegründet 1932. Laden und Lagerräume, Samstag Nachmittag geschlossen. Sehr grosser Vorrat, auch neue Bücher. Spec: Geschichte; Kulturgeschichte; Hansische Geschichte; Wirstschaftsund Sozialwissenschaften; Lübeck. Cata: 2 pro Jahr. Corresp: English. B. Handelsbank in Lübeck. CP: Hamburg 32683-207. V.D.A., B.V.D.B.

ANTIQUARIAT AMELANG, CRANACHSTRASSE 45, 2 HAMBURG 52. Prop: Hans Benecke. TN: (040) 897 484. TA: Buchamelang, Hamburg. Gegründet 1806. Wohnung, nur nach Vereinbarung. Kleiner Vorrat. Spec: Pressendrucke und illustrierte Bücher; Erstausgaben seit 1800; alte Kinderbücher; Exilliteratur. Cata: 6 oder 7 pro Jahr. Corresp: English. B: Dresdner Bank Konto 5 220 440. CP: 365 566 Hamburg. V.D.A.

ADOLF AUER, VOLGERSWEG 43/1, 3 HANNOVER-O. TN: 21327. Gegründet 1929. Wohnung 10–18 Uhr, auch nach Vereinbarung. Nur alte Graphik. Sehr grosser Vorrat. Cata: Corresp: English. B: Deutsche Bank, Konto 0-76355. CP: Hannover 19717. V.D.A.

PETER BABENDERERDE, DANZIGER STRASSE 49, 24 LÜBECK. TN: (0451) 63485. Gegründet 1840. Laden und Lagerräume. Sehr grosser Vorrat an dekorativer Graphik, Städteansichten und Landkarten. Cata. Corresp: English, Français. B: Handelsbank. Lübeck, Konto 21075. CP: Hamburg 617. V.D.A., B.V.D.B.

BÄRENREITER ANTIQUARIAT, HEINRICH-SCHUTZ-ALLEE 35, 35 KASSEL-WILHELMSHÖHE. Prop: Dr. Karl Vötterle. Gegründet 1946. B: Deutsche Bank, Kassel. CP: Frankfurt-am-Main 531 12. V.D.A.

21

GERTRUD IRIS BERGER, Finkenau 30, 2 Hamburg 76. TN: 22 02 504. Spec: Alte und Moderne Graphik. CP: Hamburg 21 93 15. V.D.A.

WOLFGANG BRANDES o.H.G., Kleine Campestrasse 2, 33 Braunschweig. Prop: Eduard Obenaus und Ulrich Schneider. TN: (0531) 73732. TA: Buchbrandes, Braunschweig. Gegründet 1949. Wohnung, nur nach Vereinbarung. Auktionen zweimal Jährlich. Corresp: English, Français. V.D.A.

DAS BÜCHERKABINETT, Postrasse 14–16, 2 Hamburg 36. Prop: Albert und Carlota Simon, Dr. Maria Conradt. TN: 34 03 85, und 34 42 19. TA: Buecherkabinett Hamburg. Gegründet 1931. Laden, Samstag Nachmittag geschlossen. Sehr grosser Vorrat, auch neue Bücher. Spec: Alte Drucke aller Gebiete; Illustrierte Bücher; Deutsche Literatur; Alte Stadtansichten und Landkarten; alte dekorative Graphik; Noten. Corresp: English, Français, Italiano. B: Commerzbank, Hamburg, Konto 22-10706. CP: Hamburg 735 66. V.D.A.

F. DÖRLING, Neuer Wall, 2 Hamburg 36. TN: 36 46 70. TA: Doerlingant, Hamburg. Gegründet 1797. Laden, Samstag geschlossen. Sehr grosser Vorrat. Spec: alte und seltene Bücher; Graphik; Städteansichten. Auktionen zweimal Jährlich. Cata. Corresp: English, B: Deutsche Bank Hamburg Konto 02-02127. CP: Hamburg 1825-203. B.V.D.B.

RUDOLF EBBEL, Postfach 243, 29 Oldenburg: TN: (0441) 214792. Gegründet 1836. Spec: Freimauerei; Mystik. B: Landessparkasse zu Oldenburg. CP: Hannover 132692. V.D.A.

ALICE ELCHLEPP, Schillerstrasse 14, 3360 Osterode a. Harz. Spec: Alte Graphik; Militaria; Geschichte. Cata. V.D.A.

N. G. ELWERT UNIVERSITÄTSBUCHHANDLUNG, Reitgasse 7-9, 355 Marburg (Lahn). Prop: Dr Wilhelm Braun-Elwert. TN: (06421) 25024. TA: Elwert, Marburg, Gegründet 1726, priviligiert 1783. Laden und Lagerräume, Samstag Nachmittag geschlossen; vorzugsweise nach Vareinbarung. Sehr grosser Vorrat, auch neue Bücher. Spec: Deutsche Orts- und Landeskunde; Geschichte; Germanistik; Geographie; Theologie. Cata: 2 oder 3 pro Jahr. Corresp: English, Français. B: Stadtsparkasse Marburg, Konto 4000 0169. CP: Frankfurt am Main 3899-605. B.V.D.B., V.D.A., Hessiche Verleger- und Buchhandlerverband, Arbeitsgemeinschaft wissenschaftlicher Sortimenter.

KLAUS VON FRANCHEVILLE, Marktstrasse 45, 3 Hannover. TN (0511) 321645. Gegründet 1949. Laden, Samstag Nachmittag geschlossen. Spec. Ansichten Topographie; dekorative Graphik. Corresp

English, Français. B. Hallbaum, Meier & Co., Hannover, Konto 062265.
CP. Hannover 153409. B.V.D.B.

M. GLOGAU, BLEICHENBRÜCKE 6, 2 HAMBURG 36. Prop: Arthur Müller.
TN: 36 75 49. B. Vereinsbank Hamburg. CP: Hamburg 8172. V.D.A.

HAMBURGENSIEN-MEYER, POSTSTRASSE 2–4, 2 HAMBURG 36. Prop:
Franz H. Meyer. TN: 35 25 96. Spec: Graphik; Landkarten; Topographie V.D.A.

HORST HAMECHER, GOETHESTRASSE 74, 35 KASSEL. TN: (0561) 131 79.
Gegründet 1947. Wohnung und Lagerräume, nach Vereinbarung.
Sehr grosser Vorrat. Spec: Geisteswissenschaften. Cata: 5 pro Jahr.
Corresp: English. B: Stadtsparkasse Kassel (BLZ 520 501 51) Konto
016 295. CP: Frankfurt am Main 31013-602. V.D.A., B.V.D.B.

Dr. ERNST HAUSWEDELL & ERNST NOLTE, PÖSELDORFERWEG 1, 2
HAMBURG 13. TN: 44 83 66. TA: Philobiblon, Hamburg. Gegründet
1927. Wohnung, vorzugsweise nach Vereinbarung. Kleiner Vorrat.
Spec: Erstausgaben; Kunstwissenschaft, Graphik und Handzeich-
nungen; Buch- und Kunstauktionen seit 1930. Cata: 8–10 pro Jahr.
Corresp: English, Français. B: Vereinsbank Hamburg, Konto 43-0125.
CP: 137 207-204. V.D.A., S.L.A.M. (Frankreich), VEBUKU (Schweiz),
Bundesverband Deutscher Kunstversteigerer.

ANTIQUARIAT PAUL HENNINGS, ALTSTÄDTER STRASSE 15, 2 HAM-
BURG 1. Prop. Rüdiger Fritsche, TN: (040) 32 58 84. Gegründet 1931.
Laden. Samstag Nachmittag geschlossen. Sehr grosser Vorrat, auch
neue Bücher. Cata: 4 pro Jahr. Corresp: English, Français. B: Bank für
Gemeinwirtschaft, Hamburg. (BLZ 200 101 11) Konto: 1 166 481 2.
CP: Hamburg 518 48-207.

ROLF KERST, MAUERSTRASSE 16/17, 34 GÖTTINGEN, Prop. Erich Gross.
TN: (0551) 57503. Gegründet 1946. Laden, Samstag Nachmittag
geschlossen. Sehr grosser Vorrat. Spec: Geisteswissenschaften;
Geschichte der Naturwissenschaft; Alte Bucher. Cata: alle 2 Wochen.
Corresp: English, Français. B: Kreissparkasse, Göttingen, Konto 81702.
CP: Hannover 126290. V.D.A., B.V.D.B.

HORST HAMECHER
ANTIQUARIAT
D-35 KASSEL, Goethestrasse 74

23

DETLEV KURTH, VERLAG UND ANTIQUARIAT, AM MARKT 24, 2202 BARMSTEDT. (Postfach 29). TN: (04123) 4766. Gegründet 1973. Lagerräume, nur nach Vereinbarung. Kleiner Vorrat. Spec. Zoologie, Botanik, Ethnologie, Archäologie. Cata: 2 pro Jahr. Corresp: English. CP: Hamburg 27 29 21-204.

FRANZ LEUWER, AM WALL 171, 28 BREMEN. Prop: Werner Siebert. TN: 32 18 28. Gegründer 1905. Laden. Mittelgrosser Vorrat, auch neue Bücher. Spec: Deutsche Literatur; Topographie—Bremen und Norddeutschland. CP: Hamburg 6480. V.D.A., B.V.D.B.

ACHIM MAKROCKI, QUELLENSTRASSE 14, 35 KASSEL. TN: (0561) 45609. Gegründet 1966. Sech Lagerräume, Mittwoch Morgen geschlossen: vorzugsweise nach Vereinbarung. Sehr grosser Vorrat. Spec: Zeitschriften, Geographie, Literatur. Corresp: English. B: B.H.F. Bank A.G. Konto 20-10628-2. CP: Frankfurt am Main 2598 33-609.

KARL PFANKUCH, KG., KLEINE BURG 12–13, 33 BRAUNSCHWEIG. TN: 45303 Gegründet 1919. B: Volksbank und Braunschweigische Stadtsbank. CP: Hannover 41000. V.D.A.

HERBERT PREIDEL, BISMARCKSTRASSE 20, 3011 GEHRDEN. TN: (05108) 4766. TA: Preidelbuch Gehrden. Gegründet 1959. Wohnung, nur nach

Vereinbarung. Mittelgrosset Vorrat, auch neue Bücher. Spec: Medizin; Geschichte der Medizin. Corresp: English. B: Stadtsparkasse Hannover, Konto 155 446. CP: Hannover 1178 79. V.D.A., B.V.D.B., J.L.A.B.

BERNHARD SCHÄFER, Conradistrasse 2, 3522 Karlshafen. TN: 05672–503. Gegründet 1957. Laden. Mittelgrosser Vorrat. Spec: Graphik (Ex-libris Bookplates). Corresp: English, Français. B: Stadtsparkasse Karlshafen. CP: Frankfurt am Main 188 643-601. V.D.A.

B. SCHRAMM, Willestrasse 4–6, 23 Kiel. TN: (0431) 44005. V.D.A.

HELMUT GERHARD SCHULZ, Ost-West-Strasse 47, 2 Hamburg 11. TN: 33 67 74. Gegründet 1923. Spec: Militaria. B: Commerzbank, Hamburg. CP: Hamburg 57620. V.D.A.

J. A. STARGARDT, Universitätsstrasse 27, 355 Marburg. Prop: Günther und Klaus Mecklenburg. TN: 23452. Gegründet 1830. Laden und Lagerräume, Samstag Nachmittag geschlossen. Mittelgrosser Vorrat. Spec: Autographen; Auktionen; Genealogie und Heraldik. Cata: 2–3 pro Jahr. Corresp: English, Français. B: Commerzbank, Marburg. CP: Frankfurt-am-Main 116 02. V.D.A., B.V.D.B.

HARTWIG STRÜCK, Baringerstrasse 4, 338 Goslar. TN: 5825. Gegründet 1958. Laden, nur Vormittags 9 bis 13. Mittelgrosser Vorrat. Spec: Harz. Cata. B: Volksbank, Goslar, Konto 7622. CP: Hannover 212898. V.D.A., B.V.D.B.

THEATRUM ANTIQUARIAT, Ole Hoop 9, 2 Hamburg-Blankenese.

FRIEDRICH TRÜJEN, Parkstrasse 83, 28 Bremen. TN: 34 18 47. Gegründet 1931. CP: Hamburg 62514.

III

RHEIN & RUHR   Postcodes: Postleitzahlen 4+ & 5+

- 51 AACHEN (Aix-la-Chapelle)
- 5070 BERGISCH GLADBACH
- 48 BIELEFELD
- 463 BOCHUM
- 53 BONN
- 3441 DATTERODE
- 41 DUISBURG
- 4 DÜSSELDORF
- 43 ESSEN

- 5 KÖLN (Cologne)
- 415 KREFELD
- 44 MÜNSTER
- 4054 NETTETAL
- 404 NEUSS
- 45 OSNABRÜCK
- 4542 TECKLENBURG
- 5620 VELBERT
- 56 WUPPERTAL

"ARMARIUM" BUCHHANDLUNG UND ANTIQUARIAT, JAHN-STRASSE 116, 4 DÜSSELDORF 1. Prop: Hermann Kullmann. TN: 346378 Gegründet 1961. Laden und Lagerräume, Samstag Nachmittag geschlossen. Mittelgrosser Vorrat. Spec: Geschichte; bes. historische Hilfwissenschaften. Cata. Corresp: English, Français. B: Stadt-Sparkasse Düsseldorf, Konto 1009 2914. CP: Köln 12 2098. V.D.A., B.V.D.B.

JOSEF BEYER, AHORNWEG 15, 5070 BERGISH GLADBACH. TN: (02202) 32 222. Wohnung. Kriegspropagandazettel; Psychologischer Krieg. Corresp: English, Français.

BOCHUMER ANTIQUARIAT G.m.b.H. & Co., K.G. VOSSKUHLSTRASSE 74, 4630 BOCHUM-STIEPEL. Prop: Jürgen Henning und Oskar Loewe. TN: (0234) 79 12 97. Gegründet 1969. Wohnung, nur nach Verein-barung. Sehr kleiner Vorrat. Corresp: English. B: Deutsche Bank, Bochum. Konto 105–0467. CP: Essen (43) 1187 51–439.

C. G. BOERNER, KASERNENSTRASSE 14, 4 DÜSSELDORF. Prop: Ruth-Maria Mithmann und Dr. Eduard Trautscholdt. TN: 37 49 81. TA: Boernerkunst Düsseldorf. Gegründet 1826. Laden, Samstag nach Vereinbarung. Spec: Alte Graphik; alte Handzeichnungen. Cata: 2 pro Jahr. Corresp: English, Français. B: Bankhaus C. G. Trinkaus & Burkhardt, Düsseldorf. (BLZ 300 30880) Konto 739–014. CP: Essen 21446–437.

BOUVIER UNIVERSITÄTSBUCHHANDLUNG G.m.b.H., AM HOF 32, 53 BONN. Prop: Herbert Grundmann K.G. TN: 65 44 45. Gegründet 1828. Laden und Lagerräume. Grosser Vorrat, auch neue Bücher. Spec: Geisteswissenschaft; Bibliophilie. Cata: periodische. Corresp: English, Français. B: Stadt Sparkasse Bonn. CP: Köln 16 667. B.V.D.B.

BÜCHERSTUBE AM DOM, HANS MEYER & CO., NEUMARKT 2, 5 KÖLN 1. TN: 234 234. Gegründet 1931. B: Dresdner Bank und Deutsche Bank. CP: Köln 537 92. V.D.A.

FRIEDRICH BURCHARD, SONNBORNERSTRASSE 144, 56 WUPPERTAL-SONNBORN. TN: 740337 und 742696. TA: Burchard Wuppertal.

Gegründet 1907. Laden und Lagerräume, Samstag Nachmittag geschlossen. Sehr grosser Vorrat, auch neue Bücher. Spec: Naturwissenschaften. Corresp: English, Français. B: Deutsche Bank AG., Wuppertal-Elberfeld, Konto 11/8083. CP: Köln 23935–502. V.D.A., B.V.D.B.

CARL F. CHRISPEELS, COMBAHNSTRASSE 15, 53 BONN-BEUEL 1. (Postfach 510 260). TN: 438 37- Gegründet 1964. Lagerräume, Samstag geschlossen. Mittelgrosser Vorrat, auch neue Bücher. Spec: Kunst und Geschichte bis 15. Jahrhunderts. Cata: 4 pro Jahr. Corresp: English, Français, Español, Italiano. B: Deutsche Bank, Bonn-Beuel, Konto 095 4917; Crédit Lyonnais, Paris, Konto 6070 J. CP: Köln 1720 89. V.D.A.

H. D. VON DIEPENBROICK-GRÜTER, HAUS MARK, 4542 TECKLENBURG. TN: 291. Gegründet 1923. Wohnung, nur nach Vereinbarung. Vorrat: 200,000 Porträts. Cata: 1 pro Jahr. Corresp: English, Français. B: Sparkasse Tecklenburg, Konto 134. CP: Dortmund 26139. V.D.A., B.V.D.B.

ANTIQUARIAT GÜNTER FUCHS, CRANACHPLATZ 1 4 DÜSSELDORF. TN: (0211) 66 65 28. Gegründet 1969. Lagerraum und Wohnung, nur nach Vereinbarung. Kleiner Vorrat, auch neue Bücher. Spec: moderne Kunst (1880–1975). Cata: ? pro Jahr. Corresp: English, Français. B: Deutsche Bank, Düsseldorf, Konto 58 203 11. CP: Köln 23 94 32–509.

NEUE BÜCHERSTUBE R. FUNCK, KENNEDY-PLATZ 5, 43 ESSEN. TN: (02141) 224841.

GOECKE & EVERS, DÜRERSTRASSE 13, 415 KREFELD. Prop: Alfons Evers. TN: 25025. Gegründet 1928. Grosser Vorrat, auch neue Bücher. Spec: Biologie, Zoologie, Botanik, Geologie. Cata: 1–2 pro Jahr. Corresp: English, Français, Español. B: Kreisbank, Krefeld, Konto 35717. CP: Essen 62258 433. B.V.D.B.

DR. RUDOLF HABELT, G.m.b.H., AM BUCHENHANG 1, 53 BONN 5. (Postfach 5004). TN: 23 20 15. TA: Buchhabelt Bonn. Gegründet 1948. Lagerräume, nur nach Vereinbarung. Sehr grosser Vorrat. Spec: Archäologie; Altertumswissenschaft; Ostasien. Cata: 4–6 pro Jahr. Corresp: English, Français. B: Deutsche Bank, Bonn, Konto 0320481. CP: Köln 52676. V.D.A., B.V.D.B.

WERNER HEYBUTZKI, PFEILSTRASSE 8, 5 KÖLN. TN: 21 61 31. Laden. Grosser Vorrat, auch neue Bücher. Spec: Kunst; Bibliophilie; Geschichte; Literatur. CP: Köln 90922. V.D.A.

THEO HILL, SCHILDERGASSE 107, 5 KÖLN. TN: 21 29 72. Spec: Alte und moderne Graphik. CP: Köln 56412. V.D.A.

WILHELM KUHRDT, PAULUSSTRASSE 28. 48 BIELEFELD. Spec: Literatur; Geschichte; Erstausgaben. V.D.A.

KUNSTANTIQUARIAT AM RATHAUS, NIEDERWALL 14, 48 BIELEFELD. TN: (0521) 64420.

WILH. KUTSCH, AM DOM/HAUPTBAHNHOF, 5 KÖLN 1.

WALTER KUTTNER, 5620 VELBERT. TN: 3670. Gegründet 1949. Wohnung. Grosset Vorrat. Cata: 6 pro Jahr. Corresp: English, Français. B: Deutsche Bank, Neviges, Konto 154–0616. CP: Köln 543 54–501.

GÜNTHER LEISTEN, IN DER HÖHLE 6, 5 KÖLN. TN: 23 27 47. Gegründet 1951. Shop, Samstag Nachmittag geschlossen. Kleine Vorrat. Spec: schöne und seltene Bücher; Graphik. Corresp: English, Français. B: Dresdner Bank, Köln. CP: Köln 1230 66. V.D.A., B.V.D.B., I.L.A.B.

DR. KONRAD LIEBMANN, LÜRMANNSTRASSE 47, 45 OSNABRÜCK. TN: (0541) 67237. Gegründet 1972. Wohnung, vorzugsweise nach Vereinbarung. Kleiner Vorrat. Spec: Erstausgaben; Philosophie und Wissen-

schaft; Einbäande. Cata: 1 pro Jahr. Corresp: English, Français. B:
Deutsche Bank, Osnabrück, Konto 38–83162. B.V.D.B. Landesverband
der Niedersächsischen Buchhändler und Verleger.

CLAUS LINCKE, KÖNIGSALLEE 96, 4 DÜSSELDORF. TN: 329257. Gegründet
1846. (als Deiters Buchhandlung). Spec: Alte und seltene Bücher;
Erstausgaben; Topographie und Reisen; Alte und moderne Graphik;
Illustrierte Bücher. CP: Köln 1977. V.D.A.

HANS MARCUS, GRABENSTRASSE 11 A, 4 DÜSSELDORF. TN: 32 11 40.
Gegründet 1936. Spec: Alte illustrierte, Bücher Graphik. B: Commerzbank, Düsseldorf. V.D.A.

HANS K. MATUSSEK, HOCHSTRASSE 9, 4054 NETTETAL. TN: (02153)
3057. V.D.A.

F. und A. MEHREN, MAURITZSTRASSE 3, 44 MÜNSTER. TN: 26517.
Lagerräume. Spec: Geschichte; Orts- und Landesgeschichte. Cata:
Monatlich. Corresp: English, Français. B: Kreissparkasse Westfalen,
Konto 15 1746. CP: Dortmund 19163. V.D.A., B.V.D.B.

KONRAD MEUSCHEL, KAISERPLATZ 5, 53 BONN. TN: 65 34 28. Gegründet 1969. Wohnung, nach vorheriger Vereinbarung. Spec: Goetheana; autographen; alte und seltene Bücher. Corresp: English, Français.
B: Dresdner Bank, Bonn, Konto 2 227 022. CP: Köln 2 389–500.
V.D.A., VEBUKU (Schweiz) L.I.L.A.

CLEMENS MÜLLER, KAPELLENWEG 59, 56 WUPPERTAL-BARMEN. TN:
42 23 81. Gegründet 1955. Spec: Topographie; Theologie. B: Bankhaus
v. d. Heydt, Wuppertal-Elberfeld. CP: Essen 85333. V.D.A.

HORST NIBBE, AUF DEM BERLICH 9, 5 KÖLN. TN: 23 14 27. Gegründet
1965. Laden, Samstag Nachmittag geschlossen. Grosser Vorrat. Spec:
Expressionismus; Deutsche Literatur; Kunst; Illustrierte Bücher. Cata:
2 pro Jahr. Corresp: English. CP: Köln 184–877.

GALERIE ORANGERIE, HELENENSTRASSE 2, 5 KÖLN. TN: 234684. V.D.A.

**Autographs
Old and Rare Books
Humanism, History of Sciences
Old Master Prints**

Konrad Meuschel, 53 Bonn 1, Kaiserplatz 5

JOACHIM REINHARDT, Burgfreiheit 8, 48 Bielefeld. TN: 649 76. Gegründet 1949. Laden und Lagerräume, Samstag Nachmittag geschlossen. Mittelgrosser Vorrat. Spec: Judaica; Zeitgeschichte 1914–1945; Occulta; Masonica; Westphalica. Cata: alle 3 Wochen. Corresp: English, Français. B: Dresdner Bank, Bielefeld, Konto 2090910. CP: Hannover 621 12–309. V.D.A., B.V.D.B.

C. ROEMKE & CIE., Apostelnstrasse 7, 5 Köln 1 (Buch- und Kunsthandlung Friedrich Tacke o.H.G.) prop: Friedrich Tacke und Ingrid Mennenöh. TN: (0221) 21 76 36 und 21 45 16. Gegründet 1865. Laden. Sehr kleiner Vorrat, auch neue Bücher (Sortimentsbuchhandlung). Corresp: English, Français. B: Dresdner Bank, Köln, CP: Köln 3440–503. B.V.D.B.

LUDWIG RÖHRSCHEID G.m.b.H., am Hof 28, 53 Bonn. TN: 63 12 81. Telex: 088 69523. Gegründet 1818. Laden, Samstag nachmittag geschlossen. Sehr grosser Vorrat, auch neue Bücher. Spec: Geschichte; Erstausgaben; Graphik. Cata. Corresp: English, Français. B: Dresdner Bank, Bonn, Konto 207 76 81. CP: Köln 34118–507. V.D.A., B.V.D.B.

KARL SCHMETZ, Kleinmrschierstrasse 5, 51 Aachen. TN: 31 369. Gegründet 1951. Laden, Samstag Nachmittag geschlossen. Mittelgrosser Vorrat, auch neue Bücher. Spec: Natur- und Geisteswissenschaften. B: Stadtsparkasse, Aachen, Konto-Nr. 695. CP: Köln 119 525. B.V.D.B.

WALTER SCHMIDT, Falltor 179, 3441 Datterode. TN: (05658) 467.

FERDINAND SCHÖNINGH, Domhof 4c, 45 Osnabrück. (Postfach 4020). TN: 285 24. Gegründet 1888. Laden und Lagerräume, Montag bis Freitag 15.00–18.000 und nach Vereinbarung. Sehr grosser Vorrat. Spec: Geschichte; Literatur; Kunst; Graphik. Cata: 6 pro Jahr. Corresp: English, Français. B: Deutsche Bank, Osnabrück, Konto 6–02342 und Commerzbank, Osnabrück, Konto 53–415 32. CP: Hannover 946 46. V.D.A.

HANNO SCHREYER, Euskirchenerstrasse 57–59, 53 Bonn 1. TN: 621059: TA: Buchschreyer Bonn. Gegründet 1953. Laden und Lagerräume, Samstag Nachmittag geschlossen. Grosser Vorrat. Spec: Alte Lankarten, alte dekorative Graphik, illustrierte Bücher 15. bis 20. Jahrhundert. Corresp: English, Français. B: Sparkasse Bonn, Konto 9035. CP: Köln 121364–503. V.D.A., L.L.A.B.

EMIL SEMMEL, Meckenheimerstrasse 45, 53 Bonn. TN: 636528. TA: Mediaevist Bonn. Gegründet 1956. Lagerräume, Samstag geschlossen. Spec: Mittelalter. Cata. B: Dresdner Bank, Bonn. CP: Köln 45261. V.D.A., B.V.D.B.

Th. STENDERHOFF & CO., ALTER FIRSCHMARKT 21, 44 MÜNSTER. Prop:
Theo. Hobbeling. TN: 44749. Gegründet 1913. Laden, Samstag Nach-
mittag geschlossen. Sehr grosser Vorrat. Spec: Alte Bücher, Theologie,
Philosophie, Geschichte, Literatur, dekorative Graphik, Städteansich-
ten, Landkarten. Cata: 8 pro Jahr. Corresp: English, Français. B:
Deutsche Bank, Münster, Konto 104 901. CP: Dortmund 858 20–461.
V.D.A.

STERN-VERLAG JANSSEN & CO., FRIEDRICHSTRASSE 26, 4 DÜSSEL-
DORF. Prop: H. und K. Janssen. TN: (0211) 373033. Gegründet 1900.
Laden, Samstag Nachmittag geschlossen. Sehr grosser Vorrat, auch
neue Bücher. Spec: Geiteswissenschaften; Modernes Antiquariat. Cata:
4 pro Jahr. Corresp: English, Français. B: Stadtsparkasse Düsseldorf.
Konto 47 00 00 13. CP: Köln 13976. B.V.D.B.

WOLFGANG SYMANCZYK, HUBERTUSWEG 32, 404 NEUSS. TN: 46 43
23. Gegründet 1958. Wohnung und Lagerräume, Samstag Nachmittag
geschlossen. Mittelgrosser Vorrat, auch neue Bücher. Spec: Klassische
Philologie; Geschichte der Wissenschaften. Cata: 12 pro Jahr. Corresp:
English. B: Stadtsparkasse Neuss, Konto 23 46 09. CP: Köln 220 954–
505. V.D.A., B.V.D.B.

HEINZ TATTERMUSCH, BERGIUSSTRASSE 10, 41 DUISBURG-RUHRORT.
TN: 81426. Gegründet 1947. Laden, Samstag Nachmittag geschlossen.
Mittelgrosser Vorrat. Spec: Niederrhein und Ruhrgebiet; Rhein-
schiffahrt; Frühsozialismus. Corresp: English. B: Rhein-Ruhr Bank,
Ruhrort, Konto-Nr. 17 114. CP: Essen 697 43. V.D.A., B.V.D.B.

HANS TROJANSKI, BLUMENSTRASSE 11, 4 DÜSSELDORF. TN: 36 92 04.
Gegründet 1924. B: Bankhaus Simon, Düsseldorf. CP: Essen 3895–436.

URBS & ORBIS, ENDENICHER ALLEE 52, 53 BONN. TN: (02221) 652668.

VENATOR, KG., ST. APERNSTRASSE 56–62, 5 KÖLN. Prop: Rolf Venator.
TN: 23 29 62. Gegründet 1946. Laden, Samstag Nachmittag geschlossen.
Sehr kleiner Vorrat. Spec: Alte und moderne Bibliophilie; Dekorative
Graphik; Auktionen. Cata. Corresp: English, Français. B: Bankhaus
J. H. Stein, Köln, Konto 34002. CP: Köln 12010. V.D.A.

DR. HELMUT VESTER, FRIEDRICHSTRASSE 7, 4 DÜSSELDORF. TN:
382843. Gegründet 1954. Spec: Medizin, Naturwissenschaften. B:
Kreissparkasse, Düsseldorf. CP: Köln 21149. V.D.A.

GALERIE VÖMEL, KÖNIGSALLEE 30, 4 DÜSSELDORF. Prop: Alex. und
Edwin Vömel. TN: (0211) 32 41 22. TA: Galerievoemel Düsseldorf.
Spec: Gemälde, Handzeichnungen, Skulpturen, Graphik. CP: Köln
68204. V.D.A.

H. TH. WENNER, GROSSE STRASSE 69, 45 OSNABRÜCK. (Postfach 4307). TN: (0541) 28102. TA: Buchwenner Osnabrück. Gegründet 1945. Laden und lagerräume, Samstag Nachmittag geschlossen. Grosser Vorrat. Spec: Alte Drucke; Literatur; Orts- und Landesgeschichte; Zeitschriften. Cata: 2–3 pro Jahr. Corresp: English. B: Commerzbank, Osnabrück, Konto 53/74897. CP: Hannover 17182. V.D.A.

OTTO ZELLER, JAHNSTRASSE 15, 45 OSNABRÜCK. TN: 41217. Gegründet 1961. Spec: Geschichte der Wissenschaften. CP: Stuttgart 92610. V.D.A.

IV

MAIN & TAUNUS	Postcodes; Postleitzahlen 6+
61 DARMSTADT	67 LUDWIGSHAFEN
6 FRANKFURT-AM-MAIN	65 MAINZ
63 GIESSEN	637 OBERURSEL
69 HEIDELBERG	6226 WALLUF
	6731 WEIDENTHAL
675 KAISERSLAUTERN	62 WIESBADEN
624 KÖNIGSTEIN	652 WORMS

"BIBLIOGRAPHICUM", HAUPTSTRASSE 194, 69 HEIDELBERG. Prop: Erna Tenner. V.D.A.

GALERIE SIEGFRIED BRUMME, BRAUBACHSTRASSE 34, 6 FRANKFURT-AM-MAIN. TN: (0611) 28 72 63. Gegründet 1950. Laden, Samstag Nachmittag geschlossen. Mittelgrosser Vorrat. Spec: Landkarte, alte Graphik, Topographie. Cata: 1 pro Jahr. Corresp: English, Français. B: Bethmann Bank, Frankfurt, Konto 15714–4–00. CP: Frankfurt 361 63–605. V.D.A., Verband Hessischer Antiquitätenhändler.

EUGEN CRUSIUS, KARL-MARX-STRASSE 15, 675 KAISERSLAUTERN. TN: 2144. Gegründet 1881. Spec: Pfalzliteratur. B: Vereinsbank, Kaiserslautern, Konto 3043. CP: Ludwigshafen 2265. V.D.A.

HARRI DEUTSCH, GRAEFSTRASSE 47, 6 FRANKFURT-AM-MAIN 3. TN: 77 73 90 und 70 24 67. Laden. Mittelgrosser Vorrat, auch neue Bücher. Spec: Naturwissenschaften. Corresp: English. B: Frankfurter Sparkasse, Konto 50/325 309. CP: Frankfurt-am-Main 112 722.

JOSEPH FACH, OHG, FAHRGASSE 8, 6 FRANKFURT-AM-MAIN. Prop: Joseph und Werner Fach. TN: 287761. Gegründet 1928. Mittelgrosser Vorrat. Spec: Graphik; Handzeichnungen; Illustrierte Bücher. Corresp: English, Français. CP: Frankfurt-am-Main 115 607. V.D.A.

34

FRANKFURTER BÜCHERSTUBE, Börsenstrasse 2–4. 6 Frankfurt-am-Main. Prop: Richard Schumann. TN: 28 14 94. Gegründet 1920. Spec: Kunstgeschichte; Illustrierte Bücher; Alte Kinderbücher. B: Georg Hauck & Sohn, Frankfurt-am-Main. CP: Frankfurt-am-Main 47420. V.D.A.

FRANKFURTER KUNSTKABINETT, HANNA BEKKER VOM RATH, G.m.b.H., Börsenplatz 13–15, 6 Frankfurt-am-Main. TN: 281085. Gegründet 1947. Laden und Lagerräume. Spec: Kunst des 20. Jahrhunderts. Cata. Corresp: English, Français. B: Dresdner Bank AG, Frankfurt-am-Main, Konto 522 150 und Bank für Gemeinwirtschaft AG, Frankfurt-am-Main, Konto 1074 6602. V.D.A.

KARL GERLINGHAUS, Schloss Platz 1, 652 Worms. TN: 22159. Gegründet 1911. Sehr kleiner Vorrat. Corresp: English. B: Kreis und Stadtsparkasse, Worms, Konto 152. V.D.A.

HANS J. VON GOETZ, Wörthstrasse 28, 62 Wiesbaden. TN: 37 23 58. Gegrundet 1928. Laden, Samstag Nachmittag geschlossen. Mittelgrosser Vorrat, auch neue Bücher. Spec: Bibliophilie; Kunstgeschichte; Geschichte. Corresp: English, Français. B: Nassauische Sparkasse, Wiesbaden, Konto 100 040 999. V.D.A.

JOHANNES GUTENBERG, Grosse Bleiche 29, 65 Mainz. (Auch In der Universität). Prop: Josef A. Kohl. TN: 24890. Gegründet 1946. B: Mainzer Volksbank, Mainz. CP: Ludwigshafen 27790. V.D.A.

OTTO HARRASSOWITZ, Taunusstrasse 5, 62 Wiesbaden. Prop: Felix Oswald Weigel. TN: 52 10 46. Gegründet 1872. Lagerräume. Grosser Vorrat, auch neue Bücher. Spec: Deutsche Literatur; Orientalistik. Cata. Corresp: English, Français. B: Deutsche Bank, Wiesbaden. CP: Frankfurt-am-Main, 654 27. V.D.A.

AUGUST HASE, im Trutz 2, 6 Frankfurt-am-Main. TN: 55 37 77. Gegründet 1932. Spec: Autographen; Graphik; Postgeschichte. Cata: periodische. B: Stadtsparkasse, Frankfurt-am-Main. CP: Frankfurt-am-Main 524 89. V.D.A.

WILHELM HENRICH, Schumannstrasse 57, 6 Frankfurt-am-Main. TN: 77501. B: Deutsche Effecten- und Wechselbank, Frankfurt-am-Main. CP: Frankfurt-am-Main 91568. V.D.A.

ERNST HOFFMANN, Weissadlergasse 3, 6 Frankfurt-am-Main. Prop: Klaus Peter Hoffmann. TN: 28 37 81. TA: Buchhoffmann Frankfurt-am-Main. Gegründet 1929. Laden, Samstag Nachmittag geschlossen. Grosser Vorrat. Spec: Inkunabeln; Holzschnittbücher; Humanismus; Reformation; Alte Drucke; Deutsche Literatur; Dekorative Graphik. Cata: 2 pro Jahr. Corresp: English, Italiano. B: Bankhaus Gebrüder Bethmann, Konto 15404–5–00. CP: Frankfurt-am-Main 22760. V.D.A., I.L.A.B.

WILHELM HOFMANN, BISMARCKSTRASSE 98, 67 LUDWIGSHAFEN. TN: 0621/516001. Gegründet 1889. Laden. Spec: Landkarten und Literatur, Pfalz und Rhein. CP: Ludwigshafen 4663. V.D.A.

JÜRGEN HOLSTEIN, GERICHTSSTRASSE 7a, 6240 KÖNIGSTEIN. (Postfach 1220). TN: (06174) 3693. Gegründet 1966. Laden, Samstag geschlossen; vorzugsweise nach Vereinbarung. Grosser Vorrat, auch neue Bücher. Spec: Kunst und Kunstgewerbe. Cata: 4 pro Jahr. Corresp: English. B: Bethmann Bank, Frankfurt, Konto 15638 600. CP: Frankfurt 207 187–607. V.D.A.

FERDINAND KEIP, HAINERWEG 46–48, 6 FRANKFURT-AM-MAIN. TN: 61 18 42, und 68 90 49. Gegründet 1959. Sehr grosser Vorrat. Spec: Recht; Wirtschaft und Gesellschaft. Corresp: English. B: Deutsche Länderbank AG, Frankfurt-am-Main. CP: Frankfurt-am-Main 213810. V.D.A.

RUDOLF KLEINERT, RÜDESHEIMERSTRASSE 21, 62 WIESBADEN. Spec: Alte Medizin. CP: München 200791. V.D.A.

OTTO KOELTZ, HERRNWALDSTRASSE 6, 624 KÖNIGSTEIN-TAUNUS. TN: 4492. Gegründet 1900 in Leipzig. Lagerräume, Samstag geschlossen, nur nach Vereinbarung. Mittelgrosser Vorrat, auch neue Bücher. Spec: Botanik; Zoologie; Paleontologie; Geologie. Cata. Corresp: English, Français. B: Effectenbank-Warburg AG, Frankfurt-am-Main, Konto 30 771. CP: Frankfurt-am-Main 86 791. B.V.D.B.

FRIEDRICH KOHLHOFF, HOLZWEG 14/I, 637 OBERURSEL. TN: (06171) 54506. Gegründet 1949. Spec: Kunst; Philosophie. B: Georg, Hauck & Sohn, Oberursel. CP: Frankfurt-am-Main 10441. V.D.A.

PETER NAACHER, SCHWEIZERSTRASSE 25, 6 FRANKFURT-AM-MAIN. TN: 287641. TA: Buecherhaus Frankfurt. Gegründet 1909. B: Frankfurter Volksbank. CP: Frankfurt-am-Main 445 68. V.D.A.

GÜNTER NOBIS, FORSTSTRASSE 12, 62 WIESBADEN. TN: (06121) 54 11 06. Gegründet 1962. Büro und Lagerräume, nur nach Vereinbarung. Sehr grosser Vorrat. Spec: Erstausgaben; Geschichte; illustrierte Bücher; alte und wertvolle Bücher. Cata. Corresp: English, Français. B: Nassauische Sparkasse, Wiesbaden, Konto 100 028 123. CP: Frankfurt-am-Main 688 36. V.D.A.

RUDOLF PATZER, MAINZER BERG 23, 6731 WEIDENTHAL. TN: 06329–362, TA: Patzer, Weidenthal (Pfalz). Gegründet 1698. Lagerräume, nur nach Vereinbarung. Grosser Vorrat. Spec: Bibliographie und Buchwesen; Zeitschriften. Cata: 2, und 3–4 Listen pro Jahr. Corresp: English. B: Deutsche Bank, Neustadt/Weinstr. Konto 06/02060. CP: Frankfurt/Main 184 381–609. V.D.A.

HELMUT H. RUMBLER, BRAUBACHSTRASSE 36, 6 FRANKFURT-AM-MAIN. TN: (0611) 291142.

DR. MARTIN SÄNDIG, G.m.b.H., NELKENSTRASSE 2, 6226 WALLUF 1. (Postfach 89). Prop: Kraus-Thomson-Organisation. TN: (06123) 710 38. Telex: 4 182 915 (saen d). TA: Sandiquar, Walluf. Gegründet 1923. Lagerräume. Mittelgrosser Vorrat. Spec: Mathematik; Naturwissenschaften; Technik; Geschichte der Wissenschaften. Cata: 2 pro Jahr. Corresp: English. B: Nass. Sparkasse, Walluf. Konto 472 01 4811; Chemical Bank Frankfurt-am-Main. Konto 120 306 781. CP: Frankfurt 26780–600. B.V.D.B., V.D.A.

GESCHWISTER SCHMIDT, KARL-MARX-STRASSE 15, 675 KAISERSLAUTERN. TN: (0631) 2144. V.D.A.

KARL FRIEDRICH SCHNEIDER, SELTERSWEG 38, 63 GIESSEN. TN: 5152. V.D.A.

RENÉ SIMMERMACHER, TURNSEESTRASSE 4a, 6 FRANKFURT-AM-MAIN. TN: (0761) 73676. Spec: Illustrierte Bücher.

TECHNISCHES ANTIQUARIAT, LAUTESCHLAGERSTRASSE 4, 61 DARMSTADT. Prop: Dipl.-Wirtsch.-Ing. Rudolf Wellnitz. TN: 76548. Gegründet 1948. Laden und Lagerräume, Samstag Nachmittag geschlossen. Sehr grosser Vorrat, auch neue Bücher. Spec: Mathematik; Naturwissenschaft; Technik. Cata. Corresp: English, Français. B: Sparkasse, Darmstadt, Konto 557269. CP: Frankfurt-am-Main 77213. V.D.A.

ERNA TENNER, HAUPTSTRASSE 194, 69 HEIDELBERG. TN: (06221) 26252.

HELMUT TENNER, BAHNHOFSTRASSE 63, 69 HEIDELBERG. TN: 24237. TA: Buchtenner Heidelberg. Gegründet 1864. Büroräume im I Stock. Samstag Nachmittag geschlossen. Kleiner Vorrat. Spec: Erstausgaben; Deutsche Literatur; Naturwissenschaften; Auktionen. Corresp: English, Français. B: Deutsche Bank, Heidelberg, Konto 46324. CP: Karlsruhe 18302. V.D.A.

TRÉSOR DE LIVRES ET GRAPHIQUES, DARMSTÄDTER LANDSTRASSE 119, 6 FRANKFURT-AM-MAIN 70. TN: (0611) 682551. Cata.

BUNDESREPUBLIK DEUTSCHLAND

KARL VONDERBANK, KG., GOETHESTRASSE 11, 6 FRANKFURT-AM-MAIN.
TN: 28 24 90. Gegründet 1866. Laden, Samstag Nachmittag geschlossen.
Spec: Moderne Graphik; Kunst. Corresp: English, Français. CP:
Frankfurt-am-Main 9758. V.D.A.

WOLFGANG WEIDLICH, SAVIGNYSTRASSE 61, 6 FRANKFURT-AM-MAIN.
TN: (0611) 7462 15. Gegründet 1945. Lagerräume und Wohnung.
Mittelgrosser Vorrat, auch neue Bücher. Spec: Ost- und Mittel-
deutschland. Cata: 6 oder 7 pro Jahr. Corresp: English. B: Gebrüder
Bethmann Bank, Frankfurt, Konto 17498 7–00. CP: Frankfurt 18 26 00.
B.V.D.B.

ELISABETH WELLNITZ, SACHSENSTRASSE 35, 61 DARMSTADT-EBER-
STADT. TN: (06151) 54716. Gegründet 1959. Wohnung, nur nach
Vereinbarung. Sehr kleiner Vorrat. Spec: Geschichte; Politik; Wehr-
wesen. Cata: 2 pro Jahr. Corresp: English. B: Stadt-u. Kreis Sparkasse,
Darmstadt, Konto 54 56 51. CP: Frankfurt-am-Main 6409–606.

RUDOLF WELLNITZ, LAUTESCHLÄGERSTRASSE 4, 61 DARMSTADT. TN:
(06151) 76548.

WIENER BÜCHERSTUBE, ESCHERSHEIMER LANDSTRASSE 18, 6 FRANK-
FURT AM-MAIN, Prop: Dr. Maria Sieber. TN: 55 60 43. Spec: Deutsche
Literatur; Wissenschaften; Dekorative Graphik. V.D.A.

AKADEMISCHE BUCHHANDLUNG WÖTZEL, PAUL-EHRLICH-
STRASSE 24, 6 FRANKFURT-AM-MAIN, Prop: Irene Wötzel. TN: 612657
und 682430. Gegründet 1951. Laden und Lagerräume, Samstag Nachmittag geschlossen. Grosser Vorrat, auch neue Bücher. Spec: Medizin;
Naturwissenschaften; Psychologie. Cata. Corresp: English. B: Stadtsparkasse, Frankfurt-am-Main, Konto 66–17515. CP: Frankfurt-am-
Main 37 133. V.D.A., B.V.D.B.

HANS WÜNDISCH, KORNMARKT 9, 69 HEIDELBERG. TN: 23100. TA:
Wuendisch Heidelberg. Cata. CP: Karlsruhe 78459. V.D.A.

V

SOUTH WESTERN GERMANY: SUDWEST-
DEUTSCHLAND: ALLEMAGNE (SUDOUEST)

Postcode: Postleitzahl 7+

747 ALBSTADT

757 BADEN-BADEN

7847 BADENWEILER

73 ESSLINGEN

78 FREIBURG in BR.

734 GEISLINGEN

38

71 HEILBRONN
775 KONSTANZ
7947 MENGEN
741 REUTLINGEN
7407 ROTTENBURG

7811 ST. PETER
SCHWARZWALD
7 STUTTGART
74 TÜBINGEN
79 ULM
7987 WEINGARTEN

EBERHARD ALBERT, KAISER-JOSEPH-STRASSE 179, 78 FREIBURG/
BREISGAU. TN: 4 42 88. Gegründet 1828. Laden, Samstag Nachmittag
geschlossen. Sehr grosser Vorrat, auch neue Bücher. Spec: Jura;
Wirtschaft; Philologie; Geschichte; Baden; Elsass. Cata: 3–4 pro Jahr.
Corresp: English, Français. B: Bankhaus Krebs, Freiburg. CP: Karls-
ruhe 166 53. V.D.A.

HERBERT BLANK, TRAUBERGSTRASSE 30, 7 STUTTGART. TN: (0711)
463068.

B.M.C.F. ANTIQUARIAT, LANGER WEG 35, 7901 ULM-GÖGGLINGEN.
Prop: Rainer Feucht. Gegründet 1975. Wohnung, nur nach Vereinbarung. Kleiner Vorrat. Spec: Bibliotheca magica, curiosa et Folkloristica. Cata: unregelmässig. Corresp: English, Français, Español.
B: Ulmer Volksbank.

WALTHER BREINERSDORF, EBITZWEG 7, 7 STUTTGART-BAD CANN-
STADT. TN: 56 57 53. Gegründet 1949. Spec: Theologie, Volkskunde;
Geschichte; Philologie. B: Bank für Gemeinwirtschaft, Stuttgart,
Konto 73267. V.D.A.

F. A. BROCKHAUS (ABTEILUNG ANTIQUARIUM), RÄPPLENSTRASSE
20, 7000 STUTTGART. (Postfach 1164). TN: 29 55 51. TA: Fab, Stuttgart. Spec: Geographie, Ethnologie, Geistes und Naturwissenschaften,
Cata. Corresp: English. B: Deutsche Bank, Stuttgart, Konto 11–28 818.
CP: Stuttgart 24 35–708. V.D.A., B.V.D.B.

FRITZ EGGERT, FELIX DAHN STRASSE 53, 7 STUTTGART, TN: 62 26 97.
Gegründet 1953. Spec: Illustrierte Bücher; deutsche Literatur. B:
Bankhaus Anselm, Stuttgart. CP: Stuttgart 59 77 7. V.D.A.

KUNSTGALERIE ESSLINGEN, GRÜNERWEG 17, 73 ESSLINGEN. Prop:
Ralph D. I. Jentsch. TN: (0711) 371985. Gegründet 1968. Wohnung:
nur nach Vereinbarung. Sehr kleiner Vorrat. Spec: illustrierte Bücher
des 20. Jahrhunderts; Karikaturen. Corresp: English. B: Kreissparkasse
Esslingen, Konto 909417. CP: Stuttgart 142 550–701. B.V.D.B.

ERWIN FLUHRER, WIESENSTEIGERSTRASSE 17, 7340 GEISLINGEN/STEIGE.
(Postfach 10). TN: (07331) 41620. Lagerräume und Wohnung. Mittelgrosser Vorrat, auch neue Bücher (wenig). Spec: Naturwissenschaften;

Länder und Ortsbde von Westdeutschland. Cata: 3 oder 4 pro Jahr. Corresp: English, Français. B: Deutsche Bank, Konto 712 182. CP: 11 56 46 Stuttgart.

ANTIQUARIAT FRITSCH, POSTFACH 1830, 79 ULM/DONAU. Prop: G. Fritsch. TN: 51283. Wohnung, nur nach Vereinbarung. Kleine Vorrat, auch neue Bücher. Spec: Geschichte d. Wissenschaften, Cata: 2–3 pro Jahr. Corresp: English, Français. B: Ulmer Volksbank. Konto 13130. CP: Stuttgart 72187. V.D.A., B.V.D.B.

KARL GESS, KANZLEISTRASSE 5, 7750 KONSTANZ. (Postfach 190). Prop: Eberhard Gess. TN: (07531) 22320. TA: Buch Gess Konstanz. Gegründet 1842. Laden. Mittelgrosser Vorrat. Spec: Geschichte; Philosophie; Literaturwissenschaft. Cata: 8 bis 10 pro Jahr. Corresp: English, Français. B: Deutsche Bank, Kontonummer 124 800, Komstanz; Midland Bank Account 557 619, London. CP: Karlsruhe 305. V.D.A.

ERNST GROSSER, REBBACHSTRASSE 11, 7987 WEINGARTEN (WÜRTTEMBERG) TN: (0751) 41347. Gegründet 1871. Laden. (Samstag nur nach Vereinbarung). Spec: dekorative Graphik. Corresp: English, Français. B: Volksbank Weingarten Konto 800 402 006. CP: Stuttgart 186 96–705. V.D.A.

J. J. HECKENHAUER, HOLZMARKT 5, 74 TÜBINGEN. (Posttach 1728). Prop: Herbert Friedrich Sonnewald. TN: 23018. Gegründet 1823. Laden. Sehr grosser Vorrat. Spec: Theologie Geschichte; Slavischen Länder. Cata: 2 pro Jahr. Corresp: English, Français, Español Russisch. B: Württ. Landessparkasse, Tübingen, Konto 1741. 011337 CP: Stuttgart 929. V.D.A., B.V.D.B.

HECKENHAUER-SONNEWALD, WALDHOF 1, 7947 MENGEN. Prop Herbert Friedrich Sonnewald. TN: (07572) 8231. Gegründet 1823. Nur nach Korrespondenz. Spec: Theologie; Geschichte; Slavischen Länder Corresp: English, Français, Español, Russisch. B: Württ. Landessparkasse, Tübingen, Konto 1741, 011337. CP: Stuttgart 929. V.D.A. B.V.D.B.

ADOLF KAPP, BAHNHOFSTRASSE 17, 7407 ROTTENBURG. (Postfach 46) Prop: Alfons Unteregger. TN: 5560. Gegründet 1923. Laden und Lagerräume, Samstag Nachmittag geschlossen. Mittelgrosser Vorrat Spec: Katholische Theologie. Cata: periodische. Corresp: English Français. B: Volksbank Rottenburg, Konto 10974008. CP: Stuttgart 40766, B.V.D.B.

HEINRICH KERLER, PLATZGASSE 26, 7900 ULM. (Postfach 2668). Prop Winfried Bader. TN: (0731) 63978. Gegründet 1877. Laden, Samstag

Nachmittage geschlossen. Mittelgrosser Vorrat. Spec: Landeskunde Baden-Württemberg. Cata: 4 oder 5 pro Jahr. Corresp: English, Français. B: Sparkasse Ulm, Konto 113 674. Ulmer Volksbank, Konto 185 0008. CP: Stuttgart 12143–700. B.V.D.B.

KARL KNÖDLER, KATHERINENSTRASSE 8–10, 7410 REUTLINGEN. TN: 35004. Gegründet 1936. Laden und Lagerräume, Samstag Nachmittag geschlossen. Grosser Vorrat, auch neue Bücher. Cata: Listen für Spezialgebiete. Corresp: English. B: Dresdner Bank, Reutlingen. CP: Stuttgart 180 09. V.D.A., B.V.D.B.

VALENTIN KOERNER G.m.b.H. IBERSTSTRASSE 36, 757 BADEN-BADEN. (Postfach 304). TN: (07221) 22 423. Gegründet 1954. Wohnung, nur nach Vereinbarung. Mittelgrosser Vorrat. Spec: Bibliographie 16 Jahhunderts. Corresp: English, Français. B: Dresdner Bank, Konto 622 39 77. CP: 92121–757. V.D.A., B.V.D.B.

KURBUCHHANDLUNG UND ANTIQUARIAT B. KROHN, KAISER-STRASSE 10, 7847 BADENWEILER. (Postfach 229). TN: 290. Laden, Mitwoch Nachmittag geschlossen. Kleiner Vorrat, auch neue Bücher. Spec: Illustrierte Bücher. Cata: 2 pro Jahr. Corresp: English, Français. B: Volksbank Badenweiler, Konto 485. CP: Karlsruhe 17269. V.D.A.

DR. LUISE KROHN, HUSSENSTRASSE 18, 775 KONSTANZ. TN: (07531) 23360. V.D.A.

MARGOT LOERCHER O.H.G., HEUBERGSTRASSE 42, 7000 STUTTGART-OST. TN: 46 12 48. Gegründet 1971. Wohnung, nur nach Vereinbarung. Sehr kleiner Vorrat, auch neue Bücher. Spec: Japanische Farbholzschnitte. Cata: 4 pro Jahr. B: Württembergische Landessparkasse, Stuttgart, Konto 10 230 10 275. CP: Stuttgart 1296 89–708. V.D.A., Landesverband der Kunst- und Antiquitätenhäandler Baden-Württemberg.

KLAUS LUX, IM HAUSGARTEN 33, 7800 FREIBURG. TN: 07664–1361. Gegründet 1967. Wohnung: nur nach Vereinbarung. Kleiner Vorrat. Spec: Geographie, Geschichte, Kinderbücher. Cata: 8 pro Jahr. Corresp: English. B: Raiffeisenbank Tuniberg, Freiberg-Opfingen, Konto 2300 14. CP: Karlsruhe 136 741–753. B.V.D.B.

OTTO MOSER, OLMENWEG 15, 7340 GEISLINGEN. TN: 64795. V.D.A.

MÜLLER & GRÄFF, CALWERSTRASSE 54, 7 STUTTGART-1. TN: 29 41. 74. Gegründet 1802. Spec: Buchwesen; Architektur; Geschichte; Theologie. B: Dresdner Bank, Stuttgart. CP: Stuttgart 18709. V.D.A.

FRITZ NEIDHARDT, RELENBERGSTRASSE 20, 7 STUTTGART. TN: 22 33 20. Gegründet 1952. Lagerräume, Samstag gesclossen. Kleiner Vorrat.

Spec: Schöne illustrierte Bücher und Graphik. Cata: Jährlich. Corresp: English. B: Girokasse Stuttgart Konto 2035626. V.D.A.

S. & P. NESER (BÜCHERSTUBE AM SEE), KREUZLINGERSTRASSE 11, 775 KONSTANZ-BODENSEE. TN: 2176. TA: Bücherstube Konstanz. Gegründet 1925. Laden, Mittwoch Nachmittag geschlossen. Mittelgrosser Vorrat, auch neue Bücher. Spec: Gechichte; Deutsche Literatur; Politik; alte Drucke. Cata: 8 pro Jahr. Corresp: English. B: Volksbank, Konstanz. V.D.A.

GUSTAV NEUWIRTH, FRANKFURTERSTRASSE 16/1, 71 HEILBRONN. TN: (07131) 81 036. Gegründet 1933. Wohnung. Kleiner Vorrat, auch neue Bücher. Spec: alte Stiche (Städteansichten) von Deutschland und Osteuropa. Cata: 2 oder 3 pro Jahr. Corresp: English, Français. B: Kreissparkasse Heilbronn, Giro Konto 11600–4, CP: Stuttgart 62866. B.V.D.B.

ANTIQUARIAT GERH. RENNER, HECHINGERSTRASSE 34, 747 ALBSTADT 2. TN: (07432) 6381. Gegründet 1957. Laden, Samstag Nachmittag geschlossen, vorzugsweise nach Vereinbarung. Sehr grosser Vorrat, auch neue Bücher. Spec: alte Wissenschaften, Mathematik. Cata: 2 pro Jahr. Corresp: English, Français. B: Kreissparkasse Albstadt, Konto 809 108. CP: Stuttgart 104 328. B.V.D.B.

LUDWIG H. SCHILLER, BIRKENRAIN 28, 7811 ST. PETERSCHWARZWALD. TN: 308. TA: Schillerbuch St. Peter-Schwarzwald. Gegründet 1961. Lagerräume, nur nach Vereinbarung. Mittelgrosser Vorrat. Spec: Baden, Elsass; Theologie, Philosophie; Alte Drucke. Cata: 5–6 pro Jahr. Corresp: English, Français. B: Sparkasse St. Peter, 3351. CP: Karlsruhe 118138. V.D.A., B.V.D.B.

HANS FERDINAND SCHULZ, FRIEDRICHRING 13, 78 FREIBURG. (Postfach 1463). TN: (0761) 36570. Gegründet 1893. Laden, Samstag Nachmittag geschlossen. Sehr kleiner Vorrat, auch neue Bücher. Spec: wissenschaft medizin. Cata: 2 pro Jahr, Corresp: English, Français. B: Städt. Sparkasse, Freiburg, Konto 2028 200. CP: Karlsruhe 18846. B.V.D.B.

RENÉ SIMMERMACHER, TALSTRASSE 5, 7800 FREIBURG. (Postfach 1452). TN: (0761) 73676. Wohnung. Sehr kleiner Vorrat, auch neue Kunstbücher. Spec: Kunst, Illustrierte Naturwissenschaft. Cata. Corresp: English, Français. B: Sparkasse Freiburg/Breisgau, Konto 2013105. CP: Karlsruhe 3276–751. V.D.A. Kunst- und Antiquitäten Händler Verband.

J. F. STEINKOPF, HERMANNSTRASSE 5, 7 STUTTGART 1. TN: 77941 Gegründet 1792. Cata. V.D.A.

STUTTGARTER ANTIQUARIAT, RATHENAUSTRASSE 21, 7000 STUTT-
GART 1. Prop: Dr. F. Kocher-Benzing. TN: (0711) 22 44 02. Gegründet
1959. Wohnung, nur nach Vereinbarung. Mittelgrosser Vorrat. Spec:
16. Jahhunderts; deutsche Literatur; Erstausgaben. Cata: 5 pro Jahr.
Corresp: English, Français. B: Württembergische Bank, Stuttgart,
Konto 2371. CP: Stuttgart 9641–707. V.D.A., I.L.A..B

GALERIE VALENTIEN, KÖNIGSBAU, 7 STUTTGART. Prop: Dr. Fritz C.
Valentien. TN: 29 27 09. Gegründet 1933. Laden und Lagerräume,
Samstag Nachmittag geschlossen. Mittelgrosser Vorrat, auch neue
Bücher. Spec: Kunstgeschichte; christlich Archäologie; angewandt
Kunst. Cata: 2 pro Jahr. Corresp: English, Français. B: Städt. Giro-
kasse, Stuttgart, Konto 1693. CP: Stuttgart 10125. V.D.A.

J. VOERSTER, RELENBERGSTRASSE 33, 7 STUTTGART. TN: (0711) 297186.
Laden. Spec: Musik; Theater; Deutsche Literatur. Corresp: English.
B: Deutsche Bank, Stuttgart, 14–56888. CP: Stuttgart 779 55. V.D.A.

JULIUS WEISE'S HOFBUCHHANDLUNG, KÖNIGSTRASSE 17, 7
STUTTGART-N. Prop: Martha Erpf. TN: 22 17 46. Gegründet 1826.
Laden, Samstag Nachmittag geschlossen. Sehr grosser Vorrat, auch
neue Bücher. Spec: Württembergica; Deutsche Literatur; Naturwissen-
schaften; Graphik. Cata. Corresp: English, Français. B: Deutsche
Bank, Stuttgart, Konto 45896. CP: Stuttgart 8262. V.D.A.

GALERIE ELFRIEDE WIRNITZER, LUDWIG-WILHELM-STRASSE 17a,
757 BADEN-BADEN. TN: (07221) 267 25. Gegründet 1955. Wohnung,
normale Geschäftsstunden, aber Montag geschlossen. Spec: Graphik.
Cata: unregelmässig. Corresp: English, Français. B: Dresdner Bank,
Baden-Baden, Konto 6 233 284. CP: Karlsruhe 120 194–755. V.D.A.

VI

BAYERN: BAVIÈRE: BAVARIA   Postcode: Postleitzahl 8+

88 ANSBACH	8002 GRÄFELFING
86 BAMBURG	8022 GRÜNWALD
8081 BUCH-AM-	807 INGOLSTADT
AMMERSEE	8205 KIEFERSFELDEN
8201 DETTENDORF	8 MÜNCHEN (Munich)
8501 ECHING	85 NURNBERG
8011 EGLHARTING	8673 REHAU
8805 FEUCHTWANGEN	8132 TUTZING
8210 GIEBINGPOSTPRIEN	87 WÜRZBURG

THEODOR ACKERMANN, Promenadeplatz 11, 8 München. TN: 22 65 60. Gegründet 1865. Laden, Samstag Nachmittag geschlossen. Sehr grosser Vorrat. Spec: Geisteswissenschaften; Alte Drucke; Graphik. Cata: 3–4 pro Jahr. Corresp: English, Français. Dutch. B: Merck, Finck & Co., München. CP: München 116 25. V.D.A., B.V.D.B.

ANGLIA ENGLISH BOOKSHOP, Schellingstrasse 3, 8 München 40. Prop: David Conolly-Smith. TN: 28 36 42. Gegründet 1952. Laden, Samstag Nachmittage geschlossen. Sehr kleiner Vorrat, auch neue Bücher. Corresp: English. B: Merck, Finck & Co., München, Konto 20237 A. CP: München 106855–802.

A. VON DER BECKE & SOHN, Widenmayerstrasse 43, 8 München 22. Prop: Bernhard J. von der Becke. TN: 29 26 84. Gegründet 1931. Wohnung. Kleiner Vorrat. Spec: Alte illustrierte; dekorative Graphik. Corresp: English. B: Deutsche Bank München, Konto 65–25596. CP: München 1166 28. V.D.A.

HELMUT BOLENZ, Türkenstrasse 48, 8 München. TN: 28 42 23. Gegründet 1964. Laden. Mittelgrosser Vorrat. Spec: Deutsche Literatur; Kunstwissenschaft; Illustrierte Bücher; Alte Drucke; Dekorative Graphik. Cata: 3 pro Jahr. B: Aufhäuser, München, Konto 113670. CP: München 174065. V.D.A., B.V.D.B.

KLAUS VON BRINCKEN, Theresienstrasse 56, 8 München 2. TN: (0811) 287268. V.D.A.

HERMAN E. BUB, Kürschnerhof 7, 87 Würzburg 2. (Postfach 783). TN: (0931) 93675 und 12876. TA: Bucherbub. Gegründet 1969. Laden. Kleiner Vorrat, auch alte Städteansichten und Landkarten. Spec: Ortsgeschichte; Africana. Cata: 5 pro Jahr. Corresp: English. CP: Nürnberg 167 063–852.

HELMUTH DOMIZLAFF, Martiusstrasse 5/II, 8 München. TN: 34 91 60. Gegründet 1933. Wohnung, nur nach Vereinbarung. Sehr kleine Vorrat. Drucke des 15 und 16 Jahrhunderts. B: Merck, Finck & Co., 21791C. CP: München 18633. V.D.A.

M. EDELMANN, Breitgasse 52, 85 Nürnberg 1. Prop: Erwin Kistner. TN: 22 65 59. Gegründet 1886. B: Bayerische Vereinsbank, Nürnberg. CP: Nürnberg 16019. V.D.A.

HEINRICH GILSING, Kaiserstrasse 3, 8205 Kiefersfelden. TN: 8354. Gegründet 1957. Wohnung, nur nach Vereinbarung. Mittelgrosser

Vorrat. Spec: Rechts- und Staatswissenschaften; Geschichte; Periodica. Cata. Corresp: English, Français, Italiano. B: Sparkasse Kiefersfelden, Konto 305912. CP: München 137507. V.D.A., B.V.D.B.

GERARD GOLDAU, GASTEIGWEG 4, 8022 GRÜNWALD. TN: (089) 641 30 23. Gegründet 1957. Lagerräume, nur nach Vereinbarung. Mittelgrosser Vorrat. Spec: Militaria, Geschichte. Cata: 3 oder 4 pro Jahr. Corresp: English, Italiano. B: Raiffeisenbank, Grünwald, Konto 226 513. CP: München 123 201–801.

ELSE HAAS, OHG., DOLLSTRASSE 7, 807 INGOLSTADT 21. (Postfach 2402). Prop: Else Haas und Dr. Max Haas. TN: (0841) 2506. Gegründet 1946. Laden, Samstag Nachmittag geschlossen, nur nach Vereinbarung. Mittelgrosser Vorrat. Spec: Alte Drucke vor 1750; Bavarica; Kulturgeschichte; Kunst; Bayerische; Städtegrafik. Cata. Corresp: English, Français. B: Stadt u. Kreissparkasse 10975. Volksbank Ingolstadt 8053 5. CP: München 829 18–808. V.D.A.

HARTUNG & KARL, KAROLINENPLATZ 5a, 8 MÜNCHEN 2. TN: (0811) 284034. V.D.A.

ELSA HAUSER, SCHELLINGSTRASSE 17, 8 MÜNCHEN 13. TN: 28 11 59. Gegründet 1911. Spec: Alte und Moderne Graphik; Alte Drucke; Bibliophilie. V.D.A.

HANS HÖCHTBERGER, ELSENHEIMERSTRASSE 18. 8 MÜNCHEN 21. TN: 57 23 61. Gegründet 1969. Lagerräume und Wohnung, nur nach Vereinbarung. Mittelgrosser Vorrat. Spec: Erstausgaben Deutscher Literatur; Illustrierte Bücher; Kunstwissenschaft Buchwesen; Literatur- und Kunstzeitschriften. Cata: 2–3 pro Jahr. Corresp: English, Français. B: Bayerische Hypotheken- und Wechselbank, München, Konto 3841006. CP: München 226945–807.

H. HUGENDUBEL, SALVATORPLATZ 2, 8 MÜNCHEN. TN: 22 66 46. TA: Hugendubel München. Telex: 529 651. Gegründet 1880. Laden und Lagerräume. Sehr grosser Vorrat, auch neue Bücher. Spec: Bavarica; Bibliophilie; Alte Drucke; Militaria. Cata: 2–3 pro Jahr und spezial Listen. Corresp: English, Français. B: Bayerische Hypotheken und Wechselbank, München, Konto 85-1457, CP: München 15 500. V.D.A., B.V.D.B.

KARL & FABER, KAROLINENPLATZ 5A, 8 MÜNCHEN 2. Prop: George und Louis Karl. Karl Hartung. TN: 28 30 24. TA: Karlanti München. Spec: Alte Bücher: Kunst; Graphik. B. H. Aufhäuser, München. CP: München 7268. V.D.A.

DR. EMIL KATZBICHLER, 8210 GIEBING POST PRIEN. TN: (08051) 2595. Gegründet 1962. Büro und Lagerräume, nur nach Vereinbarung. Grosser Vorrat. Nur Musikliteratur, Musikdrucke und Musikautographen. Cata: 3–4 pro Jahr. Corresp; English, Français. B. Sparkasse, Prien, Konto 252 411. CP: München 18 5254. V.D.A. Deutscher Musikalienwirtschafts-Verband.

GALERIE WOLFGANG KETTERER, PRINZREGENTENSTRASSE 60, VILLA STUCK, 8 MÜNCHEN 80. TN: (0811) 45 45 45. V.D.A.

ERWIN UND ROLF KISTNER, BREITE GASSE 52–54, 85 NÜRNBERG. TN: (0911) 22 55 89. Gegründet 1886. Laden. Sehr grosser Vorrat. Apec: alte und dekorative; Graphik; Naturwissenschaften; seltene und wertvolle Bücher. Cata: sehr selten. Corresp: English. B: Bayerische Vereinsbank, Nürnberg, Konto 6311 857. CP: Nürnberg 12881-857. V.D.A.

J. KITZINGER, SCHELLINGSTRASSE 25, 8 MÜNCHEN 13. Prop: A. Kitzinger. TN: (0811) 28 35 37. Gegründet 1892. Laden, Samstag Nachmittag geschlossen. Grosser Vorrat. Spec: alle Geisteswissenschaften; Kunst; Altphilologie. Cata: 2 pro Jahr. Corresp: English, Italiano. B: Bayerische Hypotheken u. Wechselbank, München, Konto 89-32107. CP: München 10841. V.D.A., B.V.D.B.

ANTIQUARIAT KLAUSSNER, PROFESSOR-KURT-HUBER-STRASSE 19, 8032 GRÄFELFING (MÜNCHEN). Prop: Inge Klaussner. TN: (089) 85 26 02. Spec: ältere Jugendbücher; Bavarica. V.D.A.

GALERIE KLIHM, FRANZ-JOSEPH-STRASSE 9, 8 MÜNCHEN 13 TN: 33 16 88. Gegründet 1946. Laden, Samstag geschlossen. Spec: Expressionistische Grafik und Bilder. Cata. 4 pro Jahr. CP: München 21550. V.D.A.

RAINER KÖBELIN, Amalienstrasse 53, 8 München 40. TN: 285 640. Laden. Spec: Militaria; Alte Naturwissenschaft; Literatur; Dekorative Graphik. B: Bayerische Vereinsbank, München, Konto 883 691. CP: München 216 745.-803

CARL-ERNST KOHLHAUER, Graser Weg 2, 8805 Feuchtwangen. TN: (09852) 9292. Gegründet 1957. Wohnung, nur nach Vereinbarung. Mittelgrosser Vorrat. Spec: alte Medizin und Naturwissenschaften (Graphik, Bücher und Autographen) Cata: Unregelmässig. Corresp: English. B: Spartkasse Feuchtwangen Konto 42. CP: Frankfurt-am-Main 185 256-609. V.D.A.

OTTO KOLB, Bahnhofstrasse 3/I, 8673 Rehau. (Postfach 140). TN: (09283) 438. Lagerräume. Sehr kleiner Vorrat, auch neue Bücher. Spec: Antiquariat Bücher, Städtansichten. Cata: 10 pro Jahr. Corresp: English, Français. B: Schmidt-Bank, Rehau, Konto 666. CP: Nürnberg 723–96. V.D.A., B.V.D.B.

UNIVERSITÄTSBUCHHANDLUNG KORN UND BERG, Haupt-markt 9, 85 Nürnberg. Prop: W. D. Berg. TN: 22980. Gegründet 1588. Laden. Mittelgrosser Vorrat, auch neue Bücher. B: Bayerische Vereinsbank, Nürnberg, Konto 260 1311: Stadtsparkasse Nürnberg, Konto 1007 208: Hypothekenbank Nürnberg, Konto 156 234 125: Dresdner Bank Konto 480 1 711–235. CP: Nürnberg 146 93–851. B.V.D.B.

"JOURNALFRANZ" ARNULF LIEBING, Werner von Siemens-Strasse 5, 87 Würzburg 2. (Postfach 1136). Prop: Arnulf und Gertrud Liebing und Hildgund Holler. TN: (0931) 21120. TA: Journalfranz Würzburg. Gegründet 1923. Lagerräume, nur nach Vereinbarung. Samstag geschlossen. Sehr grosser Vorrat. Spec: Zeitschriften und Bücher. Cata: 1 pro Jahr und Listen. Corresp: English. B: Dresdner Bank, Würzburg, Konto 10022. CP: Nürnberg 922–855. B.V.D.B., V.D.A.

AUGUST MÜLLER, Maximiliansplatz 20, 8 München 2. Prop: Franz Rauscher. TN: 22 64 70. Laden. Spec: Städteansichten; Landkarten; Englische Sportblätter; Pferde. CP: München 14185. V.D.A.

ANTIQUARIAT KARLHEINZ MURR, Karolinenstrasse 4, 86 Bamberg. (Postfach 4037) TN: (0951) 277 28. Gegründet 1954. Zwei Läden. (telefonisch immer au sprechen). Grosser Vorrat. Spec: alte Graphik, Städte-Ansichten und Landkarten, Betand ca. 30,000 Originalstiche, auch neue Bücher. Cata: 3 bis 5 pro Jahr. Corresp: English. B:

Bayerissche Vereinsbank Bamberg, Konto 372 84 98. CP: Nürnberg 215 88–851. B.V.D.B., V.D.A., Bayerischer Buchhäandler- und Verlegerverband.

Dr. KARL H. PRESSLER, HERZOGSTRASSE 58, 8 MÜNCHEN 40. TN: (089) 34 13 31 Gegrüdet 1954. Wohnung und Lagerräume; nur nach Vereinbarung. Sehr grosser Vorrat. Spec: Literatur, Geschichte, Bibliographie, Schöne und seltene Bücher. Corresp: English. B: Dresdner Bank, Mainz, Konto 2 343 952. CP: Frankfurt 1518 48–602. B.V.D.B., V.D.A., Editor of *Aus dem Antiquariat*.

KLAUS RENNER, KONRAD-CELTIS-STRASSE 33, 8 MÜNCHEN 25. TN: 760 8459. Gegründet 1957. Büro, Samstag geschlossen; nur nach Vereinbarung. Kleiner Vorrat, auch neue Bücher. Spec: Ethnologie; Archäologie, Anthropologie. Cata: 12 pro Jahr. Corresp: English. B: Städt. Sparkasse, München, Konto 908–166002. CP: München 962 17. B.V.D.B.

JACQUES ROSENTHAL, FRÜHLINGSTRASSE 12, 8051 ECHING. Prop: Hans Koch. TN: München 319 2813. Gegründet 1895. Laden und Lagerräume. Grosser Vorrat. Spec: Alte Drucke. Cata. Corresp: English, Français, Español. B: H. Aufhäuser. München. CP: München 5021. V.D.A., B.V.D.B.

LUDWIG ROSENTHAL-DÜRR, SACHSENKAMSTRASSE 26, 8 MÜNCHEN 70. TN: (0811) 760 6787. V.D.A.

OSCAR ROTHACKER, PETTENKOFERSTRASSE 18, 8 MÜNCHEN 15. Prop: Dr. H. Urban, E. Urban und M. Urban. TN: 53 24 36. Telex: Urbanbuch 05-23864. Gegründet 1872. Spec: Medizin; Naturwissenschaften; Periodica. Cata: circa monatlich. Corresp: English. B: Deutsche Bank, München, Konto 51-35 207. CP: München 222 032. V.D.A., B.V.D.B.

GERHARD SCHEPPLER, GISELASTRASSE 25, 8000 MÜNCHEN 40. TN: (089) 34 81 74. Gegründet 1966. Lagerraum, nach Vereinbarung (Nachmittags). Mittelgrosser Vorrat. Spec: seltene Bücher des 15. bis 20. Jahrhunderts. Cata: 2 pro Jahr. B: Bayerische Hypothekenbank, München. CP: München 67 163-809. B.V.D.B.

WALTER SCHMIDT, 8201 BAD FEILNBACH (DETTENNDORF). TN: (08064) 630. Spec: Zeitschriften.

HANS SCHNEIDER, MOZARTWEG 1, 8132 TUTZING ÜBER MÜNCHEN. TN: 475. TA: Musikantiquar Tutzing. Gegründet 1949. Lagerräume, nur nach Vereinbarung. Musik (ausschliessl.) sehr grosser Vorrat. Cata.

Corresp: English, Français. B: Gewerbebank, Tutzing, Konto 475.
CP: München 14602. V.D.A., B.V.D.B. Gesellschaft für Musik-
forschung.

J. SCHWEITZER SORTIMENT, MARSSTRASSE 4, 8 MÜNCHEN 2. (Postfach 37 01 04) TN: 591 502 und 591 608. Spec: Recht, Wirtschaft und
Steuern.

GALERIE STANGL, BRIENNERSTRASSE 11, 8 MÜNCHEN. Prop: Otto
Stangl. TN: 29 99 11. Gegründet 1947. Galerie, Samstag Nachmittag
geschlossen. Kleiner Vorrat, auch neue Bücher. Spec: Kunst. Corresp:
English, Français. CP: München 13512. V.D.A., B.V.D.B.

M. A. STEINBACH, HIRSCHENWEG 36, 8011 EGLHARTING. (Postfach 88)
TN: (08091) 2259. Wohnung, nur nach Vereinbarung. Kleiner Vorrat.
Spec: Kunst; illustrierte Bücher des 20. Jahrhunderts. Cata: 2 pro Jahr.
Corresp: English, Français, Español. B: Aufhäuser 357 774, München.
CP: München 256 556-802.

HORSTSTOBBE, OTTOSTRASSE 11–12, 8 MÜNCHEN 2. TN: 55 31 93.
Gegründet 1904. Laden. Spec: Kunst; Deutsch Literatur; Graphik.
B: Merck, Finck & Co., München. CP: München 59752. V.D.A.

CARL WILLY TROEGER, WILHELMSTRASSE 11/0, 8 MÜNCHEN 23.
Gegründet 1920. Laden. Spec: Dekorative Graphik; Naturwissenschaften. V.D.A.

E. VON DEN VELDEN, NEUREUTHER STRASSE 1, 8 MÜNCHEN 13. TN:
37 70 91. Spec: Zeitschriften. B: Bayerische Hypotheken- und Wechselbank, München, Konto 353 863. CP: München 482 78. V.D.A.

ED. WALZ, LERCHENFELDSTRASSE 4-11, 8 MÜNCHEN 22. Prop: Anneliese
Jamin. Spec: Graphik und Zeichnungen des 15–20 Jahrhunderts;
Städteansichten und Landkarten. CP: München 15921. V.D.A.

**BERNHARD WENDT, 8081 BUCH-AM-AMMERSEE-OBERBAYERN. ÜBER
MÜNCHEN.** TN: Inning (Ammersee) (08143) 342. Gegründet 1953.
Wohnung, nur nach Vereinbarung. Mittelgrosser Vorrat. Spec:
Inkunabeln; alte Drucke; Humanismus; Reformation und Gegen-
reformation; Theologie vor 1850; Geisteswissenschaften. Corresp:
English, Français. B: H. Aufhäuser, München, Konto 379 077. V.D.A.,
B.V.D.B.

ROBERT WÖLFLE OHG., AMALIENSTRASSE 65, 8 MÜNCHEN 13. Prop:
Gertrud Wölfle. TN: 28 36 26. Laden, Samstag Nachmittag geschlossen.
Spec: Alte Drucke; Alte Naturwissenschaften; Geisteswissenschaften;
Kunst; Graphik des 15–20 Jahrhunderts. CP: München 31781. V.D.A.

DEUTSCHE DEMOKRATISCHE REPUBLIK
GERMAN DEMOCRATIC REPUBLIC
RÉPUBLIQUE ALLEMAGNE DEMOCRATIQUE

BERLIN: DRESDEN: LEIPZIG: ROSTOCK

ANTIQUARIAT DER KARL-MARX-BUCHHANDLUNG, KARL-MARX-ALLEE 78–84, DDR-1017 BERLIN. TN: 58 14 55.

ANTIQUARIAT PANKOW, SCHÖNHOLZER STRASSE 1, DDR-110 BERLIN. TN: 48 39 71.

ANTIQUARIATS-BUCHHANDLUNG, FRIEDRICHSTRASSE 127, DDR-104 BERLIN. TN: 422 77 38.

ANTIQUARIAT UNTER DEN LINDEN, UNTER DEN LINDEN 37/45, 108 BERLIN. TN: 22 919 39.

ANTIQUARIATS-BUCHHANDLUNG, MUNZSTRASSE 1, DDR-102 BERLIN. TN: 42 90 61.

DRESDENER ANTIQUARIAT, BAUTZNER STRASSE 27, 806 DRESDEN. TN: 53368. Gegründet 1953. Laden, Sonnabend geschlossen. Sehr grosser Vorrat. Spec: Bibliophile; Kunstwissenschaft. Cata: 5 pro Jahr. B: I.H.B. Dresden, Konto 5151-13-31. CP: Dresden 14043. Borsenverein Dt. Buchhändler zu Leipzig.

NORDDEUTSCHES ANTIQUARIAT, KRÖPELINER STRASSE 14, DDR-25 ROSTOCK. (Postfach 30). TN. 34052. TA: Nordantiquariat Rostock. Laden und Lagerräume. Sehr grosser Vorrat. Cata: 15 pro Jahr. Corresp: English, Russisch. Börsenverein der Deutschen Buchhändler zu Leipzig.

ZENTRALANTIQUARIAT DER DDR, TALSTRASSE 1080, 701 LEIPZIG. (Postfrach 1080). TN: 23641–3. TA: Zentralanti Leipzig. Gegründet 1949. Laden und Lagerräume. Sehr grosser Vorrat. Spec: Wissenschaften, Kunst und Graphik. Cata: 6–7 pro Jahr. Corresp: English, Français, Russian. B: I.H.B., Leipzig 5611-18-15. CP: Leipzig 56226.

ZENTRALES ANTIQUARIAT BERLIN, RUNGERSTRASSE 20, DDR-102 BERLIN. TN: 27 92 195. Lagerräume, nur nach Vereinbarung. Sehr grosser Vorrat. Corresp: English.

ELLAS

GREECE   GRÈCE   GRIECHENLAND

ATHENS (Athènes)

ACADEMIC BOOKSTORE, HIPPOCRATUS STREET 33, ATHENS. Prop: Efthimiou D. Triantafyllou. TN: 25996. Established 1927. Shop. Also new books.

LES AMIS DU LIVRE, 9 VALAORITIS STREET, ATHENS 134. Prop: Julia & Augusto Spandonaro. TN: 615 562. TA: Esmo Athens. Established 1960. Very large stock. Spec: travel books; engravings; maps; views and landscapes. Corresp: English, Français, Deutsch, Italiano.

PANAYIOTIS GEORGIOU & COMPANY, P.O. 622, ATHENS. TN: 632.891. Spec: encyclopedias and dictionaires; books on Greece; old maps. Also publishers' representatives. Corresp: English, Français.

LIBRARIE KAUFFMANN, 28 STADIUM STREET, ATHENS-132. Spec: Greece, Turkey, maps, engravings.

ANGELOS ZAMBAKIS, LE BIBLIOPHILE, 84 SOLONIS, ATHENS 144. TN: 614:531. Shop. Spec: maps; prints; old and rare books. Also new books. Corresp: English, Français.

ESPAÑA

SPAIN ESPAGNE SPANIEN

ALMERIA: BARCELONA: MADRID:
PALMA DE MALLORCA: ZARAGOZA (Saragossa)

LIBRERIA ANTICUARIA ARISTEUCOS, Paseo de la Bonanova 14
G. Barcelona 6. TN: 2478255. Prop: Mariano Castells Plandiura.
Spec: Hispánica old and rare; Spanish, Catalan and Latin language
books 15th to 19th; Gastronomy; Chartography of Catalonia. Cata:
occasionally. Corresp: English, French, German and Catalan. B: Banca
Catalana.

LIBRERIA PARA BIBLIOFILOS LUIS BARDON, Plaza de San
Martin 3, Madrid. (Apartado Postal 7092). TN: 21 55 14. TA:
Lnbardon Madrid. Established 1946. Shop. Very large stock, also new
books. Cata. Corresp: English. B: Banco de Santander, Sucursal, Calle
de Galdo 1, Madrid, Account No. 815. A.B.A.

LIBRERIA ANGEL BATLLE Y TEJEDOR, Calle de la Paja 23,
Barcelona (2). TN: 222 8115. Established 1900. Shop. Very large
stock. Spec: engravings; ex-libris; antiquarian; popular art. Cata.

LA CASA DE LA TROYA, Luna 21 (portada roja), Madrid. TN:
2219478. Cata.

LIBRERIA M. FIOL, Olmos 119-A Palma de Mallorca. Prop: Miguel
Fiol Roig. TN: 221428. Established 1950. Shop, early closing Saturday.
Large stock. Spec: rare books on Majorca; English paperbacks.
Corresp: English, Français. B: Banco Central, No. 10168. Instituto
Nacional del Libro Español.

LIBRERIA GRANATA, Reyes Carolicos 8, Almeria. Manager: Antonio
Moreno, A.B.A.

LIBRERIA HESPERIA, Plaza Jose Antonio 10, Zaragoza. (Apartado
Postal 272). Prop: Luis Marquina y Marin. TN: 235367 and 228239.
Established 1953. Shop and storeroom. Very large stock, also new books.
Spec: Hispanica old and rare; Americana. Cata: 2 a year. Corresp:
English, Français, A.B.A.

LIBRERIA MIRTO, Ruiz de Alarcon 27, Madrid 14. Prop: Señora Herminia Allanegui. TN: 239 83 31. Established 1950. Shop. Large stock. Spec: Spanish literature and fine arts. Cata: occasionally. Corresp: English. B: Banco Español de Crédito. A.B.A.

GABRIEL MOLINA—SUCESORA, Travesia del Arenal 1, Madrid. Prop: Señora Antonia Molina Rico. TN: 266 44 43. Established 1870. Shop. Spec: old and rare; curious; also new books. Cata. Corresp: Français. B: Banco Hispano Americano. A.B.A.

PARA BIBLIOFILOS, Pl. San Martin 3, Madrid.

PORTER-LIBROS, Avenida Puerta del Angel 9, Barcelona. A.B.A.

FRANCE

FRANKREICH

Association: Verband

S.L.A.M. = Syndicat de la Librairie Ancienne et Moderne 117 Boulevard Saint-Germain, 75005 Paris, TN: 329 2101.

Public Holidays: Jour de Fête: Feiertage

Jan. 1: Easter Monday: May 1: Ascension: Whitmonday: Jul. 14: Aug. 15: Nov 1 and 11: Christmas Day.

Jan. 1: lundi de Pâques: Mai 1: Ascension: lundi de Pentecôte: Jul. 14: Août 15: Nov. 1 et 11: Déc. 25.

Jan. 1: Ostermontag: Mai 1: Himmelfahrt: Pfingstmontag: Jul. 14: Aug. 15: Nov. 1 und 11: Dez. 25.

Banks: Banques: Banken

B.F.	= Banque de France
B.I.C.S.	= Banque Industrielle et Commerciale
B.N.C.I.	= Banque National de Commerce et Industrie
C.C.F.	= Crédit Commercial de France
C.F.C.B.	= Compagnie Française de Crédit et de Banque
C.I.C.	= Crédit Industriel et Commercial
C.L.	= Crédit Lyonnais
C.N.	= Crédit du Nord
C.N.E.P.	= Comptoire National d'Escompte de Paris
S.G.	= Société Générale

I PARIS: Arondissements 1er—4e; 5e; 6e; 7e; 8e; 9e; 10e—20e Districts

II FRANCE (NORD): NORDFRANKREICH: NORTHERN FRANCE
Postcodes: Postleitzahlen: 14; 50; 59; 76; 78; 91; 92; 95.

III FRANCE (OUEST): WESTFRANKREICH: WESTERN FRANCE
Postcodes: Postleitzahlen: 17; 24; 28; 29; 33; 35; 37; 41; 44; 45; 49; 72.

IV FRANCE (EST): OSTFRANKREICH: EASTERN FRANCE
Postcodes: Postleitzahlen: 21; 25; 38; 42; 54; 57; 67; 68; 69; 71; 73; 89.

V FRANCE (SUD): SUDFRANKREICH: SOUTHERN FRANCE
Postcodes; Postleitzahlen: 06; 11; 13; 30; 31; 34; 64; 81; 82; 83; 84.

I

PARIS Arrondissements 1er-4e

DENYSE CHERTIN, 14 RUE DE RICHELIEU, 75001 PARIS. TN: 742 64 18. Fondée en 1949. Boutique. Spec: sciences anciennes; érudition, livres d'enfants; curiosités; gravures. CP: Paris 795 172. S.L.A.M.

MAURICE DUSSARP, 36 RUE DU MONT THABOR 75001 PARIS. TN: 073 6303. Spec: autographes; gravures; dessins. CP: Paris 51355. S.L.A.M.

LIBRAIRIE LE FOUINEUR, 34 RUE VIVIENNE, 75002 PARIS. TN: 236 2311. S.L.A.M.

ANTOINE GRANDMAISON, LIBRAIRIE "LES ARCADES", 8 RUE DE CASTIGLIONE, 75001 PARIS. TN: 073 1519. Fondée en 1884. Boutique. Moyen stock, aussi les livres neufs. Spec: belles reliures et reliures aux arms; histoire; beaux-arts. Corresp: English. B: Morgan Guaranty Trust Company. CP: Paris 1803–75. S.L.A.M.

LA GUILDE, 18 RUE DE TURBIGO, 75002 PARIS. Prop: K. Gumz. TN: 231 39 09. Fondée en 1945. Boutique. Très important stock. Spec: sciences humaines. Cata: 12 par an. Corresp: English, Deutsch. CP: Paris 55 44 59. S.L.A.M.

PAUL HENNEBERT, 44 RUE DE TURBIGO, 75003 PARIS TN: 887 71 39. Fondée en 1943. Boutique, fermè lundi et août en entier. Restreint stock. B: Crédit du Nord, rue St.-Martin. Paris 3e, Compte 6598. S.L.A.M.

LIBRAIRIE A. PETIT-SIROUX, 6 RUE VIVIENNE, 75002 PARIS. TN: 231 7264. S.L.A.M.

JEAN ROUSSEAU-GIRARD, 7 RUE DE LA BOURSE, 75002 PARIS. TN: 742 34 84. TA: Roosbooks Paris. Fondée en 1939. Boutique. Très important stock. Spec: sciences naturelles et exacts, littérature. Cata: 8 par an. Corresp: English, Deutsch, Italiano, Español. B: Banco di Roma à Paris. CP: Paris 2359 75. S.L.A.M.

SOCIÉTÉ HÉBRAICA JUDAICA, 12 RUE DES HOSPITALIÈRES ST.-GERVAIS, 75004 PARIS. Gérant: B. Liebermann. TN: 887 32 20. Fondée en 1920. Boutique, fermé Samedi. Restreint stock. Spec: Judaica et Hebraica; en toutes langues Corresp: English, Deutsch, Español. B: Société Génerale, Agence F. S.L.A.M.

B. P. ZIJLSTRA, 85 RUE DE RIVOLI, 75001 PARIS. TN: 236 8833. Boutique. Moyen stock, aussi les livres neufs. CP: Paris 5442–04. S.L.A.M.

PARIS Arrondissement 5e

EMILE BALABANIAN, 3 RUE DE CLUNY, 75005 PARIS. TN: 326 27 54. Fondée en 1937. Boutique. B: C.L., Agence U-421, 22 boulevard Saint-Michel, Paris 75006. Compte 54 707 E. S.L.A.M.

LIBRAIRIE DU CAMÉE, RUE DE VALENCE, 75005 PARIS. Prop: Michel Trochon. TN: 707 62 31. Fondée en 1950. Boutique, fermé lundi. Moyen stock. Spec: ouvrages documentaires. Cata: 5 par an. Corresp: English. B: B.I.C.-R.N.P. Saint Denis, 14 21 04577 1. CP: Paris 2931 11. S.L.A.M., L.I.L.A.

FERNAND CAVELOT, 12 bis AVENUE DES GOBELINS, 75005 PARIS. TN: 587 0116. Domicile, sur rendezvous seulement. CP: Paris 11078–66. S.L.A.M.

CHAUNY ET QUINSAC, 18 RUE SOUFFLOT, 75005 PARIS. TN: 033 79 16. Fondée en 1868. Boutique. Très important stock, aussi les livres neufs. Spec: droit; économie politique. B: B.N.P., Agence Sorbonne, Compte 259005. CP; Paris 586.80. S.L.A.M.

MICHEL DE COURVAL, 20 RUE DES FOSSÉS-ST.-BERNARD, 75005 PARIS. TN: 325 2520. S.L.A.M.

MARCEL DOMMERGUES, 23 RUE DES ÉCOLES, 75005 PARIS. TN: 033 9518. Boutique. Restreint stock. S.L.A.M.

LIBRAIRIE DUCHEMIN, 18 RUE SOUFFLOT, 75005 PARIS. Prop: A. Chauny et P. Quinsac. TN: (33-1) 033 79 16. Fondée en 1868. Boutique. Très important stock, nous faisons aussi des livres neufs. Spec: droit. B: B.N.P., Agence Sorbonne, compte 259005. CP: Paris 586 80. S.L.A.M.

LIBRAIRIE ELEK, 21 RUE SAINT-JACQUES, 75005 PARIS. TN: 033 4899. Cata.

LIBRAIRIE DE LA FACULTÉ DES SCIENCES, 12 RUE PIERRE ET MARIE CURIE, 75005 PARIS. TN: 033 23 04. Fondée en 1961. Boutique. Spec: ouvrages tirés a part, périodiques de sciences naturalles. Cata. Corresp: English, Español. B: B.I.C.S., 64 rue Monge, 75005 Paris, Compte 4014-017249. S.L.A.M.

À L'IMAGERIA, 9 RUE DANTE, 75005 PARIS. Galerie.

L'INVITATION AU VOYAGE, 15 QUAI SAINT-MICHEL, 75005 PARIS. Prop: Claude Menetret. TN: 033 94 74. Fondée en 1952. Boutique. Assez restreint stock. Spec. voyages. B: C.I.C. CP: Paris 7922-31. S.L.A.M.

GIBERT JEUNE, 23 QUAI SAINT-MICHEL, 75005 PARIS. TN: 033 5732. Fondée en 1886. Très important stock. Spec: beaux-arts; luxe. Aussi les livres neufs. Cata: 2 par an. Corresp: English, Deutsch, Italiano. B: B.N.P. CP: Paris 5837–11. S.L.A.M.

LIBRAIRIE J. JOLY, 6 RUE VICTOR-COUSIN, 75005 PARIS. TN: 326 58 15. Fondée en 1937. Sur rendezvous dépot. Très important stock. Spec: droit ancien et moderne; periodiques juridiques. Cata. B: Crédit Lyonnais, Agence U, 22 boulevard St.-Michel, Paris. CP: Paris 1409–14. S.L.A.M.

LIBRAIRIE LARCHON, 18 RUE DES FOSSES-SAINT-JACQUES, 75005 PARIS.

ALFRED MADER, 67 RUE SAINT-JACQUES, 75005 PARIS. TN: 326 3323. Boutique. Moyen stock, aussi les livres neufs. Spec: philosophie; occultisme. Cata. B: Crédit Lyonnais, Agence U., Paris. CP: Paris 74995. S.L.A.M.

MAISONNEUVE & LAROSE, S.A., 11 RUE VICTOR-COUSIN, 75005 PARIS. TN: 033 3270. S.L.A.M.

R.-G. MICHEL, 17 QUAI SAINT-MICHEL, 75005 PARIS. TN: 033 77 75. Spec: éstampes; dessins. B: Crédit Lyonnais, Agence U, Compte 6057–W. CP: Paris 569–24. S.L.A.M.

LIBRAIRIE NICAISE S.A., 145 BOULEVARD SAINT GERMAIN, 75005 PARIS. TN: 325 5238. Fondée en 1943. Boutique. Important stock, aussi livres neufs. Spec: éditions originales et illustrés; surrealisme et livres-objets; gravures modernes. Cata: 1 par an. Corresp: English. B: B.I.C.S., 226 bd Saint Germain, 75007 Paris. CP: Paris 892494. S.L.A.M., L.I.L.A.

LIBRAIRIE A.-G. NIZET, 3 bis PLACE DE LA SORBONNE, 75005 PARIS. TN: 033 79 76. Fondée en 1922. Boutique. Très important stock. Spec: érudition; belles-lettres. Cata: 2 ou 3 par an. Corresp: English. B: C.I.C. Agence M, Paris. Compte 14 677/51. CP: Paris 473 88.

LIBRAIRIE SCIENTIFIQUE ANCIENNE, 20 RUE DES FOSSÉS, 75005 PARIS. Prop: M. de Courval. TN: 325 25 20. Fondée en 1967. Boutique, fermé samedi apresmidi. Moyen stock. Spec: geologie, paleontologie, prehistoire, speleologie. Cata: 4 par an. B: U.B.P. CP: 5011 11. S.L.A.M.

SHAKESPEARE & COMPANY, 37 RUE DE LA BUCHERIE, 75005 PARIS. Prop: George Whitman. TN: ODE 32 62. Fondée en 1961. Boutique, ouverte chaque jour de l'année, de 12 a 24 heur. Important stock, aussi les livres neufs. Spec: éditions originales. Corresp: English, Español, Italiano. B: Banque Populaire Industrielle et Commerciale, Compte 4041 00 1096. CP: Paris 88 75-34.

JEAN VIARDOT, 13 RUE DE L'ECHAUDÉ, 75005 PARIS. TN: 633 60 07. Fondée en 1957. Boutique, fermé Samedi. Moyen stock. Spec: éditions originales. livres illustrés; sciences; voyages. Cata 1 par an. Corresp: English. B: Crédit du Nord, Bd. Raspail 28, 75007 Paris. Compte 1829-6. CP: 16 663 63. S.L.A.M., L.I.L.A.

LIBRAIRIE PHILOSOPHIQUE J. VRIN, 6 PLACE DE LA SORBONNE, 75005 PARIS. Prop: Andrée Vrin. TN: 033 03 47. Fondée en 1843. Boutique, fermé Samedi. Très important stock, aussi les livres neufs. Spec: philosophie, littérature; médecine; histoire; économie politique. Cata: 10 par an. B: B.N.P., Agence Sorbonne, Compte 270 061. CP: Paris 196 30. S.L.A.M.

MRS S. E. WARD, 35 RUE DE LA HARPE, 75005 PARIS.

PARIS Arrondissement 6e

LIBRAIRIE D'ARGENCES, 38 RUE SAINT-SULPICE, 75006 PARIS. TN: 033 05 60. Spec: histoire; religion; philologie. Cata. B: B.N.P. CP: Paris 8114-70. S.L.A.M.

LIBRAIRIE GARNIER ARNOUL, 39 RUE DE SEINE, 75006 PARIS. TN: 033 8005. Fondée en 1951. Boutique. Stock important, aussi livres neufs. Spec: théâtre; musique; danse; mime; etc. Cata: 2–3 par an. Corresp: English, Deutsch, Sveg. CP: Paris 8124-40. S.L.A.M.

MAURICE BAUDON, 27 RUE DE SEINE, 75006 PARIS. TN: 326 7300. Boutique. Spec: gravures. CP: Paris 77441.

A. BLANCHARD, 9 RUE DE MÉDICIS, 76006 PARIS. TN: 326 90 34. Fondée en 1922. Boutique. Restreint stock. Spec: mathematique, physique, chenie, sciences naturelles. Corres: English, Deutsch. B: Crédit Lyonnais, Agence U, boulevard St.-Michel, Paris. CP: Paris 72 32 64. S.L.A.M.

SERGE BOGHOSSIAN, 25 RUE DU CHERCHE-MIDI, 75006 PARIS. TN: 548 4817. S.L.A.M.

LIBRAIRIE BONAPARTE, S.A.R.L., 31 RUE BONAPARTE, 75006 PARIS. Prop: Madame G. Ripert. TN: 326 9756. Fondée en 1942. Boutique. Restreint stock, aussi les livres neufs. Spec: Spectacles; théâtre; danse; cinéma; etc. Cata. Corresp: English. B: C.I.C., Succursale F, Compte 18.012.73. CP: Paris 925 80. S.L.A.M.

PAUL BOULINIER, 20 BOULEVARD SAINT-MICHEL, 75006 PARIS. TN: 326 9057. Boutique, fermé Lundi matin. Spec: beaux-arts, médecine; technique. CP: Paris 30929. S.L.A.M.

ROBERT BOURDON, 75 RUE DE RENNES, 75006 PARIS. TN: 548 9018. Boutique, fermé Lundi et Samedi. Moyen stock. Spec: histoire religieuse; moyen age. Cata: 5 par an. Corresp: English. CP: Paris 15821.51. S.L.A.M.

ALAIN BRIEUX, 48 RUE JACOB, 75006 PARIS. TN: 260 2198. TA: Alibri, Paris. Fondée en 1960. Boutique. Restreint stock, aussi livres neufs. Spec: médecine; sciences. Cata: Corresp: Deutsch, English. B: Banque Worms, Compte 401 35 390 A. CP: Paris 16 528 04. S.L.A.M.

LOUIS BRODER, 187 BOULEVARD SAINT-GERMAIN, 75006 PARIS. TN: 222 2031. Domicile. Spec: beaux-arts; éditions originales; livres illustrés. S.L.A.M.

DANIEL BRUN, EDITION ET DIFFUSION M.P. 34 RUE SERPENTE, 75006 PARIS.

CLAUDE BUFFET, 7 RUE SAINT-SULPICE, 75006 PARIS. TN: 326 61 79. Boutique. Moyen stock. Spec: littérature française et traductions. Corresp: English. B: B.N.P., Agence Boulevard Saint-Germain, No. 213743. CP: La Source 3378740.

ROBERT CAYLA, 28 RUE SAINT-SULPICE, 75006 PARIS. TN: 326 4887. Boutique. Spec: éditions originales modernes; romantiques; manuscrits; autographes. S.L.A.M.

HENRI CAZER, 49 RUE DE SEINE, 75006 PARIS. TN: 326 45 19. Spec: beaux-arts; livres illustrés; éditions originales. S.L.A.M.

LIBRAIRIE CELTIQUE, 108 bis RUE DE RENNES, 75006 PARIS. Prop: Mme Henriette Antonelli. TN: 548 54 08. Boutique, fermé lundi matin. Restreint stock. Spec: régionalisme. Cata: 2 par an. B: C.I.C. CP: Paris 8833–07. S.L.A.M.

PHILIPPE CHABANEIX, 33 RUE MAZARINE, 75006 PARIS. TN: 326 8483. Boutique, fermé Lundi. Spec: éditions originales modernes; littérature générale; poésie. S.L.A.M.

MAISON CHARAVAY, 3 RUE DE FURSTENBERG, 75006 PARIS. Prop: Michel Castaing. TN: 033 59 89. TA: Charautographe Paris. Fondée en 1830. Boutique. Très important stock. Spec: autographes et documents historiques. Cata: 4 par an. B: Crédit Lyonnais. CP: Paris 54 04 22. S.L.A.M.

GEORGES CHAUVIN, 78 RUE MAZARINE, 75006 PARIS. TN: 326 1066. Boutique. Spec: histoire; géographie; philosophie; religions. CP: Paris 11019–67. S.L.A.M.

LIBRAIRIE I. CHMELJUK, 1 RUE DE FLEURUS, 75006 PARIS. TN: 548 36 68. Fondée en 1930. Magasin. Moyen stock. Spec: Slavisme, Europe de l'Est. Cata: 5 par an. Corresp: anglais. B: Union Bancaire, 21 rue de Vaugirard, 75006 Paris. CP: Paris 1290 91. S.L.A.M.

RAYMOND CLAVREUIL, 36 RUE SAINT-ANDRÉ-DES-ARTS, 75006 PARIS. TN: 326 7117. Boutique. Spec: histoire. CP: Paris 1277–01. S.L.A.M.

GASTON COLAS, 84 BOULEVARD RASPAIL, 75006 PARIS. TN: 548 1958. Boutique. Spec: beaux-arts; architecture; archéologie; costumes. CP: Paris 19401. S.L.A.M.

PIERRE COLAS, 38 RUE DE VAUGIRARD, 75006 PARIS. TN: 033 0085. Fermé Août. Spec: beaux-arts; voyages. CP: Paris 12258–82. S.L.A.M.

MAXIME COTTET-DUMOULIN, 3 RUE SÉGUIER, 75006 PARIS. TN: 033 6796. Boutique. Très important stock. Spec: livres illustrés, beauxarts; semantiques; éditions originales; régionalisme. Cata. S.L.A.M.

JEAN COULET, 1 RUE DAUPHINE, 75006 PARIS. TN: 326 4240. Boutique. Spec: livres illustrés; modes; art militaire. CP: Paris 2126–52. S.L.A.M.

C. COULET & A. FAURE, 5 RUE DROUOT, 75006 PARIS. TN: 770 84 87 et 770 86 38. Fondée 1883. Boutique. Important stock. Spec: editions originales; livres illustrés. Cata: 10 par an. B: B.F.C.E., 21 boulevard Haussman, Paris 9e. CP: Paris 9401–86. S.L.A.M.

LIBRAIRIE DU CYGNE, 17 RUE BONAPARTE, 75006 PARIS. TN: 326 3245. Boutique. Spec: livres anciens; gravures.

FRANCIS DASTÉ, 16 RUE DE TOURNON, 75006 PARIS. TN: 326 52 89. Fondée en 1942. Shop, fermé Samedi aprésmidi. Moyen stock. Spec: Histoire et topographie de Paris; bibliophilie. Cata: 1 par an. Corresp: English. CP: Paris 5222–31. S.L.A.M.

JEAN DESCHAMPS, 22 RUE VISCONTI, 75006 PARIS. TN: 326 9797. Spec: éditions originales et illustrés. CP: Paris 97543. S.L.A.M.

GALERIE DOCUMENTS, RUE DE SEINE 53, 75006 PARIS. Prop: Michel Romand. TN: 033 50 68. Fondée en 1954. Boutique, fermé Lundi. Moyen stock. Spec: Affiches originales "Fin de Siecle". Corresp: English. B: Union de Banques a Paris, Compte 88 107 520 00 8. CP: Paris 11 629 48. S.L.A.M., Chambre Syndicale de l'Éstampe et du Dessin.

LUCIEN DORBON, 156 BOULEVARD SAINT-GERMAIN, 75006 PARIS. Prop: Pierre Berès. TN: 326 4598. Fondée en 1877. Boutique, fermé Samedi aprésmidi. Très important stock, aussi les livres neufs. Spec: bibliographie; érudition; beaux-arts; histoire. Cata. CP: Paris 16083. S.L.A.M.

LIBRAIRIE DUPONCHELLE, 27 RUE MAZARINE, 75006 PARIS. TN: 326 5585. S.L.A.M.

CHEZ DURTAL, S.A.R.L., 12 RUE JACOB, 75006 PARIS. TN: 633 7314. Fondée en 1927. Boutique. Moyen stock. Soec: médicine; science; l'horlogerie. Listes. Corresp: English, Italiano. CP: Paris 1023 45. S.L.A.M.

LIBRAIRIE FLAMMARION, 4 RUE CASIMIR DELAVIGNE, 75006 PARIS. TN: 033 3014. Spec: éditions originales; beaux-arts. CP: Paris 81424. S.L.A.M.

CHRISTIAN GALANTARIS, 11 RUE DE VAUGIRARD, 75006 PARIS. TN: 033 69 79. Fondée en 1974. Boutique. Spec: éditions originales; livres illustrés; reliures. Cata: 3 par an. Corresp: English, Español. B: B.N.P., 1 rue de Médicis, 75006 Paris. Compte 210 010 16. S.L.A.M.

S.A. LIBRAIRIE ORIENTALISTE PAUL GEUTHNER, 12 RUE VAVIN, 75006 PARIS. TN: 326 58 62, et 326 90 27. TA: Liborient Paris. Fondée en 1902. Fermé samedi. Spec: Afrique; archéologie; Assyriologie; Egypte; Islam; Extrême Orient; voyages; linguistique; religion; périodiques. Corresp: English, Deutsch. B: Banque Jordaan, Paris. CP: Paris 1524–50 (France) et 9897–97 (Etranger).

FRANÇOIS GIRAND, 76 RUE DE SEINE, 75006 PARIS. TN: 326 0761. Boutique. Spec: géographie; régionalisme livres á gravures. CP: Paris 15279–95. S.L.A.M.

LIBRAIRIE GIRAUD-BADIN, 128 BOULEVARD SAINT-GERMAIN, 75006 PARIS. TN: 326 0708. Boutique, fermé Lundi. Spec: ventes aux enchéres; bibliographie. Cata. B: B.N.P. CP: Paris 50247. S.L.A.M.

LIBRAIRIE GUÉNÉGAUD, S.A., 10 RUE DE L'ODÉON, 75006 PARIS. TN: 326 07 91. Prop: Marc Pénau. Fondée en 1947. Boutique. Important stock. Spec: régionalisme. Cata: 4 par an. Corresp: English. B: Banque A. de Saint Phalle, Compte 6751. CP: Paris 6027 86. S.L.A.M.

J. HUETZ DE LEMPS, 70 RUE DU CHERCHE-MIDI, 75006 PARIS. TN: 222 61 31. Boutique, fermé lundi matin. Moyen stock. Corresp: English, Español, B: Banque de France, compte 317221. CP: Paris 827716. S.L.A.M.

JEAN HUGUES, 1 RUE DE FURSTENBERG, 75006 PARIS. TN: 326 7476. Spec: manuscrits; reliures; beaux livres anciens. S.L.A.M.

L'INTERMÉDIAIRE DU LIVRE, 88 RUE BONAPARTE, 75006 PARIS. Prop: Bernard Hiard. TN: 633 00 50. Fondée en 1952. Boutique. Important Stock. Spec: Réligion, Philosophie, Histoire. Cata: 2 par an. B: C.L. 5363 D. CP: 814021. S.L.A.M.

PAUL JAMMES, 3 RUE GOZLIN, 75006 PARIS. TN: 326 47 71. Fondée en 1925. Sur rendezvous. Important stock. Spec: littérature; livres anciens; typographie; bibliographie estampes. Corresp: English, Deutsch, Italiano, Español. B: Banque de France, Paris-Raspail, Compte 323 612. CP: Paris 1361 80. S.L.A.M.

LIBRAIRIE RENE KIEFFER, 46 RUE SAINT-ANDRÉ DES ARTS, 75006 PARIS. Prop: Michel Kieffer. TN: 326 47 11. Fondée en 1903. Boutique.

Important stock. Spec: illustrés modernes; éditions originales; atelier de reliure. Cata: 4 par an. B: C.C.F., Agence Saint-Germain. CP: Paris 370 147. S.L.A.M.

C. F. LABARRE, 22 RUE DAUPHINE, 75006 PARIS. TN: 033 72 62. Fondé en 1945. Boutique. Spec: imagerie; jeux; livres anciens et modernes. Corresp: English. B: B.N.P. Agence A. CP: 5344–25. S.L.A.M.

J. B. LAFFITTE, 13 RUE DE BUCI, 75006 PARIS. TN: 326 6828. Spec: périodiques. S.L.A.M.

LIBRAIRIE LEONCE LAGET, 75 RUE DE RENNES, 75006 PARIS. TN: 548 90 18. TA: Liblaget Paris 110. Fondée en 1955. Boutique, fermé samedi. Moyen stock, aussi les livres neufs. Spec: beaux-arts, architecture. Cata. Corresp: English. B: Union de Banques á Paris, and Westminster Foreign Bank, Paris. CP: La Source 3154500. S.L.A.M., L.I.L.A.

JACQUES LAMBERT, LIBRAIRIE DE L'ABBAYE, 27 RUE BONAPARTE, 75006 PARIS. TN: 033 89 99. Fondée en 1904. Boutique, fermé Lundi matin. Très important stock. Spec: autographes. Cata: 12 par an. B: B.N.P., Agence 387. S.L.A.M.

MARCEL LECOMTE, 17 RUE DE SEINE, 75006 PARIS. TN: 326 8547. Fondée en 1928. Magasin, fermé lundi. Très important stock. Spec: livres illustrés; beaux-arts; estampes originales. B: C.I.C., 57 rue de Rennes, Paris. CP: Paris 341 652. S.L.A.M.

LOUIS LECONTE, 73 RUE DES SAINTS-PÈRES, 75006 PARIS. TN: 548 8837. Boutique. Spec: sciences naturelles; médecine ancienne. Cata. B: C.I.C., 57 rue de Rennes, Paris. CP: Paris 8429–79. S.L.A.M.

ALEXANDRE LOEWY, 85 RUE DE SEINE, 75006 PARIS. TN: 033 1195. Boutique. Moyen stock, gravures, dessins. Cata. B: C.C.F., 2 Carrefour de l'Odéon, Paris 6e. CP: Paris 1518–91. S.L.A.M.

BERNARD LOLIÉE, 72 RUE DE SEINE, 75006 PARIS. TN: 326 5382. Boutique. Spec: Surrealisme; éditions originales; livres illustrés; autographes. B: C.C.F., 2 Carrefour de l'Odéon, Paris 6e. CP: Paris 6697–19. S.L.A.M.

JEAN-JACQUES MAGIS, 12 RUE GUENÉGAUD, 76006 PARIS. TN: 326 50 57. TA: Magislibri. Fondée en 1925. Boutique, fermé Samedi. Très important stock. Spec: livres anciens en sciences économiques, politiques et juridiques. Cata: 2 par an. Corresp: English, Español, Deutsch, Italiano. B: C.I.C. Agence M. Copmte 11 050 47. CP: Paris 7929 26. S.L.A.M., Compagnie des experts specialisés.

LIBRAIRIE D'AMERIQUE ET D'ORIENT ADRIEN MAISONNEUVE, 11 RUE ST. SULPICE, 75006 PARIS. Prop: Jean Maisonneuve. TN: 326 86–35. Fondée en 1926. Boutique, fermé samedi. Très important stock, aussi les livres neufs. Spec: l'Orient et l'Orientales. Cata: sans pèriodicité. Corresp: English, Español, Deutsch. B: Crédit Lyonnais, Agence V Paris, Compte 6534 J et 6535 K. CP: Paris 849–13. S.L.A.M., Syndicat des Editeurs, Cercle de la Librairie.

YVES MARGOTAT, 8 RUE DE L'ODÉON, 75006 PARIS. TN: 326 9818. Fondée en 1963 (ancien Librairie René Colas 1913). Boutique. Moyen stock. Spec: bibliographie, typographie; livres rares; littérature du XVe au XVIIIe siècle; histoire. Cata: 1 par an. Corresp: English. B: Banque de France, W 350 006. CP: Paris 1492. S.L.A.M.

JEAN-CLAUDE MARTINEZ, 53 bis QUAI DES GRANDS-AUGUSTINS, 75006 PARIS. TN: 326 6311. S.L.A.M.

ALAIN MAZO, 15 RUE GUÉNÉGAUD, 75006 PARIS. TN: 326 3984. Spec: beaux-arts; livres illustrés; gravures modernes. CP: Paris 5721–88. S.L.A.M.

LES MEILLEURS LIVRES, 18 BOULEVARD SAINT-MICHEL, 75006 PARIS. Boutique. Stock important. Spec: érudition.

LIBRAIRIE MONGE, 5 RUE DE L'ECHAUDÉ, 75006 PARIS. Prop: G. Zyssman. TN: 633 1984. Fondée en 1952. Boutique. Spec: histoire de la science et médecine (seulement). Cata. CP: Paris 7019–40. S.L.A.M.

CHARLES MORIN, 102 RUE DU CHERCHE-MIDI, 75006 PARIS. TN: 548 0391. Fondée 1939. Boutique, Ouverte la première semaine commerciale de chaque mois, l'après-midi. Restreint stock. Cata: 1 par an. CP: Paris 3315 79.

G. MORSSEN, 14 RUE DE SEINE, 75006 PARIS. TN: 326 7809. Fondée en 1954. Boutique. Important stock. Spec: autographes. Cata. Corresp: English, Deutsch, Italiano. CP: Paris 5923–72. S.L.A.M.

F. DE NOBELE, RUE BONAPARTE 35, 75006 PARIS. TN: 326 0862. TA: Denobelef, Paris. Fondée en 1920. Boutique, fermé Samedi. Important stock, aussi les livres neufs. Cata: parfois. Corres: English. B: B.N.P. 133 Bd St Germain, 75006 Paris, Compte 210 791. CP: Paris 394–22. Cercle de Librairie. S.L.A.M. Syndicat librairie ancienne Suisse, Belgique.

J.-P. PARROT, 59 RUE DE RENNES, 75006 PARIS. TN: 548 5638. Fondée en 1905. Boutique. Restreint stock. Spec: littérature; histoire; beaux-arts. Cata. Corresp: English, Deutsch. B: U.B.P. 62 rue Bonaparte, Paris 6e. CP: Paris 11221–80. S.L.A.M.

HENRY PETIET, 8 RUE DE TOURNON, 75006 PARIS. TN: 033 6855. Spec: livres illustrés; gravures. S.L.A.M.

EDITIONS A. & J. PICARD, 82 RUE BONAPARTE, 75006 PARIS. Prop: Jacques Picard. TN: 326 96 73. Fondée en 1869. Boutique. Important stock. Spec: archéologie; histoire; religions; régionalisme. Cata: 6 par an. Corresp: English. B: C.I.C. Agence F, 57 rue de Rennes, Paris, Compte 16 691–37. CP: Paris 19164. Syndicat des Editeurs, Cercle de la Librairie.

L. & J.-H. PINAULT, 36 RUE BONAPARTE, 75006 PARIS. TN: 633 0424. Fondée en 1917. Boutique. Moyen stock. Spec: littérature française; marine; livres en petit format. Cata. B: U.B.P., Compte 88–131070. CP: Paris 2.854.86. S.L.A.M., L.I.L.A.

JEAN POLAK, 8 RUE DE L'ÉCHAUDÉ, 75006 PARIS. TN: 326 05 91. Fondée en 1938. Boutique. Très important stock. Spec: marine; voyages. Cata. Corresp: English, Deutsch. B: Crédit Lyonnais, Agence U, 22 boulevard St-Michel, Paris 6e. CP: Paris 6282–10. S.L.A.M., L.I.L.A.

JEANNE POMAREDE, 19 QUAI DES GRANDS-AUGUSTINS, 75006 PARIS. TN: 326 1480. Boutique. Spec: musique et littérature musicale. CP: Paris 12148–84. S.L.A.M.

LA PORTE ETROITE, 10 RUE BONAPARTE, 75006 PARIS. TN: 033 26 03. Fondée en 1921. Boutique. Moyen stock. Livres neufs et anciens. Spec: beaux-arts; tous les écrits sur les arts plastiques. Corresp: English, Español, Deutsch, Italiano. CP: Paris 7725 59.

LIBRAIRIE POURSIN, 21 RUE SAINT-SULPICE, 75006 PARIS. Dir: Anne-Marie Poursin. Fondée en 1925. Boutique. Très important stock. Spec: littérature, histoire, beaux-arts. Cata: 2 par an. B: Banque Parisienne de Crédit, Compte 2 16 7025 0. CP: Paris 1657 64. S.L.A.M.

PAUL PROUTÉ S.A. 74 RUE DE SEINE, 75006 PARIS. TN: 326 89 80. Fondée en 1896 (1920). Boutique. Restreint stock, aussi gravures. Cata: 2 par an. Corresp: English, Deutsch. B: C.C.F. 070 2132920. C.P. Paris 508 79. S.L.A.M. Syndicat des antiquaires; Chambre Syndicale de l'estampe.

ROBERT PROUTÉ, 12 RUE DE SEINE, 75006 PARIS. TN: 326 9322. Boutique, fermé Lundi matin. Spec: gravures. CP: Paris 47057. S.L.A.M.

LIBRAIRIE QUATRE CHEMINS—EDITART, 3 PLACE SAINT-SULPICE. 75006 PARIS. TN: 033 40 73. TA: Waledit Paris. Fondée en 1924. Boutique. Spec: beaux-arts. Cata. Corresp: English, Deutsch. B: B.N.P., 133 boulevard Saint-Germain, Paris 6e. CP: Paris 3239–56. S.L.A.M.

EMILE ROSSIGNOL, 8 RUE BONAPARTE, 75006 PARIS. TN: 326 7431. Boutique. Spec: editions anciennes; incunables; manuscrits. Cata. CP: Paris 12884–21. S.L.A.M.

LIBRAIRIE EUGÉNE ROSSIGNOL, 4 RUE DE L'ODÉON, 75006 PARIS. TN: 033 68 20. Fondée en 1880. Fermé lundi matin, samedi. Très important stock. Spec: 16, 17, 18 siecles; et tous livres rares. CP: Paris 204138. S.L.A.M.

MAURICE ROUAM, 29 RUE MAZARINE, 75006 PARIS. TN: 326 1271. Boutique, fermé Lundi. Spec: éditions originales; bibliographie; livres illustrés. CP: Paris 1899–41. S.L.A.M.

FRANCIS ROUX-DEVILLAS, 12 RUE BONAPARTE, 75006 PARIS. TN: 033 6932. Boutique. Spec: sciences anciennes; autographes; americana. CP: Paris 14473–12. S.L.A.M.

SAFFROY, 3 QUAI MALAQUAIS, 75006 PARIS. Prop: Mme Naert. TN: DAN 09 19. Fondée en 1880. Spec: autographes; documents historiques. Cata: autographes, 6 par an. Corresp: English. S.L.A.M.

GASTON SAFFROY, 4 RUE CLÉMENT, 75006 PARIS. TN: 326 25 92. Fondée en 1880. Boutique. Spec: généalogie; héraldique; histoire régionale. Cata: 4 par an. CP: Paris 883 09. S.L.A.M.

SAGOT LE GARREC & CIE, 24 RUE DU FOUR, 75006 PARIS. TN: 326 4338. S.L.A.M.

LIBRAIRIE SAINT-LOUIS, 21 RUE SERVANDONI, 75006 PARIS. TN: 033 7813. Spec: beaux-arts; régionalisme; histoire. S.L.A.M.

LIBRAIRIE ORIENTALE H. SAMUELIAN, 51 RUE MONSIEUR-LE-PRINCE, 75006 PARIS. Prop: Hrand Samuelian. TN: 326 88 65. Fondée en 1930. Boutique. Moyen stock, aussi les livres neufs. Spec: Orientalisme; Arabie; Arménie; Extr. Orient; etc. Corresp: English, Deutsch. B: B.N.P., Siège Sorbonne. Cte Dépôt 270.589, Cte Export 270.593. CP: Paris 1278-35. S.L.A.M., L.I.L.A.

SARTONI & CERVEAU, 101 RUE DE SEINE, 75006 PARIS. TN: 326 8289. Boutique. Spec: cartes; atlas; vues; gravures. CP: Paris 14414-62. S.L.A.M.

EDMOND TAMIZ, "A LA COLOMBE", 30 RUE MADAME, 75006 PARIS. TN: 548 7641. Spec: érudition; histoire; voyages. CP: Paris 7869-00. S.L.A.M.

THÉODORE TAUSKY, 33 RUE DAUPHINE, 75006 PARIS. TN: 734 4065. Spec: autographes; manuscrits; documents historiques. S.L.A.M.

LIBRAIRIE THOMAS-SCHELER, 19 RUE DE TOURNON, 75006 PARIS. Prop: Lucien Scheler. TN: 326 9769. TA: Thomlib, Paris. Fondée en 1932. Boutique. Moyen stock. Spec: médecine, sciences, voyages, incunables, gothiques. Cata. Corresp: English. CP: Paris 271-41. S.L.A.M., L.I.L.A., Cercle de la Librairie.

MICHÈLE TROCHON, 76 RUE DU CHERCHE-MIDI, 75006 PARIS. TN: 222 18 53. Spec: tiers-monde francophone. Cata. 4 par an. Corresp: English, Español. B: B.I.C.–R.N.P. Saint Denis. CP: 31 409 91, La Source. S.L.A.M. Cercle National des Armées. Société Française d'Histoire d'Outre-Mer.

ALPHONSE VIDAL, 55 RUE BONAPARTE, 75006 PARIS. TN: 633 5790. Boutique. Spec: éditions anciennes; voyages; histoire; sciences. Cata. CP: Paris 5553-48. S.L.A.M.

RENÉ VIGNERON, LES ARGONAUTES, 74 RUE DE SEINE, 75006 PARIS. TN: 326 7069. Spec: autographes; manuscrits; éditions originales, livres illustrés. CP: Paris 7965-83. S.L.A.M.

VINCENT, FREAL & CIE, 4 RUE DES BEAUX-ARTS, 75006 PARIS. TN: 326 5402. Spec: architecture; beaux-arts. Cata. CP: Paris 76900. S.L.A.M.

ROBERT VIVIEN, 41 RUE MAZARINE, 75006 PARIS. TN: 033 0470. Spec: occultisme; gastronomie; médecine. Cata. CP: Paris 10050-63. S.L.A.M.

MME. ANDRÉ WAHL, LIBRAIRIE DES ALPES, 6 RUE DE SEINE, 75006 PARIS. TN: 326 90 11. Fondée en 1935. Boutique, fermé Lundi. Ouvrages anciens et livres neufs. Moyen stock. Spec: alpinisme; speleologie; Jules Verne. Cata. Corresp: English, Italiano. CP: Paris 3678 91. S.L.A.M.

D. WEIL, 1 RUE DU DRAGON, 75006 PARIS. TN: 222 19 14. Fondée en 1949. Domicile, par correspondance et sur rendez-vous. Stock important; recherches de livres épuisés. Spec: périodiques anciens et modernes, littéraires, scientifiques. Cata: sans pèriodicité. Corresp: English. B. B.I.C.S., Compte 313/1 Agence St.-Germain. CP: Paris 10 384 69. S.L.A.M., L.I.L.A.

LUCIE ET PIERRE-ANDRÉ WEILL, AU PONT DES ARTS. 6 RUE BONAPARTE, 75006 PARIS. TN: 033 7195. Spec: beaux-arts; reliures; gravures. CP: Paris 2097–67. S.L.A.M.

MADAME S. ZLATIN, 46 RUE MADAME, 75006 PARIS. TN: 222 06 47. Fondée en 1950. Domicile; 3 ème étage droite; ouvert de 14 á 18 heure et sur rendez-vous. Fermé du 15 juillet au 5 septembre. Spec: livres sur le théâtre, danse, cirque, marionnettes, cinéma, musique et architecture théâtrale. Cata. CP: Paris 93–7473. S.L.A.M.

PARIS Arrondissement 7e

MADAME GILBERTE SIMONE BARBIER, 14 RUE DE L'UNIVERSITÉ, 75007 PARIS. TN: 548 2714. Boutique, fermé mercredi aprésmidi. CP: Paris 1733.64. S.L.A.M.

GILBERTE COURNAND, 14 RUE DE BEAUNE, 75007 PARIS. TN: 222 4388. Boutique. Spec: éstampes et sculptures sur la danse et les ballets. CP: Paris 11726–78. S.L.A.M.

ANDRÉ DERUELLE, 30 RUE DES SAINTS-PÈRES, 75007 PARIS. TN: 548 7290. Fermé Lundi. Spec: régionalisme; archéologie; héraldique. CP: Paris 16815. S.L.A.M.

JEAN FOURNIER & CIE, 22 RUE DU BAC, 75007 PARIS. TN: 222 36 45. Fondée en 1952. Fermé lundi matin. Moyen stock, aussi les livres neufs. Spec: livres sur les arts. Cata. Corresp: English. B: Société Générale, Agence D. CP: Paris 3606 42. S.L.A.M.

LIBRAIRIE GALLIMARD, 15 BOULEVARD RASPAIL, 75007 PARIS. TN: 548 2484. Boutique. Spec: éditions originales; beaux-arts; livres illustrés. CP: Paris 408–80. S.L.A.M.

MADAME ANTOINE GRIMMER, 15 RUE DUPONT DES LOGES, 75007 PARIS. TN: 468 6607. Spec: littérature générale. CP: Paris 34140. S.L.A.M.

JACQUES HOUSSAIS, RUE JEAN NICOT, 75507 PARIS. Seulement par correspondance. S.L.A.M.

LIBRAIRIE LAFFONT, 58 RUE DE BABYLONE, 75007 PARIS. Prop: Robert Laffont. TN: 551 63 42. Fondée en 1960. Domicile, sur rendez-vous seulement. S.L.A.M.

EDMOND LASSARE, 1 bis RUE DE LA CHAISE, 75007 PARIS. TN: 532 7664. S.L.A.M.

LIBRAIRIE MARC LOLIÉE, RUE DES SAINTS-PÈRES, 75007 PARIS. TN: 548 40 19. Fondée en 1920. Boutique. Moyen stock. Spec: livres illustrés; éditions originales; livres anciens; autographes. Cata. Corresp: English. B: B.N.P., 133 boulevard Saint Germain, 75006 Paris. Compte. 210 419. CP: Paris 1002 80. S.L.A.M.

PIERRE PETITOT, 234 BOULEVARD SAINT-GERMAIN, 75007 PARIS. TN: 548 0527. Fondée en 1877. Boutique. Moyen stock, aussi les livres neufs. Spec: beaux livres anciens; XVIIe–XIXe siecle; art militaire. Cata. Corresp: English. B: Crédit Lyonnais, Agence X-424, Compte 5840A. S.L.A.M.

PIERRE SIEUR, 3 RUE DE LA UNIVERSITÉ, 75007 PARIS. TN: 260 75 94.
Fondée en 1945. Boutique. Moyen stock. Spec: jouets anciens et cartes
á jouer anciennes et modernes; numismatique; autographes; documents
historiques; curiosités. CP: Paris 6 803 26. S.L.A.M.

EDGAR SOETE, LIBRAIRIE SALET, 5 QUAI VOLTAIRE, 75007 PARIS. TN:
548 72 41. Fondée en 1930. Boutique, fermé Lundi. Important stock.
Spec: XVe au XIX siecle; bibliophilie; documentation; reliures;
gastronomie. Cata: 2 par an. Corresp: English. B: B.N.P. CP: Paris
2108 87. S.L.A.M.

PARIS Arrondissement 8e

PIERRE BERÉS, 14 AVENUE DE FRIEDLAND, 75008 PARIS. TN: 227 0099
TA: Piby Paris. Spec: manuscrits; beaux livres; reliures. Cata. CP:
Paris 1593.68. S.L.A.M.

LIBRAIRIE AUGUSTE BLAIZOT S.A., 164 FAUBOURG SAINT-HONORÉ
75008 PARIS. Président: Claude Blaizot. TN: 359 36 58. Fondée en 1840
Boutique. Spec: littérature française; éditions originales, livres illustrés
manuscrits et autographes. Cata: 3 ou 4 par an. B: B.N.P., CP: Paris
517-97. S.L.A.M.

PIERRE CHRÉTIEN, 178 FAUBOURG SAINT-HONORÉ, 75008 PARIS. TN
359 5266. Boutique, fermé Samedi. Spec: manuscrits; reliures; éditions
originales; livres illustrés. CP: Paris 28546. S.L.A.M.

MADAME COUTURIER, 7 RUE DE DURAS, 75008 PARIS. TN: 265 4480
Fondée en 1940. Fermé Samedi. Spec: livres anciens et modernes. Cata
4-5 par an. Corresp: English. B: Crédit Lyonnais. CP: Paris 2639-84
S.L.A.M.

MAURICE DAMBOURNET, L'ARGUS DUE LIVRE, 4 AVENUE FRANKLIN
ROOSEVELT, 75008 PARIS. TN: 225 3829. Spec: beaux livres; édition
originales. CP: Paris 1587-53. S.L.A.M.

MADAME VEUVE RONALD DAVIS, 12 AVENUE FRANKLIN-ROOSEVELT
75008 PARIS. TN: 359 1943. Spec: éditions originales; autographes
Cata. CP: Paris 38310. S.L.A.M.

GÉRARD FLEURY, LIBRAIRIE FRANÇOIS 1er, 34 AVENUE MONTAIGNE
75008 PARIS. TN: 359 7077. Spec: voyages; livres illustrés; reliures
S.L.A.M.

RENÉ GONOT, LIBRAIRIE SAINT-AUGUSTIN, 99 Boulevard Haus-mann, 75008 Paris. TN: 26527 31. Fondée en 1926. Boutique, fermé Samedi. Spec: littérature; histoire, et tous ouvrages en langue anglaise. Corresp: English. B: Société Générale, A.M. S.L.A.M., A.B.A.

LIBRAIRIE GONOT, 22 rue de Miromesnil, 75008 Paris. TN: 265 6603. Boutique. Moyen stock, aussi les livres neufs. Spec: histoire; moderne et XVIIIe et XIXe siecle; gastronomie. CP: Paris 17845–63. S.L.A.M.

JACQUES HERBINET, 39 rue de Constantinople, 75008 Paris. TN: 522 61 15. Domicile. Important stock. Spec: ancien; modernes illustrés. B: Banque de France. CP: Paris 17 337 72. S.L.A.M.

LIBRAIRIE LARDANCHET, 100 rue de Faubourg Saint-Honoré, 75008 Paris. TN: 266 68 32. B: Société Générale. *Aussi* a Lyon.

ROBERT LEGOUIX, 4 rue Chauveau-Lagarde, 75008 Paris. TN: 265 3678. Fermé Samedi. Spec: musique ancienne. CP: Paris 69944. S.L.A.M.

EDOUARD LOEWY, 184 boulevard Haussmann, 75008 Paris. TN: 924 5450. TA: Ardlowy Paris. Spec: éditions originales; livres illustrés; autographes. Cata. CP: Paris 84212. S.L.A.M.

GALERIE MAEGHT, 13 rue de Téhéran, 75008 Paris. TN: 387 6149. S.L.A.M.

LIBRAIRIE DE MONTBEL, 1 rue Paul Cézanne, 75008 Paris. Prop: Jacqueline Frachon. TN: 359 06 47. Fondée en 1947. Boutique, fermé Samedi. Restreint stock, aussi les livres neufs. Spec: chasse, équitation, vénerie, pêche. Corresp: English. B: B.N.P. Agence St. Philippe de Roule, Compte 270 160. CP: Paris 16742–38. S.L.A.M.

LIBRAIRIE DU MONT-DORE, 72 rue du Faubourg-St.-Honoré, 75008 Paris. TN: 265 6429. S.L.A.M.

HENRI PICARD FILS, 126 Faubourg Saint-Honoré, 75008 Paris. TN: 359 2811. Spec: beaux livres anciens; reliures. CP: Paris 28200. S.L.A.M.

PIERRE PICARD, 60 Boulevard Malesherbes, 75008, Paris. TN: 387 3882. Fondée en 1937. Boutique. Spec: lavage, restauration de livres et gravures. CP: Paris 2154 83. S.L.A.M.

LIBRAIRIE GEORGES PRIVAT, 162 boulevard Haussman, 75008 Paris. Prop: B. et D. Privat. TN: 227 14 49. Fondée en 1902. Boutique. Moyen stock. Cata. B: Crédit Lyonnais, Agence W. CP: Paris 557–78. S.L.A.M.

71

V.R.I.L.L.E. EDITIONS PRO-FRANCIA, 3 RUE SAINT-PHILIPPE DU ROULE, 75008 PARIS. TN: 225 4354. Fondée en 1955. Boutique. Moyen stock, aussi les livres neufs. Spec: beaux-arts; archéologie; littérature française. Corresp: English. B: Crédit Lyonnais. CP: Paris 16365–88. S.L.A.M.

PARIS Arrondissement 9e

LIBRAIRIE FERNAND CAFFIN, S.A., 80 RUE SAINT-LAZARE, 75009 PARIS. TN: 874 2313. Spec: beaux-arts; éditions modernes; technique. CP: Paris 42200. S.L.A.M.

FRANÇOIS CHAMONAL, 40 RUE LE PELETIER, 75009 PARIS. TN: 878 14 41. Spec: Beaux livres anciens; medecine et sciences; voyages; géographie; marine; Cata. S.L.A.M.

LIBRAIRIE DORBON-AINÉ, 19 BOULEVARD HAUSSMANN, 75009 PARIS. Prop: Jean Guille. TN: 770 8968. Spec: occultisme; histoire; beaux-arts. CP: Paris 15122–13. S.L.A.M.

PAUL EPPE, 49 RUE DE PROVENCE, 75009 PARIS. TN: 874 6668. Spec: éditions originales; livres illustrés. CP: Paris 17764–49. S.L.A.M.

MICHEL FAURON, 10 bis RUE DE CHATEAUDUN, 75009 PARIS. TN: 878 2011. Fondée en 1937. Boutique, fermé Samedi. Assez restreint stock. Spec: livres modernes illustrés; éditions originales. B: Jordaan. CP: Paris 5297–21. S.L.A.M.

GÉRARD FERHADIAN, 36 RUE MONTHOLON, 75009 PARIS. TN: 878 2825. Boutique. Spec: periodiques; musique. CP: Paris 3204–05. S.L.A.M.

PIERRE GIRARD, 17 RUE DE CHATEAUDUN, 75009 PARIS. TN: 878 7469. Boutique, fermé Lundi matin. Fondée en 1869. Spec: musique; théâtre; histoire. CP: Paris 2722–37. S.L.A.M.

ROBERT GOUMY, 6 bis RUE DE CHATEAUDUN, 75009 PARIS. TN: 878 77 84. Fondée en 1938. Boutique. Important stock. Spec: éditions anciennes et modernes illustrés. Cata. CP: Paris 596 149. S.L.A.M.

CLAUDE JAVELLE, 32 RUE DE PROVENCE, 75009 PARIS. TN: 828 2174. Boutique. Moyen stock. S.L.A.M.

XAVIER JEHANNO, 12 PLACE BUDAPEST, 75009 PARIS. Boutique. Important stock. Spec: politique; histoire; voyages; régionalisme;

beaux-arts; romans; cartes postales. Corresp: English. B: Crédit Lyonnais.

LIBRAIRIE LEGUELTEL, 17 RUE DROUOT, 75009 PARIS. TN: 770 33 00. Fondée en 1886. Magasin. Très important stock. Spec: beaux-arts, aussi les livres neufs. Cata: 2 par an. Corresp: English, Deutsch. B: Banque Jordaan, 26937 W. CP: La Source 34 135 06. S.L.A.M.

LOUIS LOEB-LAROCQUE, 36 RUE LE PELETIER, 75009 PARIS. TN: 878 11 18. Boutique. Important stock. Spec: atlas; topographie; voyages; estampes. Corresp: English, Deutsch. B: Crédit Lyonnais, Agence F, Paris, Compte 6803. A. S.L.A.M.

PAUL-ROBERT MARIN, 18 BOULEVARD HAUSSMANN, 75009 PARIS. TN: 770 1840. Boutique. Restreint stock. Spec: beaux-arts; reliures; livres d'enfants. CP: Paris 49284. S.L.A.M.

SOCIÉTÉ LIVRES & MUSIQUE, 6 RUE LAMARTINE, 75009 PARIS. Gérante: Mme. Elisabeth Simon. TN: 744 71 22. Fondée en 1936. Boutique. Restreint stock. Spec: Partitions P. & Ch. Orchestre— Classique et Lyriques. B: Crédit Lyonnais, Agence F.406, 50 rue Lafayette, Paris 9e., Compte 5468–Q. CP: Paris 21 356 91. S.L.A.M.

LIBRAIRIE VASILIU DU LYCÉE EDGAR QUINET, 67 RUE DES MARTYRS, 75009 PARIS. Prop: Virgil Vasiliu. TN: 878 90 47. Fondée en 1960. Boutique. Assez restreint stock, aussi les livres neufs. Spec: classiques; tourisme. Corresp: Deutsch, Italiano. B: C.L., Agence AI, 62 74 H.

LIBRAIRIE PAUL VULIN, 48 PASSAGE JOUFFROY, 75009 PARIS. Prop: Louis Ribot-Vulin. TN: 824 9889. Fermé lundi matin. CP: Paris 68396. S.L.A.M. (Aussi a 8 RUE DE ROME, PARIS 8e.)

PARIS Arrondissements 10e-20e

AUX AMATEURS DE LIVRES, 62 AVENUE DE SUFFREN, 75015 PARIS. Président: Marcel Blancheteau. TN: 567 1838 et 566 6091. Fondée en 1926. Boutique, fermé Samedi. Important stock, aussi les livres neufs. Spec: aéronautique; littérature française; beaux-arts; érudition. Cata: 1 par an. Corresp: English, Deutsch, Español. B: Société Nancèienne de Crédit, 11 rue d'Aguesseau 75008 Paris. CP: Paris 969–35. S.L.A.M.

ALEXANDRE BAER (J. BAER & CO.,) 2–6 RUE LIVINGSTONE, 75018 PARIS. TN: 255 0144 aussi 606 1466. Fondée en 1785 à Francfort, la plus ancienne maison toujours entre les mains d'une même famille et pendant de longues années la plus importante librairie ancienne du monde). Bureau, fermée les lundis: sur rendez vous seulement. Spec: Livres très rares concernant les Ameriques. Cata: prochain No. 3131 en 1977. Corresp: English, Deutsch. B: Crédit Lyonnais, Agence U, Paris: B.N.P., et Chase Manhattan Bank. CP: Paris 7040 74. S.L.A.M.

FERNAND BEAUFILS, 169 AVENUE VICTOR-HUGO, 75016 PARIS. TN: 727 9370. Spec: beaux-arts; éditions originales. CP: Paris 16233.29. S.L.A.M.

PIERRE LA BRELY, 108 RUE DU RANLAGH, 75016 PARIS. TN: 527 2237. Spec: autographes; manuscrits; éditions originales. Cata. S.L.A.M.

DANIEL BRUN, 6 RUE CLODION, 75015 PARIS. TN: 211 6573. Par correspondance seulement. Spec: érudition; histoire, philosophie. S.L.A.M.

JOSÉ CORRADINI, 18 RUE VINEUSE, 75016 PARIS. TN: 870 65 84. Domicile, sur rendezvous. Spec: Americana; voyages; beaux livres. Corresp: English, Italiano, Español. S.L.A.M.

MAX-PHILIPPE DELATTE, 133 RUE DE LA POMPE, 75116 PARIS. TN: 553 70 93 Fondée en 1939. Boutique. Restreint stock, aussi les livres neufs. Spec: éditions originales; beaux-arts, littérature; érudition. Cata. B: B.N.P. Agence Victor Hugo, Compte 210 397. CP: 5286–51. A.L.A.M. Association culturelle des libraires de litterature générale. Cercle de la Librairie.

EDOUARD HAMPARTZ, 90 RUE DE LEVIS, 75017 PARIS. TN: 622 1468. S.L.A.M.

FRANÇOIS JANICOT, 32 AVENUE NIEL, 75017 PARIS. TN: 227 3340. Cata. CP: Paris 5274–29. S.L.A.M.

AU JARDIN DES COLLECTIONNEURS, 130 BOULEVARD MURAT, 75016 PARIS. TN: 647 4826. S.L.A.M.

BORIS KAPLANSKI, 8 RUE DU LOING, 75014 PARIS. TN: 587 05 58 et 707 55 55. Fondée en 1950. Par correspondance seulement. Moyen stock. Spec: Rossica; bibliographie; éditions anciennes; érudition; histoire. Cata: 2–3 par an. Corresp: English, Russian. B: Banque Nationale de Paris, Agence Général Leclerc, Paris 14e, Compte CC No. 213.931. CP: Paris 7739 18. S.L.A.M. I.L.A.B.,

JACQUES LEVY, 46 RUE D'ALÉSIA, 75014 PARIS. TN: 331 68 79. Fondée en 1940. Boutique, fermé Lundi. Moyen stock. Spec: littérature générale; Judaica; Hebraica; histoire; curiosités. Cata: 5–6 par an.

B: C.I.C., Succarsale B.O., 99 avenue du Général Leclerc, Paris 14e, Compte 14379 64. CP: Paris 5634 31. S.L.A.M.

LIVRES ET REVUES DE FRANCE, 37 RUE DESBORDES-VALMORE, 75016 PARIS. (B.P. 146–16 75763 Paris Cedex 16) Prop: Danielle Bordes-Audineau. TN: 504 02 12 (répondeur automatique). TA: Livrevues, Paris. Fondée en 1970. Domicile; sur rendez-vous seulement. Moyen stock. Spec: littérature, sciences humaines. Cata: 3 ou 4 par an. Corresp: English. B: B.N.P. Excelmans, Paris, Compte 210 368–10. S.L.A.M., I.L.A.B.

STÉ. MANY, 12 RUE DELAMBRE, 75014 PARIS. Prop: J. Bessières. TN: 633 07 61. Fondée en 1962. Boutique, fermé Lundi. Moyen stock. Spec: littérature, beaux-arts, histoire (Revolution). Corresp: English. CP: Paris 12 869 39. S.L.A.M.

LIBRAIRIE MONTMARTROISE, 29 RUE DURANTIN, 75018 PARIS. TN: 076 4125. S.L.A.M.

II

FRANCE (NORD): NORDFRANKREICH: NORTHERN FRANCE

27800 BRIONNE	27340 PONT DE L'ARCHE
14 CAEN	76 ROUEN
76200 DIEPPE	92210 SAINT CLOUD
94120 FONTENAY-SOUS-BOIS	93400 SAINT-OUEN
91400 GOMETZ LE CHATEL	50700 VALOGNES
92130 ISSY LES MOULINEAUX	92170 VANVES
59000 LILLE	78 VERSAILLES
78 LOUVECIENNES	95450 VIGNY
95270 LUZARCHES	91 VILLEBON SUR YVETTE

L'ANE D'OR, BOITE POSTALE 6, 95450 VIGNY. Prop: Yves Lévy. TN: 466 20 66. Fondée en 1968. Domicile, sur rendez-vous seulement. Important stock. Spec: littérature, médicine, sciences humaines. Cata: 4 par an. Corresp: English, Deutsch, Español, Italiano. B: B.I.C.S., 1 rue Danté, 75005 Paris. Compte 404 1000 755. CP: 18 104–38 Paris. S.L.A.M., L.I.L.A.

ERNEST DARGENT, 11 RUE ALAIN-BLANCHARD, 76000 ROUEN. Boutique. Spec: Normandie. CP: Rouen 24339. S.L.A.M.

DAWSON-FRANCE, S.A., ZONE INDUSTRIELLE "LA PRAIRIE", 9112**1**
VILLEBON-SUR-YVETTE. (B.P. 40). TN: 909 01 22. Telex: 60394. Fondée
en 1925. Bureaux et depôt, fermé samedi. Important stock. Spéc:
périodiques. Cata: 2 par an. Corresp: English. B: Lloyds Bank Europe
Ltd., 43 bd. des Capucines, 75002 Paris, Compte 121 643 017. CP: Paris
1071 62. S.L.A.M., L.I.L.A.

HENRI DUPONT, 141 BOULEVARD DE LA LIBERTÉ, 59000 LILLE. TN: 54
85 60. Fondée en 1949. Boutique, fermé lundi matin. Assez restreint
stock, aussi les livres neufs. Spec: éditions originales, gravures, estampes,
tableaux. Corres: English. B: Banque Worms, rue du Molinel, Lille.
CP: 199–399. S.L.A.M.

CÉCILE ELUARD-VALETTE, 43 AVENUE DE LA DAME-BLANCHE, 94120
FONTENAY-SOUS-BOIS. TN: (873) 4662. S.L.A.M.

EUROPERIODIQUES, S.A., 31 AVENUE DE VERSAILLES, 78170 LA CELLE
SAINT CLOUD. Prop: Charles Blackburn. TN: 969 32 01. Telex: 69865.
Fondée en 1964. Dépôt et bureaux, fermé samedi. Sur rendez-vous s.v.p.
Restreint stock. Spec: régionalisme, extrême Orient, Japan; biblio-
graphie; périodiques. Cata: 8–10 a year. Corresp: English, Japon. B:
Lloyds Bank International (France) Ltd., 43 bd. Capucines, 75002
Paris, Compte 121 646 547. CP: Paris 19 878 34. S.L.A.M. L.I.L.A.,,

EMILE FAVEREAUX, 19 RUE DE L'HÔPITAL-MILITAIRE, 59000 LILLE. TN:
(20) 544031. S.L.A.M.

JEAN GOSSELIN, 4 RUE ALAIN-BLANCHARD, 76000 ROUEN. Boutique
fermé en Août. CP: Rouen 8288. S.L.A.M.

MICHEL GUILLAUME & CIE., S.A.R.L., 98 RUE SAINT-PIERRE, 14000
CAEN. TN: (31) 81 23 13. Boutique. Spec: histoire; droit; sciences. CP
Paris 19007–28. S.L.A.M.

HACHETTE, DEPARTMENT INTERNATIONAL ANTIQUARIAT LUXE, 58 RUE JEAN-BLEUZEN 92170 VANVES. TN: 645–21–62. TA: Aglibrairi Vanves. Fondée en 1826. Dépôt, sur rendez-vous, Stock important. Spec: beaux-arts, érudition, histoire, littérature. Cata: 4 par an. Corresp: English. CP: Paris 1063–81. S.L.A.M.

XAVIER JEHANNO, 4 PLACE DE L'EGLISE, 78430 LOUVECIENNES. TN: 969 8037. Fondée en 1945. Boutique, Ouverte: Samedi et Dimanche. Important stock. Spec: politique, histoire, voyages, régionalisme, beaux-arts, romans, cartes postales. Corresp: English. B: Société Générale.

LESTRINGANT, 123 RUE GÉNÉRAL-LECLERC, 76000 ROUEN. TN: 71 03 98. Fondée en 1702. Boutique, fermé Lundi. Livres rares par correspondance seulement. Assez restreint stock, aussi les livres neufs. Spec: histoire; Normandie. Corresp: English. CP: Rouen 269 W.

ARNOLD LEVILLIERS, 118 ROUTE DE CHARTRES (RN 188), 91400 GOMETZ-LE-CHATEL (ESSONE). TN: 592 02 24 (Paris). Fondée en 1923. Domicile, par rendezvous seulement. Moyen stock. Spec: arts et métiers; gravures; dessins; beaux-arts. Corresp: English, Deutsch. B: Barclays Bank, Paris, Compte 02–41789–14. CP: Paris 30 38 87. S.L.A.M., S.L.A.C.E.S.

JULES LORIEUL, 3 RUE DE POTERIE, 50700 VALOGNES. TN: (33) 354. Boutique. Spec: régionalisme; histoire; éditions originales. Cata. CP: Paris 2306–13. S.L.A.M.

LIBRAIRIE CHARLES LUCAS, 10 RUE ARMENGAUD, 92210 SAINT-CLOUD. TN: (Paris) 602 44 39. Fondée en 1947. Domicile, par rendezvous seulement. Restreint stock. Cata. Corresp: English, Deutsch. B: Banque de France, Bureau Central, 75001 Paris, Compte H 350 887. CP: 6913 38. S.L.A.M.

METAIS, 12 RUE JEAN PRIEUR, 27340 PONT DE L'ARCHE. TN: (35) 92 01 85. Fondée en 1961. Boutique. Restreint stock. Spec: regionalisme Normand. B: Société Générale. S.L.A.M., Syndicat National des Antiquaires.

GÉRARD MONFORT, ST.-PIERE-DE-SALERNE, 27800 BRIONNE. S.L.A.M.

DANIEL MORCRETTE, 4 AVENUE JOFFRE, 95270 LUZARCHES. (B.P. 26) TN: 471 0158. Fondée en 1954. Domicile, par rendezvous seulement Tres important stock. Spec: gastonomie; critique littéraire; livres rares: autographes. Cata. Corresp: English. CP: Paris 795470. S.L.A.M.

GUY PROUTÉ, 15 RUE DU 18-JUIN, 92210 SAINT-CLOUD. TN: (602) 5115 Spec: estampes.

LIBRAIRIE PUZIN, 30 RUE DE LA PAROISSE, 78 VERSAILLES. TN: 950 43 75 Fondée en 1900. Boutique, fermé Lundi matin. Important stock. Spec histoire; livres anciens.

G. RAFFY, 85 RUE DES ROSIERS (STAND 83 MARCHÉ BIRON), 93400 SAINT-OUEN (SEINE-ST. DENIS). TN: 770 36 51. Boutique, ouvert Samedi Dimanche, Lundi. Moyen stock, Spec: topographie. Cata: Corresp Español. S.L.A.M.

LIBRAIRIE RAOUST, 11 RUE NEUVE, 59000 LILLE. TN: (20) 54 64 79. Fondée en 1822. Boutique, fermé lundi matin. Restreint stock, aussi les livres neufs. Spec: histoire; régionalisme, Flandre-Artois. B: S.G., Lille, Compte CCD 4649. CP: Lille 1729 16. S.L.A.M.

WLADIMIR TIRASPOLSKY, 69 AVENUE VICTOR-CRESSON, 92130 ISSY-LES-MOULINEAUX. Spec: langues étrangères; sciences naturelles. S.L.A.M.

GALERIE VAUQUELIN, 4 RUE VAUQUELIN, 76200 DIEPPE. Prop: Michel Burollaud. TN: (35) 84 31 78. Boutique, ouvert tous les jours. Moyen stock. Spec: régionalisme; histoire; beaux-arts; littérature. Cata. B: Crédit Lyonnais, 76 Dieppe. Compte 8332 71298 P. CP: Rouen 226621 F. S.L.A.M.

III

FRANCE (OUEST): WESTFRANKREICH: WESTERN FRANCE

49 ANGERS	89 LIMOGES
17 ANGOULEME	44 NANTES
33120 ARCACHON	45 ORLEANS
41 BLOIS	24 PERIGNEUX
33 BORDEAUX	29 QUIMPER
28 CHARTRES	35 RENNES
17 LA ROCHELLE	37 TOURS
72 LE MANS	

LIBRAIRIE ANCIENNE ET MODERNE, 50 RUE SCELLERIE, 37000 TOURS. Boutique. Moyen stock, aussi les livres neufs.

PIERRE BACHELIER, 6 RUE NEUVE-DES-CAPUCINS, 44000 NANTES. TN: (40) 715367. S.L.A.M.

A. BELLANGER, 5 PLACE DU BON PASTEUR, 44000 NANTES. TN: (40) 73 20 03 et 71 36 88. Fondée en 1942. Dépôt, 4 étages, fermé lundi matin. Important stock aussi les livres neufs. Spec: littérature, voyages, Régionalisme, gravures. Cata: 4 ou 5 par an. B: B.N.P., et C.C.F. CP: Nantes 10997–4 S.L.A.M.

PIERRE H. LE BODO, 31 RUE DE BORDEAUX, 37000 TOURS (INDRE-ET-LOIRE). Fondée en 1895. Boutique, fermé Juillet et Août, ouvert diamanches et fétes. Important stock. Spec: livres anciens; gravures; timbres poste; vieux papiers; archives. CP: Nantes 1724–29. S.L.A.M.

LIBRAIRIE-GALERIE BRETONNE, 1 RUE DES FOSSÉS, 3500 RENNES. Prop: G. L. Thomas. TN: 30 98 80. Fondée en 1950. Boutique. Spec: Bretagne, folklore, gravures anciennes, Marine. Cata: 2 par an. Corresp: English. B: B.N.P. à Rennes. CP: Rennes 1702–15. S.L.A.M.

MARIE & REINE CAILLON, 10 RUE MONTAULT, 49000 ANGERS. Spec: livres illustrés; régionalisme. CP: Nantes 34416. S.L.A.M.

CANDIDE, 7 RUE MONTAULT, 49000 ANGERS. TN: 88 66 02. Fondée en 1969. Boutique, fermé Lundi. Important stock. Spec: regionalisme; beaux-arts; musicologie. Cata: 1 par an. Corresp: English. B: Crédit Lyonnais, Angers.

LIBRAIRIE CISNEROS, 4 RUE CHARLES-MARCEL PÉNARD, 33000 BORDEAUX. TN: 48 24 88. CP: Bordeaux 4373. S.L.A.M.

HENRI DANIGO, 17 RUE MARC-SANGNIER, 29000 QUIMPER. Fondée en 1953. Domicile. Restreint stock. Spec: Bretagne et varia. Cata. B: C.L., Quimper. CP: Nantes 1549 15. S.L.A.M.

MADAME LEON DENIS, 50 RUE DE LA SCELLERIE, 37000 TOURS. S.L.A.M.

GABRIEL DURANCE, 5 ALLÉE D'ORLÉANS, 44000 NANTES. TN: 73 28 12. Fondée en 1815. Boutique, fermé lundi matin. Très important stock. Spec: régionalisme; histoire; voyages. Cata: 2–3 par an. Corresp: English, Deutsch, Italiano, Español. B. C.L. CP: Nantes 295–59. S.L.A.M.

JEAN MICHEL DE FLOESSER, 28 RUE DES REMPARTS, 33000 BORDEAUX (GIRONDE). TN: 48 77 71. Boutique. Expert organisation vente publique. Spec: érudition; médecine ancienne. Cata: CP: Bordeaux 23 23 05. S.L.A.M.

LIBRAIRIE GIRON, 4 RUE TROIS-ECRITOIRE, 37000 TOURS. Boutique.

MADAME L'HUILLIER, 24 RUE DE LA CLOCHE VERTE, 16000 ANGOULÉME. TN: 2039. Boutique. S.L.A.M.

JEAN JUHEL-DOUET, 3 RUE D'ANGLETERRE, 41000 BLOIS. TN: 79 18 84. Boutique. Moyen stock. Spec: régionalisme. Cata. Corresp: English. CP: Paris 5461–99. S.L.A.M.

GEORGES LAMONGIE, 2 RUE DE LA NATION, 24 PERIGUEUX. TN: 53 22 45. Fondée en 1924. Boutique. Moyen stock. Cata. 12 par an. CP: Limoges 2986. S.L.A.M.

MARCEL LAUCOURNET, 45 BOULEVARD CARNOT, 87000 LIMOGES. TN: (55) 774339. S.L.A.M.

MADAME E. J. LEGRAND, 48 RUE DU MAIL, 49000 ANGERS.

PIERRE LELANT, 18 RUE BERTIN, 49000 ANGERS. TN: 43 89 70. Fondée en 1962. Boutique. Très important stock. Spec: érudition, études litteraires. Cata: 3 par an. Corresp: English. B: C.L., Angers, Compte 070 025. CP: Paris 18 791 98 M. S.L.A.M.

MAURICE LESTER, 13 bis RUE DU CYGNE (MARCHÉ AUX FLEURS), 28000 CHARTRES. TN: 667. Spec: éditions modernes; gravures; régionalisme. CP: Paris 87045. S.L.A.M.

JEAN LETERRIER, 20 RUE JEANNE D'ARC, 45000 ORLEANS. TN: 87 50 60. Boutique. CP: Orleans 64984. S.L.A.M.

LA MAISON DU LIVRE, 24 RUE DE LA CLOCHE VERTE, 16000 ANGOULÉME. Prop: Mme Guillaume. TN: (45) 92 20 39. Fondée en 1947. Boutique, fermé Lundi; de préférence sur rendez-vous. Important stock, aussi quelques livres neufs de documentation, beaux-arts et régionalisme. Cata: parfois. S.L.A.M., L.I.L.A.

MME. E. MARONNE, 37 RUE BOUFFARD, 33000 BORDEAUX. Fondée en 1930. Boutique, fermé Lundi. Moyen stock. CP: Bordeaux 416-07.

CHARLES MORIN, 9 RUE AUVRAY, 72000 LE MANS. TN: 84 62 12. Fondée en 1920. Boutique, fermé Lundi. Moyen stock. Cata. CP: Rennes 1 174 72. S.L.A.M.

LIBRAIRIE MORVRAN, 16 bis RUE RENÉ MADEC, 29000 QUIMPER. (succ. Librairie le Dault, fondée 1923). TN: (98) 95 31 63. Boutique, fermé le Lundi. Spec: Bretagne et pays celtiques. aussi en livres neufs: gravures et cartes. Cata: 2 par an. Corresp: English. B: C.I.O., Quimper Compte 058 053320 W. CP: Rennes 485 07.

HÉLÈNE PELLERIN, 7 RUE DUPATY, 17000 LA ROCHELLE. Spec: régionalisme. CP: Bordeaux 69528. S.L.A.M.

QUARTIER LATIN, 21 RUE ALBERT-1er, 17000 LA ROCHELLE. Prop: Roger La Blanc. Fondée en 1950. TN: (46) 28 21 54. Magasin, fermé lundi. Restreint stock, aussi les livres neufs. Spec: régionalisme; enseignement. B: Banque de l'Union Parisienne, Agence de la Rochelle, Compte Y 17 272-2. CP: Bordeaux 119 036. S.L.A.M. Syndicat des libraires classiques de France.

"VIEILLE FRANCE", 65 BOULEVARD GÉNÉRAL-LECLERC, 33120 ARCA-CHON. Prop: Georges Berthier. TN: (56) 83 19 14. Fondée en 1947. Boutique. Restreint stock. Spec: livres anciens–romantiques; médecine; varia; curiosités. Cata: 8–9 par an. Corresp: English, Español. B: B.F., 302142 Arcachon. CP: Bordeaux 31 02 20. S.L.A.M.

IV

FRANCE (EST): OSTFRANKREICH: EASTERN FRANCE

71400 AUTUN	71 MACON
25 BESANÇON	73550 MÉRIBEL-LES-ALLUES
73 CHAMBERY	57 METZ
21 DIJON	68 MULHOUSE
38 GRENOBLE	54 NANCY
69 LYON	42 SAINT-ETIENNE
	67 STRASBOURG

LIBRAIRIE DU BAT D'ARGENT, 3 RUE DU BAT D'ARGENT, 69 LYON (RHÔNE). Prop: Madame Chartier. TN: 28 18 08. CP: Lyon 2004 47. S.L.A.M.

PAUL BISEY, 35 PLACE DE LA RÉUNION, 68100 MULHOUSE. TN: (89) 44 72 91. Fondée en 1906. Boutique, fermé lundi. Restreint stock. Spec: régionalisme. Cata. Corresp: English, Deutsch. B: C.M.D.P., St Paul. CP: Strasbourg 1977 J. S.L.A.M. Syndicat des librairies Alsace. Cercle de la Librairie, Paris.

LIBRAIRIE ANCIENNE CHAMBEFORT, 26 PLACE BELLECOUR, 69 LYON.

LIBRAIRIE DU CHARIOT D'OR, 38 RUE DES REMPARTS D'AINAY, 69002 LYON. TN: (78) 374 153. Fondée en 1970. Boutique, fermée le matin. Spec: livres anciens; littérature; histoire, régionalisme. Cata: 2 par an. CP: 5 265 59.

CITÉ DES VIEUX LIVRES, 139 GRANDE RUE, 25000 BESANÇON. Prop: Raymond Cartier. TN: (81) 83 40 67. Fondée en 1950. Boutique, fermé lundi. Moyen stock. Spec: histoire locale; numismatique. Corresp: English. B: C.M.D.P. Besançon-Centre, Compte 10854 845. CP: Dijon 710 61 D. S.L.A.M.

JEAN COLLIARD, 11 RUE AUGUSTE-COMTE, 69 LYON (RHÔNE). TN: 42 44 83. Fondée en 1958. Boutique fermé Lundi et tous les matins. Moyen stock. Spec: beaux livres anciens. Cata: 2 par an. B: Crédit Lyonnais. CP: Lyon 4643 20. S.L.A.M.

BOUQUINERIE COMTOISE, 9 RUE MORAND, 25000 BESANÇON (DOUBS). Prop: Jean Louis Cariage. TN: (81) 83 21 91. Boutique, fermé Lundi. Moyen stock, aussi les livres neufs. Spec: régionalisme (Franche-Comté); gravures. B: B.N.P. CP: Dijon 219–95W. S.L.A.M.

LIBRAIRIE DUBOUCHET, 2 RUE GÉNÉRAL FOY, 42 SAINT-ÉTIENNE. (LOIRE). Prop: Yves Dubouchet. TN: (77) 32 36 59. Fondée en 1828. Boutique, fermée Lundi. Moyen stock. aussi les livres neufs. Spec: livres illustrés et anciens; erudition; régionalisme; varia. Cata: 6 par an. Corresp: English, Italiano. B: B.N.P., Compte 223. 006, et Crédit Lyonnais, Compte 642.840 R. CP: Lyon 57.90. S.L.A.M., L.I.L.A.

LOUIS FILLET, 13 RUE DE BOIGNE, 73 CHAMBÉRY. TN: 33 27 60 Spec: régionalisme; érudition. S.L.A.M.

LIBRAIRIE GANGLOFF, 13 AVENUE AUGUSTE-WICKY, 68100 MULHOUSE. Prop: François Gangloff. TN: 44 62 04. Fondée en 1932. Boutique. Important stock. Spec: régionalisme (Alsace); littérature, aussi les livres neufs. B: B.N.P. CP: Strasbourg 2 18 90. S.L.A.M., L.I.L.A.

LOUIS GANGLOFF, 20 PLACE DE LA CATHÉDRALE, 67000 STRASBOURG. TN: (88) 32 40 52. Fondée en 1927. Magasin, fermé lundi matin. Important stock, aussi les livres neufs. Spec: régionalisme, Alsace. Cata: 4 par an. Corresp: Deutsch. B: C.I.A.L., Strasbourg. CP: Strasbourg 148–48. S.L.A.M.

L'HOMME DE FER, 32 RUE DES DOMINICAINS, 54000 NANCY. Prop: Jean Pierre André. TN: 24 35 28. Fondée en 1886. Boutique. Important stock. Spec: Lorraine, Alsace. CP: Nancy 212 45. S.L.A.M.

LIBRAIRIE LARDANCHET, 10 RUE PRÉSIDENT CARNOT, 69002 LYON. Prop: Mme Armand Lardanchet. TN: (78) 37 41 34. Fondée 1899. Boutique, fermée lundi matin. Restreint stock, aussi les livres neufs. Spec: beaux livres anciens et modernes; manuscrits; gravures. B: Crédit Lyonnais. CP: Lyon 6091. S.L.A.M.

JEAN-LOUIS LEFEBVRE, 73550 MÉRIBEL-LES-ALLUES. TN: 248. S.L.A.M.

PIERRE LEMALLIER, 4 RUE DES ORFÈVRES, 67000 STRASBOURG. Magazin. Spec: romantiques; mémoires; voyages; médecine; Judäisme. CP: Strasbourg 61865. S.L.A.M.

MARCEL LE MEUR, 12 PLACE DU THÉÂTRE, 21000 DIJON. TN: 32 32 90. Fendée en 1900. Boutique, fermé Lundi matin. Moyen stock. B: Société Générale, Dijon. CP: Dijon 28054. S.L.A.M.

LIBRI, 6 RUE DU PONT, 71000 MACON. Prop: André Ruel, TN: 38 15 09 (le matin jusqu'à 9.30). Fondée en 1961. Boutique, fermé dimanche, lundi et mardi. Assez restreint stock. Spec: Régionalisme seulement. B: B.N.P., S.L.A.M., L.I.L.A.

GUY METRA, 43 GRAND-RUE CHAUCHIEN, 71400 AUTUN. TN: 240.

FERDINAND MOSCHENROSS, 31 QUAI DES BATELIERS, 67000 STRAS-BOURG. TN: 365051. S.L.A.M.

JEAN PEYSSON, 7 RUE DU PLAT, 69002 LYON. TN: 37 73 32. Boutique, fermé en Août. Spec: régionalisme; héraldique. CP: Lyon 4790–43. S.L.A.M.

PIERRE POSOT, 28 QUAI JONVIN, 38000 GRENOBLE. TN: (76) 874324. S.L.A.M.

LIBRAIRIE A. REMY, 25 RUE STANISLAS, 54000 NANCY. Fondée en 1912. Boutique, fermé lundi. Important stock. Spec: littérature; histoire; régionalisme. CP: 20 18 75 E. S.L.A.M.

LIBRAIRIE STENDHAL, 4 RUE DE SAULT, 38000 GRENOBLE. Prop: Jean Menagé. TN: (76) 44 41 69. Fondée en 1940. Boutique, fermé lundi. Moyen stock. Spec: Stendhal; littérature ancienne et moderne; alpinisme; voyages; éstampes. Corresp: English. B: C.L., Grenoble (Jean Menagé, 112 059 Y). CP: Grenoble 375 86 M. S.L.A.M., L.I.L.A.

JEAN ZALC, RUE MAZELLE 37, 5700 METZ. TN: (97) 740014. S.L.A.M.

V

FRANCE (SUD): SUDFRANKREICH: SOUTHERN FRANCE

83460 LES ARCS
13100 AIX EN PROVENCE
30100 ALES
06600 ANTIBES
84000 AVIGNON
45190 BEAUGENCY
06 CANNES
83330 LE CASTELLET
81100 CASTRES
13001 MARSEILLE

82200 MOISSAC
34000 MONTPELIER
06000 NICE
30000 NÎMES
64000 PAU
13000 PELISSANNE
64500 SAINT-JEAN-DE-LUZ
83100 TOULON
31000 TOULOUSE

ERNEST ARTIGUE, 6 RUE DU LORGUES, 83100 TOULON. Spec: régional-isme; marine. CP: Marseille 82473. S.L.A.M.

ARTS ET LETTRES, "LE VIEUX CHATEAU", 83330 LE CASTELLET. Prop: Mme A. Cadéo de Iturbide. TN: (94) 98 74 73. Fondée en 1950.

Domicile, sur rendezvous seulement. Restreint stock. Spec: érudition; livres anciens; travail et littérature générale. Cata: 6–8 par an. Corresp: Deutsch, Italiano, Español. B: Caisse Régionale de Crédit Agricole, Olliovles (83), Compte 66590.00.0.2. CP: Mme Cadéo de Iturbide, Marseille 3982–68. S.N.C.A.O.

PAUL BATAILLE, "CALENDAL", 14 RUE CHÂTEAUREDON, 13 MARSEILLE. TN: 54 07 68. Spec: beaux-arts; voyages; histoire; sciences. S.L.A.M.

ANDRE BOTTIN, LIBRAIRIE NICOISE, 2 RUE DÉFLY, 06 NICE. TN: 85 36 39. Fondée en 1930. Boutique, fermé Lundi; ouvert tous les jours de 9 h. á 19 h. Très important stock. Spec: érudition; critique littéraire; éditions originales; Provence. Cata. Corresp: English. B: Banque Commerciale Italienne. CP: Marseille 32652. S.L.A.M.

ROBERT BOURDON, 184 bis ROUTE DE CHATEAUDUN, 45190 BEAUGENCY. TN: 89 27 78. Dépôt, sur rendez-vous. Moyen stock. Spec: histoire et sciences auxiliaires; livres ancien français; religion. Cata: 4 par an. Corresp: English, Deutsch, Italiano, Español. S.L.A.M.

PIERRE BRUN, 68 RUE CARNOT, 13 PELISSANNE. TN: (90) 56 28 16. Fondée en 1930, Domicile, sur rendez-vous seuelement. Important stock. Spec: médicine, sciences, economie politique. B: B.U.P. Agence de Marseille. CP: Marseille 226–85. S.L.A.M., L.I.L.A.

PIERRE CLERC, 13 RUE ALEXANDRE-CABANEL, 34000 MONTPELLIER. TN: (67) 72 82 31. Fondée en 1967. Boutique. Très important stock. Spec: régionalisme; histoire; littérature. Cata. B: C.C.F., place aristide briant, Montpellier, Compte 305 203 9890. CP: Montpellier 943 17. S.L.A.M., L.I.L.A., C.N.E.S.

MARCEL COLAS, PASSAGE AGARD, 13100 AIX-EN-PROVENCE. TN: 398. S.L.A.M.

JEANNE LAFITTE, 106 BOULEVARD LONGCHAMP, 13001 MARSEILLE. TN: (91) 643885. Fondée en 1847. Stock important. Spec: folklore; editions originales, beaux-arts. Corresp: English. B: Barclays. CP: Marseille 589847. S.L.A.M.

BOUQUINERIE DU LANGUEDOC, 12 RUE DE L'UNIVERSITÉ, 34000 MONTPELLIER. Prop: Gérard Collin. TN: (67) 72 47 65. Fondée en 1906. Shop, fermé lundi matin. Très important stock. Spec: régionalisme; érudition; livres universitaires; numismatique. Cata: 2 par an. Corresp: English, Español. B: B.F., Montpellier. CP: Paris 11 89 573. S.L.A.M., L.I.L.A.

G. DE LUCENAY, 15 RUE PETITE-FUSTERIE, 84000 AVIGNON. TN: (90) 82 15 69. Fondée en 1920. Boutique, fermé lundi. Restreint stock. Spec: musique ancienne; Provence. Cata. Corresp: English, Español. B: Crédit Agricole, Avignon. S.L.A.M., L.I.L.A.

HENRI MARTIN-BRES, 60 RUE GRIGNAN, 13000 MARSEILLE. TN: (91) 37 02 92. S.L.A.M.

JACQUES MATARASSO, 2 RUE LONGCHAMP, 06 NICE. TN: (93) 87 74 55. Fondée en 1941. Boutique. Restreint stock. Spec: éditions originales; livres illustrés; beaux-arts; autographes; éstampes modernes. Cata. CP: Marseille 1535–01. S.L.A.M.

PAUL MAUREL, 104 RUE PARADIS, 13001 MARSEILLE. TN: (92) 375481. S.L.A.M.

LIBRAIRIE-GALERIE PAUL MAUREL, 27–29 BOULEVARD ALBERT 1er, 06600 ANTIBES. TN: (93) 34 60 78. Fondée en 1967. Boutique (1er étage). Restreint stock. Spec: livres illustrées modernes; éditions originales; beaux-arts. Cata: 3 par an. Corresp: English. S.L.A.M.

JACQUELINE MONDANGE, 7 AVENUE NOTRE-DAME, 06000 NICE. TN: (93) 80 08 29. Fondée en 1950. Boutique, fermé Lundi matin. Moyen stock. Spec: ancienne. CP: Marseille 40535. S.L.A.M.

EDOUARD MONTBARBON, 29 RUE D'ALGER, 83100 TOULON TN: (94) 922363. S.L.A.M.

LIBRAIRIE OCCITANIA, 46 RUE DU TAUR, 31000 TOULOUSE. Prop: Claude Thourel. TN: 21 00. Fondée en 1947. Boutique. Spec: Estampes, Occitan (littérature). CP: Toulouse 48213 X. S.L.A.M.

LIBRAIRIE RIVARÈS, 3 RUE RIVARÈS, 64000 PAU. Prop: Madame Roth. TN: 27 26 23. Fondée en 1954. Boutique. Important stock, aussi les livres neufs. Spec: régionalisme; pyrénées; lithogravures. B: Société Bordelaise, Pau, Compte 1 14 0543.V. CP: Bordeaux 225.100. S.L.A.M.

JEAN ROCCA, 7 RUE MEYERBEER, 06000 NICE. Boutique. CP: Marseille 59296. S.L.A.M.

HENRI ROSSIGNOL, 1 AVENUE DE GRASSE, 06400 CANNES. TN: (93) 39 70 55. Fondée en 1928. Magasin, fermé samedi et mercredi apres-midi. Restreint stock. Cata: 4–5 par an. Corresp: English. B: S.G., 2001 4886. CP: Marseille 276 35. S.L.A.M.

LIBRAIRIE ANCIENNE L. D. ROSSIGNOL, DOMAINE SAINT PIERRE, 83460 LES ARCS. TN: (93) 73 30 17. Fondée en 1974. Magasin. Stock restreint. Cata: 3–4 par an. Corresp: English. B: S.G., Les Arcs. CP: Marseille 36 39 92. C.N.E.S.

LIBRAIRIE SAINT-JACQUES, 10 RUE SAINT-JACQUES, 64500 SAINT-JEAN-DE-LUZ. TN: 261619. S.L.A.M.

JEAN-LOUIS SAINTE-MARIE, 43 BOULEVARD ALSACE-LORRAINE, 82200 MOISSAC. TN: 1 04 00 93. Boutique, fermé Lundi matin. Moyen stock. Spec: histoire; documentation; livres anciens. Cata: 12 par an. B: S.G., Compte 3915. CP: Toulouse 2105–04. S.L.A.M.

ETIENNE SANSONETTI, 9 RUE GUIZOT, 3000 NîMES. Boutique, fermé jeudi et du ler au 25 Août. CP: Montpellier 49777. S.L.A.M.

JEAN TASSY, 20 RUE DE BRESIS, 30100 ALES. TN: (66) 86 12 39. Fondée en 1942. Restreint stock. Spec: régionalisme; religions. Cata: 4 par an. B: Banque de Paris. CP: Montpellier 954 05. S.L.A.M.

ANDRÉ THÉROND, 40 RUE VICTOR HUGO, 81100 CASTRES. TN: (63) 59 31 43. Domicile, de preference sur rendez-vous. Important stock. Cata: 5 par an. Corresp: English. B: B.P.T.A. CP: Toulouse 1167 65 K. S.L.A.M.

CLAUDE THOUREL, LIBRAIRIE OCCITANIA, 46 RUE DU TAUR, 31000 TOULOUSE. TN: 21 49 00. Fondée en 1945. Boutique. Important stock. Spec: régionalisme; varia; gravures. Cata: 10 par an. CP: Toulouse 48213 X. S.L.A.M.

MARCEL THOUREL, 61 RUE DU TAUR, 31000 TOULOUSE. TN: (61) 22 09 02. Spec: histoire; régionalisme. S.L.A.M.

A. F. VOLTAIRE, 30 RUE ADOLPHE-THIERS, 13001 MARSEILLE. TN: (91) 48 60 58. Fondée en 1941. Magasin. Important stock. Cata. Corresp: English. CP: Marseille 286–81. S.L.A.M.

ISLAND

ICELAND   ISLANDE

REYKJAVÍK

FORNBOKVERZLUNIN, KLAPPERSTIG 37, REYKJAVÍK.

FORNBOKAVERZLUN KRISTJANSSONAR, HVERFISGOTU 26, REYKJAVÍK.

SNAEBJORN JONSSON & CO. H.F. HAFNARSTRAETI 4 and 9, REYKJAVÍK. (P.O. Box 1131.) TN: 11936, 13133 and 14281. TA: Books Reykjavik. Established 1927. Two shops. Very small stock, also new books. Cata: 1 a year .Corresp: English. B: National Bank of Iceland.

ISRAEL
ISRAËL

JERUSALEM: TEL AVIV

LOGOS BOOKSHOP, 38 Ben Yehuda Street, Tel Aviv. Prop: Walter Zadek. TN: 22 23 37. Established 1940. Shop, early closing Friday. Very large stock, also new books. Spec: anything about Palestine (old books, maps, engravings). Corresp: Ivrith, English, Deutsch, Français, Dutch. B: Bank Leumi Leisrael, Branch: Trumpeldor.

LUDWIG MAYER, LIMITED, Shlomzion Hamalka 4, Jerusalem. (P.O. Box 1174.) TN: 222628. Established 1908. Spec: Archaeology; Orientalia; mathematics; natural history. A.B.A.

F. PINCZOWER, 83 Sokolow Street, Tel Aviv. (P.O. Box 6008). TN: 443 448. TA: Pincbooks Tel-Aviv. Established 1939. House Premises, closed Friday 16.00 hours. Medium stock, also new books. Spec: military; contemporary history; Middle East. Cata: 3 a year. Corresp: English, Deutsch. B: Barclays Bank, Tel-Aviv, Account No. 13374. CP: Tel-Aviv 4128.

NISSEN PREMINGER, LTD., 9 Montefiore Street, Tel Aviv. (P.O. Box 29001). TN: 53027. TA: Promedice Tel Aviv. Spec: horology.

THE UNIVERSITAS-BOOKSELLERS, 9 Shlomzion Hamalka, Jerusalem. (P.O. Box 1086.) Prop: Hermann N. Z. Meyer. TN: 24050. Established 1935. Shop, open 10–13 or by appointment. Spec: archaeology; Palestine geography and travels; ancient cartography. Corresp: English, Deutsch, Français.

ZOHAR, 3 Nahalat Benyamin, Tel Aviv. (P.O. Box 4814.) Prop: E. Sheftl. TN: 621106 (after hours 263045). Established 1940. Shop, open 8–13 hours. Very large stock, also new books. Spec: Hebraica; Judaica; Orientalia. Cata: about 4 a year. Corresp: Hebrew, Yiddish, English, Français, Deutsch, Russian. B: Barclays Bank, Tel Aviv, Account No. 133571.

ITALIA

ITALY ITALIE ITALIEN

Association: Verband

C.L.A. = Circolo dei Librai Antiquari, via Consolata
8, Torino.

Public Holidays: Jours de Fête: Feiertage

Jan. 1 and 6: Mar. 19: Easter Monday: Apl. 25: May 1: Ascension: Corpus
Christi: Jun. 2 and 29: Aug. 15: Nov. 1 and 4: Dec. 8, 25 and 26.

Jan. 1 et 6: Mar. 19: lundi de Pâques: Avr. 25: Mai 1: Ascension: Fête-
Dieu: Jun. 2 et 29: Août 15: Nov. 1 et 4: Déc. 8, 25 et 26.

Jan. 1 und 6: Marz 19: Ostermontag: Apr. 25: Mai 1: Himmelfahrt:
Fronleichnam: Juni 2 und 29: Aug. 15: Nov. 1 und 4: Dez. 8, 25 und 26.

I

ROMA (ROM, RÔME)

LIBRERIA S. AGOSTINO, Via S. Agostino 17/A, Roma. Prop: Michelli
Chezubina. TN: (06) 655470. Established 1955. Shop. Medium stock.
Spec: spectacle, music, art. Cata. Corresp: Français. CP: Roma 1/
34465.

LIBRERIA ALESSANDRIA, Via Alessandria 216/a, Roma. Prop: Carlo
Misasi. TN: 858142. Established 1960. Shop. Small stock. Spec: occult;
science. Cata. Corresp: Français. CP: Roma 1/39793.

LIBRERIA LA BANCARELLA, Via Cavour 119, Roma. Prop: Felice
Bertocchi. TN: (06) 462541. Established 1932. Shop, closed during
August. Small stock. Corresp: Français.

LIBRERIA ANTIQUARIA M. T. CICERONE, Via Cicerone 39–41,
00193 Roma. Prop: G. Brotrini. TN: (06) 312465. Cata.

LIBRERIA DOTTI, Via Della Scrofa 58, 00186 Roma. Prop: Sergio Dotti. TN: (06) 564755. Established 1960. Shop, closed Monday morning. Large stock. Spec: sciences and literature. Cata: 6 a year. Corresp: English, Français. B: Banca Nazionale Lavoro, Ag. 15. CP: Roma 1/20390. A.L.A.I.

LIBRERIA ANTIQUARIA DELL'IMPERO, Corso Rinascimento 63, 00186 Roma. Cata.

LIBRERIA PASQUALE LOMBARDI, Via San Eufemia 11, 00187 Roma. Established 1940. Shop. Large stock, also new books. Spec: religion; law. Cata: 1 a year. Corresp: English, Français, Deutsch. B: Credito Italiano, Roma. CP: Roma 1/36606. A.L.A.I.

LIBRERIA GIA NARDECCHIA, S.p.A., Piazza Cavour 25, 00193 Roma. TN: (06) 352235. Established 1921. Shop, closed Saturday. Very large stock. Spec: Italian periodicals, old Italian books. Corresp: English, Deutsch.

LIBRERIA ANTIQUARIA QUERZOLA, 153 Via Del Babuino, 00187 Roma. Prop: Clara Querzola. TN: 6790 568. Shop. Very small stock. Corresp: English, Français. B: Banca Commerciale Italiana. CP: Roma 1/24606. A.L.A.I., S.L.A.M.

LIBRERIA ANTIQUARIA C. E. RAPPAPORT, Via Sistina 23, Roma. Prop: Elisabeth and James Seacombe. TN: 483826. TA: Libreria Rappaport Roma. Established 1906. Shop, closed Saturday. Medium stock Spec: medicine; science; fine arts; literature. Cata: about 3 a year. Corresp: English, Français, Deutsch. B: Banco di Sicilia, Agenzia 2 Roma, No. 41 00 98 450. CP: Roma 1/15558. A.L.A.I., L.I.L.A.˙ A.B.A. (int.).

LIBRERIA MARESCA RICCARDI, Piazza Ponte San Angelo 29 Roma.

GIUSEPPE SCARPIGNATO, Via Ripetta 156, 00186 Roma. TN: (06) 655923.

LIBRERIA SFORZINI, Via Della Vite 43, 00187 Roma. Cata.

FIAMMETTA SOAVE, Via Guiseppe Cuboni 12, 00197 Roma. Cata.

II

BOLOGNA
CHIVARI
COMACCHIO
COMO

FIRENZE (Florence)
GENOVA (Genoa, Genua)
LUCCA
LUCIGNANO

MILANO (Milan, Mailand)
NAPOLI (Naples, Neapel)
PADOVA (Padua)
PARMA
PERUGIA
RAVENNA

REGGIO EMILIA
RIMINI
TORINO (Turin)
TRIESTE
VENEZIA (Venice, Venedig)
VERONA

LIBRERIA "ACHILLE" DI A. MISAN, Piazza Vecchia 4, 34121
Trieste. TN: (040) 68525. A.L.A.I.

A. DEGLI ALBIZI, Piazza Duomo 22r, Firenze. TN: 21237. Spec: fine
arts; old prints; illustrated books. Cata. C.L.A.

DANILO ALLEGRETTI, 17 Viale Rosselli, 22100 Como. TN: 559801.
Established 1950. Private premises, appointment necessary. Small stock.
Cata: monthly. Corresp: English, Français. B: Banco di Roma,
Account No. C.538. CP: Como 18/3689.

LIBRERIA ALPINA, Via Savioli 39/2, 40137 Bologna. Prop: Gastone
and Mario Mingardi. TN: (051) 345715. Established 1961. Storeroom,
open normal business hours. Small stock, also new books. Spec: old
and new books, prints and maps on mountaineering. Cata: 2–3 a year.
Corresp: English. B: Banca Cooperativa di Bologna, Sede., No. 12833.
CP: Bologna 8/24566.

BOTTEGA AMBROSIANA, Via Vitruvio 47, 20124 Milano. TN: 227936.
Spec: fine arts; religions; science. Cata. CP: Milano 3/51932. A.L.A.I.

LIBRERIA GIURIDICA ARDY, Piazza Sauli 4–2, 16123 Genova. TN:
(010) 295508. Cata.

L'ARTE ANTICA, Via A. Volta 2, 10121 Torino. Prop: Teresa Salamon.
TN: (011) 515834. A.L.A.I.

LIBRERIA ANTIQUARIA LUIGI BANZI, Via Borgonuovo 10, 40125
Bologna. Prop: Dott. Mario Tamburello. TN: (051) 269088. Shop,
early closing Saturday. Very small stock. Spec: autographs. Corresp.:
Français. B: Banco di Napoli-Filiale di Bologna. CP: Bologna 8/20182.
A.L.A.I.

LIBRERIA S. BARDINI, Via XII Ottobre, 16121 Genova. TN: (010)
298956.

LIBRERIA VINCENZO BERISIO, Via Medina 14, 80133 Napoli. TN:
(081) 328922. Cata.

LIBRERIA BERRUTO, VIA SAN FRANCESCO DA PAOLA 10 bis, 10123 TORINO. Prop: Serafino Berruto. TN: (011) 542569. Established 1939. Shop, closed Monday. Large stock. Spec: bibliography, Italian literature, topography (Italy, Piedmont). Cata. Corresp: English, Français. B: Credito Italiano. CP: Torino 2/20571. A.L.A.I.

LIBRERIA BERTOCCHI, STRADA MAGGIORE 70, 40125 BOLOGNA. Prop: Romeo Bertocchi. TN: (051) 229799. Spec: old and modern medicine and periodicals.

LIBRERIA ANTIQUARIA "BIANCHINO DEL LEONE", PIAZZA ÁNSIDEI 4, 06100 PERUGUIA. (C.P. 25). Prop: Silvestri Lodovico. TN: 66.323. Established 1946. Private premises, open normal business hours. Medium stock. Spec: libri; stampe; autografi. Corresp: English, Français, Tedesco. B: Banca Commerciale Italiana. CP: Perugia 12046-0. A.L.A.I.

LA BIBLIOFILA, CORSO PORTA NUOVA 2, 20121 MILANO. Prop: Carla Marzoli. TN: 669248. Spec: Americana; incunabula; manuscripts; geography; old prints. A.L.A.I.

LIBRERIA BONFANTI, VIA MACEDONIO MELLONI 19, 20129 MILANO. TN: 74 61 81. Spec: law; political science. CP: Milano 3/38504. A.L.A.I.

LE BOUQUINISTE, VIA PRINCIPE AMEDEO 29, 10123 TORINO. Prop: dott. Carla Viotto Maccono. TN: 876782. TA: Bouquiniste Torino. Spec: old and rare; old prints; Italian topography; history. CP: Torino 2/37491. A.L.A.I.

BICE BOURLOT, PIAZZA CASTELLO 9, TORINO, 10123. TN: 53 48 65. TA: Bourlot Stampe Torino. Spec: prints—arts and crafts; costumes, sports and pastimes; atlases, maps and views. B: Credito Italiano. CP: Torino 2/22492. A.L.A.I.

LIBRERIA ANTIQUARIA BOURLOT, PIAZZA SAN CARLO 183, I–10123 TORINO. Prop: Gian Vittorio Bourlot. TN: 53 74 05. Established 1848. Shop, closed Monday morning and during August. Large stock. Spec: old and rare; Italian literature and topography; old science; geography; old prints. Cata: 2 a year. Corresp: English, Français. B: Banco di Roma, Torino. CP: Torino 2/18001. A.L.A.I., S.L.A.M.

LIBRERIA ANTIQUARIA BRIGHENTI, VIA GUIDO RENI 4, 40125 BOLOGNA. (P.O. Box 506). Prop: Gino Brighenti. TN: 236101. Established 1952. Office and storeroom, appointment necessary. Medium stock, also new books. Spec: early medicine and science; economics; bibliography. Cata: 1 a year. Corresp: English, Français, Deutsch. B:

Banca Commerciale Italiana, Bologna. CP: Bologna 8–9603. A.L.A.I., L.I.L.A.

G. BUZZANCA, Piazzetta Pedrocchi 4, 35100 Padova. TN: (049) 651831. Spec: prints, maps, drawings, illustrated books. A.L.A.I.

LIBRERIA INTERNAZ. C. CALDINI, Via Tornabuoni 89–91 rosso, 50123 Firenze. TN: (055) 24474.

LUIGI CARPANETO, Via Burlamacchi 31, 55100 Lucca.

LIBRERIA GASPARE CASELLA, Piazza Municipio 84, 80133 Napoli. Prop: Dott. Guido Lo Schiavo. TN: (081) 324579. TA: Libri Napoli. Storeroom, early closing Saturday. Medium stock. Cata: 1 a year. Corresp: English. B: Banca Commerciale Italiana. CP: Napoli 6/25409. A.L.A.I., L.I.L.A., A.B.A.

GIOCONDO CASSINI, San Marco 2424, 30124 Venezia. TN: 31815. Spec: geography; old prints; Italian literature; Italian topography. A.L.A.I.

CAVALIERI D'ORO, Via Mazzini 84, 44022 Comacchio. Spec: autographs. B: Casa di Risparmio di Ferrara. CP: Comacchio 8/10879. A.L.A.I.

CARLO ALBERTO CHIESA, Via Bigli 11, 20121 Milano. TN: 79 86 78. Spec: old and rare; first editions and illustrated books 15th to 19th centuries; manuscripts; incunabula. L.I.L.A.

LIBRERIA ANTIQUARIA DALLAI, Piazza de Marini 11 rosso, 16123 Genova. Prop: Giovanna and Norma Dallai. TN: (010) 298338. Established 1939. Shop, closed Monday, and during August. Very small stock. Corresp: English, Français, Deutsch. B: Cassa di Risparmio, No. 7369/80.

"DOCETT", Via A. Righi 9/A, 40126 Bologna. TN: 23 07 57. Spec: old and rare books; prints. A.L.A.I.

DOMSCH & C., Viale Milton 73, Firenze. Prop: Ewald and Ruth Domsch. TN: 48 68 42. TA: Domsch Firenze. Established 1948. Private premises. Corresp: English, Français, Deutsch. B: Banco di Roma and Banco di Sicilia. CP: Firenze 5/6134 and Frankfurt 300257. Associazione Librai Italiani.

BOTTEGA D'ERASMO, Via Gaudenzio Ferrari 9, 10124 Torino. Prop: dott. Angelo Barrera. TN: 80331 and 81264. TA: Erasmus Torino. Spec: law; philology; philosophy; religion. CP: Torino 2/34095. A.L.A.I.

BANCO LIBRI DI FIAMMENGHI, Via Marsala 6, 40126 Bologna. Cata.

LIBRERIA C. FIAMMENGHI, Via Malcontenti 11, 40126 Bologna. Cata.

LUIGI FINZI, Foro Buonaparte 12, 20121 Milano. TN: 86 25 79. Spec: fine arts; Italian literature and topography; theatre; old prints. Cata: B: Banca Vonwiller. CP: Milano 3/26748. A.L.A.I.

LIBRERIA FAUSTO FIORENTINO, Calata Trinita Maggiore 36, 80134 Napoli. Cata.

LIBRERIA FLUMEN DANTIS di P. ZALI, Piazza Mazzini 12/1, 16043 Chivari (Genova). Cata.

IL GABINETTO DELLE STAMPE, Via Montenapoleone 3, 20121 Genova. TN: (02) 708082. A.L.A.I. Prop: Harry Salamon.

NATALE GALLINI, Via Del Conservatorio 17, 20122 Milano. TN: 70 98 20 and 70 28 58. Spec: music and music literature. B: Banco Ambrosiano. A.L.A.I.

GARISENDA LIBRI & STAMPE, S.L.S., Strada Maggiore 14/A, 40125 Bologna. Prop: Maria Fiammenghi. TN: 231893. TA: Garisenda Bologna. Established 1959. Shop. Very small stock. Spec: geography; old prints; science; fine arts; illustrated books. Corresp: English, Français. B: Credito Romagnolo, Ag.13, n.437. CP: Bologna 8/25491. A.L.A.I.

LUIGI GONNELLI & FIGLI, Via Ricasoli 14 rosso, Firenze. Prop: Aldo Gonnelli. TN: 216835. Spec: autographs; old and rare books, manuscripts; old and modern prints; paintings. B: Monte dei Paschi di Siena and Banca Steinhauslin. CP: Firenze 5/11376. A.L.A.I.

LIBRERIA ORESTE GOZZINI di PIETRO CHELLINI, Via Ricasoli 49, 50122 Firenze. Prop: Pietro Chellini. TN: 212433. Established about 1870. Shop, closed Saturday afternoon. Very large stock. Spec: fine arts; history; jurisprudence; literature. Corresp: Français. Cata: 3 a year. B: Credito Italiano-Firenze, No. 38161. CP: Firenze 5/1631. A.L.A.I.

G. C. GRIFONI, Via Emilia Levante 13, 40139 Bologna. TN: (051) 231893. A.L.A.I.

LIBRI DI IERI, Casella Postale 524, 50100 Firenze. Cata.

LIBRERIA "IL DEFINO", Via Cesare Battisti 19/A, 10123 Torino. Prop: Merys Vidani. TN: (011) 540411. A.L.A.I.

LEONARDO LAPICCIRELLA, Lungarno Vespucci 18, 50123 Firenze. TN: 27 65 98. Spec: manuscripts; woodcut books; engravings. C.L.A.

LICOSA ANTIQUARIATO, Via Lamarmora 45, 50121 Firenze. Cata.

STUDIO BIBLIOGRAFICO LIDIS, Foro Bonaparte 12, 20121 Genova. Prop: Lea Boldi. TN: (02) 802073. A.L.A.I.

LIBRERIA LUIGI LOMBARDI, V. Costantinopolis 4 bis, 80138 Napoli. TN: (081) 211921. Cata.

GAETANO MANUSÉ, Via Ciovasso 17, Milano. T: 80 72 46, 539 31 52. Established 1945. Storeroom, open normal business hours. Medium stock. Cata: 3 or 4 a year. Corresp: Deutsch, Français. B: Banca Popolare di Bergamo, Milano. Account No. 10241. CP: Milano 3–14395.

LIBRERIA ANTIQUARIA MARTELLI, Via Santo Stefano 43, 40125 Bologna. Prop: Guiseppe Nociti. TN: (051) 227453. Established 1846. Studio, appointment necessary, closed Monday morning. Medium stock. Spec: Incunabula; first editions; Italian literature: folklore; art; history. Cata. Corresp: English, Français. CP: Bologna, 8/17495.

LIBRERIA MARZOCCO, Via Martelli 22 rosso, 50129 Firenze. TN: (055) 24568 and 298575.

C. MARZOLI, Corso Porta Nuova 2, 20121 Milano. TN: (02) 669248. A.L.A.I.

LIBRERIA MATTEUZZI, Piazza Aldrovandi 5/B, 40125 Bologna. TN: (051) 221687. Cata.

LIBRERIA ANTIQUARIA MEDIOLANUM, Via Montebello 30, 20121-Milano. Prop: Dr. Elfo Pozzi. TN: 65 36 37. Established 1928. Shop, early closing Saturday. Very large stock. Spec: old books; autographs; engravings. Corresp: Français. B: Banca Morgan Vonwiller, Milano, Cto. 41113/7. CP: Milano 3/37004. C.L.A., L.I.L.A.

IL MERCANTE DI STAMPE, Corso Venezia 29, 20121 Milano. TN: (02) 879148. A.L.A.I.

WALTER MICHELONI, Vico Falamonica 15 rosso, 16123 Genova. TN: 20 38 21. CP: Genova 4/8256. A.L.A.I.

LIBRERIA MONTANINI, Via Nino Bixio 58, Parma. Prop: Gian Paolo Montanini. TN: (0521) 68662. Cata. CP: 25/1378.

LIBRERIA ANTIQUARIA MORETTI, Via Lusardi 8, 20122 Milano. TN: (02) 8391 275. Spec: illustrated books; incunabula; atlases and travel. Cata. A.L.A.I.

LEO S. OLSCHKI=STUDIO BIBLIOGRAFICO, 52046 Lucignano (Arezzo). Prop: M. and F. Witt. TN: (0575) 84715. TA: Librosc Lucignano. Established 1886. Private premises, appointment necessary. Large stock. Spec: art, architecture: classics, history; medicine, science; theology. Corresp: English, Français, Deutsch. B: American Express Bank, Florence, No. 7425. A.L.A.I., A.B.A.

LIBRERIA ANTIQUARIA PALMAVERDE, Via Castiglione 35, 40124 Bologna. Prop: dott. Roberto Roversi. TN: 232085. Shop. Large stock. Spec: modern first editions; erudition; philology. Cata: 6 a year. CP: Bologna 8/3319. C.L.A.

LIBRERIA ANTIQUARIA PERINI, Via A. Sciesa 9, 37100 Verona. TN: (045) 30073. Cata.

DOTT. ADA PEYROT, Via Consolata 8, 10122 Torino. TN: 54 74 38. Spec: illustrated books; topography; economics. A.L.A.I.

LIBRERIA DI PIAZZA S. BABILA, Corso Monforte 2, 20122 Milano. Prop: Peppi Battaglini. TN: (02) 799219. Established 1952. Shop. Old and modern prints. A.L.A.I.

IL POLIFILO, Via Borgonuovo 3, 20121 Milano. Prop: A. M. Vigevani. TN: 87 11 89. TA: Polifilo Milano. Established 1941. Shop. Spec: old Italian books. Cata. Corresp: English, Français. A.L.A.I.

IL POZZO DEL BIBLIOFILO, Via S. Lorenzo 19, 16123 Genova. Cata.

LIBRERIA ANTIQUARIA PRANDI, Viale Timavo 75, Reggio Emilia. Prop: Dino, Dante and Paolo Prandi. TN: 34973. Established 1927. TA: Libreria Prandi Reggio-E. Spec: fine arts, modern prints, modern illustrated books; philology; folklore. Corresp: English, Français. CP: Reggio Emilia 25/5326. A.L.A.I., S.L.A.M.

LIBRERIA ANTIQUARIA ARTURO PREGLIASCO, Via Accademia Albertina 3 bis, 10123 Torino. TN: (011) 877114. TA: Preliber Torino. Established 1912. Shop, closed Saturday afternoon. Large stock. Spec: old and rare; fine arts, old prints; autographs. Cata: 4–5 a year. Corresp: English, Français. B: Credito Italiano, AG., 7, Torino. CP: Torino 2/23883. A.L.A.I.

GIORGINA PREGLIASCO-MATHES, Via Po 14, 10123 Torino. TN: (011) 515386. Spec: autographs, manuscripts. Cata.

LEO S. OLSCHKI

STUDIO BIBLIOGRAFICO
LUCIGNANO (AREZZO)
ITALY

ITALIAN BOOKS

INCUNABLES, ART, ARCHITECTURE
HISTORY, THEOLOGY, CLASSICS
MEDICINE, SCIENCE, LITERATURE
FINE BOOKS

CATALOGUES ISSUED

ANTIQUARIATO LIBRARIO RADAELI, Via A. Manzoni 39, 20121 Milano. Prop: dott. Francesco Radaeli. TN: 630055. Established 1964. Shop, closed Monday morning. Spec: manuscripts; miniatures; incunabula; Italian XV–XVIII century books. Cata: 2 a year. Corresp: English, Français, Deutsch. A.L.A.I.

RICORDI, Negozio di Via Berchet 2, 20121 Milano. Spec: music.

LIBRERIA M. RIGATTIERI, Calle Della Mandola 3713, 30124 Venezia. TN: (041) 31321. A.L.A.

LIBRERIA RIMINESE, Via IV Novembre 46, 47037 Rimini (Forli). TN: (0541) 26417.

RENZO RIZZI, Via Cernaia 4, I–20121 Milano. TN: 666 705. TA: Librire Milano. Established 1954. Storeroom, appointment preferred. Small stock. Spec: manuscripts, old Italian books; palaeography. Cata. B: Banca Belinzaghi. CP: Milano 3/26430. A.L.A.I., L.I.L.A.

UMBERTO SABA, Via San Nicolo 30, 34121 Trieste. Prop: Carlo Cerne. TN: (040) 31741. Established 1904. Shop, closed Monday. Medium stock, also new books. Spec: old and rare books, incunabula. Cata: 4 a year. Corresp: English, Deutsch. B: Banca Commerciale Italiana, No. 26990. CP: Trieste 11/7847. A.L.A.I.

CESARE SALETTA, Casella Postale 390, 40100 Bologna. Cata.

GUSTAVO & VITALIANO SALIMBENI, Via Matteo Palmieri 10 e 14r, 50122 Firenze. TN: 29 20 84 and 29 89 05. Spec: fine arts; topography. CP: Firenze 5/16746. C.L.A.

SALOTTO DEL BIBLIOFILO, Via Luccoli 21, 16123 Genova. TN: (010) 294480. Cata.

LIBRERIA ANTIQUARIA M. SGATTONI, Via Vivaio 22, 20122 Milano. Cata.

SIBRIUM LIBRI E MANOSCRITTI, Via Bigli 21, Milano. Prop: Dr. A. Martegani. TN: 705969. Established 1966. Office, appointment preferred. Small stock. Spec: autographs, manuscripts; old and rare books; science. Cata. Corresp: Français, Deutsch. B: Italo–Israeliana cc. 1321. C.L.A.

LIBRERIA ANTIQUARIA SOAVE, Via Po 48, I–10123 Torino. Prop: Mrs. Elena Soave Médail, Litt.D. TN: 87 89 57. Established 1935. Shop, open Monday to Saturday from 15.30 to 19.30. Large stock. Spec: old books on sciences, history and literature; old prints and engravings. Cata: about twice a year. Corresp: English, Français. CP: Torino 2/28555. C.L.A.

MATTEO TONINI, Via Antica Zecca 26, 48100 Ravenna. TN: (0544 30397. Established 1965. Shop. Small stock. Cata 2 a year. Corresp English, Français. B: Cassa di Risparmio di Ravenna. CP: Ravenna 8/4820. A.L.A.I.

LIBRERIA VALLERI, Via Ricasoli 68 rosso, 50121 Firenze. Prop Giovanni Valleri. TN: (055) 296192. Shop. Very large stock. Cata monthly. Corresp: English, Deutsch. B: Banca Toscana, Firenze. CP Firenze 5/11097. A.L.A.I.

LIBRERIA SANTO VANASIA, Via M. Macchi 58, 20124 Milano. TN (02) 266917. Spec: mathematics, physics, chemistry.

LIBRERIA ANTIQUARIA A. VIGLONGO, Via Genova 266, 10127 Torino. TN: (011) 660 421. A.L.A.I.

LIBRERIA VINCIANA, Via Monte Napoleone 23, 20121 Milano. TN: (02) 701582. Prop: Alessandro Piantanida. Spec: old and rare books. A.L.A.I.

JUGOSLAVIJA

YUGOSLAVIA   JUGOSLAWIEN

BEOGRAD (Belgrade, Belgrad): LJUBLJANA: ZAGREB.

CANKARJEVA ZALOZBA, Kopitarjeva 2, 61001 Ljubljana. (P.O. Box 201–IV). TN: 323–841. Established 1945. Shop, early closing Saturday. Small stock. Spec: Slavica; rarities. Cata: irregularly. Corresp: English, Deutsch. B: Ljubljanska banka.

"MATICA HRVATSKA", 2 Maticine, Zagreb.

ANTIKVARIJAT "TIN UJEVIC", TRG N. Zrinjskoga br. 16, Zagreb.

SRPSKA KNJIZEVNA ZADRUGA, 19 Marsala Tita, Beograd.

ZALOZBA MLADINSKA KNJIGA "EMKA", 38 Capova, Ljubljana.

KYPRIAKI DIMOKRATIA
KIBRIS CUMHURIYETI
CYPRUS   CHYPRE   ZYPERN

NICOSIA

"M A M", 192 LEDRA STREET, FLAT 4, NICOSIA. (P.O. BOX 1722). Prop: Mrs. Thelma M. Michaelidou. TN: 64562. TA: Mam, Nicosia. Established 1965. Storeroom and office, open normal business hours. Medium stock. Spec: Cyprus. Cata. B: Greek & English Bank of Cyprus Ltd., 10–01–101036. Booksellers Association of Cyprus.

LIECHTENSTEIN

INTERLIBRUM ESTABLISHMENT, Schloss-Strasse 6, FL 9490
Vaduz. (P.O. Box 1344). Director: Walter Alicke. TN: (075) 23261.
TA: Interlibrum Vaduz. Established 1961. Shop, appointment neces-
sary. Large stock. Spec: history of science and ideas; illustrated books;
Helvetica. Cata: 4–6 a year. Corresp: English, Français, Deutsch. B:
Bank in Liechtenstein AG., 417 830.0 and Midland Bank Ltd., London,
30476285. CP: St. Gallen 90–19707 and Stuttgart 3691–705. S.L.A.M.,
V.D.A., I.L.A.B.

LUXEMBOURG

EDI-CENTRE J.-P. KRIPPLER-MULLER, 17 rue Gibraltar, Luxembourg. Prop: J.-P. Krippler. TN: 42 709. Fondée en 1949. Dépôt. Important stock. Spec: livres Luxembourgeois de tout genre. Corresp: English, Deutsch. B: Banque Internationale à Luxembourg. CP: Luxembourg 40.608.

MAGYARORSZÁG

HUNGARY   HONGRIE   UNGARN

BUDAPEST

KULTURA, P.O. Box 149, Budapest 62. Fé 11. 32, Budapest 1. TN: 159
450. TA: Kulturpress Budapest. Established 1950. Offices and store-
rooms, appointment necessary. Closed Saturday. Very large stock.
Spec: scientific and literary books and journals. Corresp: English,
Français, Deutsch. B: National Bank of Hungary.

MALTA

SLIEMA VITTORIOSA

PAUL BEZZINA, 114 SAINT LAWRENCE STREET, VITTORIOSA. Private premises, but no appointment necessary. Spec: Maltese books, maps, engravings; anything about Knights of Jerusalem and Malta. Corresp: English, Français, Italiano. B: Barclays Bank International Limited.

FRANK KIRKOP, 106 BLANCHE STREET, SLIEMA. TN: 33 166. Private premises; by appointment only. Very small stock. Spec: everything about Malta. Corresp: English, Français, Deutsch, Italiano. B: Bank of Valletta; and Barclays Bank International Limited.

NEDERLAND

NETHERLANDS   HOLLAND
PAYS-BAS   NIEDERLAND

Associations: Verbände

N.V.A. = Nederlandsche Vereeniging van Antiquaren, Delilaan 5. Hilversum 1304. TN: (02150) 1 42 32.

Public Holidays: Jours de Fête: Feiertage

Jan. 1: Easter Monday: April 30: May 5: Whitmonday: Dec. 25 and 26.

Jan. 1: Pâques: Avril 30: Mai 5: lundi de Pentecôte: Dec. 25 et 26.

Jan. 1: Ostermontag: April 30: Mai 5: Pfingstmontag: Dez. 25 und 26.

I	AMSTERDAM
II	's-GRAVENHAGE (La Haye, The Hague, Den Haag)

III

APELDOORN	LEIDEN
ARNHEM	LISSE
BAARN	LOCHEM
BILTHOVEN	MIDDELBURG
BUREN	NIEUWKOOP
EDE	NIJMEGEN
EINDHOVEN	ROTTERDAM
GRONINGEN	SOEST
GROUW	
HAARLEM	UTRECHT
HILVERSUM	VLISSINGEN
KAMPEN	WASSENAAR
LEEUWARDEN	ZANDVOORT

I AMSTERDAM

ANTIQUARIAAT ANTIQUA, HERENGRACHT 159, AMSTERDAM. Prop: R. van der Peet. TN: (020) 245998. Established 1960. Postal business only. Large stock. Spec: history of medicine and science; musicology; philology; philosophy. Cata: 4 a year. Corresp: English. B: Amro, Amsterdam, No. 46 66 00 100. CP: Den Haag 258600. N.V.A.

A. ASHER & CO., B.V., KEIZERSGRACHT 526, AMSTERDAM. Prop: Nico Israel. TN: (020) 22 22 55. TA: Asherbooks Amsterdam. Established 1825. Shop and storeroom. Medium stock. Spec: natural history. Cata: 4 a year. Corresp: English, Français, Deutsch. B: Hollandse Koopmansbank N.V., Account No. 6 350 141 30. CP: The Hague 511662. N.V.A., S.L.A.M., I.L.A.B., Graphic Export Centre.

ATHENAEUM ANTIQUARIAN BOOKSELLERS, KEIZERSGRACHT 6008, 1002 AMSTERDAM. TN: (020) 226210. TA: Athbooks Amsterdam. Spec: political science; humanistica; autographs. N.V.A.

JOHN BENJAMINS, B.V., AMSTELDIJK 44, AMSTERDAM. Prop: John L. Benjamins. TN: 738156. TA: Benper Amsterdam. Telex: 15798. Established 1964. Storeroom, closed Saturday, appointment necessary. Very large stock of periodicals. Spec: periodicals in the domain of liberal arts and social science. Cata: irregularly. Corresp: English, Français, Deutsch, Italiano, Español. B: Hollandse Koopmansbank-Lippmann Rosenthal. CP: Den Haag 289615. N.V.A., I.L.A.B.

VAN BERG ANTIQUARIAAT, OUDE SCHANS 8–10, AMSTERDAM. TN: (020) 24 08 48. TA: Bergbooks Amsterdam. Spec: fine art; topography; biography. Cata. CP: Amsterdam 657269. N.V.A.

LEO BISTERBOSCH, ST. LUCIENSTEEG 22, and N.Z. VOORBURGWAL 349, AMSTERDAM-C. TN: (020) 24 64 39. Established 1939. Shops. Spec: Catholic books and prints; also new books. Corresp: Deutsch. B: Amro, Rokin, Amsterdam. CP: Amsterdam 45837. N.V.A.

TON BOLLAND, PRINSENGRACHT 493, 1002 AMSTERDAM. TN: (020) 221921. N.V.A.

ANTIQUARIAAT HIERONYMUS BOSCH, SPUISTRAAT 125, AMSTERDAM. (P.O. Box 12018). Prop: P. H. Kerssemakers. TN: (020) 993920 and 226682. Established 1970. Shop, closed Monday, open other days 12.00 to 17.30. Medium stock, also new books. Spec: Dutch history and art before 1800. Cata: 8 a year. Corresp: English, Français, Deutsch. CP: Arnhem 166 24 21.

ANTIQUARIAAT BROEKEMA, 28 Titiaanstraat, Amsterdam. Prop:
C. Broekema. TN: (020) 725933. TA: Artbrug Amsterdam. Established
1950. House premises, appointment necessary. Medium stock. Spec:
geography, cartography, travel. Cata: 4 a year. Corresp: English,
Français, Deutsch. B: Algemene Bank Nederland, Amsterdam, No.
53 90 37 893. CP: Amsterdam 458267. N.V.A.

S. EMMERING, N.Z. Voorburgwal 304, Amsterdam. TN: (020)
231476. Established 1905. Shop and storeroom. Spec: political sciences;
Judaica; Americana (West Indies); Old Master prints. Cata. Corresp:
English, Français, Deutsch. B: Algemene Bank Nederland, N.Z.
Voorburgwal 304, Amsterdam, No. 54 15 10 037. N.V.A., I.L.A.B.

ERASMUS ANTIQUARIAAT EN BOEKHANDEL, Spui 2, Amsterdam.
Prop: Dr. A. Horodisch. TN: 229147. Established 1934. Shop. Large
stock, also new books. Spec: book history and bibliography; history of
art; German literature; 16th century books; Judaica. Cata: 5–6 a year.
Corresp: English, Français, Deutsch. B: Pierson, Heldring & Pierson,
Amsterdam, 24.08.18.660.0. CP: Den Haag 234079, Milano 7715,
München 120134.

A. L. VAN GENDT & CO., N.V., Keizersgracht 610, Amsterdam. Prop:
A. L. van Gendt. TN: 234107. TA: Rightbook Amsterdam. Established
1947. Spec: manuscripts, incunabula; medicine, old science. Also
auctioneers. B: Banque de Suez (Nederland), N.V. CP: Amsterdam
46542.

B. R. GRÜNER, B.V., Nieuwe Herengracht 31, Amsterdam-C. TN:
(020) 64371. TA: Viriditas Amsterdam. Established 1967. Shop, early
closing Saturday. Small stock, also new books. Spec: Orientalia;
linguistics; law; classical antiquity. Cata: 6 a year. Corresp: English,
Deutsch. B: Hollandse Koopmansbank, Amsterdam. CP: Den Haag
115419.

B. HAGEN, Herengracht 26, 1002 Amsterdam. TN: (020) 953335.
N.V.A.

ADOLF M. HAKKERT, B.V., Spuistraat 90A, Amsterdam. (P.O. Box
10944). TN: (020) 64359. Established 1952. Very small stock. Spec:
classical philology, ancient history, Byzantium. Corresp: English,
Deutsch. CP: Amsterdam 126525. N.V.A.

BERNARD HOUTHAKKER, Rokin 98, Amsterdam. Prop: L. A.
Houthakker. TN: (020) 23 39 39. Spec: drawings (15th to 18th centuries); Rembrandt etchings; old painting. B: Amro. CP: Amsterdam
3636. N.V.A.

M. L. HUIZENGA, O.Z.ACHTERBURGWAL 156, AMSTERDAM. TN: (020) 23 75 66. Established 1945. Private premises. Large stock. Spec: antiquity; philosophy; anthropology; science. Cata. Corresp: English, Deutsch. B: Algemene Bank Nederland, Spuistraat, Amsterdam 644836. N.V.A.

B. M. ISRAEL, N.V., BOEKHANDEL EN ANTIQUARIAAT, N.Z. VOORBURGWAL 264, AMSTERDAM. TN: 24 70 40. TA: Israelbook Amsterdam. Established 1899. Private premises, open Monday to Friday. Large stock. Spec: old and rare; medicine; sciences; travel. Cata: 2–6 a year. Corresp: English, Français, Deutsch. B: Amro Bank, Head Office, Amsterdam. CP: Amsterdam 49 03 89. N.V.A.

N. ISRAEL, KEIZERSGRACHT 526, AMSTERDAM. TN: (020) 64031. Telex: 14070. TN: Ennibook Amsterdam. Established 1950. Shop and storeroom, early closing Saturday. Medium stock. Spec: rare books, manuscripts; cartography, travel and voyages. Cata: 1 a year. Corresp: English, Français, Deutsch. B: Hollandse Koopmansbank, Amsterdam, No. 63 50 141 30. CP: Amsterdam 433 275. N.V.A., S.L.A.M.

C. KOOLEMANS, WILLEMSPARKWEG 164, AMSTERDAM. TN: (020) 73 28 42. Established 1957. Spec: 16th and 17th centuries; ethnography; Africa; Australia; natural history. CP: Amsterdam 563417. N.V.A.

A. KOK, 4 AND 11 HOOGSTRAAT, AMSTERDAM. Shops.

P. F. KREMERS, COMMELINSTRAAT 52, AMSTERDAM. (P.O. BOX 10704). TN: 943055. CP: Amsterdam 2730205.

HANS MARCUS, KEIZERSGRACHT 574, AMSTERDAM. TN: (020) 23 45 44. Established 1953. Spec: old illustrated books. B: Amro Bank. CP: Amsterdam 599999. N.V.A.

RUDOLF MULLER INTERNATIONAL BOOKSELLERS, B.V., P.O. Box 9016, AMSTERDAM. (Overtoom 487). Managing Director: R. Muller. Est: 1969. TN: 16 59 55. Shop, appointment necessary. Very small sec. and antiq. stock, also new books. Spec: geography, geology, cartography.

Cata: 6 a year. Corresp: English, Français, Deutsch, Italiano, Español. B: Algemene Bank Nederland—Amsterdam, London and New York. CP: 18 06 019. I.C.B.A.

GÉ NABRINK & ZOON, BOEKHANDEL EN ANTIQUARIAT, KORTE KORSJESPOORTSTRAAT 8, AMSTERDAM–C. Prop: G. Nabrink and F. R. Nabrink. TN: (020) 22 30 58. Established 1924. Shop and storeroom, early closing Saturday. Very large stock, also new books. Spec: Orientalia. Cata: weekly list and 10 catalogues a year. Corresp: English, Français, Deutsch. B: Algemene Bank Nederland N.V., Account No. 54 02 75 719. CP: The Hague 114143. N.V.A.

P. C. NOTEBAART, POSTBOX 7289, AMSTERDAM. Established 1967. Postal business only. Small stock. Spec: humaniora; Dutch 17th century books; theology; surrealism. Cata: 4 a year. Corresp: English. CP: Amsterdam 12 53 799. N.V.A., I.L.A.B.

C. P. J. VAN DER PEET, B.V., 33–35 NIEUWE SPIEGELSTRAAT, AMSTERDAM. TN: (020) 235763. TA: Mobin Amsterdam. Established 1947. Shop, Monday to Friday 9 to 17.30, Saturday 14 to 17 hours. Large stock, also new books. Spec: Indonesia, Africa, Americana, Asiatica, Orientalia; Oriental and primitive arts; decorative arts; old maps and prints. Cata: 2 a month. Corresp: English, Français, Deutsch. B: A.B.N. CP: 529581. N.V.A., S.L.A.M. *Also at* 39 Jansweg, Haarlem.

H. D. PFANN, (3 shops), ROKIN 112, N. Z. VOORBURGWAL 127, and HERENGRACHT 329, AMSTERDAM. TN: (020) 24 62 04. Established 1919. Large stock, also new books and remainders. Spec: geography; old and modern prints and drawings; illustrated books (15th to 18th centuries); manuscripts. B: Amro Bank. CP: Amsterdam 672174. N.V.A.

G. POSTMA, O.Z. VOORBURGWAL 249, AMSTERDAM. TN: (020) 24 57 81. Spec: languages. N.V.A.

ANTIQUARIAAT W. N. SCHORS, REGULIERSGRACHT 52–54, AMSTERDAM–C. TN: (020) 64121 and 250813. Established 1953. Shop, closed Monday morning, appointment necessary for antiquarian department Medium antiquarian stock, also new books on specialities. Spec: alchemy, comparative religion, freemasonry, medicine, occult, psychology, sexuology, witchcraft. Cata: 5–6 a year. Corresp: English, Français, Deutsch. B: Kas-Associatie, Spuistraat 172, Amsterdam, No. 22 26 50 974. CP: Den Haag 447730. N.V.A.

ANTIQUARIAAT SCHUHMACHER, GELDERSCHEKADE 107, AMSTERDAM. Prop: Wilma and Max Schuhmacher. TN: (020) 221604. TA: Shoebooks Amsterdam. Established 1962. Shop, closed Saturday. Very large stock. Spec: language and literature—Dutch, English, French,

German. Cata: 2 a year. Corresp: English, Français, Deutsch. B: Algemene Bank Nederland, Amsterdam, No. 54 54 10 339. CP: The Hague 388801. N.V.A., I.L.A.B.

JACQUES SCHULMAN, B.V., Keizersgracht 448, Amsterdam–C. TN: 23 33 80. TA: Numismatique Amsterdam. Established 1880. Shop. Numismatics only. Cata: occasionally. Corresp: English, Français, Deutsch, Italiano, Spanish. B: Amro-Bank, Amsterdam. CP: Amsterdam 29 73 61. N.V.A. International Association of Professional Numismatists.

J. DE SLEGTE, Kalverstraat 11–13, Amsterdam. TN: (020) 23 25 40. Established 1900. Shop. Very large stock. Spec: art,; travels; old maps; views and prints; colour-plate books; remainders. Corresp: English, Français, Deutsch, Español. B: Algemene Bank Nederland, Amsterdam. CP: Amsterdam 120646. N.V.A.

M. SOTHMANN, N.Z.Voorburgwal 284, Amsterdam. TN: (020) 23 69 20. CP: Amsterdam 513709. N.V.A.

II 's-GRAVENHAGE

HET A.B.C. DER BOEKEN, 142 Wagenstraat, 's-Gravenhage. TN: (070) 606044. Shop. Medium stock

BOEKEN, 34a, STATIONWEG, 's-GRAVENHAGE. Shop.

JURIDISCH ANTIQUARIAAT, LAAN VAN MEERDERVOORT 45, 's-GRAVENHAGE. Prop: K. P. Jongbloed. TN: (070J 336317. Established 1925. Spec: law, economics. B: Mees & Hope. CP: 's-Gravenhage 114195. N.V.A.

LOOSE, PAPESTRAAT 3, 's-GRAVENHAGE. TN: 11 03 42. Established 1946. Shop. Medium stock. Spec: children's books; topography. Corresp: English, Français, Deutsch. B: Amro Bank, Kneuterdijk, 's-Gravenhage. CP: 's-Gravenhage 170 159.

ANTIQUARIAAT MEIJER ELTE, KORTE POTEN 13, 's-GRAVENHAGE. TN: (070) 639781. Established 1899. Shop, early closing Saturday. Large stock. Spec: fine arts; illustrated books 15th–19th century. Cata: 1 a year. Corresp: English, Français, Deutsch. B: Algemene Bank Nederland, account 51.36.12.084. CP: 's-Gravenhage 66874. N.V.A.

ANTIQUARIAAT MINERVA, ZEESTRAAT 48, 's-GRAVENHAGE. (Postbox 1853). Prop: Hans J. Hanselaar. TN: 11 15 11 (After 18h: 55 80 16). Established 1940. Storeroom, open to public, 10 to 17.30 hours, closed Mondaymorning. Medium stock. Spec: literature; geography; art. Cata: 6 a year. Corresp: English, Français, Deutsch. CP: 35 43 33. N.V.A.

MARTINUS NIJHOFF, N.V., LANGE VOORHOUT 9–11, 's-GRAVENHAGE. TN: 46 94 60. TA: Books 's-Gravenhage. Established 1853. Shop, closed on Saturday. Very large stock, also new books. Spec: collections; periodicals; humanities in all languages; Russian books. Cata: 8 a year. Corresp: English, Français, Deutsch. B: Algemene Bank Nederland. CP: 's-Gravenhage 4165. N.V.A.

J. DE SLEGTE, SPUISTRAAT 9, 's-GRAVENHAGE. TN: (070) 63 97 12. Shop. Medium stock, also new books and prints. N.V.A.

VAN STOCKUM'S ANTIQUARIAAT, PRINSEGRACHT 15, 's-GRAVENHAGE. Prop: J. Kuipers. TN: (070) 11 64 02. Established 1833. Spec: public sales. CP: 's-Gravenhage 5154. N.V.A.

MARTIN VEENEMAN, NOORDEINDE 100, 's-GRAVENHAGE. TN: (070) 11 78 77. TA: Artbooks 's-Gravenhage. Established 1940. Spec: art; old prints. CP: 's-Gravenhage 343020. N.V.A.

H. A. VLOEMANS, ANNA PAULOWNSTRAAT 10, 's-GRAVENHAGE. TN: (070) 607886. Established 1932. House premises, appointment necessary. Spec: modern arts and architecture; German exile literature. Cata: 3 a year. Corresp: English, Français, Deutsch. B: Nederlandsche Middesnstandsbank, No. 66 83 60 070. CP: Den Haag 226330. N.V.A.

W. R. VOS, LAAN VAN MEERDERVOORT 394, 2026 's-GRAVENHAGE. TN: (070) 331063. N.V.A.

III

ALFA ANTIQUARIAN BOOKSELLERS, P.O. BOX 1116, NIJMEGEN. (Van Welderenstraat 17 *and* L. Hezelstraat 6). Prop: Leo J. H. Kerssemakers. TN: (080) 23 15 64. Established 1970. Two shops. Medium stock. Spec: The Middle Ages and comparative religion. Cata: 8 a year. Corresp: English, Français, Deutsch, Español. B: Algemene Bank Nederland N.V., Account No. 53 70 12 672. CP: Arnhem 19686.57.

ARGUS ANTIQUARIAN BOOKSELLERS, PROF. DRIONLAAN 6, 2670 BAARN. Prop: W. J. Hommerson. TN: (02154) 5820. N.V.A.

J. L. BEIJERS, B.V., ACHTER SINT PIETER 14, UTRECHT. Prop: H. L. Gumbert and Mrs. N. A. Franco. TN: (030) 310958. TA: Bookbee Utrecht. Established 1865. 17th century house, open to the public, closed Saturday except by appointment. Very large stock. Spec: humaniora; history of learning, 16th and 17th century books; political economy; emblem and other illustrated books, art nouveau. Also auctioneers. Cata: irregularly. Corresp: English, Français, Deutsch. B: Amro Bank, Utrecht, No. 45 60 09 035. CP: Utrecht 7245. N.V.A.

VAN BENTHEM EN JUTTING, LANGE DELFT 64, MIDDEL-BURG. TN: (01180) 2630. Spec: topography; geography. B: Algemene Bank Nederland. CP: Middelburg 309834. N.V.A.

E. J. BONSET, PATRIJZENSTRAAT 8, ZANDVOORT. (Postbox 136). TN: (02507) 3906. Established 1955. Private premises. Large stock. Spec: psychology; social sciences. Also reprints. Cata: 10 a year. Corresp: all European languages. B: Algemene Bank Nederland. CP: Amsterdam 646 084. N.V.A.

BOUMA'S BOEKHUIS, N.V., TURFSINGEL 3, GRONINGEN. Prop: B. & E. Forsten. TN: (050) 23037. TA: Boumaboek Gronigen. Shop, early closing Saturday. Very large stock, also new books. Spec: philology; theology; history; philosophy. Cata: 6–8 a year. Corresp: English, Français, Deutsch. B: Amro Bank, Groningen, Account 44.60 07.730. CP: Arnhem 806445 and Köln 194840. N.V.A.

E. J. BRILL, OUDE RIJN 33A, LEIDEN. Prop: F. C. Wieder. TN: 071-46646. Telex: 33129. Established 1683. Spec: Orientalia; Slavonica; ethnography. CP: Leiden 13921. N.V.A.

BURGERSDIJK & NIERMANS, NIEUWSTEEG 1, LEIDEN. Prop: M. Stam-Hommes. TN: 071–21067. Established 1894. Shop. Very large stock.

Spec: antiquity; regional. Cata: 5–6 a year. Corresp: English, Français, Deutsch. B: Algemene Bank Nederland. CP: The Hague 14408. Auctions. N.V.A.

H. COEBERGH, GEDEMPTE OUDE GRACHT 74, HAARLEM. (P.O. BOX 98). TN: (023) 313 750. Established 1892. Spec: religion in general; philosophy. B: Nederlandse Credietbank. CP: Den Haag 85843. N.V.A.

ANTIQUARIAAT VAN COEVORDEN, VARENSTRAAT 41, SOEST. Prop: J. W. van Coevorden. TN: (02155) 18099. TA: Millbooks Soest. Established 1968. House premises, appointment necessary. Medium stock. Spec: fine arts, archaeology. Cata: 3 a year. Corresp: English, Deutsch. B: Amro Bank, 48 22 15 631. CP: 60 01 09. N.V.A.

COSMOS ANTIQUARIAN BOOKS, KASTANJELAAN 3, 6570 LOCHEM. (P.O. Box 30). Prop: A. Bouwer. Established 1972. Private premises, appointment necessary. Medium stock. Spec: natural history (old and modern); history of medicine, history of physics, chemistry and astronomy. Cata: 2 a year. Corresp: English, Français, Deutsch. B: Algemene Bank Nederland, Lochem, No. 53 27 14 148. CP: Arnhem 22 52 789.

CREYGHOTON:MUSICOLOGY-MUSICA ANTIQUA, 45 LASSUSLAAN, BILTHOVEN. (Postbox 38). Prop: A. B. Creyghton. TN: (030) 783 714. TA: Musicant Bilthoven. Established 1949. Storeroom, open usual business hours. Medium stock. Spec: musicology and theatre. Cata: 6 a year. Corresp: English, Français, Deutsch. B: Algemene Bank Nederland, Bilthoven. CP: Bilthoven 137225 and Köln 160967. N.V.A.

BOEKHANDEL EN ANTIQUARIAAT "DE TILLE", FA. SIPKE DYKSTRA, WIRDUMERDIJK 24–28, LEEUWARDEN. Prop: S. G. Dykstra. TN: 25129. Established 1948. Medium stock, also new books. Spec: theology. Cata: 3 a year. B: Nederlandse Middenstandsbank, Leeuwarden. CP: Leeuwarden 825 323. N.V.A.

W. C. VAN DIJK, BURGWAL 75, KAMPEN. TN: (05292) 3437. Established 1927. Spec: textbooks; students' books. B: Amro. CP: Kampen 875004. N.V.A.

"FRISCO" ANTIQUARIAT, HOOFDSTRAAT 5, 9064 GROUW. Prop: L. and N. Brolsma. TN: (05662) 1316. N.V.A.

H. G. GERRITSEN, VAN WELDERENSTRAAT 88, NIJMEGEN. Prop: A. G. Gerritsen. TN: 224387—224385. Established 1915. Shop, early closing Monday. Large stock. Spec: literature; history; sciences. Cata: 5 a year. Corresp: English, Français, Deutsch. CP: Nijmegen 839095.

ANTIQUARIAAT DE GRAAF, Zuideinde 40, Nieuwkoop. Prop: B. de Graaf. TN: (01725) 1461. TA: Degraaf Nieuwkoop. Established 1959. Private premises, appointment necessary. Medium stock, also new books and publishing. Spec: bibliography; Reformation books; books printed 1500 to 1700. Cata: about 3 a year. Corresp: English, Français, Deutsch, Italiano. B: Amsterdam-Rotterdam Bank. CP: Nieuwkoop 274 890. N.V.A.

GYSBERS EN VAN LOON, Bakkerstraat 7A, Arnhem. TN: (085) 424 421. Established 1942. Shop. Large stock, also new foreign books. Spec: fine arts; folklore; Dutch topography and history; automobiliana. Cata: once a week. Corresp: English, Français, Deutsch. B: Algemene Bank Nederland. CP: Arnhem 883 309. N.V.A.

MENNO HERTZBERGER, Eemnesserweg 81, Baarn. (P.O. Box 91). TN: 02154–4938. TA: Bibliopola Baarn. Eestablished 1920. Private premises, appointment preferred. Small stock. Spec: incunabula; medicine, sciences; illustrated books; humanism. Cata: 4 a year. Corresp: English, Français, Deutsch, Italiano. B: Algemene Bank Nederland, Baarn, No. 55 27 43 437. CP: 1494972. N.V.A., A.B.A., I.L.A.B

ANTIQUARIAAT C. HOVINGH & ZN., KLEINE HOUTSTRAAT 50, HAARLEM. Prop: C. & C. W. Hovingh. TN: (023) 31 07 14. Established 1940. Shop, closed Monday. Very large stock. Spec: art, history. Cata: 6 a year. Corresp: English, Deutsch, Français, Italiano. B: Mees & Hope, N.V., Haarlem. N.V.A., I.L.A.B.

ANTIQUARIAAT JUNK, DR. R. SCHIERENBERG & SONS, B.V., WALDERSTRAAT 10, LOCHEM. (P.O. Box 5). Prop: D. & E. Schierenberg. TN: (05730) 1725. Telex: 49513. T.A. Junk Lochem. Established 1899. Storeroom, closed Saturday. Very large stock. Spec: natural history, anthropology. Cata: 10 a year. Corresp: English, Français, Deutsch. B: Algemene Bank Nederland, Lochem, No. 53 27 10 622. CP: Lochem 909200. N.V.A., I.L.A.B.

ANTIQUARIAAT FRITZ KNUF, P.O. Box 20, 2707 BUREN. TN: (03447) 691. TA: Librorum Buren. Private premises, appointment necessary. Medium stock. Spec: bibliography. Cata: 4 a year. Corresp: English, Français, Deutsch, Español. N.V.A.

L. M. C. NIERYNCK, VERDILAAN 85, VLISSINGEN. TN: 01184–4172. Private premises, appointment necessary. Spec: early newspapers from 16th to 19th century. Cata: 3 a year. Corresp: English, Français. B: Algemene Bank Nederland.

C. P. J. VAN DER PEET, B.V., JANSWEG 39, HAARLEM. TN: (023) 320216. Shop. Spec: Indonesia, Africa, Americana, Asiatica, Orientalia. N.V.A., S.L.A.M.

OTTO PICKER, GROOT HOEFIJZERLAAN 3, WASSENAAR. TN: (01751) 9782. Spec: topography. N.V.A.

LUDWIG ROSENTHAL'S ANTIQUARIAAT, BUSSUMERGRINTWEG 4, HILVERSUM. Prop: H. B. Rosenthal and E. Petten-Rosenthal. TN: (02150) 47951. TA: Ludros Hilversum. Established 1859. Storeroom

EARLY NEWSPAPERS

permanent wanted from 16th to 19th century in single copies or runs

L. M. C. Nierynck
Verdilaan 85 — VLISSINGEN, Netherlands

and office, open usual business hours. Very large stock. Spec: Reformation; Protestant and Catholic theology; humanism; incunabula. Cata: Corresp: English, Français, Deutsch. B: Algemene Bank Nederland, Hilversum. CP: Hilversum 309771. N.V.A., V.D.A.

J. DE SLEGTE, JANSTRAAT 28, ARNHEM. TN: (08300) 20597. N.V.A.

J. DE SLEGTE, RECHESTRAAT 36, EINDHOVEN. TN: (040) 63240. N.V.A.

J. DE SLEGTE, COOLSINGEL 83, ROTTERDAM. TN: (010) 13 83 05. N.V.A.

J. DE SLEGTE, OUDE GRACHT 121, UTRECHT. TN: (030) 313001. N.V.A.

SWETS & ZEITLINGER, B.V., HEEREWEG 374B, LISSE. TN: (02521) 19113. TA: Swezeit Lisse. Est: 1901. Storeroom, appointment necessary. Very large stock. Spec: periodicals, reprints and antiquarian books. Cata: 6 a year. Corresp: English, Français, Deutsch, Español, Portuguese. B: Amro Bank, Amsterdam, Account No. 46.69.74.418. CP: Holland 13984. N.V.A.

H. DE VRIES, GEDEMPTE OUDE GRACHT 27, HAARLEM. (Postbox 274). TN: (023) 31 14 40. Established 1905. Shop, closed Monday. Small stock, also new books. Spec: sports and physical education. Corresp: English, Français, Deutsch. B: A.D.N., Haarlem, Account No. 560, 919 654. CP: Haarlem 5404. N.V.A., V.B.B., N.B.B.

F. W. VAN DER WAL, NASSAULAAN 16, 6100 EDE. TN: (08380) 13983. N.V.A.

H. DE WEERD, MIDDELLAAN 34, APELDOORN. TN: (05760) 52181. Established 1961. Private premises, open irregular hours. Small stock, also new books. No catalogues. Corresp: English, Français, Deutsch. B: Amro Bank, Apeldoorn. CP: 11 47 864.

J. WRISTERS, MINREBROEDERSTRAAT 13, UTRECHT. Prop: J. and D. Wristers. TN: 31 02 82. Established 1887. Shop, early closing Monday. Large stock, also new books. Spec: theology; medicine. Corresp: English, Deutsch. B: C.E.B.U., Kromme Nieuwe Gracht 6, Utrecht, Account No. 69 90 11 620. CP: 's-Gravenhage 43991. N.V.A., V.B.B., N.B.

NORGE

NORWAY NORVÈGE NORWEGEN

Associations: Verbände

N.A.B.F. = Norsk Antikvarbokhandlerforening
Ullevålsveien 1, OSLO 1

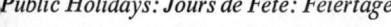

Public Holidays: Jours de Fête: Feiertage

Jan. 1: Easter: May 1: May 17: Ascension Day: Whitmonday: Dec. 25 and 26.

Jan. 1: Pâques: Mai 1: Mai 17: Ascension: Pentecôte: Dec 25 et 26.

Jan. 1: Karfreitag and Ostermontag: Mai 1: Mai 17: Pfingstmontag: Dez. 25 und 26.

BEKKESTUA: BERGEN: OSLO.

BERGENSANTIKVARIATET K. J. TØSSE, Store Markevei 8–10, Bergen. Prop: Olav Tøsse. TN: 21 04 23. Established 1947. Shop, early closing Saturday. Small stock; also new books. Corresp: English.

BØRSUMS FORLAG OG ANTIKVARIAT A-S, Fr. Nansensplass 2, Oslo 1. Prop: Baltzer M. Børsum. TN: 41 04 33. TA: Bokbør Oslo. Shop and storeroom, early closing Saturday. Very large stock, also new books. Spec: facsimile editions; marine; old and rare; first editions. Corresp: English, Français, Deutsch. B: Bergens Privatbank, Oslo. CP: Oslo 14052 .N.A.B.F.

J. W. CAPPELENS ANTIKVARIAT, Kirkegatan 15, Oslo 1. Manager: Paul M. Bottn. TN: 33 62 80. Established 1829. Shop, early closing Saturday. Large stock, also new books. Spec: old and rare; maps and views relating to Scandinavia, Iceland and Greenland; travel and topography. Cata: 12 a year. Corresp: English. B: Christiania Bank og Kreditkasse, 24100-163. CP: Oslo 113 02. I.L.A.B.

DAMMS ANTIKVARIAT A/S, Tollbodgaten 25, Oslo 1. Prop: Claes Nyegaard. TN: 42 62 75. TA: Dammantikk Oslo. Spec: old and rare; atlases and maps; topography. B: Oslo Sparebank. *Also at:* Eckersbergsgaten 14, Oslo. N.A.B.F.

A. LUNGELARSEN, ØYGARDVEIEN 16E, BEKKESTUA. TN: 53 65 06. Private premises, appointment necessary. Spec: Scandinavica; old and rare. N.A.B.F.

BJØRN RINGSTRØMS ANTIKVARIAT, ULLEVÅLSVEIEN 1, OSLO 1. TN: 20 78 05. Established 1965. Shop, open Tuesday and Thursday 12–17, other days 9.30–17, Saturday 9.30–15. Medium stock. Spec: Norwegian 1st editions and topography; history in general. Cata: 8 a year. Corresp: English. B: Bergens Privatbank 5024.05. 17067. CP: Oslo 3 00 94. N.A.B.F.

STRØMS ANTIKVARIAT, HEGDEHAUGSVEIEN 34, OSLO 3. Prop: Rolv Lie. TN: 47 2 606684. N.A.B.F.

ÖSTERREICH

AUSTRIA   AUTRICHE

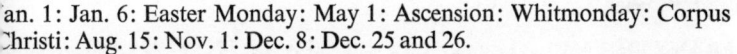

Associations: Verbände
V.A.Ö. = Verband der Antiquare Österreichs
Grünangergasse 4, Wien 1.

Public Holidays: Jours de Fête: Feiertage
Jan. 1: Jan. 6: Easter Monday: May 1: Ascension: Whitmonday: Corpus
Christi: Aug. 15: Nov. 1: Dec. 8: Dec. 25 and 26.
Jan. 1: Jan. 6: lundi de Pâques: Mai 1: Ascension: lundi de Pentecôte:
Fête-Dieu: Août 15: Nov. 1: Dec. 8: Dec. 25 et 26.
Jan. 1: Jan. 6: Ostermontag: Mai 1: Christi Himmelfahrt: Pfingstmontag:
Fronleichnam: Aug. 15: Nov. 1: Dez. 8: Dez. 25 und 26.

I

WIEN (Vienna, Vienne)

IOS. ABHEITER, WAHRINGERSTRASSE 83, 1018 WIEN. Laden. Kleiner
Vorrat, auch neue Bücher.

AKADEMISCHE BUCHHANDLUNG KUPPITSCH, SCHOTTENRING 8,
WIEN. Prop: Dr. M. Beer und Dr. Z. Seidl. TN: 63 02 77 and 63 94 30.
Laden, grosser Vorrat auch neue Bücher. Spec: Rechtswissenschaften;
Literatur; Philosophie. Cata: selten. Corresp: English, Français. B:
Creditanstalt-Bankverein, Wien, Konto 24–96727. CP: Wien 49917 und
München 1 201 47. V.A.Ö.

BECK'SCHE UNIVERSITÄTS BUCHHANDLUNG, WÄHRINGERSTRASSE
12, WIEN 1009. Laden. Grosser Vorrat, auch neue Bücher.

4. BERGER, KOHLMARKT 3, 1010 WIEN. TN: 52 23 60. Spec: Einbände,
Kunst; Archäologie. CP: Wien 53653. V.A.Ö.

BOURCY+PAULUSCH, WIPPLINGERSTRASSE 5, 1010 WIEN. Prop: Otto
Bourcy und Hans Paulusch. TN: 63 71 49. Gegründet 1917. Laden,
Samstag geschlossen. Sehr grosser Vorrat. Spec: Alpinismus; Austriaca;
Genealogie; Medizin. Cata: B: Schoeller & Co., Wien. PSK Wien
2319.012 München 1208.87. V.A.Ö.

DIE BÜCHER FUNDGRUBER, 24 WAHRINGERSTRASSE, WIEN 9. Laden. Mittelgrosser Vorrat.

F. DEUTICKE, HELFERSTORFERSTRASSE 4, WIEN 1. TN: 63 64 29 und 63 1. 35. Spec.: Folklore; Kunst; Naturwissenschaften; Philologie; Philosophie. V.A.Ö.

LUDWIG DOBLINGER (Bernhard Herzmansky) K.G., DOROTHEERGASSE 10, 1010 WIEN. TN: 0222/ 52 35 04. TA: Musikdob Wien. Gegründe 1816. Laden, Samstag Nachmittag geschlossen. Kleiner Vorrat, auch neue Bücher. Spec: Musikbücher und Musikalien. Cata. Corresp English, Français. B: Creditanstalt-Banverein, Wien 1, Konto 52–12360 CP: Wien 22523. V.A.Ö.

FRANZ FRIEMEL, GABLENZGASSE 4, 1160 WIEN. TN: 92 22 18. Gegründe 1926. Laden, Samstag Nachmittag geschlossen. Kleiner Vorrat, auch neue Bücher. B: Creditanstalt Bankverein 71–11768. CP: Wien 7605.518 und München 1201 07–808. V.A.Ö. Österreichischer Buchhändlerverband.

GEROLD & CO., GRABEN 31, 1011 WIEN. TN: 52 22 35. TA: Geroldbuch Wien. Laden. Spec: Philologie; Philosophie; Psychologie. CP: Wien 32108. V.A.Ö.

H. GEYER, HOFMÜHLGASSE 14, WIEN 6. Prop: Hannes Geyer. TN: 57 81 46. TA: Buchgeyer Wien. Gegründet 1946. Laden und Lagerräume; Samstag geschlossen. Sehr grosser Vorrat. Spec: Austriaca; Jus; Soziologie; Periodic; Geschichte. Cata: 6 pro Jahr. Corresp: English, Français Español, Hungarian. B: Zentralsparkasse der Gemeinde, Wien 7. CP: Wien 191 954 und Frankfurt 300 029. V.A.Ö.

GILHOFER BUCH- UND KUNSTANTIQUARIAT K.G., BOGNERGASSE 2, 1010 WIEN. Prop: W. Taeuber und R. Hoffmann. TN: 63 42 85. TA: Gilburg, Wien. Gegründet 1883. Laden. Sehr grosser Vorrat. Spec: Austriaca, Bohemica; Wissenschften; alte und seltene Bücher; Graphik. Cata. Corresp: English. B: Erste Österreichische Spar-Casse, Konto 002–93385. V.A.Ö., V.D.A.

H. GODAI, MARIAHILFERSTRASSE 169, 1150 WIEN. TN: 83 82 95. Laden. Spec: Deutsche Literatur und Erstausgaben. CP: Wien 153924. V.A.Ö.

LEO GODAI, TALGASSE 11, WIEN 1015. Laden.

DR. HANS EBERHARD GOLDSCHMIDT, DÖBLINGER HAUPTSTRASSE 61, WIEN 19. TN: 36 56 83. Gegründet 1958. Laden, Samstag Nachmittag geschlossen. Kleiner Vorrat. Spec: Literatur; Kunst; Geschichte. Corresp: English, Français, Russian. CP: Wien 48 642. V.A.Ö.

M. & L. GRASEL, WÄHRINGERSTRASSE 41, WIEN 1009. Laden.

KARL M. HALOSAR, MARGARETENSTRASSE 35. 1040 WIEN. TN: 56 13 53. Gegründet 1947. Zwei Läden. Sehr grosser Vorrat, auch neue Bücher. Spec: alte Kinderbücher; illustrierte Bücher; Literatur; Erstausgaben; Cata: unregelmässig. Corresp: English. B: Creditanstalt Bankverein Wien, Konto 64 133 71. CP: Wien 126 1886. V.A.Ö.

A. L. HASBACH, WOLLZEILE 9 und 29, WIEN 1. Prop: Dr. Herbert Borufka. TN: 52 88 76 und 52 89 32. Gegründet 1876. Laden und Lagerräume, Samstag Nachmittag geschlossen. Mittelgrosser Vorrat. Spec: Geschichte; Kunst; Sprachwissenschaft. Cata: 4–5 pro Jahr. Corresp: English, Français, Italiano. B: Österreichischer Landerbank 222–103–239. CP: Wien 7041.660. V.A.Ö.

V. A. HECK, KÄRNTNER RING 12, 1010 WIEN. Prop: Dr. Christa Demelius. Hans D. Paulusch. TN: 65 51 52. TA: Heckbooks Wien. Gegründet 1870. Laden, Samstag Nachmittag geschlossen. Grosser Vorrat. Spec: Austriaca; Deutsche Literatur; Autographen; alte Landkarten. Cata: 4–6 pro Jahr. Corresp: English, Français. B: Creditanstalt, Konto 66–16999. CP: Wien 7038453 und Frankfurt 3000 10. V.D.A.

RUDOLF HEGER, WOLLEZEILE 2, 1010 WIEN 1. Prop: Christl und Olga Wagner. TN: 52 63 98. Laden, Samstag Nachmittag geschlossen. Grosser Vorrat, auch neue Bücher. Spec: Deutsche Literatur; Kunst; Folklore. Cata: 3 pro Jahr. Corresp: English, Français. B: Österreichischer Landerbank, Wien, Konto 2,201,026. CP: Wien 30 903. V.A.Ö.

LEOPOLD HEIDRICH, PLANKENGASSE 7, WIEN 1. Prop: Erwin Heidrich. TN: 52 37 01 und 52 29 93. Gegründet 1914. Laden, Samstag Nachmittag geschlossen. Mittelgrosser Vorrat, auch neue Bücher. Spec: Kunst; Deutsche Literatur; Austriaca; Viennennsia. Cata: 2–4 pro Jahr. Corresp: English, Français. B: Pinschof & Co., Spiegelgasse 3, Wien 1. CP: Wien 103 763, und Frankfurt 300 043. V.A.Ö.

HEINRICH HINTERBERGER, HEGELGASSE 17 Mezz., WIEN 1001.

OSKAR HÖFELS, OHG., SEILERSTÄTTE 18, 1010 WIEN. TN: 52 18 28. V.A.Ö.

KARL HÖLZL, K.G., SEILERGASSE 3, 1010 WIEN. TN: 52 28 96, Spec: Graphik; alte Landkarten; Bibliophile Ausgaben. V.A.Ö.

WALTER KLÜGEL, Gumpendorferstrasse 33, 1060 Wien. TN: 57 3(
342. Gegründet 1921. Laden und Lagerräume, Samstag Nachmitta;
geschlossen. Grosser Vorrat, auch neue Bücher. Spec: Erotica; Sitten
geschte; Bibliophile; Kubiniana. CP: Wien 77 46 570. V.A.Ö.

ANTON KÖNIG, Josefstäderstrasse 71, Wien 1008. Laden.

R. KREY, Ges.m.b.H., Graben 13, 1010 Wien 1. Laden. Spec: Militaria

WALTER KRIEG, Kärntnerstrasse 4, 1010 Wien. Prop: M. Krieg. TN
52 11 93. TA: Buchkrieg Wien. Gegründet 1923. Laden, Samsta;
geschlossen. Grosser Vorrat, auch neue Bücher. Spec: Bibliophilie
Geschichte. Corresp: English. B: Pinschof & Co., Wien, Konto 8066
CP: Wien 42154. V.A.Ö. Österreichischer Buchhändlerverband.

KURY & CO., Landstrasse Hauptstrasse 33, Wien 3. Laden. Mittel
grosser Vorrat.

FRANZ MALOTA'S ENKELIN A. STERN, Wiedner Hauptstrasse 22
Wien 4. Prop: Anni Stern. TN: 57 92 75. Gegründet 1901. Laden unc
Lagerräume, Samstag Nachmittag geschlossen. Sehr grosser Vorrat
auch neue Bücher. Cata: 4–6 pro Jahr. Corresp: English, Français. CP
Wien 160 169. V.A.Ö.

MANZ, Kohlmarkt 16, Wien 1. Laden. Mittelgrosser Vorrat, auch neu
Bücher.

LEOPOLDINE MATHIS, Nussdorferstrasse 10, Wien 9. Laden
Kleiner Vorrat.

W. MAUDRICH, Alserstrasse 19, 1080 Wien. TN: 42 72 21. Spec
Medizin; Naturwissenschaften. V.A.Ö.

CHRISTIAN M. NEBEHAY, Annagasse 18, 1015 Wien. (Postfach 303)
TN: 52 18 01. TA: Nebehaybooks Wien. V.A.Ö.

WILHELM PUSKAS, Weihburggasse 16, 1010 Wien. TN: 52 88 53
Spec: Austriaca; Folklore; Geschichte; Philosophie. CP: Wien 39496
V.A.Ö.

A. REICHMANN, Wiedner Hauptstrasse 18, Wien 1041. TN: 57 81 58
Spec: Literaturwissenschaft; Mathematik; Naturwissenschaften; Spiele
Zeitschriften. CP: Wien 76482. V.A.Ö.

HEINRICH RIMANEK, Kaiserstrasse 6, 1070 Wien. TN: 93 98 764
Spec: Austriaca; Naturwissenschaften; Sprachwissenschaft; Theater
Tanz. V.A.Ö.

WALTER R. SCHADEN, Sonnenfelsgasse 4, 1010 Wien. TN: (222) 524 856. V.D.A.Ö.

FRIEDRICH SCHALK, Mariahilferstrasse 97, Wien 1006. Gegründet 1895. Laden.

RINGBUCHHANDLUNG A. SEXL & CO., Dr. Karl-Lueger-Ring 6, 1010 Wien. TN: 634440. Laden.

M. F. STEINBACH, Salmannsdorferstrasse 64, 1190 Wien. TN: 44 11 39. Gegründet 1932. Lagerräume, nur nach Vereinbarung. Grosser Vorrat. Spec: Kunst; Literatur; Naturwissenschaften; Graphik. Cata. Corresp: English. B: Credit-Anstalt-Bankverein, Wien. V.A.Ö.

DR. KARL STROPEK, Währingerstrasse 122, 1181 Wien. Spec: Recht; Staatswissenschaften. CP: Wien 28493. V.A.Ö.

J. WELKHAMMER, Burggasse 123, 1070 Wien. (Auch Neubaugürtel 48). TN: 93 41 35. V.A.Ö.

WIENER ANTIQUARIAT, Seilergasse 16, Wien. Prop: Ingo Nebehay. TN: (0222) 52 54 66. TA: Ingobooks Wien. Gegründet 1962. Laden, Samstag Nachmittag geschlossen. Mittelgrosser Vorrat. Spec: Autographen; Kunst; Graphik. Cata: 6 pro Jahr. Corresp: English, Français, Italiano. B: BPS Bank, Wien, Konto 3060.2303. V.A.Ö.

TH. WILD, Mariahilferstrasse 158, Wien 1015. Laden.

KUNSTVERLAG WOLFRUM, Augustinerstrasse 10, 1010 Wien. TN: 52 53 98 und 52 41 78. TA: Witwolf Wien. Laden. Sehr kleiner Vorrat, auch neue Bücher. Spec: Kunst. Cata: unregelmässig. Corresp: English, Français, Italiano, Español. B: Creditanstalt Konto 50–16282–01. CP: Wien 1191 107. Hauptverband der Österreichischer Buchhandels.

II

GRAZ: INNSBRUCK: KLAGENFURT: LINZ: SALZBURG: S. POLTEN: STIFT ZWETTL.

EDUARD HÖLLRIGL, Sigmund-Haffner-Gasse 10, 5020 Salzburg. (Postfach 239). TN: 41146. Spec: Austriaca. V.A.Ö.

JOS. A. KIENREICH, Sackstrasse 6 (im Halbstock), 8011 Graz. TN: 96121. Spec: Austriaca; Geschichte; Kulturgeschichte; Literaturwissenschaft; Philosophie. CP: Wien 45180. V.A.Ö.

MAYRISCHE BUCHHANDLUNG, THEATERGASSE, 5020 SALZBURG
Prop: Gerhard Neugebauer. TN: 73 596. Gegründet circa 1595. Laden
und Lagerräume, Samstag Nachmittag geschlossen. Sehr grosser Vorrat
auch neue Bücher. Cata. Corresp: English, Français. B: Spängler Bank
CP Wien 76 22 508 und München 1,200.72.807. V.A.Ö.

WERNER NEUGEBAUER O.H.G., LANDSTRASSE 1 4020 LINZ. Prop
Werner und Inge Neugebauer. TN: (07222) 22713. Gegründet 1935
Laden. Mittelgrosser Vorrat, auch neue Bücher. Corresp: English
Français. B: Oberbank Linz Konto 401 5699; Sparkasse Linz Konto
127 862. CP: Wien 772 80 93. München 1205 49–806. Verband de
Österreichischer Buchhandels. I.A.S.V.

J. G. SYDYS, WIENERSTRASSE 19, 3100 ST. PÖLTEN. TN: 3189. Prop: L
Schubert. Spec: Austriaca. CP: Wien 11673. V.A.Ö.

J. E. THOMA, 3910 STIFT ZWETTL. Gegründet 1914. Nur Post-Vekehr
Cata. CP: Wien 1831 577.

MATTHÄUS TRUPPE, STUBENBERGGASSE 7, 8011 GRAZ. TN: 79552
Spec: Graphik; Wissenschaftliche Bücher. CP: Wien 104163. V.A.Ö.

WAGNER'SCHE UNIVERSITÄTS BUCHHANDLUNG OHG.
MUSEUMSTRASSE 4, 6021 INNSBRUCK. TN: 22316. Spec: Wissenschaften
Dekorative Graphik; Austriaca; Alpinismus. CP: Wien 22316. V.A.Ö

GALERIE WELZ SALZBURG, SIGMUND-HAFFNERGASSE 16, SALZBURG
Prop: Prof. Friedrich Welz. TN: 87031. Gegründet 1899. Laden
Samstag Nachmittag geschlossen. Sehr kleiner Vorrat, auch neu
Bücher. Spec: Graphik; Kunst. Corresp: English, Français. B: Bank
haus Berger & Co., Salzburg, Konto 1921. CP: Vienna 91.156. V.A.Ö

WILDNER BUCHANTIQUARIAT, STEMPFERGASSE 8, 8010 GRAZ. TN
(03122) 74216. V.D.A.Ö.

POLSKA

POLAND   POLOGNE   POLEN

BYDGOSZCZ (Bromberg): KRAKÓW (Cracovie, Krakau): POZNAŃ (Posen): RADOM: WARSZAWA (Warsaw, Varsovie, Warschau). WROCLAW (Breslau).

ANTYKWARIAT, 8 PL. UNIVERSYTECKI, WROCŁAW. Shop, secondhand and antiquarian stock.

ANTYKWARIAT NAUKOWY, ULICA SWIĘTOKRZYSKA 14, WARSZAWA. Shop, secondhand and antiquarian stock.

ANTYKWARIAT NAUKOWY, ULICA STARY RYNEK 53/54, POZNAN. Shop, secondhand and antiquarian stock.

ANTYKWARIAT NAUKOWY, ZEROMSKIEGO 89, RADOM. Shop, secondhand and antiquarian stock.

ANTIKWARIAT NAUKOWY, ULICA SLAWKOWSKA 10, KRAKÓW. Shop, secondhand and antiquarian stock.

ANTYKWARIAT NAUKOWY, ULICA PODWALE 4, KRAKÓW. Shop, secondhand and antiquarian stock.

BYDGOSKI ANTYKWARIAT NAUKOWY, "DOM KSIAZKI", STARY RYNEK 16, 85–105 BYDGOSZCZ. Established 1952. Shop and storeroom. Very large stock. Spec: humanistic. Cata: 4 a year. Corresp: English, Esperanto, German, Russian.

DOM KSIAZKI ANTYKWARIAT, 6 RYNEK (kom M.O.I), WROCŁAW. Shop, secondhand and antiquarian stock.

KSIEGARNIA ANTYKWARYCZNA, NOWY SWIAT 61, WARSZAWA. Shop, secondhand and antiquarian stock.

PORTUGAL

LISBOA (Lisbon, Lissabon). PORTO

LIVRARIA ANTIQUARIA, Rua da Misericordia 147, Lisboa. TN: 32 72 72.

BIBLARTE, LIMITADA, Rua de Sao Pedro de Alcantara 71, Lisboa 2. Prop: Ernesto Martins. TN: 363702. Established 1950. Very large stock, also new books. Spec: periodicals; history; art; literature. Cata: 2 a year. Corresp: English, Français, Español.

LIVRARIA A BIBLIÓFILA LTDA., Rua da Misericórdia 102, Lisboa. TN: 33476. Established 1942. Shop. Small stock, also new books. Corresp: English, Français, Italiano, Deutsch. B: 242 Banco Espirito Santo (Camoes).

LIVRARIA BRASÍLIA, Rua da Misericordia 79, Lisboa. TN: 32 03 20.

A. TAVARES DE CARVALHO, Avenida da Republica 46–3, Lisboa. TN. 77 03 77. Established 1960. House premises, appointment necessary. Large stock. Spec: early rare books on Brazil; sciences; Italian Renaissance; chess. Corresp: English, Français. B: Banco Totta & Açores, No. 97777/001. A.B.A. (Int.).

LIVRARIA CASTRO E SILVA, Rua da Rosa 31, Lisboa. Prop: Ezequiel de Castro e Silva. TN: 367380. Established 1957. Shop and storeroom. Very large stock. Spec: Portuguese literature; history; art; foreign. Cata: 6 a year. Corresp: English, Français, Español. B: Banco Nacional Ultramarino, (Camoes), 210/8705.

DIAS & ANDRADE LDA, LIVRARIA PORTUGAL, Rua do Carmo 70, Lisboa 2. TN: 36 05 82, 32 82 20. Established 1941. Shop. Very large stock. Spec: literature; technical; sports. Cata: monthly bibliographical bulletin. Corresp: English, Français, Español.

LIVRARIA FÉRIN, Rua Nova do Almada 74, Lisboa. TN: 32 44 22.

MANUEL FERREIRA, Rua Formosa 19, Porto. TN: 313356. Established 1959. Shop and storeroom, early closing Saturday. Large stock. Spec: Portuguese general bibliography. Cata: Corresp: English, Français. B: Banco Portugués do Atlantico, Dep. Padrão, Porto. A.B.A.

LIVRARIA HISTÓRICA E ULTRAMARINA (J. C. SILVA), Travessa da Queimada 28, Lisboa 2. Prop: José Maria da Costa e Silva. TN: 368 589. Established 1951. Shop. Very large stock. Spec: Africana; Judaica; history; engravings; maps; manuscripts. Cata: monthly. Corresp: English, Français, Español. B: Banco Nacional Ultramarino and Banco Espirito Santo e Commercial de Lisboa. A.B.A.

AMERICO F. MARQUES, Rua da Misericordia 92–1, Lisboa. TN: 36 49 77. Shop.

LIVRARIA EDUARDO ANTUNES MARTINHO, Rua Voz do Operario 7–B, Lisboa. TN: 86 64 86.

O MUNDO DO LIVRO, Largo da Trindade 11–13, Lisboa 2. Prop: João Rodrigues Pires. TN: 369951. Established 1946. Shop and storeroom. Large stock. Cata: 12 a year. Corresp: English, Français. B: Crédit Franco-Portugais, 21.171, and Banco Borges & Irmão, 2100–5544315. A.B.A.

LIVRARIA D. PEDRO V., Rua D. Pedro V. 16, Lisboa. TN: 36 89 04.

R. B. ROSENTHAL, Rua do Alecrim 47–4 Salas D, Lisboa. Spec: Africa.

P. GUEDES DA SILVA, Livraria Academica, Rua Martires da Liberdade 8–12, Porto.

J. A. TELLES DA SYLVA, Travessa do Marquês de Sá da Bandera 19–3, Lisboa 1. Prop: Dom José Antonio Telles da Sylva. TN: 77 48 24 and 65 00 81. Established 1966. Private premises, appointment necessary. Very small stock. Spec: navigation; Portuguese and Spanish explorations overseas and commerce. Cata: 1 a year. Corresp: English, Français, Italiano, Español. B: Totta & Açores, No. 1.199,870/002. A.B.A.

ROMINA

ROUMANIA   ROUMANIE   RUMANIEN

BRAŞOV (Kronstadt): BUCUREŞTI (Bucharest, Bukarest): CON-STANTA.

ANTICARIAT C.L.D.C., STRADA REPUBLICII 24, BRAŞOV. Shop.

ANTICARIAT UNITATEA Nr. 18, TOMIS STRADA, CONSTANTA. Shop.

ANTICARIATUL BUCUREŞTI, LIPSCANI 6, BUCUREŞTI. TN: 14 47 61. Established 1950. Shop and storeroom, open 7–15 hours. Very large stock. Spec: Roumania–history, law, economics, etc. Corresp: Français, Deutsch. B: Banca Româna de Comert Exterior.

ANTICARIATUL Nr. 2, BULEVARDUL REPUBLICII 5, BUCUREŞTI. TN: 15 87 61. Shop.

ANTICARIATUL Nr. 3, BULEVARDUL GENERAL MAGHERU 2, BUCUREŞTI. TN: 15 52 96. Shop. Medium stock, Roumainian and foreign. Hours 9–13 and 16–20.

ANTICARIATUL Nr. 4, BIS ENEI 16, BUCUREŞTI. TN: 15 48 83. Shop.

ANTICARIATUL Nr. 6, CALEA VICTORIEI 45, PASAJ KRETZULESCU, BUCUREŞTI. TN: 13 08 97. Shop, open 8–13.30 and 17–19.30 Monday, Thursday and Saturday, 8–14 Tuesday, Wednesday and Friday. Very large stock, also new books and maps, engravings and prints.

ANTICARIATUL Nr. 9, POLIZII 2, BUCUREŞTI. TN: 15 35 93. Shop.

S.S.S.R (C.C.C.P.)
SOYUZ SOVYETSKIH SOZIALISTICHESKIH RESPUBLIK
U.S.S.R.   U.R.S.S.   U.d.S.S.R.

LENINGRAD: MOSKVA (Kyrillic=MOCKBA) Moscow: Moscou: Moskau: RIGA.

MOSCOW

"BUKINIST", Stoleshnikov Lane, Moscow. Shop. Secondhand and antiquarian stock.

MAGAZIN No. 1. AKADEMKNIGA (BUKINISTICHESKI), Ulitsa Gorkogo d.8, Moscow.

MAGAZIN No. 7 (BUKINISTICHESKI), Ulitsa Sretyenka d.9, Moscow.

MAGAZIN No. 9 (BUKINISTICHESKI), Ulitsa Kirova d.13, Moscow.

MAGAZIN No. 14 (BUKINISTICHESKI), Proyezd Khydojestveve-nogo Teatra d.5, Moscow.

MAGAZIN No. 28 (BUKINISTICHESKI), Stoleshnikov Perbylok d.14, Moscow.

MAGAZIN No. 32 (BUKINISTICHESKI), Kutaiski Proyezhd d.1, Moscow.

MAGAZIN No. 34 (BUKINISTICHESKI), Dobrininskaya Ulitsa d.32/2, Moscow.

MAGAZIN No. 35 (BUKINISTICHESKI), Ulitsa Arbat d.10, Moscow.

MAGAZIN No. 36 (BUKINISTICHESKI), Ulitsa Arbat d.8, Moscow.

MAGAZIN No. 45 (BUKINISTICHESKI), Prospekt Marksa d.1, Moscow. Spec: antiquarian.

MAGAZIN No. 54 (BUKINISTICHESKI), ULITSA CHERNISHEVSKOGO d.50, MOSCOW.

MAGAZIN No. 121 (BUKINISTICHESKI), LENINSKI PROSPEKT d.69, MOSCOW.

LENINGRAD

LENKNIGI MAGAZIN No. 10 (BUKINISTICHESKI), ULITSA ZHUKOV- SKOGO 2, LENINGRAD. TN: 63 33 84.

LENKNIGI MAGAZIN No. 26 (BUKINISTICHESKI), BOLSHOI PROSPEKT 19, LENINGRAD. TN: 32 17 65.

LENKNIGI MAGAZIN No. 40 (BUKINISTICHESKI), VASILEVSKI OSTROV, LENINGRAD. TN: 13 43 47.

LENKNIGI MAGAZIN No. 53 (BUKINISTICHESKI), ULITSA GERTSENA 12, LENINGRAD. TN: 19 78 62.

LENKNIGI MAGAZIN No. 61 (BUKINISTICHESKI), LITEINI PROSPEKT 59, LENINGRAD. TN: 62 97 14.

RIGA, LATVIAN S.S.R.

ANTIKVARIATS, PETERIS STUCKAS ILEA 5, RIGA. Shop, new and second- hand stock.

CENTRALIS ANTIKVARIATS, LENINA ILEA 46, RIGA. Shop, new and secondhand stock.

SUISSE SCHWEIZ SVIZZERA

SWITZERLAND

Languages—Langues—Sprache Français, Deutsch, Italiano
Associations: Verbände

SLACES = Syndicat de la Librairie Ancienne et du Commerce de l'Estampe en Suisse.

VEBUKU = Vereinigung der Buchantiquare und Kupferstichhändler der Schweiz.
Trittligasse 19, 8001 Zürich.

SBVV = Schweizer Buchhändler und Verleger Verein.
SKV = Schweizer Kunsthandelsverband.
SLESR = Société des Libraires et Editeurs de la Suisse Romande.
SZBV = Schweizer und Zürcher Buchhändlervereine.
VSAK = Verband Schweizer Antiquare und Kunsthändler.

Public Holidays: Jours de Fête: Feiertage
Jan. 1: Good Friday: Ascension Day: Dec. 25.
Jan. 1: Vendredi-Saint: Ascension: 25 Déc.
Jan. 1: Karfreitag: Christi Himmelfahrt: Weihnachtstag.

English	Français	Deutsch	Italiano
—	ARAN	—	—
—	—	BURGDORF	—
BASLE	BALE	BASEL	BASILEA
—	BERNE	BERN	—
GENEVA	GENÈVE	GENF	GINEVRA
—	LAUSANNE	—	LOSANNA
—	—	LIESTAL	—
—	—	—	LUGANO
—	LUCERNE	LUZERN	—
—	NEUCHATEL	—	—
—	—	OLTEN	—
—	SAINT GALLEN	—	—
—	SAINT PREX	—	—
—	—	THUN	—
—	YVERDON	—	—
—	—	ZURICH	ZURIGO

ROBERT ALDER, Junkerngasse 41, Bern. TN: 22 41 02. Gegründet 1936. Etagengeschäft, 2. Stock (Aufzug). Grosses Lager. Spec: Geisteswissenschaften; Geschichte; Kunst; Literatur; Helvetica. Corresp: Français. B: Kantonalbank von Bern, und Bank von Ernst & Cie, A.G., Bern. CP: 30 10 955. BEBUKU.

L'ART ANCIEN S.A., Signaustrasse 6, 8008 Zürich. TN: 479229. TA: Artancien Zürich. Lagerräume, Samstag geschlossen. Wertvolle Bücher, Graphik und Zeichnungen grosser Meister. Cata: 2–3 a year. Corresp: English, Français. B: Julius Baer & Cie., Postfach, 8022 Zürich. CP: Zürich 80–29905. VEBUKU, SBVV, ZBV, VSAK, SKV, ABA.

FÉLIX BLOCH, 10 Route de Rolle, 1162 Saint-Prex. (Boite Postale 58). TN: (021) 76 16 62. Fondée en 1973. Domicile, sur rendez-vous. Restreint stock. Spec: Histoire de médice et science. Cata: 1 par an. Corresp: English, Deutsch. B: Banque cantonale vaudoise, Lausanne. Swiss Banking Corporation, New York. CP: 10 323 52. S.L.A.C.E.S., S.L.E.S.R.

HANS BOLLIGER, Lenggstrasse 14, 8008 Zürich. TN: (01) 535888. S.L.A.C.E.S.

LIVRES ANCIENS MAURICE BRIDEL, S.A., avenue du Théâtre 1, 1000 Lausanne. (Case Postale 1662). TN: (021) 23 77 35. TA: Livrancien Lausanne. Fondée en 1948. Boutique. Restreint stock, aussi les livres neufs. Spec: beaux livres anciens et modernes; equitation. Cata: mensuel. Corresp: English. B: Société de Banque Suisse, Lausanne. CP: Lausanne 10–9155. SLACES, SLAM.

BUCHANTIQUARIAT BRITSCHGI, Rämistrasse 33, Zürich. Prop: Melchior Britschgi. TN: (051) 575632. Gegründet 1943. Laden, Samstag Nachmittag geschlossen. Mittelgrosser Vorrat. Corresp: English, Français. CP: Zürich VIII 29990. VEBUKU.

BÜCHER-SCHMIDT ANTIQUARIAT, Torgasse 4, 8000 Zürich. TN: (051) 32 85 27. TA: Bucherschmidt Zürich. Gegründet 1913. Prop: Max Schmidt. Laden. Grosser Vorrat, auch neue Bücher. Spec: Zoologie; Botanik; Philosophie. B: Schweiz Bankverein, Depka Bellevue, Zürich. CP: Zürich 80–25354. VEBUKU.

GALERIE GÉRALD CRAMER, 13 rue de Chantepoulet, Genève. TN: 32 54 32. TA: Bibliocramer Genève. Fondée 1945. Galerie. Spec: éstampes modernes et livres de peintres modernes; sculptures modernes. Cata. Corresp: English. B: Société de Banques Suisse, Agence Cornavin, Genève. SLACES, SKV.

PAUL DESCOMBES, RUE DU VIEUX-COLLÈGE 6, 1204 GENEVE. TN: (022) 240443. SLACES.

GALERIE ENGELBERTS, 11 GRAND RUE, 1204 GENÈVE. Prop: Edwin Engelberts. TN: 28 37 32. TA: Cantabile, Genève. Fondée en 1960. Galerie, fermée lundi. Spec: art contemporain; tableaux, dessins, gravures, livres illustrés par les peintres. B: Banque de l'harpe, Leclerc et Cie., Bd Théâtre 2, 1211 Genève 11. CP: Genève XII-579. SLACES.

LA FIERA DEL LIBRO, VIA MARCONI 2, 6900 LUGARNO. Prop: Moghini & Nesa. TN: 27649. Spec: fine arts, maps and views, prints and drawings.

EDUARD FINK, METZERGASSE 18, 3400 BURGDORF. TN: (034) 24711. SLACES.

PAUL & ARTHUR FISCHER, HALDENSTRASSE 19, 6006 LUZERN. TN: (041) 225712. SLACES.

FUCHS & REPOSO, LIBRAIRIE WEGA, VIA NASSA 21, 6900 LUGANO. TN: 23514. TA: Wega Lugarno. Fondée en 1935. Boutique, early closing Saturday. Moyen stock. Spec: moderne bibliophile. Corresp: English, Français, Deutsch, Italiano. B: Unione de Banche Svizzere. CP: Lugano 69 1911. SBVV. VEBUKU.

GILHOFER & RANSCHBURG G.m.b.H., HALDENSTRASSE 9, 6006 LUZERN. Leiter: Axel Erdmann. TN: (041) 23 64 66. TA: Gilhag, Luzern. Laden, aber vorzugsweise nach Vereinbarung. Gegründet 1924. Kleiner Vorrat. Spec: Inkunabeln; XVI Jahrhundert; Manuskripte; Geschichte d. Wissenschaften und Medizin. Cata: 4 pro Jahr. Corresp: Deutsch, Français, English, Italiano. B: Schweiz. Kreditanstalt, Luzern. CP: 60 2786. ILAB, VEBUKU.

LIBRAIRIE DU GRAND-CHÊNE, 1603 ARAN. Prop: Ernest Abravanel. TN: (021) 99 25 21. Domicile, sur rendez-vous. Restreint stock. Spec: Stendhal, Balzac, Proust, Rilke; critique littéraire. Cata: 6 par an. Corresp: English, Français, Deutsch. B: Banque populaire suisse, Lausanne, Compte 167 160. CP: Lausanne 10 177 69. VEBUKU, LILA.

DAS GUTE BUCH, ROSENGASSE 10, 8001 ZÜRICH. Prop: Gebrüder Seidenberg. TN: 327072. Gegründet 1940. Laden. Sehr grosser Vorrat. Spec: alle Gebiete; Okkulta. Cata. Schweizer Kreditanstalt, Rathaus, Zürich. CP: Zürich 80 22853. Schweizische Buchhändlervereinigung.

DR. ANNEMARIE GUYER-HALTER, AUF DER MAUER 1, 8000 ZÜRICH 1.
TN: (051) 47 33 43. Spec: Geschichte; Philosophie; Wissenschaften. B:
Schweiz. Kreditanstalt. CP: Zürich 80–33053. VEBUKU.

HAUS DER BÜCHER, AG, "ERASMUSHAUS", BÄUMLEINGASSE 18, BASEL.
Dir: Adolf Seebass. TN: 23 30 88. TA: Bücherhaus Basel. Spec:
Auktionen; alte Bücher; Manuskripte. B: Crédit Suisse. CP: Basel
40–604. VEBUKU.

EDUARD HEGNAUER, KRAMGASSE 16, 3000 BERN. TN: (031) 22 64 15
und 22 74 00. Gegründet 1944. Laden, Montag geschlossen. Sehr
grosser Vorrat. Corresp: English, Français, Deutsch. B: Schweizer
Creditanstalt, Konto 339160. Schweizerische Bankgessellschaft, Konto
479 204 01 P. CP: 30 15595. VEBUKU, LILA.

P. H. HEITZ, POSTFACH 80, BASEL 4006. TN: 42 88 60. TA: Heitzverlag
Basel. Gegründet 1483 (Strasbourg, France). Domicile, par rendez-
vous seulement. Spec: Helvetica; Alsatica; Incunabula. Corresp:
English, Français, Italiano. B: Schweizer Kreditanstalt, Basel. CP: V
8905 Basel. SLAM.

ANTIQUARIAT IBERIA, HIRSCHENGRABEN 6, BERNE. Prop: Jaime
Romagosa, jr. TN: 25 59 43. Fondée 1950. Boutique. Moyen stock.
Littérature espagnole, littérature générale, philosophie. Corresp:
English, Français, Deutsch, Español, Italiano. B: Union de Banque
Suisse, Berne. CP: Berne 30–22065. SLACES.

KORNFELD & KLIPSTEIN, LAUPENSTRASSE 49, BERN. Prop: Eberhard
W. Kornfeld. TN: 25 46 73. TA: Artus Bern. Spec: Kunst; Graphik.
VEBUKU.

M. KREBSER & CO., BÄLLIZ/BAHNHOFBRÜCKE, 3600 THUN. Prop:
Markus Krebser. TN: 220 48. TA: Krebserco Thun. Laden, Samstag
Nachmittag geschlossen. Spec: Naturwissenschaft; illustrierte Bücher.
B: Banque cantonale de Berne à Thun et Spar und Leihkasse, Thun.
CP: Thun 30 5181. VEBUKU.

HERBERT LANG & CIE. A.G., MUNZGRABEN 2 (ECKE AMTHAUSGASSE).
3000 BERN. TN: (031) 22 88 71. TA: Herbertbook, Bern. Gegründet
1921. 3 Lagerräume, nur nach Vereinbarung. Grosser Vorrat. Spec:
Rechts-, Wirtschafts- und Sozialwissenschaften; Geschichte, Philosophie; Zeitschriften. Cata: 6 pro Jahr. Corresp: English, Français,
Deutsch. B: Schweiz. Kreditanstalt, Bern. Dresdner Bank, Hamburg.
Swiss Credit Bank, New York, Crédit Lyonnais, Paris. CP: Bern
30 4108; Frankfurt am Main 300 376–607. SLACES.

AUGUST LAUBE & SOHN, TRITTLIGASSE 19, 8001 ZÜRICH. TN: 25 82 24. TA: Buchlaube Zürich. Spec: Illustrierte Bücher. alte Graphik; Auktionen. B: Schweitzerische Kreditanstalt, Zürich. CP: Zürich 80–9245. VEBUKU, SLACES.

LIEHBIBLIOTHEK, GERBERGÄSSLEIN, BASEL. TN: (061) 237354. Laden. Kleiner Vorrat.

GALERIE ANNIE MURISET, 4 PLACE DU MOLARD, 1200 GENÈVE. TN: (022) 24 66 72. Spec: gravures anciennes; géographie. SLACES.

F. SCHEIBER, DENKMALSTRASSE 8, LUZERN. TN: (041) 36 4823. Laden, Kleiner Vorrat.

BUCHANTIQUARIAT NEUES SCHLOSS, STOCKERSTRASSE 17, 8027 ZÜRICH. Prop: H. & R. Madliger-Schwab. TN: (01) 36 78 35. TA: Madligerschwab Zürich. Gegründet 1951. Laden, Samstag Nachmittag geschlossen (März-Okt.). Sehr grosser Vorrat, auch neue Bücher. Spec: Bibliophilie; Kunst; Geschichte; Helvetica. Corresp: Français. B: Schweiz. Kreditanstalt, Zürich. CP: Zürich 80–37.276. VEBUKU, SBVV.

ANNEMARIE PFISTER, PETERSGRABEN 18, 4051 BASEL. TN: (061) 25 75 02. Gegründet 1974. Laden. Kleiner Vorrat, auch neue Bücher. Spec: Klassiker; Kunst; Geisteswissenschaften. Corresp: English, Français. B: Schweiz. Bankverein. CP: 40 36 232.

ANTIQUARIAT PINKUS GENOSSENSCHAFT, FROSCHAUGASSE 7, 8001 ZÜRICH. (Postfach 8025 Zürich). Prop: Studienbibliothek zur Geschichte der Arbeiterbewegung. TN: 32 26 47. TA: Desiderata Zürich. Gegründet 1940. Laden und Lagerräume (Antiquariat Montag geschlossen). Grosser Vorrat, auch neue Bücher. Spec: Literatur in Erstausgaben; alte Drucke; illustrierte Bücher; Politik, Socialismus; Philosophie; Arbeiterliteratur. Cata: 6 pro Jahr. Corresp; Deutsch, Français, English, Italiano, Pycckuu. B: Schweizer Kreditanstalt Depositenkasse, Rathausplatz, 8022 Zürich. CP: Zürich 80 25 787. Stuttgart 5004. SBVV.

HANS RAUNHARDT, KIRCHGASSE 17, 8000 ZÜRICH 1. Prop: Gerhard Heinemann. TN: (051) 32 13 68. TA: Raunhardtbuch Zürich. Spec: Recht; Wirtschaft; Medizin. B: Schweiz. Kreditanstalt, (Depka Rathausplatz), Zürich. CP: Zürich 80905. VEBUKU.

MADAME EUGENE REYMOND, 14 FAUBOURG DE L'HOPITAL, NEU-CHATEL. TN: 5 45 15. TA: Libremon Neuchâtel. Fondée 1927. Fermé

Lundi. Important stock. Spec: erudition, documentation tous sujets. Cata. Corresp: English. B: Société de Banque Suisse. CP: Neuchâtel 20–2036. SLACES.

HANS ROHR, OBERDORFERSTRASSE 5, 8024 ZÜRICH 1. TN: 47 12 52. Gegründet 1921. Laden und Lagerräume, Montag geschlossen. Sehr grosser Vorrat, auch neue Bücher. Spec: Altphilologie; Philosophie; Psychologie; Helvetica; Literatur; Film. Corresp: English, Français. B: Swiss Credit, Zürcher Kantonalbank. CP: Zürich 80/9613 und Stuttgart 107 30–705. VEBUKU.

JÖRG SCHÄFER, HOTTINGERSTRASSE 5, 8032 ZÜRICH. TN: 01–32 25 85. TA: Schaeferbuch Zürich. Gegründet 1971. Laden, Samstag Nachmittag geschlossen. Spec: 15. und 16. Jahrhunderts. Bücher, Geschichte der Wissenschaften. Cata: 3 pro Jahr. Corresp: English, Français. B: Julius Bär & Co., Zürich. CP: Zürich 80–69515. VEBUKU, ILAB, VDA.

HELLMUT SCHUMANN, AG., RÄMISTRASSE 25, ZÜRICH. Manager: Hans Neubauer. TN: (051) 320272. TA: Schumannbuch Zürich. Gegründet 1828. Laden, Samstag Nachmittag geschlossen. Sehr grosser Vorrat. Spec: Bücher, Graphik. Cata: 6 pro Jahr. Corresp: English, Français, Italiano. B: Swiss Credit, Zürich, Branch Seefeld. CP: Zürich 80–2932. VEBUKU.

M. SLATKINE ET FILS, 15 COURS DE RIVE, 1200 GENÈVE. (aussi 5 Rue des Chaudronniers). Prop: Michel Slatkine. TN: 35 16 48 et 20 04 76. TA: Slatlivre, Genève. Fondée en 1914. Boutique et depôt. Très important stock. Spec: Romanica, Helvetica, périodiques. Cata: 5 par an. Corresp: English, Deutsch, Français. B: Crédit Suisse, Genève. CP: Genève 12 3238. SLACES.

LOUIS VUILLE, MAISON ROUGE 5, 1400 Yverdon. TN: (024) 21 25 44. Fondée en 1853. Boutique. Très restreint stock. Spec: gravures de vues et livres de voyages. Cata: 1 ou 2 par an. Corresp: Français, Deutsch. B: Banque vaudois de Crédit. CP: Lausanne 10–12464. SLACES.

OTTO WASER-ALBIEZ, RÜMELINSPLATZ 15, BASEL. TN: 237318. Laden. Kleiner Vorrat, auch neue Bücher.

WEISS-HESSE ANTIQUARIAT, FROBURGSTRASSE 30, 4600 OLTEN. Prop: Rudolf Weiss-Hesse. TN: (062) 21 27 05. Gegründet 1935. Wohnung. Spec: Bücher; Zeichungen; N.S.W. des 15. bis 20. fahrhunderts. Corresp: English, Français, Italiano. B: Solothurner Kantonalbank, Olten. CP: Olten 46–971. VEBUKU, VDA.

GALERIE WIDMER, Neugasse 9000 35, St. Gallen. Prop: Carl Widmer. TN: (071) 22 16 26. Gegründet 1936. Laden. Spec: Kupferstiche; Landkarten; Helvetica. B: St. Gallische Creditanstalt, Marktplatz 1, St. Gallen. CP: St. Gallen 90–2364. VEBUKU.

R. & I. WANNER-ZANDER, Kronnengasse 35, 5400 Baden. TN (056) 22 30 93 TA: ISIBOOK, Telex: 53872 (Swan). B: Schweiz. Bankgesellschaft, Baden. VEBUKU.

ALEXANDER WILD, Marktgasse 50, 3011 Bern. TN (031) 22 44 80. TA: Wildbuch. B. Kantonal Bank von Bern. VEBUKU.

SUOMI

FINLAND   FINLANDE   FINNLAND

Languages: Langues: Sprache
Finnish and Swedish.

Associations: Verbände
F.A.F. = Finska Antikvariatforeningen
Suomen Antikoariaa
Norra Magasinsgatan 6, Helsingfors.

Public Holidays: Jours de Fête: Feiertage
Easter Monday; May 1; Whitmonday; December 6: Dec. 25.
Lundi de Pâques: May 1: lundi de Penticôte: Dec. 6: Dec. 25.
Ostermontag: Mai 1: Pfinstmontag: Weihnachtstag.

HELSINKI = HELSINGFORS.

ANTIKVARIAT GORDIN, NYLANDSGATAN 11, 00120 HELSINGFORS 12.
Prop: Mr. & Mrs. I. Gordin. TN: 641551. Established 1948. Shop and
storeroom, early closing Saturday. Medium stock. Spec: Finnish books;
prints and maps; folklore; art; travels; books. maps and prints of
Baltic, Russia, Scandinavia. Corresp: English, Français, Deutsch and
Scandinavian languages. B: Nordiska Foreningsbanken, No. 2058 38
1996 1. CP: Helsingfors 11748 5.

KAMPINTORIN ANTIKVARIAATTI, FREDRIKINKATU 63, HELSINKI.
Prop: Mme Meeri Makelin. TN: 63 99 61. CP: Helsinki 77452. F.A.F.

KIRJAKUJA, KY. UUDENMAANKATU 4–6, HELSINKI. LIBRARIA, KASERN-
GATAN 23, HELSINGFORS.

KESKUSTAN ANTIKVARIAATTI, 1 YRJÖNKATU, HELSINKI. F.A.F.

NORDISKA ANTIVARISKA BOKHANDELN, NORRA MAGASINGATAN
6, HELSINGFORS. Prop: Mrs. Tove Nilsson. TN: 62 63 52. TA: Antqva
Helsingfors. Shop. Very large stock. Spec: maps; history; periodicals;
Scandinavia; prints. B: H.A.B., Helsingfors. CP: Helsingfors 6578.
F.A.F.

SVERIGE

SWEDEN   SUÈDE   SCHWEDEN

Associations: Verbände

S.A.F. =   Svenska   Antikvariatforeningen
Birger Jarlsgatan 32,1142q Stockholm.

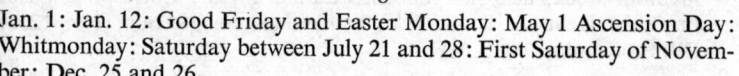

Public Holidays: Jours de Fête: Feiertage

Jan. 1: Jan. 12: Good Friday and Easter Monday: May 1 Ascension Day:
Whitmonday: Saturday between July 21 and 28: First Saturday of November: Dec. 25 and 26.

Jan. 1: Jan. 12: Pâques: May 1: Ascension: Pentecôte, 2 jours: Samedi
entre Juillet 21 et 28: Premier Samedi du Novembre: Dec. 25 and 26.

Jan. 1: Jan. 12: Karfreitag und Ostermontag: Mai 1: Himmelfahrt:
Pfingsten 2 Tage: Samstag zwischen July 21 and 28: Erstex Samstag
November: Dez. 25 und 26.

ESLÖV: GÖTEBORG (Gothenburg): KARLSTAD: LANDSKRONA:
LUND: MALMÖ: NORRKÖPING: ÖSTERBYMO: STOCKHOLM:
UPPSALA.

AKARPS ANTIKVARIAT AB, LA. TVÄRGATAN 5, 24033, LÖBERÖD.

ASPINGTONS ANTIKVARIAT AB, DROTTNINGGATAN 73 C, STOCK-
HOLM. Prop: Inga Lisa Aspington-Hyltmark. TN: 11 21 60. B: Skandinaviska Banken. CP: 45 86 46. S.A.F.

ANTIKVARISKA BOKHANDELN AB, GUSTAF ADOLFS TORG 41,
MALMÖ. Prop: Bo Sörlin. TN: 97 97 28. Established 1942. Shop, early
closing Saturday. Very large stock, also new books and remainders.
Cata: occasionally. Corresp: English, Deutsch. B: Svenska Handelsbanken, Malmö, Account No. 6776–3338. VP: Malmö 87–6350. S.A.F.

BJÖRCK & BÖRJESSON, KUNGSGATAN 5/II, STOCKHOLM-C. (Postbox
1701). TN: 20 18 60. TA: Bokbörje Stockholm. Shop and storeroom.
Very large stock. Spec: old and rare, scientific periodicals; Swedish
literature; philology; science; topography. Cata: 2–3 a year. Corresp:

SVERIGE SWEDEN

English, Deutsch, Français. B: Svenska Handelsbanken, 73–4061. CP: Stockholm 2717. S.A.F., A.B.A.

A. CEDERBERGS EFTR. AB, SYSSLOMANSGATAN 8, 752 23 UPPSALA. Prop: Sven P. Ullberg. TN: 13 80 08. TA: Upsalabok Uppsala. Established 1903. Shop, early closing Saturday. Large stock, also new books. Corresp: English, Français, Deutsch. CP: Upsala 378565. S.A.F.

DAHLSTRÖMS ANTIKVARIAT AB, STORGATAN 31, LANDSKRONA. TN: 11464. S.A.F.

FRITZES KUNGL, HOVBOKHANDEL, FREDSGATAN 2, STOCKHOLM 16. TN: 23 89 00. TA: Bokfritze Stockholm. Established 1837. Shop. Medium stock, also new books. Cata: 6 a year. Corresp: English, Français, Deutsch. B: Svenska handelsbanken, Account No. 1236. CP: Stockholm 193. S.A.F.

N. J. GUMPERTS BOKHANDEL AB, FREDSGATAN 1, GÖTEBORG. TN: 17 30 60. TA: Gumperts Göteborg. Cata. S.A.F.

O. A. HAGELIN, TEGNERGATAN 14, 11358 STOCKHOLM. Appointment necessary. Spec: Linnaeus and his disciples; natural history; history of science and medicine; travels.

WILLIE HEIMANN, LINNEGATAN 3, STOCKHOLM. A.B.A.

GRETA HOLMS ANTIKVARIAT, NORRLANDSGATAN 16, STOCKHOLM-C. Prop: Eva Margareta Holm. TN: 11 59 64. B: Skandinaviska Banken. CP: Stockholm 35–6417. S.A.F.

HULTS ANTIKVARIAT, GREVTUREGATAN 18, STOCKHOLM. TN: 67 82 82.

GUNNAR JOHANSON-THOR, AB., HALLSFARM, 24100 ESLÖV. TN: (0713) 73138. Private premises, appointment necessary. Spec: old Swedish books; topography; old science; history; old prints and maps. Cata: 5–6 a year. Corresp: English, Français, Deutsch. B: Skånska Banken 27–7903. S.A.F.

JONES ANTIKVARIAT, NORTULLSGATAN 3, 11329 STOCKHOLM. Prop: Ragnar Jones. TN: 30 76 97. Spec: illustrated books; first editions; fine arts. B: Göteborgs Bank. S.A.F.

KARLSTAD ANTIKVARIAT, ÖSTRA TORGGATAN 1, KARLSTAD. TN: 54342. S.A.F.

LENGERTZ' ANTIKVARIAT-BOKHANDEL I LUND, AB., ST. GRABRÖDSGATAN 13, 222 22 LUND. Prop: Eric Vilhelm Andersson. TN:

(046) 110345. Established 1922. Very large stock. Cata: 1 a year. Corresp: English, Deutsch. B: Bankgiro 869–2659. CP: 53 84 69–8.

LENGERTS ANTIKVARIAT, ADELGATAN 19, MALMÖ-C. Prop: G. Jansson. TN: 12 22 65. Spec: topography; illustrated books; bibliography. B: Skandinaviska Banken. CP: Malmö 13416. S.A.F.

LIBRIS ANTIKVARIATET, KOMMENDÖRSGATAN 14, 10243 STOCKHOLM. (P.O. Box 5123). Prop: Ake Andersson. TN: 62 21 31 and 60 92 62. TA: Librisantik Stockholm. Established 1960. Shop, early closing Saturday. Medium stock. Spec: old and rare books; bindings; humanities. Cata: 6–8 a year. Corresp: English. B: Skandinaviska Banken, account 57 5754. CP: Stockholm 6074–86. S.A.F.

LILLA ANTIKVARIATET, SÖDRA FÖRSTADSGATAN 20, MALMÖ-C. Prop: G. Jansson. TN: 12 04 83. CP: Malmö 43–5604. S.A.F.

LINDBERGHS ANTIKVARIAT, TEGNÉRGATAN 10, 113 58 STOCKHOLM. Prop: Nils Lindbergh. TN: 31 20 20. Established 1952. Shop, early closing Saturday. Large stock. Corresp: English, Deutsch. CP: Stockholm 50 05 85. S.A.F.

LÖWENDAHLS ANTIKVARIAT, P.O. BOX 2101, 75002 UPPSALA 2. Prop: Björn Löwendahl. TN: (018) 103670. Business by appointment only. Spec: old and rare books; geography (travels); natural history; Scandinavica. Cata. Corresp: English, Français, Deutsch. B: Skandinaviska Banken, Uppsala, Account No. 370–0366. S.A.F.

H. MELLGRENS ANTIKVARIAT, CENTRUMHUSET ÖSTRA LARMGATAN 17, 41107 GÖTEBORG. Prop: Cecilia Håkansson. TN: 105874. Established 1918. Shop. Large Stock. Spec: old and rare; illuminated manuscripts; old maps; art. Corresp: English, Deutsch. B: Sveriges Kreditbank, Göteborg, Account No. 2274. CP: Göteborg 41802. S.A.F. *Also at:* Via Hamngatan 6.

OLINS ANTIKVARIAT, KLOSTERGATAN 11, LUND. Prop: Enoch Olin. TN: 11 24 99. Established 1867. Shop, early closing Saturday. Very large stock. Corresp: English. B: Skandinaviska Banken, Account No. 66–0637. CP: Kund 33843. S.A.F.

RÖNNELLS ANTIKVARIAT, AB, BIRGER JARLSGATAN 32, 11429 STOCKHOLM. TN: 20 21 63 and 11 54 11. TA: Roennellbok Stockholm. Established 1930. Shop, early closing Saturday. Very large stock, also new books. Spec: scholarly and scientific books and periodicals in many languages; old Swedish views and maps. Cata: occasionally.

143

Corresp: English, Français, Deutsch. B: Göteborgs Bank, Stockholm, Account No. 4154:101 241–7. CP: Stockholm 50040 and Hamburg 4000 68. S.A.F., V.D.A.

ANTIKVARIAT STEN RYÖ, ARSENALSGATAN 4, 111 47 STOCKHOLM. Prop: Sten Ryö. TN: 10 16 17. Established 1954. Shop, early closing Saturday. Medium stock. Spec: art; illustrated books; old and modern prints. Cata: 1 a year. Corresp: English, Français, Deutsch, Dansk. CP: Stockholm 1238. S.A.F.

SAMLAREN ANTIKVARIAT & KONSTHANDEL, KORSGATAN 2, 41116 GÖTEBORG. Prop: S. Grauers. TN: 13 18 07. Spec: first editions (Swedish literature). fine arts; topography. CP: Göteborg 47061. S.A.F.

SETTERGARDS ANTIKVARIAT, BIRGER JARLSGATAN 44, STOCKHOLM-Ö. TN: 20 23 84. S.A.F.

THULIN & OHLSON, KUNGSGATAN 9B, 41119 GÖTEBORG. Prop: T. Ohlson. TN: 118974 and 118975. TA: Antiqva Göteborg. Established 1918. Shop. Very large stock. Spec: old Swedish children's books. 2 a year. Corresp: English. B: Skandinavska Banken, Bankgiro No. 500–2340. CP: Göteborg 124081. S.A.F.

THULINS ANTIKVARIAT, AB., 57060 ÖSTERBYMO. Prop: R. Du Rietz. TN: (0140) 83021. Very large stock. Spec: early printed; old science. Corresp: English, Français, Deutsch. S.A.F.

ANTIKVARIAT BLÅ TORNET, DROTTNINGGATAN 85, STOCKHOLM. Prop: Harald Hult. TN: 20 21 43 and 7673111 (private). Established 1967. Shop, early closing Saturday. Medium stock. Spec: old and rare books; old and new illustrated books. Corresp: English. CP: Stockholm 407158–5. S.A.F.

VARIA-ANTIKVARIAT, TIBBLE, LEKSAND. Prop. Gunnar Alfvén. TN: 62 76 83. Established 1943. Shop. Large stock. Corresp: English, Deutsch. B: Skandinaviska Banken, Account No. 57–5758. CP: Stockholm 55 28 36. S.A.F.

ALPHABETICAL LIST
LISTE ALPHABÉTIQUE
ALPHABETISCHE LISTE

ALPHABETICAL LIST

LISTE ALPHABÉTIQUE
ALPHABETISCHE LISTE

A

Aabenhus (A.) = Bøckmann's Antikvariat, Aarhus, Danmark.
A.B.C. der Boeken (Het), 142 Wagenstraat, 's-Gravenhage, Nederland.
Abheiter (Jos.), Wahringerstrasse 83, 1018 Wien, Österreich.
Abravanel (Ernest) = Librairie du Grand-Chêne, Aran, Suisse.
Academic Bookstore, Hippocratus Street 33, Athens, Ellas.
"Achille" di A. Misan (Libreria), Piazza Vecchia 4, 34121 Trieste, Italia.
Ackermann (Theodore), Promenadeplatz 11, 8 München, Deutschland.
Adler (Arno), Hüxstrasse 55, 24 Lübeck Deutschland.
Agostino (Libreris S.), Via S. Agostino 17/A, Roma, Italia.
Albert (Eberhard), Kaiser-Joseph-Strasse 179, 78 Freiburg, Deutschland.
Albizi (A. Degli), Piazza Duomo 22r, Firenze, Italia.
Alder (Robert), Junkerngasse 41, Bern, Schweiz.
Alessandria (Libreria), Via Alessandria 216/A, Roma, Italia.
Alfa Antiquarian Booksellers, P.O. Box 1116, Nijmegen, Nederland.
Alfvén (Gunnar) = Varia-Antikvariat, Stockholm, Sverige.
Alicke (Walter) = Interlibrum, Vaduz, Liechtenstein,
Allanegue (Herminia) = Libraria Mirto, Madrid, España.
Allegretti (Danilo), Viale Rosselli 17, 22100 Como, Italia.
Alpina (Libreria), Via Savioli 39/2, 40137 Bologna, Italia.
Amateurs de Livres (Aux), 62 avenue de Suffren, 75015 Paris, France.
Ambrosiana (Bottega), Via Vitruvio 47, 20124 Milano, Italia.
Amelang (Antiquariat) Cranachstrasse 45, 2 Hamburg 52, Deutschland.
Amis de la Musique S.P.R.L. (Les), Rue Dautzenberg 58, 1050 Bruxelles, Belgique.
Amis du Livre (Les), 9 Valaoritis Street, Athens 134, Ellas.
Andersen (Carl), Aboulevarden 60, 2200 København-N, Danmark.
Andersen (Kristian) = Bog-Borsen, København, Danmark.
Andersens Antikvariat (S.C.), Alhambravej 22, 1826 København-V, Danmark.
Andersson (Ake) = Libris Antikvariatet, Stockholm, Sverige.
Andersson (Eric Vilhelm) = Lengertz, Lund, Sverige.
André (Jean Pierre) = l'Homme de Fer, Nancy, France.
l'Ane d'Or, Boite Postale 6, 95450 Vigny, France.
Anglia English Bookshop, Schellingstrasse 3, 8 München 40, Deutschland.
Antikvariska Bokhandeln, AB., Gustaf Adolfs Torg 41, Malmö, Sverige.
Antiqua (Antiquariaat), Herengracht 159, Amsterdam, Nederland
Antiquariats-Buchhandlung, Friedrichstrasse 127, DDR-104 Berlin, und Münzstrasse 1, 102 Berlin, D.D.R.
Antonelli (Mme Henriette) = Librairie Celtique, Paris, France
Ardy (Libreria Giuridica), Piazza Sauli 4-2, 16123 Genova, Italia.
d'Argences (Librairie), 38 rue St.-Sulpice, 75006 Paris, France.
Argus Antiquarian Booksellers, Prof. Drionlaan 6, 2670 Baarn, Nederland.
Aristeucos (Libreria Anticuaria), Paseo de la Bonanova 14 G, Barcelona, España.

Armarium Buchhandlung und Antiquariat, Stresemannstrasse 4, 4 Düsseldorf, Deutschland.
Arnoul (Garnier), 39 rue de Seine, 75006 Paris, France.
l'Art Ancien, Signaüstrasse 6, 8008 Zürich, Schweiz.
l'Arte Antica, Via A. Volta 2, 10121 Torino, Italia.
Artigue (Ernest), 6 rue du Lorgues, 83 Toulon, France.
Arts et Lettres, Le Vieux Chateau, 83 Le Castellet, France.
Asher & Co. B.V., (A.), Zeizersgracht 526, Amsterdam, Nederland.
Aspingtons Antikvariat, AB, Drottninggatan 73 C, Stockholm, Sverige.
Athenaeum Antiquarian Booksellers, Keizersgracht 6008, 1002 Amsterdam, Nederland.
Auer (Adolf), Volgersweg 43/1, 3 Hannover-O, Deutschland.

B

Babendererde (Peter), Danziger Strasse 49, 24 Lübeck, Deutschland.
Bachelier (Pierre), 6 rue Neuve-des-Capucins, 44000 Nantes, France.
Bader (Winfried) = Heinrich Kerler, Ulm, Deutschland.
Baer (Alexandre), 2–6 rue Livingstone, 75018, Paris, France.
Balabanian (Emile), 3 rue de Cluny, 75005 Paris, France.
Bancarella (Libreria La), Via Cavour 119, Roma, Italia.
Banzi (Luigi), Via Borgonuovo 10, 40125 Bologna, Italia.
Barbier (Mme Gilberte Simone). 14 rue de l'Université, 75007 Paris, France.
Bardini (Libraria S.), Via XII Ottobre, 16121 Genova, Italia.
Bardon (Luis), Plaza de San Martin 3, Madrid, España.
Bärenreiter Antiquariat, Heinrich-Schütz-Allee 35, 35 Kassel-Wilhelmshöhe, Deutschland.
Barrera (Dott. Angelo) = Bottega d'Erasmo, Torino, Italia.
Baruch (Jacques) = Librairie-éditions Thanh-Long, Bruxelles, Belgique.
Bassenge (Galerie Gerda), Erdener Strasse 5 A, 1 Berlin 33, Deutschland.
Bassenge (Galerie Gerda), Kurfürstendamm 206, 1 Berlin 15, Deutschland.
Bataille (Paul), "Calendal", 14 rue Châteauredon, 13 Marseille, France
Bat d'Argent (Librairie du), 3 rue du Bat d'Argent, 69 Lyon, France.
Battaglini (Peppi) = Libreria di Piazza S. Babila, Milano, Italia.
Batlle y Tejedor (Angel), Calle de la Paja 23, Barcelone 2, España.
Baudon (Maurice), 27 due de Seine, 75006 Paris, France.
Beaufils (Fernand), avenue Victor-Hugo 169, 75016 Paris, France.
Becke & Sohn (A. von der), Widenmayerstrasse 43, 8 München 22, Deutschland.
Beck'sche Universitäts Buchhandlung, Währingerstrasse 12, 1009 Wien, Österreich.
Beer (Dr. M.) = Akademische Buchhandlung-Kuppitsch, Wien, Österreich.
Beijers, B.V. (J.L.), Achter Sint Pieter 14, Utrecht, Nederland.
Bellanger (A.), 5 place du Bon Pasteur, 44 Nantes, France.
Benecke (Hans) = Amelang, Hamburg, Deutschland.
Benjamins, B.V. (John), Amsteldijk 44, Amsterdam, Nederland.
Berès (Pierre), 14 avenue de Friedland, 75008 Paris, France.
Berès (Pierre) = Lucien Dorbon, Paris, France.
Berg Antiquariaat (Van), Oude Schans 8–10, Amsterdam, Nederland.
Bergensantikvariatet K.J. Tøsse, Store Markevei 8–10, Bergen, Norge.
Berger (Gertrud Iris), Finkenau 30, 2 Hamburg 76, Deutschland.
Berger (J.), Kohlmarkt 3, 1010 Wien, Österreich.

Berisio (Libreria Vincenzo), Via Medina 14, 80133 Napoli, Italia.
Berruto (Libreria), Via San Francesco da Paolo 10 bis, 10123 Torino, Italia.
Bertocchi (Libreria), Strada Maggiore 70, 40125 Bologna, Italia.
Bertocchi (Felice) = Libreria La Bancarella, Roma, Italia.
Beyer (Josef), Ahornweg 15, 5070 Bergish Gladbach, Deutschland.
Bezzina (Paul), 114 Saint Lawrence Street, Vittoriosa, Malta.
Bianchino del Leone (Libreria Antiquaria), Piazza Ansidei 4, 06100 Perugia, Italia.
Biblarte Limitada, Rua de Sao Pedro de Alcantara 71, Lisboa, Portugal.
Bibliofila (La), Corso Porta Nuova 2, 20121 Milano, Italia.
Bibliographicum, Hauptstrasse 194, 69 Heidelberg, Deutschland.
Bibliographikon (Das), Carmerstrasse 19, 1 Berlin-Charlottenberg 2, Deutschland.
Bickhardt'sche Buchhandlung, Karl-Marx-Strasse 168, 1 Berlin-Neukölln, Deutschland.
Bisey (Paul), 35 place de la Réunion, 68100 Mulhouse, France.
Bisterbosch (Leo), St. Luciensteeg 22, Amsterdam-C, Nederland.
Björck & Börjesson, Kungsgatan 5/II. Stockholm-C, Sverige.
Blackburn (Charles) = Europeriodiques, La Celle Saint-Cloud, France.
Blaizot, S.A. (Librairie August), 164 faubourg Saint-Honoré, 75008 Paris, France.
Blanc (Roger Le), = Quartier Latin, La Rochelle, France.
Blanchard (A.), 9 rue de Médicis, 76006 Paris, France.
Blancheteau (Marcel) = Aux Amateurs de Livres, Paris, France.
Blank (Herbert), Traubergstrasse 30, 7 Stuttgart, Deutschland.
Blå Tornet (Antikvariat), Drottninggatan 85, Stockholm, Sverige.
Bloch (Félix), 10 route de Rolle, 1162 Saint-Prex, Suisse.
Bloch (K.V.), Fiolstraede 34, 1171 København-K, Danmark.
B.M.C.F. Antiquariat, Langer Weg 35, 7901 Ulm-Gögglingen, Deutschland.
Bochumer Antiquariat G.m.b.H. & Co., K.G., Vosskuhlstrasse 74, 4630 Bochum-Stiepel, Deutschland.
Bøckmann's Antikvariat, Rosensgade 11, 8000 Aarhus-C, Danmark.
Bodo (Pierre H. Le), 31 rue de Bordeaux, 37 Tours, France.
Boeken, 34a Stationweg, 's-Gravenhage, Nederland.
Boerner (C.G.), Kasernenstrasse 14, 4 Düsseldorf, Deutschland.
Boerner (Frau Hilly) = Das Bibliographikon, Berlin, Deutschland.
Bog-Borsen, Studiestraede 10, 1455 København-K, Danmark.
Boghallens Antikvariat, Raadhuspladsen 37, 1585 København-V, Danmark.
Boghossian (Serge), 25 rue du Cherche-Midi, 75006 Paris, France.
Bog-Messen, Gammel Kongevej 19, 1610 København-V, Danmark.
Bolenz (Helmut), Türkenstrasse 48, 8 München, Deutschland.
Bolland (Ton), Prinsengracht 493, 1002 Amsterdam, Nederland.
Bolliger (Hans), Lenggstrasse 14, 8008 Zürich, Schweiz.
Boloukhère (J.) = Librairie de Galeries, Bruxelles, Belgique.
Bonaparte, S.A.R.L. (Librairie), 31 rue Bonaparte, 75006 Paris, France.
Bonfanti (Libreria), Via Macedonio Melloni 19, 20129 Milano, Italia.
Bonset (E. J.), Patrijzenstraat 8, Zandvoort, Nederland.
Bordes-Audineau (Danielle) = Livres et Revues de France Paris, France.
Børsums Forlag og Antikvariat, A.S., Fr. Nansens-plass 2, Oslo 1, Norge.
Borufka (Dr. Herbert) = A. L. Hasbach, Wien, Österreich.
Bosch (Antiquariaat Hieronymus), Spuistraat 125, Amsterdam, Nederland.
Botrini (G.) = Libreria Antiquaria M. T. Cicerone, Roma, Italia.
Bottin (André), Librairie Nicoise, 2 rue Défly, 06 Nice, France.

147

Bottin (Paul M.) = J. W. Cappelens Antikvariat, Oslo, Norge.
Boulinier (Paul), 20 boulevard Saint-Michel, 75006 Paris, France.
Bouma's Boekhuis, N.V., Turfsingel 3, Groningen, Nederland.
Bouquiniste (Le), Via Principe Amedeo 29, 10123 Torino, Italia.
Bourcy & Paulusch, Wipplingerstrasse 5, 1010 Wien, Österreich.
Bourdon, 75 rue de Rennes, 75006 Paris, France.
Bourdon (Robert), 184 bis route de Chateaudun, 45190 Beaugency, France.
Bourlot (Bice), Piazza Castello 9, Torino, Italia.
Bourlot (Libreria Antiquaria), Piazza San Carlo 183, 10123 Torino, Italia.
Bouvier Universitätsbuchhandlung G.m.b.H., Am Hof 32, 53 Bonn, Deutschland.
Bouwer (A.) = Cosmos Lochem, Nederland.
Brandes, o.H.G. (Wolfgang), Kleine Campestrasse 2, 33 Braunschweig, Deutschland.
Branners Bibliofile Antikvariat, Bredgade 10, 1260 København-K, Danmark.
Brasília (Livraria), Rua da Misericordia 79, Lisboa, Portugal.
Breinersdorf (Walther), Ebitzweg 7, 7 Stuttgart-Bad Cannstadt, Deutschland.
Brely (Pierre La), 108 rue du Ranelagh, 75016 Paris, France.
Bretonne (Librairie-Galerie), 1 rue des Fossés, 35000 Rennes, France.
Bridel, S.A. (Livres Anciens Maurice), 1 avenue du Théâtre, 1000 Lausanne, Suisse.
Brieux (Alain), 48 rue Jacob, 75006 Paris, France.
Brighenti (Libreria Antiquaria) Via Guido Reni 4, 40125 Bologna, Italia.
Brill, (E.J.), Oude Rijn 33 A, Leiden, Nederland.
Britschgi (Buchantiquariat), Rämistrasse 33, Zürich, Schweiz.
Brockhaus (F.A.), Kapplenstrasse 20, 7000 Stuttgart, Deutschland.
Broder (Louis), 187 boulevard Saint-Germain, 75006 Paris, France.
Broekema (Antiquariaat), 28 Titiaanstraat, Amsterdam, Nederland
Brugschen Eenhoorn (In den), Genthof 16, Brugge, Belgie.
Brumme (Galerie Siegfried), Braubachstrasse 34, 6 Frankfurt-am-Main, Deutschland.
Brumme (Siegfried), Kirschgarten 19, 65 Mainz, Deutschland.
Brun (Daniel), 6 rue Clodion, 75015 Paris, France.
Brun (Daniel), Edition et Diffusion M.P., 34 rue Serpente, 75006 Paris, France.
Brun (Pierre), 68 rue Carnot, 13 Pelissanne, France.
Bub (Herman E.), Kürschnerhof 7, Würzburg 2, Deutschland.
Bücherfass Antiquariat (Das), Muskauerstrasse 35, 1 Berlin 36, Deutschland.
Bücherkabinett (Das), Poststrasse 14, 2 Hamburg 36, Deutschland.
Bücherstube am Dom Hans Meyer & Co., Neumarkt 2, 5 Köln 1, Deutschland.

Bücherwurm, Schiffstrasse 16, 78 Freiburg, Deutschland.
Bücherwurm (Der), Motzstrasse 24, 1 Berlin 30, Deutschland.
Buffet (Claude), 7 rue Saint-Sulpice, 75006 Paris, France.
Burchard (Friedrich), Sonnbornerstrasse 144, 56 Wuppertal-Sonnborn, Deutschland.
Burgersdijk & Niermans, Nieuwsteeg 1, Leiden, Nederland.
Burollaud (Michel) = Galerie Vauquelin, Dieppe, France.
Busck (Arnold), Fiolstraede 24, 1171 København-K, Danmark.
Buzzanca (G.), Piazzetta Pedrocchi 4, 35100 Padova, Italia.
Bydgoski Antykwariat Naukowy "Dom Ksiazki", Stary Rynek 16, 85-105 Bydgoszcz, Polska.
Byens Antikvariat, Studiestraede 25, 1455 København-K, Danmark.

C

Cadéo de Iturbide (Mme. A.) = Arts et Lettres, Le Castellet, France.
Caffin, S.A. (Librairie Fernand), 80 rue Saint-Lazare, 75009 Paris, France.
Caillon (Marie & Reine), 10 rue Montault, 49 Angers, France.
Caldini (Libreria Internaz. C.), Via Tornabuoni 89–91 rosso, 50123 Firenze, Italia.
Camée (Librairie du), 3 rue de Valence, 75005 Paris, France.
Candide, 7 rue Montault 49000 Angers, France.
Cankarjeva Zalozba, Kopitarjeva 2, 61001 Ljubljana, Jugoslavija.
Cappelens Antikvariat (J.W.), Kirkegatan 15, Oslo 1, Norge.
Cariage (Jean Louis) = Bouquiniste Comtoise, Besançon, France.
Carpaneto (Luigi), Via Burlamacchi 31, 55100 Lucca, Italia.
Cartier (Raymond) = Cité des Vieux Livres, Besançon, France.
Casa de la Troya, Luna 21, Madrid, España.
Casella (Libreria Gaspare), Piazza Municipio 84, 80133 Napoli, Italia.
Cassini (Giocondo), San Marco 2424, 30124 Venezia, Italia.
Castaing (Michel) = Maison Charavay, Paris, France.
Castro e Silva (Livraria), Rua da Rosa 31, Lisboa, Portugal.
Cavelot (Fernand), 12 bis avenue des Govelins, 75005 Paris, France.
Cayla (Robert) 28 rue Saint-Sulpice, 75006 Paris, France.
Cazer (Henri), 49 rue de Seine. 75006 Paris, France.
Cederbergs Eftr. AB. (A.), Sysslomansgatan 8, 75223 Uppsala, Sverige.
Celtique (Librairie), 108 bis rue de Rennes, 75006 Paris, France.
Cerne (Carlo) = Umberto Saba, Trieste, Italia.
Chabaneix (Philippe), 33 rue Mazarine, 75006 Paris, France.
Chambefort (Librairie Ancienne), 26 place Bellecour, 69 Lyon, France.
Chamonal (François), 40 rue le Peletier, 75009 Paris, France.
Charavay (Maison), 3 rue de Furstenberg 75006 Paris, France.
Chariot d'Or (Librairie du), 38 rue des Remperts d'Ainay, 69002 Lyon, France.
Chartier (Madame) = Librairie du Bat d'Argent, Lyon, France.
Chauny (A.) = Librairie Duchemin, Paris, France.
Chauny & Quinsac, 18 rue Soufflot, 75005 Paris, France.
Chauvin (Georges), 78 rue Mazarine, 75006 Paris, France.
Chellini (Pietro) = Libreria Oreste Gozzini, Firenze, Italia.
Chertin (Denyse), 14 rue de Richelieu, 75001 Paris, France.
Chevalier (Louis) 176a rue Blaes, 1000 Bruxelles, Belgique.
Chezubina (Michetti) = Libreria S. Agostino, Roma, Italia.
Chiesa (Carlo Alberto), Via Bigli, 11, 20121 Milano, Italia.

Chmeljuk (Librairie I.), 1 rue de Fleurus, 75006 Paris, France.
Chrétien (Pierre), 178 faubourg Saint-Honoré, 75008 Paris, France.
Chrispeels (Carl F.), Combahnstrasse 15, 53 Bonn-Beuel 1, Deutschland.
Christensens Antikvariat (J.E.), L. Hammerichsvej 5, 8200 Aarhus, Danmark.
Christophé & Grothe (Antiquariat), Uhlandstrasse 50, 1 Berlin 15, Deutschland.
Cicerone (Libreria Antiquaria M.T.), Via Cicerone 39–41, 00193 Roma, Italia.
Cisneros (Librairie), 4 rue Charles-Marcel Pénard, 33 Bordeaux, France.
Cité des Vieux Livres, 139 Grande Rue, 25000 Besançon, France.
Clavreuil (Raymond), 37 rue Sainte André-des-Arts, 75006 Paris, France.
Clerc (Pierre), 13 rue Alexandre-Cabanel, 34000 Montpellier, France.
Coebergh (H.), Gedempte Oude Gracht 74, Haarlem, Nederland.
Coevorden (Antiquariaat Van), Varenstraat 41, Soest, Nederland.
Colas (Gaston), 84 boulevard Raspail, 75006 Paris, France.
Colas (Marcel), passage Agard, 13 Aix-en-Provence, France.
Colas (Pierre), 38 rue de Vaugirard, 75006 Paris, France.
Colliard (Jean), 11 rue Auguste-Comte, 69 Lyon, France.
Collin (Gerard) = Bouquinerie du Languedoc, Montpellier, France.
Comtoise (Bouquinerie), 9 rue Morand, 25 Besançon, France.
Conolly-Smith (David) = Anglia English Bookshop, München, Deutschland.
Conradt (Dr. Maria) = Das Bücherkabinett, 2 Hamburg, Deutschland.
Corradini (José), 18 rue Vineuse, 75016 Paris, France.
Cosmos Antiquarian Books, Kastanjelaan 3, 6570 Lochem, Nederland.
da Costa e Silva (José Maria) = Livraria Historica e Ultramarina, Lisboa, Portugal.
Costier (Mlle Andrée) = Les Amis de la Musique, Bruxelles, Belgique.
Cottet-Dumoulin (Maxime), 3 rue Séguier, 75006 Paris, France.
Coulet (Jean), 1 rue Dauphine, 75006 Paris, France.
Coulet & A. Faure (C.), 5 rue Drouot, 75006 Paris, France.
Cournand (Gilberte), 14 rue de Beaune, 75007 Paris, France.
Courval (M. de) = Librairie Scientifique Ancienne, Paris, France.
Courval (Michel de), 20 rue des Fossés-St.-Bernard, 75005 Paris, France.
Couturier (Madame), 7 rue de Duras, 75008 Paris, France.
Cramer (Galerie Gérald), 13 rue de Chantepoulet, Genève, Suisse.
Creyghton: Musicology-Musica Antiqua, Lassuslaan 45, Bilthoven, Nederland.
Crusius (Eugen), Karl-Marx-Strasse 15, 675 Kaiserslautern, Deutschland.
Cygne (Librairie du), 17 rue Bonaparte, 75006 Paris, France.

D

Dahlströms Antikvariat, A.B., Storgatan 31, Landskrona, Sverige.
Dallai (Libreria Antiquaria), Piazza de Marini 11, 16123 Genova, Italia.
Dam (Ole) = Boghallens Antikvariat, København, Danmark.
Dambournet (Maurice). l'Argus du Livre, 4 avenue Franklin-Roosevelt, 75008 Paris, France.
Damms Antikvariat, A/S., Tollbodgaten 25, Oslo 1, Norge.
Danigo (Henri), 17 rue Marc-Sangnier, 29000 Quimper, France.
Dargent (Ernest), 11 rue Alain-Blanchard, 76 Rouen, France.
Dasté (Francis), 16 rue de Tournon, 75006 Paris, France.
Davis (Madame Veuve Ronald), 12 avenue Franklin-Roosevelt, 75008 Paris, France.
Dawson-France, S.A., Zone Industrielle "La Prairie". 91121 Villebon-sur-Yvette, France.

Delatte (Max-Philippe), 133 rue de la Pompe, 75016 Paris, France
Dell'Impero (Libreria Antiquaria), Corso Rinascimento 63, 00186 Roma, Italia.
Delplace (Madame), 23 Boulevard de Waterloo, Bruxelles 1, Belgique.
Demelius (Dr. Christa) = V. A. Heck, Wien, Österreich.
Denis (Madame Leon), 50 rue de la Scellerie, 37 Tours, France.
Deny (Georges A.), rue du Chêne 5 1000 Bruxelles, Belgique.
Derryx (Mevrouw L.) = De Renaissance van het Boek, Gent, Belgique.
Deruelle (André), 30 rue des Saints-Pères, 75007 Paris, France.
Descombes (Paul), rue du Vieux-Collège, 6 1204 Gèneve, Suisse.
Deschamps (Jean), 22 rue Visconti, 75006 Paris, France.
"De Tille", Fa. Sipke Dykstra (Boekhandel en Antiquariat), Wirdumerdijk
    24–28, Leeuwarden, Nederland.
Deuticke (F.), Helferstorferstrasse 4, 1010 Wien, Österreich.
Deutsch (Harri), Graefstrasse 47, 6 Frankfurt-am-Main 3, Deutschland.
Dias & Andrade, Lda., Livraria Portugal, Rua do Carmo 70, Lisboa 2, Portugal.
Diepenbroick-Grüter, Haus Mark, 4542 Tecklenburg, Deutschland.
Dijk (W.C. Van), Burgwal 75, Kampen, Nederland.
Dirckinck-Holmfeld (H.), Aabenraa 29, 1124 København-K, Danmark.
Doblinger, K.G., (Ludwig), Dorotheergasse 10, 1010 Wien, Österreich.
"Docett", Via A. Righi 9/A, 40126 Bologna, Italia.
Domizlaff (Helmuth), Martiusstrasse 5/II, 8 München, Deutschland.
Dommergues (Marcel), 23 rue des Écoles, 75005 Paris, France.
Domsch & C., Viale Milton 73, Firenze, Italia.
Dorbon (Lucien), 156 boulevard Saint-Germain, 75006 Paris, France.
Dorbon-Aine (Librairie), 19 boulevard Haussmann, 75009 Paris, France.
Dörling (F.), Neuer Wall, 2 Hamburg 36, Deutschland.
Dotti (Libreria), Via Della Scrofa 58, 00186 Roma, Italia.
Dresdener Antiquariat, Bautzner Strasse 27, 806 Dresden, D.D.R.
Drewsen (Gertrude), Fredensgade 16, 2200 København-N, Danmark
Drincken (Klaus von), Theresienstrasse 56, 8 München 2, Deutschland.
Dubouchet (Librairie), 2 rue Général Foy, 42 Saint-Étienne, France.
Duchemin (Librairie), 18 rue Soufflot, 75005 Paris, France.
Duponchelle (Librairie), 27 rue Marazarine, 75006 Paris, France.
Dupont (A.) = Librairie-Galerie Ancienne et Moderne, Lille, France.
Dupont (Henri), 141 boulevard de la Liberté, 59000 Lille, France.
Durance (Galerie), 5 allée d'Orléans, 44000 Nantes, France.
Du Rietz (R.) = Thulins Antikvariat, Österbymo, Sverige.
Durtal (Chez), 12 rue Jacob, 75006 Paris, France.
Dussarp (Maurice), 36 rue du Mont Thabor, 75001 Paris, France.
Dykstra (S.G.) = Antiquariat "De Tille", Leeuwarden, Nederland.

E

Early Newspapers = L.M.C. Nierynck, Vlissingen, Nederland.
Ebbel (Rudolf), Schüttingstrasse 7, 29 Oldenburg, Deutschland.
Edelmann (M.), Breitgasse 52, 85 Nürnberg 1, Deutschland.
Edi-Centre J.-P. Krippler-Muller, 17 rue Gibraltar, Luxembourg.
Eggert (Fritz), Felix Dahn Strasse 53, 7 Stuttgart, Deutschland.
Elchlepp (Alice), Schillerstrasse 14, 3360 Osterode a. Harz, Deutschland.
Elek (Librairie), 21 rue Saint-Jacques, 75005 Paris, France.
Elte (Antiquariaat Meijer), Korte Poten 13, 's-Gravenhage, Nederland.

Eluard-Valette (Cécile), 43 avenue de la Dame-Blanche, 94120 Fontenay-sous-Bois, France.
Elwert Universitätsbuchhandlung (N.G.), Reitgasse 7–9, 355 Marburg (Lahn), Deutschland.
Emmering (S.), N.Z. Voorburgwal 304, Amsterdam, Nederland.
Encyclopedique (Librairie), rue du Luxembourg 40, 1040 Bruxelles, Belgique.
Engelberts (Galerie), 11 Grand Rue, 1204 Genève, Suisse.
Engholst (Frede), Studiesstraede 35, 1455 København-K, Danmark.
Eppe (Paul), 49 rue de Provence, 75009 Paris, France.
d'Erasmo (Bottega), Via Gaudenzio Ferrari 9, 10124 Torino, Italia.
Erasmus Antiquariaat en Boekhandel, Spui 2, Amsterdam, Nederland.
Erdmann (Axel) = Gilhofer & Ranschburg, Luzern, Schweiz.
Erpf (Martha) = Julius Weise's Hofbuchhandlung, Stuttgart, Deutschland.
Esslingen (Kunstgalerie), Grünerweg 17, 73 Esslingen, Deutschland.
l'Europe (Librairie de), 1 Val des Roses, 1000 Bruxelles, Belgique .
Europeriodiques, S.A., 31 avenue de Versailles, 78170 La Celle Saint-Cloud, France.
Evers (Alfonso) = Goecke & Evers, Krefeld, Deutschland.

F

Fach, O.H.G., (Joseph), Krögerstrasse 2, 6 Frankfurt-am-Main, Deutschland.
Faculté des Sciences (Librairie de la), 12 rue Pierre et Marie Curie, 75005, Paris, France.
Fauron (Michel), 10 bis rue de Chateaudun, 75009 Paris, France.
Favereaux (Emile), 19 rue de l'Hôpital-Militaire, 59000 Lille, France.
Ferhadian (Gérard), 36 rue Montholon, 75009 Paris, France.
Férin (Livraria), Rue Nova do Almada 74, Lisboa, Portugal.
Ferreira (Manuel), Rua Formosa 19, Porto, Portugal.
Feucht (Rainer G.) = B.M.C.F. Antiquariat, Ulm, Deutschland.
Fiammenghi (Banco Libri di), Via Marsala 6, 40126 Bologna, Italia.
Fiammenghi (Libreria C.), Via Malcontenti 11, 40126 Bologna, Italia.
Fiammenghi (Maria) = Garisenda Libri, Bologna, Italia.
Fiera del Libro (La), Via Marconi 2, 6900 Lugarno, Italia.
Fillet (Louis), 13 rue de Boigne, 73 Chambéry, France.
Fink (Eduard), Metzgergasse 18, 3400 Burgdorf, Schweiz.
Finzi (Luigi), Foro Buonaparte 12, 20121 Milano, Italia.
Fiol (Libreria M.), Olmos 119-A, Palma de Mallorca, España.
Fiorentino (Libreria Fausto), Calata Trinita Maggiore 36, 80134 Napoli, Italia.
Fischer (Paul & Arthur), Haldenstrasse 19, 6006 Luzern, Schweiz.
Flammarion (Librairie), 4 rue Casimir Delavigne, 75006 Paris, France.
Fleury (Gérard), Librairie François ler, 34 avenue Montaigne, 75008 Paris, France.
Fluhrer (Erwin), Weisensteigerstrasse 17, 7340 Geislingen/Steige, Deutschland.
Flumen Dantis di P. Zali (Libreria), Piazza Mazzini 12/1, 16043 Chivari (Genova), Italia.
Fog Musikantikvariat (Dan), Graabrødre Torv 7, 1154 Kobenhavn-K, Danmark.
Fornbokaverzlun Kristjanssonar, Hverfisgotu 26, Reykjavík, Island.
Fornbokverzlunin, Klapperstig 37, Reykjavík, Island.
Forsten (B. & E.) = Bouma's Bokhuis, Groningen, Nederland.
Fouineur (Librairie le), 34 rue Vivienne, 75002 Paris, France.
Fournier & Cie (Jean), 22 rue du Bac, 75007 Paris, France.
Frachon (Jacqueline) = Librairie de Montbel, Paris, France.

Francheville (Klaus von), Marktstrasse 45, 3 Hannover, Deutschland.
Franco (Mrs. N.A.) = J.L. Beijers, Utrecht, Nederland.
Frankfurter Bücherstube, Börsenstrasse 2–4, 6 Frankfurt-am-Main, Deutschland.
Frankfurter Kunstkabinett, Hanna Bekker vom Rath, G.m.b.H., Börsenplatz 13–15, 6 Frankfurt-am-Main, Deutschland.
Frederiksberg Antikvariat, Gammel Kongevej 120, 1850 København-V, Danmark.
Fricke Versand-und Antiquariats Buchhandlung (Roberte), Hardenbergplatz 13, 1 Berlin 12, Deutschland.
Friedländer & Sohn (R.), Nonnendammallee 92-f, 1 Berlin 13, Deutschland.
Friemel (Franz), Gablenzgasse 4, 1160 Wien, Österreich.
"Friso" Antiquariat, Hoofdstraat 5, 9064 Grouw, Nederland.
Fritsch (Antiquariat), Postfach 1830, 79 Ulm/Donau, Deutschland.
Fritsche (Rüdiger) = Antiquariat Paul Hennings, Hamburg, Deutschland.
Fuchs (Antiquariat Günter), Cranachplatz 1, 4 Düsseldorf, Deutschland.
Fuchs & Reposo, Librairie Wega, Via Nassa 21, 6900 Lugano, Suisse.
Funck (Neue Bücherstube R.), Kennedy-Platz 5, 43 Essen, Deutschland.
Fundgruber (Die Bücher), 24 Wahringerstrasse, Wien 9, Österreich.

G

Gabinetto delle Stampe (Il), Via Montenapoleone 3, 20121 Genova, Italia.
Galantaris (Christian), 11 rue de Vaugirard, 75006 Paris, France.
Gallimard (Librairie), 15 boulevard Raspail, 75007 Paris, France.
Gallini (Natale), Via Del Conservatorio 17, 20122 Milano, Italia.
Gammeltorvs Antikvariat, Gammel Torv 8, 1457 København-K, Danmark.
Gangloff (Louis), 20 place de la Cathédrale, 67000 Strasbourg, France.
Gangloff (Librairie), 13 avenue Auguste-Wicky, 68100 Mulhouse, France.
Garisenda Libri & Stampe, Strada Maggiore 14/A, 40125 Bologna, Italia.
Gendt & Co. N.V. (A.L. Van), Keizersgracht 610, Amsterdam, Nederland.
Gerlinghaus (Karl), Weilhelm Leuchnerstrasse 10, 652 Worms, Deutschland.
Gerold & Co., Graben 31, 1011 Wien, Österreich.
Gerritsen (H.G.), Van Welderenstraat 88, Nijmegen, Nederland.
Gess (Karl), Kanzleistrasse 5, 7750 Konstanz, Deutschland.
Geuthner (Librairie Orientaliste Paul), 12 rue Vavin, 75006 Paris, France.
Geyer (H.), Hofmühlgasse 14, Wien 6, Österreich.
Gibert Jeune, 23 quai Saint-Michel, 75005 Paris, France.
Gilhofer Buch- und Kunstantiquariat, K.G., Bognergasse 2, 1010 Wien, Österreich.
Gilhofer & Ranschburg G.m.b.H., Haldenstrasse 9, 6006 Luzern, Schweiz.
Gilsing (Heinrich), Kaiserstrasse 3, 8205 Kiefersfelden, Deutschland.
Girand (François), 76 rue de Seine, 75006 Paris, France.
Girard (Pierre), 17 rue de Chateaudun 75009 Paris, France.
Giraud-Badin (Librairie), 128 boulevard Saint-Germain, 75006 Paris, France.
Giron (Librairie), 4 rue Trois-Ecritoire, 37 Tours, France.
Glogau (M.), Bleichenbrücke 6, 2 Hamburg 36, Deutschland.
Godai (H.), Mariahilferstrasse 169, 1150 Wien, Österreich.
Godai (Leo), Talgasse 11, Wien 1015, Österreich.
Goecke & Evers, Dürerstrasse 13, 415 Krefeld, Deutschland.
Goetz (Hans von), Wörthstrasse 28, 62 Wiesbaden, Deutschland.
Goldau (Gerhard), Gasteigweg 4, 8022 Grünwald, Deutschland.
Goldschmidt (Dr. Hans Eberhard), Döblinger Hauptstrasse 61, Wien 19, Österreich.

154

Gonnelli & Figli (Luigi), Via Ricasoli 14, Firenze, Italia.
Gonot (René), Librairie Saint-Augustin, 99 boulevard Haussmann, 75008 Paris, France.
Gonot (Librairie), 22 rue de Miromesnil, 75008 Paris, France.
Gordin (Antikvariat), Nylandsgatan 11, 00120 Helsingfors 12, Suomi.
Gosselin (Jean), 4 rue Alain-Blanchard, 76 Rouen, France.
Gothier (Fernand), Librairie Universitaire, place du 20 Août 11, 4000 Liège, Belgique.
Gothier (Paul), Rue Bonne Fortune 3, Liege, Belgique.
Goumy (Robert), 6 bis rue de Chateaudun, 75009 Paris, France.
Gozzini (Libreria Oreste di Pietro Chellini), Via Ricasoli 49, 50122 Firenze, Italia.
Graaf (Antiquariaat De), Zuideinde 40, Nieuwkoop, Nederland.
Granata (Libreria), Reyes Catolicos 8, Almeria, España.
Grand-Chêne (Librairie du), 1603 Aran, Suisse.
Grandmaison (Antoine), Librairie "Les Arcades", 8 rue de Castiglione, 75001 Paris, France.
Grasel (M. & L.), Währingerstrasse 41, Wien 1009, Österreich.
Grauers (S.) = Samlaren Antikvariat, Göteborg, Sverige.
Grenier du Collectionneur (Le), avenue Orban 238, 1150 Bruxelles, Belgique.
Grifoni (G.C.), Via Emilia Levante 13, 40139 Bologna, Italia.
Grimmer (Madame Antoine) 15 rue Dupont des Loges, 75007 Paris, France.
Gross (Erich) = Rolf Kerst, Göttingen, Deutschland.
Grosser (Ernst), Rebbachstrasse 11, 7987 Weingarten (Württemberg), Deutschland.
Grothe (Regina) = Christophé und Grothe, Berlin, Deutschland.
Grubb's Antikvariat (J.), Nørregade 47, København-K, Danmark.
Grundmann (Herbert) = Bouvier G.m.b.H., Bonn, Deutschland.
Grüner, B.V. (B.R.), Nieuwe Herengracht 31, Amsterdam-C, Nederland.
Gsellius'sche Buch-, Antiquar- und Globehandlung, G.m.b.H., Hertastrasse 16, 1 Berlin 37, Deutschland.
Guedes Da Silva (P.), Livraria Academica, Rua Martires da Liberdade 8–12, Porto, Portugal.
Guénégard (Librairie), 10 rue de l'Odéon, 75006 Paris, France.
Guilde (La), 18 rue de Turbigo, 75002 Paris, France.
Guillaume & Cie, S.A.R.L. (Michel), 98 rue Saint-Pierre, 14 Caen, France.
Guillaume (Madame) = La Maison du Livre, Angoulême, France.
Guille (Jean) = Librairie Dorbon-Ainé, Paris, France.
Gumbert (H.L.) = J.L. Beijers, Utrecht, Nederland.
Gumz (K.) = La Guilde, Paris, France.
Günther (Max), Charlottenbrunnerstrasse 5a, 1 Berlin 33, Deutschland.
Gustafsson (J.), Volden 12, 8000 Aarhus-C, Danmark.
Gute Buch (Das), Rosengasse 10, 8001 Zürich, Schweiz.
Gutenberg (Johannes), Grosse Bleiche 29, 65 Mainz, Deutschland.
Guyer-Halter (Dr. Annemarie), Auf der Mauer 1, 8000 Zurich, Schweiz.
Gysbers en Van Loon, Bakkerstraat 7a, Arnhem, Nederland.

H

Haas, oHG, (Else), Dollstrasse 7, 807 Ingolstadt 21, Deutschland.
Habelt (Dr. Rudolf), G.m.b.H., Am Buchenhang 1, 53 Bonn 5, Deutschland.
Hachette, 58 rue Jean-Bleuzen, 92170 Vanves, France.
Hagelin (O.A), Tegnergatan 14, 11358 Stockholm, Sverige.

Hagen (B.), Herengracht 26, 1002 Amsterdam, Nederland.
Hakansson (Cecilia) = H. Mellgrens, Göteborg, Sverige.
Hakkert, B.V. (Adolf M.), Supuistraat 90/A, Amsterdam, Nederland.
Halbart, Wahle & Cie, Rue des Carmes 11, 4000 Liège, Belgique.
Halosar (Karl M.), Margaretenstrasse 35, 1040 Wien, Österreich.
Hamburgensien-Meyer, Poststrasse 2–4, 2 Hamburg 36, Deutschland.
Hamecher (Horst), Goethestrasse 74, 35 Kassel, Deutschland.
Hamel (George C.), Brandenburgerstrasse 74, 1 Berlin 31, Deutschland.
Hampartz (Edouard), 90 rue de Levis, 75017 Paris, France.
Hankard (Jean-Jacques), 25 rue de la Paix, 1050 Bruxelles, Belgique.
Hankard Librairie, S.P.R.L. (Victor), 27 rue de la Madeleine, Bruxelles 1, Belgique.
Hannmann (Heinz) = Der Bücherwurm, Berlin, Deutschland.
Hanselaar (Hans J.) = Antiquariaat Minerva, 's-Gravenhage, Nederland.
Harcks Antikvariat, Fiolstraede 33, 1171 København-K, Danmark.
Harrassowitz, Taunusstrasse 5, 62 Wiesbaden, Deutschland.
Hartinger (Hans), Xantener Strasse 14, 1 Berlin 15, Deutschland.
Hartung (Karl) = Karl und Faber, München, Deutschland.
Hartung & Karl, Karolinenplatz 5a, 8 München 2, Deutschland.
Hasbach (A.L.), Wollzeile 9 & 29, Wien 1, Österreich.
Hase (August), Im Trutz 2, 6 Frankfurt-am-Main, Deutschland.
Haus der Bücher, A.G., "Erasmushaus", Bäumleingasse 18, Basel, Schweiz.
Hauser (Elsa), Schellingstrasse 17, 8 München 13, Deutschland.
Hauswedell (Dr. Ernst) & Nolte (Ernst), Pöseldorferweg 1, 2 Hamburg 23, Deutschland.
Hébraica Judaica (Société), 12 rue des Hospitalières St.-Gervais, 75004 Paris, France.
Heck (V.A.), Kärntner Ring 12, 1010 Wien, Österreich.
Heckenhauer (J.J.), Holzmarkt 5, 74 Tübingen, Deutschland.
Heckenhauer-Sonnewald, Waldhof 1, 7947 Mengen, Deutschland.
Heger (Rudolf), Wollezeile 2, 1010 Wien, Österreich.
Hegnauer (Eduard), Kramgasse 16, 3000 Bern, Schweiz.
Heidrich (Leopold), Plankengasse 7, Wien 1, Österreich.
Heilbrun (Georges), 3 rue Gît-le-Coeur, 75006 Paris, France.
Hainemann (Gerhard) = Hans Raunhardt, Zürich, Schweiz.
Heitz (P.H.), Postfach 80, 4006 Basel, Schweiz.
"Hemus", 11 Slaveikov Square, Sofia, Bulgariya.
Hennebert (Paul), 44 rue de Turbigo, 75003 Paris, France.
Henning (Jürgen) = Bochumer Antiquariat, Bochum, Deutschland.
Hennings (Antiquariat Paul), Altstädter Strasse 15, 2 Hamburg 1, Deutschland.
Henrich (Wilhelm), Schumannstrasse 57, 6 Frankfurt-am-Main, Deutschland.
Herbinet (Jacques), 39 rue de Constantinople, 75008 Paris, France.
Hertzberger (Menno), Eemnesserweg 81, Baarn, Nederland.
Hesperia (Libreria), Plaza Lose Antonio 10, Zaragoza, España.
Hessling (Bruno), Rankestrasse 31–32, 1 Berlin 30, Deutschland.
Heybutzki (Werner), Pfeilstrasse 8, 5 Köln, Deutschland.
Hiard (Bernard) = L'Intermédiare du Livre, Paris, France.
Hildebrandt (Helmut) = Struppe und Winckler, Berlin, Deutschland.
Hill (Theo), Schildergasse 107, 5 Köln, Deutschland.
Heinrich Hinterberger, Hegelgasse 17 Mezz., Wien 1001, Österreich.
Historica e Ultramarina (J.C. Silva), Travessa da Queimada 28, Lisboa 2, Portugal.
Hobbeling (Theo) = Th. Stenderhoff & Co., Münster, Deutschland.

Höchterberger (Hans), Elsenheimerstrasse 18, 8 München 21, Deutschland.
Hoeter (Frédéric Van), 61 rue Saint-Quentin, Bruxelles 4, Belgique.
Höfels, OHG., (Oskar), Seilerstätte 18, 1010 Wien, Österreich.
Hoffmann (Ernst), Weissadlergasse 3, 6 Frankfurt-am-Main, Deutschland.
Hoffman (R.) = Gilhofer Buch- und Kunstantiquariat, Wien, Österreich.
Hofmann (Wilhelm), Bismarckstrasse 98, 67 Ludwigshafen, Deutschland.
Holler (Hildgund) = Journalfranz Arnulf Liebing, Würzburg, Deutschland.
Höllrigl (Eduard), Sigmund-Haffner-Gasse 10, 5020 Salzburg, Österreich.
Holms Antikvariat (Greta), Norrlandsgatan 16, Stockholm-C, Sverige.
Holstein (Jürgen), Gerichtsstrasse 7a, 6240 Königstein, Deutschland.
Hölzl, K.G. (Karl), Seilergasse 3, 1010 Wien, Österreich.
l'Homme de Fer, 32 rue des Dominicains, 54000 Nancy, France.
Horodisch (Dr. A) = Erasmus Antiquariaat, Amsterdam, Nederland.
Høst & Søn, (Andr. Fred.), Bredgade 35, 1260 København-K, Denmark.
Houssais (Jacques), rue Jean Nicot, 75007 Paris, France.
Houthakker (Bernard), Rokin 98, Amsterdam, Nederland.
Hovingh & Zn. (Antiquariat C.), Kleine Houtstraat 50, Haarlem, Nederland.
Huetz de Lemps (J.), 70 rue du Cherche-Midi, 75006 Paris, France.
Hugendubel (H.), Salvatorplatz 2, 8 München, Deutschland.
Hugues (Jean), 1 rue de Furstenberg, 75006 Paris, France.
l'Huillier (Madame), 24 rue de la Cloche Verte, 17 Angouléme, France.
Huizenga (M.L.), O.Z. Achterburgwal 156, Amsterdam, Nederland.
Hult (Harald) = Bla Tornet, Stockholm, Sverige.
Hults Antikvariat, Grevturegatan 18, Stockholm, Sverige.

I

Iberia (Antiquariat), Hirschengraben 6, Bern, Schweiz.
Ieri (Libri di), Casella Postale 524, 50100 Firenze, Italia.
"Il Defino" (Libreria), Via Cesare Battisti 19/A, 10123 Torino, Italia.
l'Imageria (À), 9 rue Dante, 75005 Paris, France.
Interlibrum Establishment, Schloss-Strasse 6, 9490 Vaduz, Liechtenstein.
l'Intermédiaire du Livre, 88 rue Bonaparte, 75006 Paris, France.
l'Invitation au Voyage, 15 quai Saint-Michel, 75005 Paris, France.
Israel, N.V. (B.M.), N.Z. Voorburgwal 264, Amsterdam, Nederland.
Israel (N.), Keizersgracht 526, Amsterdam, Nederland.
Israel (Nico) = A. Asher & Co., Amsterdam, Nederland.

J

Jamin (Anneliese) = Ed. Walz, München, Deutschland.
Jammes (Paul), 3 rue Gozlin, 75006 Paris, France.
Janicot (François), 32 avenue Niel, 75017 Paris, France.
Jansson (G.) = Lilla Antikvariatet, Malmö, Sverige.
Jardin des Collectionneurs (Au), 130 boulevard Murat, 75016 Paris, France.
Javelle (Claude), 32 rue de Provence, 75009 Paris, France.
Jean-Léo = Le Grenier du Collectionneur, Bruxelles, Belgique.
Jehanno (Xavier), 12 place Budapest, 75009 Paris, France.
Jehanno (Xavier), 4 place de l'Église, 78 Louveciennes, France.
Johanson-Thor, AB., (Gunnar), Hallsfarm, 24100 Eslöv, Sverige.
Joly (J.), 6 rue Victor-Cousin, 75005 Paris, France.
Jones Antikvariat, Norrlandsgatan 3, Stockholm, Sverige.

Jongbloed (K.P.) = Juridisch Antiquariaat, 's-Gravenhage, Nederland.
"Journal Franz" Arnulf Liebing, Werner von Siemans-strasse 5, 87 Würzburg 2, Deutschland.
Juhel-Douet (Jean), 3 rue d'Angleterre, 41 Blois, France.
Junk, Dr. R. Schierenberg & Sons, B.V. (Antiquariaat), Walderstraat 10, Lochem, Nederland.
Juridisch Antiquariaat, Laan van Meerdervoort 45, 's-Gravenhage, Nederland.

K

Kaabers Antikvariat, Skindergade 34, 1159 København-K, Danmark.
Kampintorin Antikvariaatti, Fredrikinkatu 63, Helsinki, Suomi.
Kaplanski (Boris), 8 rue du Loing, 75014 Paris, France.
Kapp (Adolf), Bahnhofstrasse 17, 7407 Rottenburg, Deutschland.
Karl & Faber, Karolinenplatz 5A, 8 München 2, Deutschland.
Karl-Marx-Buchhandlung (Antiquariat der), Karl-Marx-Allee 78–84, 1017 Berlin, D.D.R.
Karlstad Antikvariat, Östra Torggatan 1, Karlstad, Sverige.
Karsch (Florian) = Galerie Nierendorf, Berlin, Deutschland.
Katzbichler (Dr. Emil), 8210 Giebing Post Prien, Deutschland.
Kauffmann (Librairie), 28 Stadium Street, Athens 132, Ellas.
Keip (Ferdinand), Hainerweg 46, 6 Frankfurt-am-Main, Deutschland.
Kerler (Heinrich), Platzgasse 26, 7900 Ulm, Deutschland.
Kerssemakers (Leo J.II.) = Alfa Antiquariaat, Nijmegen, Nederland.
Kerssemakers (P.H.) = Hieronymus Bosch, Amsterdam, Nederland.
Kerst (Rolf), Maustrasse 16/17, 34 Göttingen, Deutschland.
Keskustan Antikvariaatti, 1 Yrjönkatu, Helsinki, Suomi.
Ketterer (Galerie Wolfgang), Prinzregentenstrasse 60, Villa Stuck, 8 München 80, Deutschland.
Kieffer (Librairie René), 46 rue Saint-André des Arts, 75006 Paris, France.
Kienreich (Jos. A.), Sackstrasse 6, 8011 Graz, Österreich.
Kiepert, K.G., Hardenbergstrasse 4–5, 1 Berlin 12, Deutschland.
Kirjakuja, Ky. Uudenmaankatu 4–6, Helsinki, Suomi.
Kirkop (Frank), 106 Blanche Street, Sliema, Malta.
Kistner (Erwin & Rolf), Breite Gasse 52–54, 85 Nürnberg, Deutschland.
Kistner (Erwin) = M. Edelmann, Nürnberg, Deutschland.
Kitzinger (J.), Schellingstrasse 25, 8 München 13, Deutschland.
Klaussner (Antiquariat), Professor-Kurt-Huber-Strasse 19, 8032 Gräfelfing (München), Deutschland.
Kleinert (Rudolf), Rüdesheimer Strasse 21, 62 Wiesbaden, Deutschland.
Klerstam (Sven) = Skakhuset, København, Danmark.
Klihm (Galerie), Franz-Joseph-Strasse 9, 8 München 13, Deutschland.
Klügel (Walter), Gumpendorferstrasse 33, 1060 Wien, Österreich.
Knagsteds Antikvariat, Kompagnistraede 8, 1208 København-K, Danmark.
Knapps (Gertrud) = Max Günther, Berlin, Deutschland.
Knigi (Antikvarni), 19 Ulitsa Graf Ignatiev, Sofia, Bulgariya.
Kniha, Malé Námesti No. 11, Praha 1, Ceskoslovensko.
Knizní Velkoobchod n.p., 65 Stepánská, Praha 2, Ceskoslovenko.
Knödler (Karl), Katharinenstrasse 8–10, 7410 Reutlingen, Deutschland.
Knuf (Antiquariaat Fritz), P.O. Box 20, 2707 Buren, Nederland.
Köbelin (Rainer), Amalienstrasse 53, 8 München 40, Deutschland.

Koch (Hans Horst), Hauptstrasse 7–8, 1 Berlin 62, Deutschland.
Koch (Hans) = Jacques Rosenthal, Eching, Deutschland.
Kocher-Benzing (Dr. F.) = Stuttgarter Antiquariat, Stuttgart, Deutschland.
Koeltz (Otto), Herrnwaldstrasse 6, 624 Königstein-Taunus, Deutschland.
Koerner, G.m.b.H. (Valentin), Iberststrasse 36, 757 Baden-Baden, Deutschland.
Koerner (Valentin), Yburgstrasse 36, 757 Baden-Baden, Deutschland.
Kohl (Josef A.) = Johannes Gutenberg, Mainz, Deutschland.
Kohlhauer (Carl-Ernst), Graser Weg 2, 8805 Feuchtwangen, Deutschland.
Kohlhoff (Friedrich), Holzweg 14/I, 637 Oberursel, Deutschland.
Kohls (Albert), Winterfeldstrasse 44, 1 Berlin 30, Deutschland.
Kok (A.), 4 & 11 Hoogstraat, Amsterdam, Nederland.
Kolb (Otto), Bahnhofstrasse 3/I, 8673 Rehau, Deutschland.
König (Anton), Josefstäderstrasse 71, Wien 1008, Österreich.
Koolemans (C.), Willemsparkweg 164, Amsterdam, Nederland.
Korn & Berg (Universitätsbuchhandlung), Hauptmarkt 9, 85 Nürnberg, Deutsch-
    land.
Kornfeld & Klipstein, Paupenstrasse 49, Bern, Schweiz.
Krebser & Co. (M.), Bälliz/Bahnhofbrücke, 3600 Thun, Schweiz.
Kremers (P.F.), Commelinstraat 52, Amsterdam, Nederland.
Kreuschner (Harri) = R. Friedländer & Sohn, Berlin, Deutschland.
Krey (R.), Graben 13, 1010 Wien, Österreich.
Krippler (J.-P.) = Edi-Centre, Luxembourg.
Krieg (Walter), Kärtnerstrasse 4, 1010 Wien, Österreich.
Krohn (Kurbuchhandlung & Antiquariat B.), Kaiserstrasse 10, 7847 Badenweiler,
    Deutschland.
Krohn (Dr. Luise), Hussenstrasse 18, 775 Konstanz, Deutschland.
Kubiak (Günther), Martin-Luther-Strasse 127, 1 Berlin 62, Deutschland.
Kühn (Carlos) = Carl Wegner, Berlin, Deutschland.
Kuipers (J.) = Van Stockum's Antiquariaat, 's-Gravenhage, Nederland.
Kullmann (Hermann) = "Armarium" Buchhandlung, Düsseldorf, Deutschland.
Kultura, P.O. Box 149, Budapest 62, Magyarország.
Kunstantiquariat am Rathaus, Niederwall 14, 48 Bielefeld, Deutschland.
Kuhrdt (Wilhelm), Paulusstrasse 28, 48 Bielefeld, Deutschland.
Kungl, Hovbokhandel (Fritzes), Fredsgatan 2, Stockholm 16, Sverige.
Kuppitsch (Akademische Buchhandlung), Schottenring 8, Wien, Österreich.
Kurth (Detlev), Am Markt 24, 2202 Barmstedt, Deutschland.
Kury & Co., Landstrasse Hauptstrasse 33, Wien 3, Österreich.
Kutsch (Wlh.), Am Dom/Hauotbahnhof, 5 Köln 1, Deutschland.
Kuttner (Walter), 5620 Velbert, Deutschland.

L

Labarre (C.F.), 22 rue Dauphine, 75006 Paris, France.
Lafitte (Jeanne), 106 boulevard Longchamp, 13001 Marseille, France.
Lafitte (J.B.), 13 rue de Buci, 75006 Paris, France.
Laffont (Librairie), 58 rue de Babylone, 75007 Paris, France.
Laget (Librairie Leonce), 75 rue de Rennes, 75006 Paris, France.
Lambert (Jacques), Librairie de l'Abbaye, 27 rue Bonaparte, 75006 Paris, France.
Lammens (Charles) = Librairie a Rombaut, Gand, Belge.
Lamongie (Georges), 2 rue de la Nation, 24 Perigueux, France.
Lang & Cie, A.G. (Herbert), Munzgraben 2, 3000 Bern, Schweiz.
Lange & Springer, Heidelbergerplatz 3, 1 Berlin 33, Deutschland.

Languedoc (Bouquinerie du), 12 rue de l'Université, 34000 Montpellier, France.
Lapiccirella (Leonardo), Lungarno Vespucci 18, 50123 Firenze, Italia.
Larchon (Librairie), 18 rue des Fossés-Saint-Jacques, 75005 Paris, France.
Lardanchet (Librairie), 100 rue de Faubourg Saint-Honoré, 75008 Paris, France.
Lardanchet (Librairie), 10 rue Président Carnot, 69002 Lyon, France.
Lassare (Edmond), 1 bis rue de la Chaise, 75007 Paris, France.
Laube & Sohn (August), Trittligasse 19, 8001 Zürich, Schweiz.
Laucournet (Marcel), 45 boulevard Carnot, 87000 Limoges, France.
Lecomte (Marcel), 17 rue de Seine, 75006 Paris, France.
Leconte (Louis), 73 rue des Saints-Pères, 75006 Paris, France.
Lefebvre (Jean-Louis), 73550 Méribel-les-Allues, France.
Legouix (Robert), 4 rue Chaveau-Lagarde, 75008 Paris, France.
Legrand (Madame J), 48 rue du Mail, 49 Angers, France.
Legueltel (Librairie), 17 rue Drouot, 75009 Paris, France.
Leisten (Günther), In der Höhle, 6, 5 Köln, Deutschland.
Lelant (Pierre), 18 rue Bertin, 49000 Angers, France.
Lemallier (Pierre), 4 rue des Orfèvres, 67 Strasbourg, France.
Lengertz Antikvariat-Bokhandel I Lund, A.B., St. Grabrödsgatan 13, 222 22
    Lund, Sverige.
Lengerts Antikvariat, Adelgatan 19, Malmö-C, Sverige.
Lescrauwaet (Boekhandel), Oude Burg 31, Brugge, Belgie.
Lester (Maurice), 13 bis rue du Cygne, 28 Chartres, France.
Lestringant, 123 rue Général-Leclerc, 76000 Rouen, France.
Leterrier (Jean), 20 rue Jeanne d'Arc, 45 Orleans, France.
Leuwer (Franz), Am Wall 171, 28 Bremen, Deutschland.
Levilliers (Arnold), 118 Route de Chartres, 91400 Gometz-le-Chatel, France.
Levin (Richard), Dannebrogsgade I/IV, 1660 København-V, Danmark.
Levy (Jacques), 46 rue d'Alésia, 75014 Paris, France.
Lévy (Yves) = l'Ane d'Or, Vigny, France.
Leyenberger (M.) = Librairie Encyclopedique, Bruxelles, Belgique.
Librairie Ancienne et Moderne, 50 rue Scellerie, 37 Tours, France.
Librairie des Galeries, Galerie du Roi 2, 1000 Bruxelles, Belgique.
Libri, 6 rue du Pont, 71000 Macon, France.
Libris Antikvariatet, Kommendörsgatan 14, 10243 Stockholm, Sverige.
Licosa Antiquariato, Via Lamammora 45, 50121 Firenze, Italia.
Lidis (Studio Bibliografico), Foro Bonaparte 12, 20121 Genova, Italia.
Liebermann (B.) = Sté. Hébraica-Judaica, Paris, France.
Liebmann (Dr. Konrad), Lürman-Strasse 47, 45 Osnabrück, Deutschland.
Liehbibliothek, Gerbergässlein, Basel, Schweiz.
Lilla Antikvariatet, Sädra Förstadsgatan 20, Malmö-C, Sverige.
Lincke (Claus), Königsallee 96, Düsseldorf, Deutschland.
Lind (Mrs Aly) = Madsen-Linds Antikvariat, København, Danmark.
Lindberghs Antikvariat, Tegnérgatan 10, 11358 Stockholm, Sverige.
Livraria a Bibliófila, Ltda., Rua da Misericórdia 102, Lisboa, Portugal.
Livraria Antiquaria, Rua da Misericordia 147, Lisboa, Portugal.
Livres et Revues de France, 38 rue Desbordes-Valmore, 75016 Paris, France.
Lodovico (Silvestri) = Lib. Ant. Bianchino del Leone, Perugia, Italia.
Loeb-Larocque (Louis), 36 rue le Peletier, 75009 Paris, France.
Loercher, O.H.G. (Margot), Heubergstrasse 42, 7000 Stuttgart-Ost, Deutschland.
Loewe (Oskar) = Bochumer Antiquariat, Bochum, Deutschland.
Loewy (Alexandre), 85 rue de Seine, 75006 Paris, France.
Loewy (Edouard), 184 boulevard Haussmann, 75008 Paris, France.

Logos Bookshop, 38 Ben Yehuda Street, Tel-Aviv, Israel.
Loliée (Bernard), 72 rue de Seine, 75006 Paris, France.
Loliée (Librairie Marc), rue des Saints-Pères, 75007 Paris, France.
Lombardi (Libreria Luigi), Via Constantinopolis 4 bis, 80138 Napoli, Italia.
Lombardi (Libreria Pasquale), Via San Eufemia 11, 00187 Roma, Italia.
Loose, Papestraat 3, 's-Gravenhage, Nederland.
Lorieul (Jules), 3 rue de Poterie, 50 Valognes, France.
Lo Schiavo (Libreria G. Casella di), Piazza Municipio 84, Napoli, Italia.
Lo Schiavo (Dott. Guido) = Libreria Gaspare Casella, Napoli, Italia.
"Lotus" (Librairie Le), rue Malibran, 53, 1050 Bruxelles, Belgique.
Lotz (Günther) = Hans J. von Goetz, Wiesbaden, Deutschland.
Louis (Romain), 31–33 Rue St. Jean, 1000 Bruxelles, Belgique.
Löwendahls Antikvariat, P.O. Box 2101, 75002 Uppsala 2, Sverige.
Lucas (Librairie Charles), 10 rue armengaud, 92210 Saint-Cloud, France.
Lucenay (G. de), 15 rue Petite-Fusterie, 84000 Avignon, France.
Lunge Larsen (A.), Øygardveien 16 E, Bekkestua, Norge.
Lux (Klaus), Im Hausgarten 33, 7800 Frieburg, Deutschland.
Lynge & Son, Løvstraede 8–10, 1152 København-K, Danmark.

M

Maccono (Dott. Carla Viotto) = Le Bouquiniste, Torino, Italia.
Macoir (Christian), Val des Roses 1, Bruxelles, Belgique.
Macoir (Ch.-D.) = Librairie de l'Europe, Bruxelles, Belgique.
Mäder (Alfred), 67 rue Saint-Jacques, 75005 Paris, France.
Madliger-Schwab (H. & R.) = Buchantiquariat Neues Schloss, Zürich, Schweiz.
Madsen-Linds Antikvariat, Klosterstraede 24, 1157 København-K, Danmark.
Maeght (Galerie), 13 rue de Téhéran, 75008 Paris, France.
Magis (Jean-Jacques), 12 rue Guenégaud, 75006 Paris, France.
Maison du Livre (La), 24 rue de la Cloche Verte, 16000 Angouléme, France.
Maisonneuve (Adrien), Librairie d'Amerique et d'Orient, 11 rue Saint-Sulpice, 75006 Paris, France.
Maisonneuve & Larose, S.A., 11 rue Victor-Cousin, 75005 Paris, France.
Makelin (Madame Meeri) = Kampintorin Antikvariatti, Helsinki, Suomi.
Makrocki (Achim), Quellenstrasse 14, 35 Kassel, Deutschland.
Malota's Enkelin A. Stern (Franz), Wiedner Hauotstrasse 22, Wien 4, Österreich.
"MAM", 192 Ledra Street, Flat 4, Nicosia, Cyprus.
Manusé (Gaetano), Via Ciovasso 17, Milano, Italia.
Many (Sté), 12 rue Delambre, 75014 Paris, France.
Manz, Kohlmarkt 16, Wien 1, Österreich.
Marcus (Hans), Grabenstrasse 11A, 4 Düsseldorf, Deutschland.
Marcus (Hans), Keizersgracht 574, Amsterdam, Nederland.
Maréchal (Vos,) = Boekhandel Lescrauwet, Brugge, Belgie.
Margotat (Yves), 8 rue de l'Odéon, 75006 Paris, France.
Marin (Paul-Robert), 18 boulevard Haussmann, 75009 Paris, France.
Maronne (Madame E.), 37 rue Bouffard, 33000 Bordeaux, France.
Marques (Americo F.), Rua da Misericordia 92–1, Lisboa, Portugal.
Marquina y Marin (Luis) = Libraria Hesperia, Zaragoza, España.
Martegani (Dott. A.) = Sibrium Libri e Manoscritti, Milano, Italia.
Martelli (Libreria Antiquaria), Via Santo Stefano 43, 40125 Bologna, Italia.
Martin-Bres (Henri), 60 rue Grignan, 13 Marseille, France.
Martinez (Jean-Claude), 53 bis quai des Grands-Augustins, 75006 Paris, France.

Martinho (Livraria Eduardo Antunes), Rua Voz do Operário 7-B, Lisboa, Portugal.
Martins (Ernesto) = Biblarte, Lisboa, Portugal.
Marzocco (Libreria), Via Martelli 22, 50129 Firenze, Italia.
Marzoli (Carla) = La Bibliofila, Milano, Italia.
Marzoli (C.), Corso Porta Nouva 2, 20121 Milano, Italia.
Matarasso (Jacques), 2 rue Longchamp, 06 Nice, France.
Mathis (Leopoldine), Nussdorferstrasse 10, Wien 9, Österreich.
Matteuzzi (Libreria), Piazza Aldrovandi 5/B, 40125 Bologna, Italia.
Matthiesen (Galerie), Meinekestrasse 11, 1 Berlin 15, Deutschland.
Matica Hrvatska, 2 Maticine, Zagreb, Jugoslavija.
Matussek (Hans K.), Hochstrasse 9, 4054 Nettetal, Deutschland.
Maudrich (W.), Alserstrasse 19, 1080 Wien, Österreich.
Maurel (Paul), 104 rue Paradis, 13001 Marseille, France.
Maurel (Librairie-Galerie Paul), 27–29 boulevard Albert 1er, 06 Antibes, France.
Mayer, Limited (Ludwig), Shlomzion Hamalka 4, Jerusalem, Israel.
Mayrische Buchhandlung, Theatergasse, 5020 Salzburg, Österreich.
Mazo (Alain), 15 rue Guénégaud, 75006 Paris, France.
Mecklenburg (Günther und Klaus) = J. A. Stargardt, Marburg, Deutschland.
Médail (Mrs. Elena Soave) = Lib. Ant. Soave, Torino, Italia.
Mediolanum (Libreria Antiquaria, Via Montebello 30, 20121 Milano, Italia.
Mehren (F. & A.), Mauritzstrasse 3, 44 Münster, Deutschland.
Meijer (J.) = In den Brugschen, Eenhorn, Brugge, Belgie.
Meilleurs Livres (Les), 18 boulevard Saint-Michel, 75006 Paris, France.
Mellgrens Antikvariat (H.), Centrumhuset Östra Larmgatan 17, 41107 Göteborg, Sverige.
Menagé (Jean) = Librairie Stendhal, Grenoble, France.
Menetret (Claude) = L'Invitation au Voyage, Paris, France.
Mennenöh (Ingrid) = C. Roemke & Cie, Köln, Deutschland.
Mercante di Stampe (Il), Corso Venezia 29, 20121 Milano, Italia.
Mercier (H.) = La Proué, Bruxelles, Belgique.
Metais, 12 rue Jean Prieur, 27340 Pont de l'Arche, France.
Metra (Guy), 43 Grand-Rue Chauchien, 71400 Autun, France.
Meur (Marcel le), 12 place du Théâtre, 21 Dijon, France.
Meuschel (Konrad), Kaiserplatz 5, 53 Bonn, Deutschland.
Meyer (Franz H.) = Hamburgensien-Meyer, Hamburg, Deutschland.
Meyer (Hermann N. Z.) = The Universitas-Booksellers, Jerusalem, Israel.
Michaelidou (Thelma M.) = MAM, Nicosia, Cyprus
Michel (R.-G.), 17 quai Saint-Michel, 75005 Paris, France.
Michel de Floesser (Jean), 28 rue des Remparts, 33 Bordeaux, France.
Micheloni (Walter), Vico Falamonica 15, 16123 Genova, Italia.
Minerva (Antiquariaat), Zeestraat 48, 's-Gravenhage, Nederland.
Mingardi (Gastone & Mario) = Libreria Alpina, Bologna, Italia.
Mirto (Libreria), Ruiz de Alarcon 27, Madrid, España.
Misasi (Carlo) = Libreria Alessandria, Roma, Italia.
Molina (Gabriel), Travesia del Arenal 1, Madrid, España.
Mondange (Jacqueline), 7 avenue Notre-Dame, 06 Nice, France.
Monfort (Gérard), Saint-Pierre-de-Salerne, 27800 Brionne, France.
Monge (Librairie), 5 rue de l'Echaudé, 75006 Paris, France.
Montanini (Libreria), Via Nino Bixio 58, Parma, Italia.
Montbarbon (Edouard), 29 rue d'Alger, 83100 Toulon, France.
Montbel (Librairie de), 1 rue Paul Cézanne, 75008 Paris, France.

Mont-Dore (Librairie du), 72 rue du Faubourg-Saint-Honoré, 75008 Paris, France.
Montmartroise (Librairie), 29 rue Durantin, 75018 Paris, France.
Moorthamers (Librairie Louis), Rue Lesbroussart 124, 1050 Bruxelles, Belgique.
Morcrette (Daniel), 4 avenue Joffre, 95270 Luzarches, France.
Moreno (Antonio) = Libreria Granata, Almeria, España.
Moretti (Libreria Antiquaria), Via Lusardi 8, 20122 Milano, Italia.
Morin (Charles), 9 rue Auvray, 72000 Le Mans, France.
Morssen (G.), 14 rue de Seine, 75006 Paris, France.
Morvran (Librairie), 16 bis rue René-Madec, 29000 Quimper, France.
Moschenross (Ferdinand), 31 quai des Bateliers, 67000 Strasbourg, France.
Moser (Otto), Olmenweg 15, 7340 Geislingen, Deutschland.
Morin (Charles), 102 rue du Cherche-Midi, 75006 Paris, France.
Müller (Arthur) = M. Glogau, Hamburg, Deutschland.
Müller (August), Maximiliansplatz 20, 8 München 2, Deutschland.
Müller (Clemens), Kapellenweg 59, 56 Wuppertal-Barmen, Deutschland.
Muller International Booksellers (Rudolf), P.O. Box 9016, Amsterdam, Nederland.
Müller & Gräff, Calwerstrasse 54, 7 Stuttgart 1, Deutschland.
Mundo do Livro (O), Largo da Trindade 11–13, Lisboa 2, Portugal.
Muriset (Galerie Annie), 4 place du Molard, 1200 Genève, Suisse.
Murr (Antiquariat Karlheinz), Karolinenstrasse 4, 86 Bamberg, Deutschland.
Muthmann (Ruth-Marie) = C. G. Boerner, Düsseldorf, Deutschland.

N

Naacher, O.H.G. (Peter), Steinweg 3, 6 Frankfurt-am-Main, Deutschland.
Nabrink & Zoon (Ge), Korte Korsjespoortstraat 8, Amsterdam-C, Nederland.
Naert (Madame J.) = Saffroy, Paris, France.
Nardecchia (Libreria Gia), Piazza Cavour 25, 00193 Roma, Italia.
Nebehay (Christian M.), Annagasse 18, 1015 Wien, Österreich.
Nebehay (Ingo) = Wiener Antiquariat, Wien, Österreich.
Neidhardt (Fritz), Relenbergstrasse 20, 7 Stuttgart, Deutschland.
Neser (S. & P.), Kreuzlingerstrasse 11, 775 Konstanz-Bodensee, Deutschland.
Neubauer (Hans) = Helmut Schumann, Zürich, Schweiz.
Neues Schloss (Buchantiquariat), Stockerstrasse 17, 8027 Zürich, Schweiz.
Neugebauer (Gerhard) = Mayrische Buchhandlung, Salzburg, Österreich.
Neugebauer, O.H.G., (Werner), Landstrasse 1, 4020 Linz, Österreich.
Neuwirth (Gustav), Frankfurterstrasse 16/I, 71 Heilbronn, Deutschland.
Nibbe (Horst), Auf dem Berlich 9, 5 Köln, Deutschland.
Nicaise, S.A. (Librairie), 145 boulevard Saint-Germain, 75005 Paris, France.
Nicolas (Félix), Leliestraat 61, Hove, Belgie.
Nierendorf (Galerie), Hardenbergstrasse 19, 1 Berlin 12, Deutschland.
Nierynck (L.M.C.), Verdilaan 85, Vlissingen, Nederland.
Nijhoff, N.V. (Martinus), Lange Voorhout 9–11, 's-Gravenhage, Nederland.
Nilsson (Mrs. Tove) = Nordiska Antikvariska Bokhandeln, Helsingfors, Suomi.
Nizet (Librairie A.-G.), 3 bis place de la Sorbonne, 75005 Paris, France.
Nobele (F. de), rue Bonaparte 35, 75006 Paris, France.
Nobis (Günther), Forststrasse 12, 62 Wiesbaden, Deutschland.
Nociti (Guiseppe) = Lib. Ant. Martelli, Bologna, Italia.
Noelle (Dr. M.) = Galerie Matthiesen, Berlin, Deutschland.
Nørballe (Leif) = Frederiksberg Antinvariat, København, Danmark.

Norddeutsches Antiquariat, Kröpeliner Strasse 14, 25 Rostock, D.D.R.
Nordiska Antikvariska Bokhandeln, Norra Magasingatan 6, Helsingfors, Suomi.
Nørgart (H.C.), Fiolstraede 15, 1171 København-K, Danmark.
Notebaart (P.C.), Postbox 7289, Amsterdam, Nederland.
Nyegaard (Claes) = Damms Antikvariat, Oslo, Norge.

O

Obenhaus (Eduard) = Wolfgang Brandes, Braunschweig, Deutschland.
Office International de Librairie, Avenue Marnix 30, 1050 Bruxelles, Belgique.
Olins Antikvariat, Klostergatan 11, Lund, Sverige.
Olschki—Studio Bibliografico (Leo S.), 52046 Lucignano (Arezzo), Italia.
Olsen (Marinus), Studiestraede 41, 1455 København-K, Danmark.
Orangerie (Galerie), Theodor-Heuss-Ring 62, 5 Köln, Deutschland.
d'Oro (Cavalieri), Via Mazzini 84, 44022 Comacchio, Italia.
Overdiep (Antiquariaat H. K.), Korte Gasthuisstraat 45, 2000 Antwerpen, Belge.

P

Palmaverde (Libreria Antiquaria), Via Castiglione 35, 40124 Bologna, Italia.
Paludan (Erik), Fiolstraede 10, 1171 København-K, Danmark.
Panayiotis Georgiou & Co., P.O. Box 622, Athens, Ellas.
Pankow (Antiquariat), Schönholzer Strasse 1, 110 Berlin, D.D.R.
Para Bibliofilos, Pl. San Martin 3, Madrid, España.
Parrot (J.P.), 59 rue de Rennes, 75006 Paris, France.
Patzer (Rudolf), Mainzer Berg 23, 6731 Weidenthal, Deutschland.
Paulusch (Hans D.) = V. A. Heck, Wien, Österreich.
Grønholt Pedersens Boghus, Fiolstraede 19, 1171 København-K, Danmark.
Pedro V. (Livraria D.), Rua D. Pedro V. 16, Lisboa, Portugal.
Peet (C.P.J. van der), 33–35 Nieuwe Spiegelstraat, Amsterdam, Nederland.
Peet (C.P.J. van der), Jansweg 39, Haarlem, Nederland.
Peet (R. van der) = Antiquariaat Antiqua, Amsterdam, Nederland.
Pellerin (Hélène), 7 rue Dupaty, 17 La Rochelle, France.
Pénau (Marc) = Librairie Guénégaud, Paris, France.
Perini (Libreria Antiquaria), Via A. Sciesa 9, 37100 Verona, Italia.
Persson (Stellan) = Skakhuset, København, Danmark.
Petiet (Henri), 8 rue de Tournon, 75006 Paris, France.
Petitot (Pierre), 234 boulevard Saint-Germain, 75007 Paris, France.
Petit-Siroux, 6 rue Vivienne, 75002 Paris, France.
Petten-Rosenthal (E.) = Ludwig Rosenthal's Antiquariaat, Hilversum, Nederland.
Peyrot (Dott. Ada), Via Consolata 8, 10122 Torino, Italia.
Peysson (Jean), 7 rue du Plat, 69 Lyon, France.
Pfankuch, K.G., (Karl), Kleine Burg 12, 33 Braunschweig, Deutschland.
Pfann, (H.D.), Rokin 122, N.Z. Voorburgwal 127, and Herengracht 329, Amster-
  dam, Nederland.
Pfister (Annemarie), Petersgraben 18, 4051 Basel, Schweiz.
Piantanida (Alessandro) = Libreria Vinciana, Milano, Italia.
Piazza S. Babila (Libreria), Corso Monforte 2, 20122 Milano, Italia.
Picard (A. & J.), 82 rue Bonaparte, 75006 Paris, France.
Picard Fils (Henri), 126 faubourg Saint-Honoré, 75008 Paris, France.
Picard (Pierre), 60 boulevard Malesherbes, 75008 Paris, France.

Picker (Otto), Groot Hoefijzerlaan 3, Wassenaar, Nederland.
Pilegaard (Gunnar), Algade 65, Aalborg, Danmark.
Pinault (L. & J.-H.), 36 rue Bonaparte, 75006 Paris, France.
Pinczower (F.), 83 Sokolow Street, Tel Aviv, Israel.
Pinkus Genossenschaft (Antiquariat), Froschaugasse 7, 8001 Zürich, Schweiz.
Pires (Joâo Rodrigues) = O Mundo do Livro, Lisboa, Portugal.
Plandiura (Mariano Castells) = Libraria Anticuaria Aristeucos, Barcelona, España.
Poisot (Pierre), 28 quai Jonvin, 38000 Grenoble, France.
Polak (Jean), 8 rue de l'Échaudé, 75006 Paris, France.
Polifilo (Il), Via Borgonuovo 3, 20121 Milano, Italia.
Pomarede (Jeanne), 19 quai des Grands-Augustins, 75006 Paris, France.
Porte Etroite (La), 10 rue Bonaparte, 75006 Paris, France.
Porter-Libros, Avenida Puerta del Angel 9, Barcelona, España.
Postma (G.), O.Z. Voorburgwal 249, Amsterdam, Nederland.
Poursin (Librairie), 21 rue Saint-sulpice, 75006 Paris, France.
Pozzi (Dott. Elfo) = Libreria Antiquaria Mediolanum, Milano, Italia.
Pozzo del Bibliofilo (Il), Via S. Lorenzo 19, 16123 Genova, Italia.
Prandi (Libreria Antiquaria), Viale Timavo 75, Reggio Emilia, Italia.
Pregliasco (Libreria Antiquaria Arturo), Via Accademia 3 bis, 10123 Torino, Italia.
Pregliasco-Mathes (Giorgina), Via Po 14, 10123 Torino, Italia.
Preidel (Herbert), Bismarckstrasse 20, 3011 Gehrden, Deutschland.
Preminger, Ltd. (Nissen), 9 Montefiore Street, Tel Aviv, Israel.
Presses Académiques Européenes, 98 Chaussée de Charleroi, Bruxelles 6, Belgique.
Pressler (Dr. Karl H.), Herzogstrasse 58, 8 München 40, Deutschland.
Privat (Librairie Georges), 162 boulevard Haussmann, 75008 Paris, France.
Proue (La), 6 rue des Eperonniers, 1000 Bruxelles, Belgique.
Prouté (Guy), 15 rue du 18-Juin, 92210 Saint-Cloud, France.
Prouté, S.A. (Paul), 74 rue de Seine, 75006 Paris, France.
Prouté (Robert), 12 rue de Seine, 75006 Paris, France.
Puskas (Wilhelm), Weiburggasse 16, 1010 Wien, Österreich.
Puzin (Librairie), 30 rue de la Paroisse, 78 Versailles, France.

Q

Quartier Latin, 21 rue Albert-1er, 17000 La Rochelle, France.
Quartre Chemins-Editart (Librairie), 3 place Saint-Sulpice, 75006 Paris, France.
Querzola (Libreria Antiquaria), 153 Via del Babuino, 00187 Roma, Italia.
Quinsac (P.) = Librairie Duchemin, Paris, France.

R

Radaeli (Antiquariato Librario), Via A. Manzoni 39, 20121 Milano, Italia.
Raffy (G.), 85 rue des Rosiers, 93400 Saint-Ouen, France.
Ranch's Antikvariat, Vesterbrogade 110, 1620 København-V, Danmark.
Raoust (Librairie), 11 rue Neuve, 59000 Lille, France.
Rappaport (Libreria Antiquaria C. E.), Via Sistina 23, Roma, Italia.
Raunhardt (Hans), Kirchgasse 17, 8000 Zürich, Schweiz.
Rauscher (Franz) = August Müller, München, Deutschland.
Riechmann (A.), Wiedner Hauotstrasse 18, Wien 1041, Österreich.
Reinhardt (Joachim), Burgfreiheit 8, 48 Bielefeld, Deutschland.

Relecom (Emile), rue des Chardons 19, 1030 Bruxelles, Belgique.
Remy (Librairie A.), 25 rue Stanislas, 54000 Nancy, France.
Renaissance van het Boek (De), Walpoortstraat 7, 9000 Gent, Belgie.
Renner (Antiquariat Gerh.), Hechingerstrasse 34, 747 Albstadt 2, Deutschland.
Renner (Klaus), Konrad-Celtis-Strasse 33, 8 München 25, Deutschland.
Reymond (Madame Eugene), 14 faubourg de l'Hopital, Neuchâtel, Suisse.
Ribot-Vulin (Louis) = Librairie Paul Vulin, Paris, France.
Richter (Günther), Breite Strasse 29, 1 Berlin 33, Deutschland.
Riccardi (Libreria Maresca), Piazza Ponte San Angelo 29, Roma, Italia.
Rico (Antonia Molina) = Gabriel Molina, Madris, España.
Ricordi, Negozio di Via Berchet 2, 20121 Milano, Italia.
Rigattieri (Libreria M.), Calle della Mandola 3713, 30124 Venezia, Italia.
Rimanek (Heinrich), Kaiserstrasse 6, 1070 Wien, Österreich.
Riminese (Libreria), Via IV Novembre 46, 47037 Rimini, Italia.
Ringstrøms Antikvariat (Bjørn), Ullevalsveien 1, Oslo 1, Norge.
Ripert (Madame G.) = Librairie Bonaparte, Paris, France.
Rittershofer (Horst A.), Meinekestrasse 3, 1 Berlin 15, Deutschland.
Rivarès (Librairie), 3 rue Rivarès, 64000 Pau, France.
Rizzi (Renzo), Via Cernaia 4, 20121 Milano, Italia.
Rocca (Jean), 7 rue Meyerbeer, 06 Nice, France.
Roemke & Cie (C.), Apostelnstrasse 7, 5 Köln 1, Deutschland.
Rohr (Hans), Oberdorferstrasse 5, 8024 Zürich, Schweiz.
Rohrscheid, G.m.b.H. (Ludwig), Am Hof 28, 53 Bonn, Deutschland.
Roig (Miguel Fiol) = Libreria M. Fiol, Palma de Mallorca, España.
Romand (Michel) = Galerie Documents, Paris, France.
Romagosa (Jaime) = Antiquariat Iberia, Berne, Schweiz.
Rombaut (Librairie A.), Lievestraat 14, 9000 Gent, Belgie.
Rönnells Antikvariat, A.B., Birger Jarlsgatan 32, 11429 Stockholm, Sverige.
Rosenkilde og Bagger, 3 Kron-Prinsens-Gade, 1114 København, Danmark.
Rosenthal (H.B.) = Ludwig Rosenthal's Antiquariat, Hilversum, Nederland.
Rosenthal (Jacques), Frühlingstrasse 12, 8051 Eching, Deutschland.
Rosenthal (R.B.), Rua do Alecrim 47–4, Salas D, Lisboa, Portugal.
Rosenthal's Antiquariaat (Ludwig), Bussumergrintweg 4, Hilversum, Nederland.
Rosenthal-Dürr (Ludwig), Sachsenkamstrasse 26, 8 München 70, Deutschland.
Rossignol (Emile), 8 rue Bonaparte, 75006 Paris, France.
Rossignol (Eugéne), 4 rue de l'Odéon, 75006 Paris, France.
Rossignol (Henri), 1 avenue de Grasse, 06400 Cannes, France.
Rossignol (Librairie Ancienne L.D.), Domaine Saint-Pierre, 83460 Les Arcs, France.

Roth (Marielle) = Librairie Rivarès, Pau, France.
Rothacker (Oscar), Hardenberstrasse 11, 1 Berlin 12, Deutschland.
Rothacker (Oscar), Pettenkoferstrasse 18, 8 München 15, Deutschland.
Rouam (Maurice), 29 rue Mazarine, 75006 Paris, France.
Rousseau-Girard (Jean), 7 rue de la Bourse, 75002 Paris, France.
Roux-Devillas (Francis), 12 rue Bonaparte, 75006 Paris, France.
Roversi (Dott. Roberto) = Libreria Antiquaria Palmaverde, Bologna, Italia.
Ruel (André) = Libri, Macon, France.
Rumbler (Helmut H.) = Braubachstrasse 36, 6 Frankfurt-am-Main, Deutschland.

S

Saba (Umberto), Via San Nicolo 30, 34121 Trieste, Italia.
Saffroy, 3 quai Malaquais, 75006 Paris, France.
Saffroy (Gaston), 4 rue Clément, 75006 Paris, France.
Sagot le Garrec & Cie, 24 rue du Four, 75006 Paris, France.
Saint-Louis (Librairie), 21 rue Servandoni, 75006 Paris, France.
Saint-Jacques (Librairie), 10 rue Saint-Jacques, 64500 Saint-Jean-de-Luz, France.
Sainte-Marie (Jean-Louis), 43 boulevard Alsace-Lorraine, 82200 Moissac, France.
Saletta (Cesare), Casella Postale 390, 40100 Bologna, Italia.
Salimbeni (Gustavo & Vitaliano), Via Matteo Palmieri 10, 50122 Firenze, Italia.
Salotto del Bibliofilo, Via Luccoli 21, 16123 Genova, Italia.
Samlaren Antikvariat & Konsthandel, Korsgatan 2, 41116 Göteborg, Sverige.
Samuelian (Librairie Orientale H.), 51 rue Monsieur-le-Prince, 75006 Paris, France.
Samuelson (Mrs. B.) = Thornams Antikvariat, København, Danmark.
Sändig, G.m.b.H. (Dr. Martin), Nelkenstrasse 2, 6226 Walluf 1, Deutschland.
Sansonetti (Etienne), 9 rue Guizot, 3000 Nîmes, France.
Santo Vanasia (Lbreria), Via M. Macchi 58, 20124 Milano, Italia.
Sartoni & Cerveau, 101 rue de Seine, 75006 Paris, France.
Scarpignato (Giuseppe), Via Ripetta 156, 00186 Roma, Italia.
Schaden (Walter R.), Sonnenfelsgasse 4, 1010 Wien, Österreich.
Schäfer (Bernhard), Conradistrasse 2, 3522 Karlshafen, Deutschland.
Schäfer (Jörg),Hottingerstrasse 5, 8032 Zürich, Schweiz.
Schalk (Friedrich), Mariahilferstrasse 97, Wien 1006, Österreich.
Scheppler (Gerhard), Giselastrasse 25, 8000 München 40, Deutschland.
Scheringer (Georg) = Gsellius'sche Buchhandlung, Berlin, Deutschland.
Schierenberg (D. & E.) = Antiquariat Junk, Lochem, Nederland.
Schiller (Ludwig H.), Birkenrain 28, 7811 St. Peter-Schwarzwald, Deutschland.
Schilling (Kurt) = Scientia, Aalen, Deutschland.
Schmetz (Karl), Kleinmrschierstrasse 5, 51 Aachen, Deutschland.
Schmidt Antiquariat (Bücher-), Torgasse 4, 8000 Zürich, Schweiz.
Schmidt (Geschwister), Karl-Marx-Strasse 15, 675 Kaiserslautern, Deutschland.
Schmidt (Walter), 8201 Bad Feilnbach (Dettendorf), Deutschland.
Schmidt (Walter), Falltor 179, 3441 Datterode, Deutschland.
Schmidt (Young), Osloplads 2-A, 2100 København-Ø, Danmark.
Schneider (Hans), Mozartweg 1, 8132 Tutzing über München, Deutschland.
Schneider (Jean P.) = Galerie Orangerie, Köln, Deutschland.
Schneider (Karl Friedrich), Seltersweg 38, 63 Giessen, Deutschland.
Schneider (Ulrich) = Wolfgang Brandes, Braunschweig, Deutschland.
Schöningh (Ferdinand), Domhof 4-c, 45 Osnabrück, Deutschland.
Schors (Antiquariaat W.N.), Reguliersgracht 52–54, Amsterdam-C, Nederland.

Schramm (B.), Willesstrasse 4–6, 23 Kiel, Deutschland.
Schreyer (Hanno), Euskirchenerstrasse 57–59, 53 Bonn 1, Deutschland.
Schubert (L.) = J.G. Sydys, St. Pölten, Österreich.
Schuhmacher (Antiquariaat), Gelderschekade 107, Amsterdam, Nederland.
Schulman, B.V. (Jacques), Keizersgracht 448, Amsterdam-C, Nederland.
Schulz (Hans Ferdinand), Friedrichring 13, 78 Freiburg, Deutschland.
Schulz (Helmut Gerhard), Ost-West-Strasse 47, 2 Hamburg 11, Deutschland.
Schulz (Paul) = Heinrich Heine, Berlin, Deutschland.
Schumann, A.G. (Hellmut), Rämistrasse 25, Zürich, Schweiz.
Schumann (Richard) = Frankfurter Bücherstube, Frankfurt-am-Main, Deutschland.
Schweitzer Sortiment (J.), Marsstrasse 4, 8 München 2, Deutschland.
Scientifique Ancienne (Librairie), 20 rue des Fossés, 75005 Paris, France.
Seacombe (Elisabeth) = C.E. Rappaport, Roma, Italia.
Seebass (Adolf) = Haus der Bücher, Basel, Schweiz.
Seidenberg (Gebrüder) = Das Gute Buch, Zürich, Schweiz.
Seidl (Dr. Z.) = Akademische Buchhandlung, Kuppitsch, Wien, Österreich.
Semmel (Emil), Meckenheimerstrasse 45, 53 Bonn, Deutschland.
Settergards Antikvariat, Birger Jarlsgatan 44, Stockholm-Ö, Sverige.
Seuffer (Walter), Steglitzer Damm, 1 Berlin 41, Deutschland.
Severin (Peter) = Bickhardt'sche Buchhandlung, Berlin, Deutschland.
Sexl & Co. (Ringbuchhandlung), Dr. Karl-Lueger-Ring 6, 1010 Wien, Österreich.
Sforzini (Libreria), Via Della Vite 43, 00187 Roma, Italia.
Sgattoni (Libreria Antiquaria M.), Via Vivaio 22, 20122 Milano, Italia.
Shakespeare & Co., 37 rue de la Bucherie, 75005 Paris, France.
Sheftl (E.) = Zohar, Tel Aviv, Israel.
Sibrium Libri e Manoscritti, Via Bigli 21, Milano, Italia.
Sieber (Dr. Maria) = Wiener Bücherstube, Frankfurt-am-Main, Deutschland.
Siebert (Werner) = Franz Leuwer, Bremen, Deutschland.
Sieur (Pierre), 3 rue de la Université, 75007 Paris, France.
Simmermacher (René), Turnseestrasse 4-a, 6 Frankfurt-am-Main, Deutschland.
Simmermacher (René), Talstrasse 5, 7800 Freiburg, Deutschland.
Simon (Albert & Carlotta) = Das Bücherkabinett, Hamburg, Deutschland.
Simon (Madame Elisabeth) = Sté. Livres & Musique, Paris, France.
Simonsen (C.F.) = Arnold Busck, København, Danmark.
Simonson (Librairie), 20 Avenue des Arts, 1040 Bruxelles, Belgique.
Sintermann (Carl), 258 Kaiser-Joseph-Strasse, 78 Freiburg, Deutschland.
Skakhuset (The Chess House), 24 Studiesstraede, 1455 København-K, Danmark.
Slatkine et Fils (M.), 15 Cours de Rive, 1200 Genève, Suisse.
Slegte (J. de), Kalverstraat 11, Amsterdam, Spuistraat 9, 's-Gravenhage, Janstraat 28, Arnhem, Rechestraat 36 Eindhoven, Coolsingel 83, Rotterdam, Oude Gracht 121 Utrecht, — Nederland.
Slovenský Knizný Velkoobshod, Bratislava, Ceskoslovensko.
Smith & Son (W.H.), Boulevard Adolphe Maz 71–75, 1000 Bruxelles, Belgique.
Snaebjorn Jonsson & Co., Hafnarstraeti 4, Reykjavík, Island.
Soave (Libreria Antiquaria), Via Po 48, 10123 Torino, Italia.
Soave (Fiammetta), Via Giuseppe Cuboni 12, 00197 Roma, Italia.
Société Livres & Musique, 6 rue Lamartine, 75009 Paris, France.
Soete (Edgar), Librairie Salet, 5 quai Voltaire, 75007 Paris, France.
Sonnewald Heckenhauer, 7947 Mengen, Deutschland.
Sörlin (Bo) = Antikvariska Bokhandeln, Malmö, Sverige.
Sörlin (Tor) = Norrköpings Antikvariat, Norrköping, Sverige.

Sorø Antikvariat, Frederiksvergvej 8, 4180 Sorø, Danmark.
Spandonaro (Julia & Augusto) = Les Amis du Livre, Athens, Ellas.
Springer (Rudolf J.), Fasenenstrasse 13, 1 Berlin 12, Deutschland.
Srpska knjizevna zadruga, 19 Marsala Tita, Beograd, Jugoslavija.
Stam-Hommes (M.) = Burgersdijk & Niermans, Leiden, Nederland.
Stangl (Galerie), Briennerstrasse 11, 8 München, Deutschland.
Stargadt (J.A.), Universitätsstrasse 27, 355 Marburg, Deutschland.
Staschen (Wolfgang), Bülowstrasse 11, 1 Berlin 30, Deutschland.
Steinbach (M.A.), Hirschenweg 36, 8011 Eglharting, Deutschland.
Steinbach (M.F.), Salmannsdorferstrasse 64, 1190 Wien, Österreich.
Steinkopf (J.F.), Hermannstrasse 5, 7 Stuttgart 1, Deutschland.
Stenderhoff & Co. (Th.), Alter Firschmarkt 21, 44 Münster, Deutschland.
Stendhal (Librairie), 4 rue de Sault, 38000 Grenoble, France.
Sten Ryö (Antikvariat), Arsenalsgatan 4, 11147 Stockholm, Sverige.
Stern (Annie) = Franz Malota's Enkelin, Wien, Österreich.
Stern-Verlag Janssen & Co., Friedrichstrasse 26, 4 Düsseldorf, Deutschland.
Stobbe (Horst), Ottostrasse 11, 8 München 2, Deutschland.
Stockum's Antiquariaat (Van), Prinsegracht 15, 's-Gravenhage, Nederland.
Strand (Antikvariat Gustav), St. Pedersstraede 47, 1453 København-K, Danmark.
Streisand (Hugo), Eislebener Strasse 4, 1 Berlin 30, Deutschland.
Strøms Antikvariat, Hegdehaugsveien 34, Oslo 3, Norge.
Stropek (Dr. Karl), Währingerstrasse 122, 1181 Wien, Österreich.
Strück (Hartwig), Bäringerstrasse 4, 338 Goslar, Deutschland.
Struppe und Winkler, Potsdamerstrasse 103, 1 Berlin 30, Deutschland.
Stuttgarter Antiquariat, Rathenausstrasse 21, 7000 Stuttgart 1, Deutschland.
Swets & Zeitlinger, B.V., Heereweg 347-B, Lisse, Nederland.
Sydys (J.G.), Wienerstrasse 19, 3100 St. Pölten, Österreich.
Symanczyk (Wolfgang), Hubertusweg 32, 404 Neuss, Deutschland.

T

Tacke (Friedrich) = C. Roemke & Cie, Köln, Deutschland.
Taeuber (W.) = Gilhofer Buch und Kunst-Antiquariat, Wien, Österreich.
Tamburello (Dott. Mario) = Libreria Antiquaria Luigi Banzi, Bologna, Italia.
Tamiz (Edmond), "A la Colombe", 30 rue Madame, 75006 Paris, France.
Tassy (Jean), 20 rue de Bresis, 30 Ales, France.
Tattermusch (Heinz), Bergiusstrasse 10, 41 Duisburg-Ruhrort, Deutschland.
Tausky (Théodore), 33 rue Dauphine, 75006 Paris, France.
Tavares de Carvalho (A.), Avenida da Republica 46–3, Lisboa, Portugal.
Technisches Antiquariat, Lauteschlagerstrasse 4, 61 Darmstadt, Deutschland.
Teikko (Ivan) = Antikvaarinen Kirjakauppa, Helsinki, Suomi.
Telles da Sylva (J.A.), Travessa do Marquês de Sá da Bandeira 19–3, Lisboa 1, Portugal.
Tenner (Erna) = "Bibliographicum", Heidelberg, Deutschland.
Tenner (Erna), Hauptstrasse 194, 69 Heidelberg, Deutschland.
Tenner (Helmut), Bergheimerstrasse 59, 69 Heidelberg, Deutschland.
Thanh-Long (Librairie-Editions), 34 Rue Dekens, 1040 Bruxelles, Belgique.
Theatrum Antiquariat, Ole Hoop 9, 2 Hamburg-Blankenese, Deutschland.
Thérond (André), 40 rue Victor-Hugo, 81100 Castres, France.
Thoma (J.E.), 3910 Stift Zwettl, Österreich.
Thomas (Gérard), l'Amis des Livres, 1 rue des Fossés, Rennes, France.
Thomas (G.L.) = Librairie-Galerie Bretonne, Rennes, France.

Thomas-Scheler (Librairie), 19 rue de Tournon, 75006 Paris, France.
Thornams Antikvariat, Kompagniestraede 16, 1208 København-K, Danmark.
Thourel (Marcel), 61 rue du Taur, 31 Toulouse, France.
Thourel (Claude), Librairie Occitania, 46 ru du Taur, 31000 Toullouse, France.
Thuesens Antikvariat, Fiolstraede 23, 1171 København-K, Danmark.
Thulin & Ohlson, Kungsgatan 9-B, 41119 Göteborg, Sverige.
Thulins Antikvariat, A.B., 57060 Österbymo, Sverige.
"Tin Ujevic" (Antikvarijat), Trg N. Zrinjskoga br. 16, Zagreb, Jugoslavija.
Tiraspolsky (Wladimir), 69 avenue Victor-Cresson, 92 Issy-les-Moulineaux,
    France.
Tonini (Matteo), Via Antica Zecca 26, 48100 Ravenna, Italia.
Tøsse (Olav) = Bergensantikvariet, Bergen, Norge.
Trautscholdt (Dr. Eduard) = C. G. Boerner, Düsseldorf, Deutschland.
Trésor de Livres et Graphiques, Darmstädter Landstrasse 119, 6 Frankfurt-am-
    Main 70, Deutschland.
Triantafyllou (Efthimiou D.) = Academic Bookstore, Athens, Ellas.
Trochon (Michéle), 76 rue du Cherche-Midi, 75006 Paris, France.
Trochon (Michel) = Librairie du Camée, Paris, France.
Trocki (Ch. B.) = Presses Académiques Européenes, Bruxelles, Belgique.
Troeger (Carl Willy), Wilhelmstrasse 11/0, 8 München 23, Deutschland.
Trojanski (Hans), Blumenstrasse 11, 4 Düsseldorf, Deutschland.
Trüjen (Friedrich), Parkstrasse 83, 28 Bremen, Deutschland.
Truppe (Matthäus), Stubenberggasse 7, 8011 Graz, Österreich.
Tulkens (Fl.), 21 rue du Chêne, Bruxelles 1, Belgique.

U

Ullberg (Sven P.) = A. Cederbergs, Uppsala, Sverige.
Universitas-Booksellers (The), 9 Shlomzion Hamalka, Jerusalem, Israel.
Unter den Linden (Antiquariat), Unter den Linden 37/45, 108 Berlin, D.D.R.
Unteregger (Alfons) = Adolf Kapp, Rottenburg, Deutschland.
Urban (Heinz, Ernst und Michael) = Oscar Rothacker, Berlin, Deutschland.
Urbs & Orbis, Endenicher Allee 52, 53 Bonn, Deutschland.

V

Valentien (Galerie), Königsbau, 7 Stuttgart, Deutschland.
Valleri (Libreria), Via Ricasoli 68 r., 50121 Firenze, Italia.
Van Benthem en Jutting, Lange Delft 64, Middelburg, Nederland.
Vandenbroeck (E.) = Librairie "Le Lotus", Bruxelles, Belgique.
Van de Plas (Jean-Marie), 10 Rue des Eperonniers, 1000 Bruxelles, Belgique.
Van der Perre (Paul), Rue de la Régence 21, 1000 Bruxelles, Belgique.
Van der Perre (Francine), Rue de la Madeleine 23, 1000 Bruxelles, Belgique.
Vandevelde (A.W.). Dweerstraat 6, 8000 Bruges, Belgique.
Van Loock (A.), Rue Saint-Jean 51, 1000 Bruxelles, Belgique.
Varia-Antikvariat, Tibble, Leksand, Sverige.
Vasiliu du Lycée Edgar Quinet (Librairie), 67 rue des Martyrs, 75009 Paris,
    France.
Vauquelin (Galerie), 4 rue Vauquelin, 76200 Dieppe, France.
Veeneman (Martin), Noordeinde 100, 's-Gravenhage, Nederland.
Von den Velden (E.), Neureuther Strasse 1, 8 München 13, Deutschland.
Venator, K.G., Apernstrasse 56–62, 5 Köln, Deutschland.

171

Vester (Dr. Helmut), Friedrichstrasse 7, 4 Düsseldorf, Deutschland.
Viardot (Jean), 13 rue de l'Echaudé, 75005 Paris, France.
Vidal (Alphonse), 55 rue Bonaparte, 75006 Paris, France.
Vidani (Merys) = Libreria "Il Defino", Torino, Italia.
"Veille France", 65 boulevard Général-Leclerc, 33120 Arcachon, France.
Vie Rustique, S.P.R.L. (La), Avenue Winston Churchill 40, 1180 Bruxelles, Belgique.
Vigevani (A.M.) = Il Polifilo, Milano, Italia.
Viglongo (Libreria Antiquaria A.), Via Genova 266, 10127 Torino, Italia.
Vigneron (René), 74 rue de Seine, 75006 Paris, France.
Vincent, Freal & Cie, 4 rue des Beaux-Arts, 75006 Paris, France.
Vinciana (Libreria), Via Monte Napoleone 23, 20121 Milano, Italia.
Vivien (Robert), 41 rue Mazarine, 75006 Paris, France.
Vloemans (H.A.), Anna Paulownstraat 10, 's-Gravenhage, Nederland.
Voerster (J.), Relenbergstrasse 33, 7 Stuttgart, Deutschland.
Voltaire (A.F.), 30 rue Adolphe-Thiers, 13 Marseille, France.
Vömel (Galerie), Königsallee 30, 4 Düsseldorf, Deutschland.
Vonderbank, K.G. (Karl), Goethestrasse 11, 6 Frankfurt-am-Main, Deutschland.
Vos (W.R.), Laan van Meerdervoort 394, 2026 's-Gravenhage, Nederland.
Vötterle (Dr. Karl) = Bärenreiter Antiquariat, Kassel, Deutschland.
Vries (H. de), Gedempte Oude Gracht 27, Haarlem, Nederland.
V.R.I.L.L.E., Editions Pro-Francia, 3 rue Saint-Philippe-du-Roule, 75008 Paris, France.
Vrin (J.), 6 place de la Sorbonne, 75005 Paris, France.
Vuille (Louis), Maison Rouge 5, 1400 Yverdon, Suisse.
Vulin (Paul), 48 Passage Jouffroy, 75009 Paris, France.

W

Wagner (Christl & Olga) = Rudolf Heger, Wien, Österreich.
Wagner'sche Universitäts Buchhandlung, Museumstrasse 4, 6021 Innsbruck, Österreich.
Wahl (Madame André), Librairie des Alpes, 6 rue de Seine, 75006 Paris, France.
Wal (F. W. van der), Nassaulaan 16, 6100 Ede, Nederland.
Walz (Ed.), Lerchenfeldstrasse 4, 8 München 22, Deutschland.
Ward (Mrs. S.E.), 35 rue de la Harpe, 75005 Paris, France.
Waser-Albiez (Otto), Rümelinsplatz 15, Basel, Schweiz.
Wasmuth Buchhandlung & Antiquariat, Hardenbergstrasse 9a, 1 Berlin 12, Deutschland.
Wastiau (Roger), Rue de l'Industrie, 1040 Bruxelles, Belgique.
Weerd (H. De), Middellaan 34, Apeldoorn, Nederland.
Wegner (Carl), Martin-Luther-Strasse 113, 1 Berlin 62, Deutschland.
Weidlich (Wolfgang), Savignystrasse 61, 6 Frankfurt-am-Main, Deutschland.
Weigel (Felix Oswald) = Otto Harrassowitz, Wiesbaden, Deutschland.
Weil (D.), 1 rue du Dragon, 76006 Paris, France.
Weill (Lucie & Pierre-André), Au Pont des Arts, 6 rue Bonaparte, 75006 Paris, France.
Weise's Hofbuchhandlung (Julius), Königstrasse 17, 7 Stuttgart, Deutschland.
Weiss-Hesse Antiquariat, Froburgstrasse 30, 4600 Olten, Schweiz.
Welkhammer (J.), Burggasse 123, 1070 Wien, Österreich.
Wellnitz (Elisabeth), Sachsenstrasse 35, 61 Darmstadt-Eberstadt, Deutschland.
Wellnitz (Rudolf), Lauteschlägerstrasse 4, 61 Darmstadt, Deutschland.

Wellnitz (Rudolf) = Technisches Antiquariat, Darmstadt, Deutschland.
Welz Salzburg (Galerie), Sigmund-Haffnergasse 16, Salzburg, Österreich.
Wendt (Bernhard), 8081 Buch-am-Ammersee-Oberbayern über München, Deutschland.
Wenner (H.Th.), Grosse Strasse 69, 45 Osnabrück, Deutschland.
Whitman (George) = Shakespeare & Co., Paris, France.
Widmer (Galerie), Neugasse 35, 9000 St. Gallen, Schweiz.
Wieder (F.C.) = E. J. Brill, Leiden, Nederland.
Wiener Antiquariat, Seilergasse 16, Wien, Österreich.
Wiener Bücherstube, Eschersheimer Landstrasse 18, 6 Frankfurt-am-Main, Deutschland.
Wild (Th.), Mariahilferstrasse 158, Wien 1015, Österreich.
Wildner Buchantiquariat, Stempfergasse 8, 8010 Graz, Österreich.
Wirnitzer (Galerie Elfriede), Ludwig-Wilhelm-Strasse 17-a, 757 Baden-Baden, Deutschland.
Witt (M.& F.) = Leo S. Olschki, Lucignano, Italia.
Witt (Preben), Hestemøllestraede 3, 1464 København-K, Danmark.
Wittkowski (Marlene) = Hans Hartinger, Berlin, Deutschland.
Wölfle, O.H.G. (Robert), Amalienstrasse 65, 8 München 13, Deutschland.
Wolfrum (Kunstverlag), Augustinerstrasse 10, 1010 Wien, Österreich.
Wötzel (Akademische Buchhandlung), Paul-Ehrlich-Strasse 24, 6 Frankfurt-am-Main, Deutschland.
Wristers (J.), Minrebroederstraat 13, Utrecht, Nederland.
Wündisch (Hans), Kornmarkt 9, 69 Heidelberg, Deutschland.
de Wyngaert (Madame Cécile) = La Vie Rustique, Bruxelles, Belgique.

Z

Zadek (Walter) = Logos Bookshop, Tel Aviv, Israel.
Zahn (Ernst) = Bruno Hessling, Berlin, Deutschland.
Zalc (Jean), 37 rue Mazelle, 5700 Metz, France.
Zalozba Mladinska Knjiga "Emka", 38 Capova, Ljubljana, Jugoslavija.
Zambakis (Angelos), 84 Solonis, Athens, Ellas.
Zeller (Otto), Jahnstrasse 15, 45 Osnabrück, Deutschland.
Zentralantiquariat der DDR, Talstrasse 1080, 701 Leipzig, D.D.R.
Zentrales Antiquariat Berlin, Rungerstrasse 20, 102 Berlin, D.D.R.
Zijlstra (B.P.), 85 rue de Rivoli, 75001 Paris, France.
Zlatin (Madame S.), 46 rue Madame, 75006 Paris, France.
Zohar, 3 Nahalat Benyamin, Tel Aviv, Israel.
Zukunft (Bjarne) = Sorø Antikvariat, Sorø, Danmark.
Zyssman (G.) = Librairie Monge, Paris, France.

SPECIALITIES

SPECIALITIES   SPECIALITÉS:
SPEZIALITÄTEN

Specialities are arranged under the following heads:

1. AUCTIONEERS: Ventes aux Enchères: Auktionen
2. AUTOGRAPHS and MANUSCRIPTS: Autographes et Manuscrits: Autographen und Handschriften
3. BIBLIOGRAPHY: Bibliographie: Buchwesen
4. COLLECTING: Livres pour Collectionneurs: Bücher für Sammler
5. CRAFTS and USEFUL ARTS: Arts et Mêtiers: Kunstgewerbe
6. ENTERTAINMENTS: Théâtre et Cinéma: Theater und Kino
7. EROTIC and CURIOUS: Curiosités et Érotique: Erotik
8. FINE and RARE: Beaux livres: Schöne und Seltener Bücher
9. JUVENILE: Livres d'Enfants: Kinderbücher
10. HISTORY: Histoire: Geschichte
11. LANGUAGES: Langues: Sprache
12. LAW and CRIMINOLOGY: Droit et criminologie: Recht
13. MEDICINE: Médecine: Medizin
14. MUSIC: Musique: Musik und Noten
15. NATURAL HISTORY: Sciences naturelles: Naturwissenschaften
16. PERIODICALS: Périodiques: Zeitschriften
17. PICTORIAL ART: Beaux Arts: Kunst und Graphik
18. RELIGION and PHILOSOPHY (I): RELIGIONS and PHILOSOPHIE (I): THEOLOGIE UND PHILOSOPHIE (I)
19. RELIGION and PHILOSOPHY (II): Religions et Philosophie (II): Theologie und Philosophie (II)
20. REMAINDERS and OVERSTOCKS: Soldes: Restauflage
21. SOCIOLOGY: Sociologie: Soziologie
22. SPORTS, GAMES and PASTIMES: Sports et Jeux: Sport und Spiele
23. TECHNICAL and EDUCATIONAL: Technique et Érudition: Technik
24. SCIENCE: Sciences: Wissenschaften
25. TOPOGRAPHY and TRAVEL: Régionalsime et voyages: Topographie und Reisen

SPECIALITIES

SPECIALITIES   SPECIALITÉS:
SPEZIALITÄTEN

Alchemy	19	Educational	23
Alte Drucke	8	Einband	8
Alte Bücher	8	Encadrements	17
Anthropology	15	Enfants (Livres d')	9
Archaeology	15	Engravings	17
Architecture	17	Entertainments	6
Art	17	Entomology	15
Arts et Métiers	5	Equitation	22
Atlases	25	Erotic	7
Auctioneers	1	Erotique	7
Auktionen	1	Erstausgaben	8
Autographs	2	Erudition	23
		Estampes	17
Beaux-arts	17	Ethnography	15
Beaux livres	8	Ethnology	15
Bibliography	3		
Bibliophilie	4	Facsimiles	4
Botanik	15	Farbstiche	17
Botany	15	Fine arts	17
Buchwesen	3	First editions	8
		Folklore	21
Cartes	25	Freemasonry	19
Cartography	25	Freemaurerei	19
Chasse	22		
Chemie	24	Gastronomie	5
Chess	22	Gemälde	17
Cinema	6	Genealogy	10
Circus	6	Geography	25
Cirque	6	Geschichte	10
Collecting	4	Gesellschaft	21
Collectionneurs (Livres pour)	4	Graphik	17
Costumes	17	Gravures	17
Crafts and Useful Arts	5		
Criminology	12	Handschriften	2
Curiosités	7	Handzeichnungen	17
		Hebraica	18
Danse	6	Heimatkunde	24
Dentistry	13	Heraldique	10
Dessins	17	Heraldry	10
Dictionaries	11	History	10
Droit	12	Horology	4
		Hunting	22
Editions originales	8		

Illustrated	17	Politik	21
Illustrierte	17	Pressendrucke	4
Incunabula	8	Prints	17
Inkunabeln	8	Psychology	18
Judaica	18	Recht	12
Juvenile	9	Reisen	25
		Reformation	10
Kinderbücher	9	Régionalisme	25
Kino	6	Religions	18
Kunst	17	Reliures	17
Kunstgewerbe	5	Remainders	20
		Restauflagen	20
Landkarten	25		
Languages	11	Sammler (Bücher für)	4
Langues	11	Sciences	24
Law	12	Sciences naturelles	15
		Sculptures	17
Manuscripts	2	Seltene Bücher	8
Maps	25	Sexology	7
Marine	23	Sittengeschichte	7
Marionettes	6	Sociology	21
Mathematics	24	Soldes	20
Medicine	13	Speleologie	22
Medizin	13	Sports et jeux	22
Militaria	23	Sports, games and pastimes	22
Mineralogy	15	Sprachwissenschaft	11
Mountaineering	22	Staatswissenschaften	21
Music	14	Städteansichten	25
Musique	14		
		Tanz	6
Natural History	15	Technical	23
Naturwissenschaft	15	Technik	23
Navigation	23	Technique	23
Noten	14	Theatre	6
Numismatique	4	Theology	18
		Topography	25
		Travel	25
Occult	19	Typographie	3
Old and rare	8		
		Vénerie	22
Paleontology	15	Ventes aux Enchères	1
Pêche	22	Views	25
Periodicals	16	Voyages	25
Petit Format (Livres en)	8	Vues	25
Pferde	22		
Pharmacie	13	Wertvolle Bücher	8
Philology	11	Wirtschaft	21
Philosophy	18	Wissenschaften	24
Physics	24		
Physique	24	Zeitgeschichte	10
Pictorial art	17	Zeitschriften	16
Political economy	21	Zoology	15

1. AUCTIONEERS: VENTES AUX ENCHÉRES: AUKTIONEN

J. L. Beijers, B.V., Achter Sint Pieter, 14, Utrecht, Nederland.
Wolfgang Brandes, Kleine Campestrasse 2, 33 Braunschweig, Deutschland.
Burgersdijk & Niermans, Nieuwsteeg 1, Leiden, Nederland.
F. Dörling, Neuer Wall, 2 Hamburg 36, Deutschland.
Giraud-Badin, 128 boulevard St.-Germain, 75006 Paris, France.
Haus der Bücher, "Erasmushaus", Bäumleingasse 18, Basel, Schweiz.
Hauswedell & Nolte, Pöseldorferweg 1, 2 Hamburg 23, Deutschland.
Laube & Sohn, Trittligasse 19, 8001 Zürich, Schweiz.
Jean Michel de Floesser, 28 rue de Remparts, 33 Bordeaux, France.
Horst A. Rittershofer, Meinekestrasse 3, 1 Berlin 15, Deutschland.
J. A. Stargadt, Universitätsstrasse 27, 355 Marburg, Deutschland.
Van Stockum's Antiquariaat, Prinsegracht 15, 's-Gravenhage, Nederland.
Paul van der Perre, Rue de la Régence 21, 1000 Bruxelles, Belgique.
Venator, K.G., Apernstrasse 56–62, Köln, Deutschland.

2. AUTOGRAPHS AND MANUSCRIPTS: AUTOGRAPHES ET MANU-SCRITS: AUTOGRAPHEN UND HANDSCHRIFTEN

Athenaeum Antiquarian Booksellers, Keizersgracht 6008, 1002 Amsterdam, Nederland.
Luigi Banzi, Via Borgonuovo 10, 40125 Bologna, Italia.
Pierre Berès, 14 avenue de Friedland, 75008 Paris, France.
Bianchino del Leone, Piazza Ansidei 4, 06100 Perugia, Italia.
Bibliofila, Corso Porta Nuova 2, 20121 Milano, Italia.
Blaizot, S.A., 164 faubourg St.-Honoré, 75008 Paris, France.
Boghallens Antikvariat, Raadhuspladsen 37, 1585 København-V, Danmark.
Pierre La Brely, 108 rue du Ranelagh, 75016 Paris, France.
Robert Cayla, 28 rue St.-Sulpice, 75006 Paris, France.
Charavay, 3 rue de Furstenberg, 75006 Paris, France.
Carlo Alberto Chiesa, Via Bigli, 11, 20121 Milano, Italia.
Pierre Chrétien, 178 faubourg St.-Honoré, 75008 Paris, France.
Mme Veuve Ronald Davis, 12 avenue Franklin-Roosevelt, 75008 Paris, France.
Maurice Dussarp, 36 rue du Mont Thabor, 75001 Paris, France.
Gendt & Co. N.V., Keizersgracht 610, Amsterdam, Nederland.
Gilhofer & Ranschburg, Haldenstrasse 9, 6006 Luzern, Schweiz.
Gonnelli & Figli, Via Ricasoli 14, Firenze, Italia.
Fernand Gothier, 11 place du 20 Août, 4000 Liège, Belgique.
August Hase, Im Trutz 2, 6 Frankfurt-am-Main, Deutschland.
Haus der Bücher, "Erasmushaus", Bäumleingasse 18, Basel, Schweiz.
V. A. Heck, Kärntner Ring 12, 1010 Wien, Österreich.
Historica e Ultramarina, Travessa da Queimada 28, Lisboa 2, Portugal.
N. Israel, Keizersgracht 526, Amsterdam, Nederland.
Jean Hugues, 1 rue de Furstenberg, 75006 Paris, France.
Jacques Lambert, 27 rue Bonaparte, 75006 Paris, France.
Leonardo Lapiccirella, Lungarno Vespucci 18, 50123 Firenze, Italia.
Lardanchet, 10 rue Président Carnot, 69002 Lyon, France.
Bernard Loliée, 72 rue de Seine, 75006 Paris, France.
Marc Loliée, rue des Saints-Pères, 75007 Paris, France.
Edouard Loewy, 184 boulevard Haussmann, 75008 Paris, France.
G. Casella di Lo Schiavo, Piazza Municipio 84, Napoli, Italia.

Jacques Matarasso, 2 rue Longchamp, 06 Nice, France.
Mediolanum, Via Montebello 30, 20121 Mioano, Italia.
Mellgrens Antikvariat, Centrumhuset Östra Larmgatan 17, 41107 Göteborg, Sverige.
Konrad Meuschel, Kaiserplatz 5, 53 Bonn, Deutschland.
Daniel Morcrette, 4 avenue Joffre, 95270 Luzarches, France.
G. Morssen, 14 rue de Seine, 75006 Paris, France.
Pfann, Rokin 112, Amsterdam, Nederland.
Arturo Pregliasco, Via Accademia 3 bis, 10123 Torino, Italia.
Giorgina Pregliasco-Mathes, Via Po 14, 10123 Torino, Italia.
Radaeli, Via A. Manzoni 39, 20121 Milano, Italia.
Mme Eugene Reymond, 14 faubourg de l'Hopital, Neuchâtel, Suisse.
Renzo Rizzi, Via Cernaia 4, 20121 Milano, Italia.
Emile Rossignol, 8 rue Bonaparte, 75006 Paris, France.
Francis Roux-Vellias, 12 rue Bonaparte, 75006 Paris, France.
Saffroy, 3 quai Malaquais, 75006 Paris, France.
Jean-Louis Sainte-Marie, 43 boulevard Alsace Lorraine, 82200 Moissac, France.
Sibrium Libri e Manoscritti, Via Bigli 21, Milano, Italia.
Pierre Sieur, 3 rue de la Université, 75007 Paris, France.
J. A. Stargadt, Universitätsstrasse 27, 355 Marburg, Deutschland.
Théodore Tausky, 33 rue Dauphine, 75006 Paris, France.
René Vigneron, 74 rue de Seine, 75006 Paris, France.
Wiener Antiquariat, Seilergasse 16, Wien, Österreich.

3. BIBLIOGRAPHY: BIBLIOGRAPHIE: BÜCHWESEN

Berruto, Via San Francesco da Paola 10 bis, 10123 Torino, Italia.
Bouvier Universitätsbuchhandlung, Am Hof 32, 53 Bonn, Deutschland.
Arnold Busck, Fiolstraede 24, 1171 København-K, Danmark.
Francis Dasté, 16 rue de Tournon, 75006 Paris, France.
Lucien Dorbon, 156 boulevard St.-Germain, 75006 Paris, France.
Dresdener Antiquariat, Bautzner Strasse 27, 806 Dresden, D.D.R.
Erasmus Antiquariaat, Spui 2, Amsterdam, Nederland.
Europeriodiques, S.A., 31 avenue de Versailles, 78170 La Celle St.-Cloud, France.
Manuel Ferreira, Rua Formosa 19, Porto, Portugal.
Giraud-Badin, 128 boulevard St.-Germain, 75006 Paris, France.
Hans von Goetz, Wörthstrasse 28, 62 Wiesbaden, Deutschland.
Antiquariaat de Graaf, Zuideinde 40, Nieuwkoop, Nederland.
Gsellius'sche Antiquariat, Hertastrasse 16, 1 Berlin 37, Deutschland.
Max Günther, Charlottenbrunnerstrasse 5-a, 1 Berlin 33, Deutschland.
Bruno Hessling, Rankestrasse 31, 1 Berlin 30, Deutschland.
Werner Heybutski, Pfeilstrasse 8, 5 Köln, Deutschland.
Hans Höchterberger, Elsenheimerstrasse 18, 8 München 21, Deutschland.
Karl Hölzl, K.G., Seilergasse 3, 1010 Wien, Österreich.
H. Hugendubel, Salvatorplatz 2, 8 München, Deutschland.
Paul Jammes, 3 rue Gozelin, 75006 Paris, France.
Boris Kaplanski, 8 rue du Loing, 75014 Paris, France.
Walter Klügel, Gumpendorferstrasse 33, 1060 Wien, Österreich.
Fritz Knuf, P.O. Box 20, 2707 Buren, Nederland.
Hans Horst Koch, Hauptstrasse 7, 1 Berlin 62, Deutschland.
Valentin Koerner, Iberstrasse 36, 757 Baden-Baden, Deutschland.

Walter Kreig, Kärtnerstrasse 4, 1010 Wien, Österreich.
Lengertz Antikvariat, Adelgatan 19, Malmö-C, Sverige.
Louis Loeb-Larocque, 36 rue le Peletier, 75009 Paris, France.
Yves Margotat, 8 rue de l'Odéon, 75006 Paris, France.
Müller & Gräff, Calwerstrasse 54, 7 Stuttgart 1, Deutschland.
Buchantiquariat Neues Schloss, Stockerstrasse 17, 8027 Zürich, Schweiz.
Rudolf Patzer, Mainzer Berg 23, 6731 Weidenthal, Deutschland.
Dr. Karl H. Pressler, Herzogstrasse 58, 8 München 40, Deutschland.
Edgar Soete, 5 quai Voltaire, 75007 Paris, France.
Paul Van der Perre, Rue de la Régence 21, 1000 Bruxelles, Belgique.
Venator, K.G., Apernstrasse 56, 5 Köln, Deutschland.

4. COLLECTING: LIVRES POUR COLLECTIONNEURS: BÜCHER FÜR
   SAMMLER.

Chez Durtal, 12 rue Jacov, 75006 Paris, France—*Horologie*.
Cité de vieux livres, 139 Grande Rue, 25000 Besançon, France—*Numismatique*.
Bouquinerie du Languedoc, 12 rue de l'Université, 34000 Montpellier, France—
    Numismatique.
Nissen Preminger, 9, Montefiore Street, Tel Aviv, Israel—*Horology*.
Jacques Schulman, Keizersgracht 448, Amsterdam-C, Nederland.—*Numismatics*.
Pierre Sieur, 3 rue de l'Université, 75007 Paris, France—*jouets anciens, cartes à
    jouer anciennes et modernes, Numismatique*.

5. CRAFTS AND USEFUL ARTS: ARTS ET MÉTIERS: KUNSTGEWERBE

Aristeucos, Paseo de la Bonanova 14-G, Barcelona, España—*gastronomy*.
Frederiksberg Antikvariat, Gammel Kongevej 120, 1850 København-V, Dan-
    mark—*arts and crafts*.
Librairie Gonot, 22 rue de Miromesnil, 75008 Paris, France—*gastronomie*.
Jürgen Holstein, Gerichtsstrasse 7-a, 6240 Könogstein, Deutschland—*Kunst-
    gewerbe*.
Arnold Levilliers, 118 Route de Chartres, 91400 Gometz-le-Chatel, France—*arts
    et métiers*.
Daniel Morcrette, 4 avenue Joffre, 95270 Luzarches, France—*gastronomie*.
Edgar Soete, 5 quai Voltaire, 75007 Paris, France—*gastronomie*.
Robert Vivien, 41 rue Mazarine, 75006 Paris, France—*gastronomie*.

6. ENTERTAINMENTS: THÉÂTRE ET CINÉMA: THEATER UND KINO

S. Agostino, Via S. Agostino 17/A, Roma, Italia—*spectacle*.
Garnier Arnoul, 39 rue de Seine, 75006 Paris, France—*théâtre, danse, mime*.
Bog-Messen, Gammel Kongevej 19, 1610 København-V, Danmark—*ballet*.
Libraire Bonaparte, 31 rue Bonaparte, 75006 Paris, France—*spectacles, théâtre,
    danse, cinéma*.
Creyghton, Lassuslaan 45, Bilthoven, Nederland—*theatre*.
Luigi Finzi, Foro Buonaparte 12, 20121 Milano, Italia—*theatre*.
Pierre Girard, 17 rue de Chateaudun, 75009 Paris, France—*théâtre*.
Le Grenier du Collectionneur, Avenue Orban 238, 1150 Bruxelles, Belgique—
    performing arts.

Heinrich Rimanek, Kaiserstrasse 6, 1070 Wien, Österreich—*Theater, Tanz.*
Hans Rohr, Oberdorferstrasse 5, 8024 Zürich, Schweiz—*Film.*
J. Voerster, Relenbergstrasse 33, 7 Stuttgart, Deutschland—*Theatre.*
Carl Wegner, Martin-Luther-Strasse 113, 1 Berlin 62, Deutschland—*Theater.*
Mme S. Zlatin, 46 rue Madame, 75006 Paris, France—*théâtre, danse, cirque, cinéma, marionettes.*

7. EROTIC AND CURIOUS: CURIOSITÉS et ÉROTIQUE: EROTIK

B.M.C.F. Antiquariat, Langer Weg 35, 7901 Ulm-Gögglingen, Deutschland—*Curiosa.*
Denyse Chertin, 14 rue de Richelieu, 75001 Paris, France—*curiosités.*
Le Grenier du Collectionneur, Avenue Orban 238, 1150 Bruxelles, Bruxelles—*ephemera.*
Walter Klügel, Gumpendorferstrasse 33, 1060 Wien, Österreich—*Erotik, Sittengeschichte..*
Jacques Levy, 46 rue d'Alésia, 75014 Paris, France—*curiosités.*
Gabriel Molina, Travesia del Arenal 1, Madrid, España—*curious.*
"Veille France", 65 boulevard Général-Leclerc, 33120 Arcachon, France—*curiosités.*

8. FINE AND RARE: BEAUX LIVRES: SCHÖNE UND SELTENER BÜCHER

Theodore Ackermann, Promenadeplatz 11, 8 München, Deutschland—*alte Drucke.*
Antiquariat Amelang, Cranachstrasse 45, 2 Hamburg 52, Deutschland—*Pressendrucke, Erstausgaben seit 1800.*
Alexandre Baer, 2–6 rue Livingstone, 75018 Paris, France—*livres très rares concernant les Ameriques.*
Fernand Beaufils, Avenue Victor-Hugo 169, 75016 Paris, France— *éditions originales.*
Pierre Bères, 14 avenue de Friedland, 75008 Paris, France—*beaux livres, reliures.*
La Bibliofila, Corso Porta Nuova 2, 20121 Milano, Italia—*incunabula,*
Björck & Börjesson, Kungsgatan 5/II, Stockholm-C, Sverige—*old and rare.*
August Blaizot, 164 faubourg St.-Honoré, 75008 Paris, France—*éditions originales.*
Bla Tornet, Drottningatan 85, Stockholm, Sverige—*old and rare.*
Bøckmann'a Antikvariat, Rosensgade 11, 8000 Aarhus-C, Danmark—*first editions.*
Pierre H. Le Bodo, 31 rue de Bordeaux, 37 Tours, France—*livres anciens.*
Boghallens Antikvariat, Raadhuspladsen 37, 1585 København-V, Danmark—*fine and old, finely bound English sets.*
Helmut Bolenz, Türkenstrasse 48, 8 München, Deutschland—*alte Drucke.*
Børsums Forlag og Antikvariat, Fr. Nansens-plass 2, Oslo 1, Norge—*old and rare, first editions.*
André Bottin, 2 rue Défly, 06 Nice, France—*éditions originales.*
Le Bouquiniste, Via Principe Amadeo 29, 10123 Torino, Italia—*old and rare.*
Lib. Ant. Bourlot, Piazza San Carlo, 183, 10123 Torino, Italia,—*old and rare.*
Branners Biblifile Antikvariat, Bredgade 10, 1260 København-K, Danmark—*old and rare.*

Pierre La Brely, 108 rue du Ranelagh, 75016 Paris, France—*éditions originales.*
Maurice Bridel, 1 avenue du Théâtre, 1000 Lausanne, Suisse—*beaux livres.*
Louis Broder, 187 boulevard St.-Germain, 75006 Paris, France—*éditions originales.*
Robert Cayla, 28 rue St.-Sulpice, 75006 Paris, France—*éditions originales.*
Henri Cazer, 49 rue de Seine, 75006 Paris, France—*éditions originales.*
Philippe Chabaneix, 33 rue Mazarine, 75006 Paris, France—*éditions originales modernes.*
François Chamonal, 40 rue le Peletier, 75009 Paris, France—*beaux livres anciens.*
Chariot d'Or, 38 rue des Remparts d'Ainay, 69002 Lyon, France—*livres anciens.*
Carlo Alberto Chiesa, Via Bigli 11, 20121 Milano, Italia—*old and rare, first editions, incunabula.*
Pierre Chrétien, 178 faubourg St.-Honoré, 75008 Paris, France—*éditions originales.*
Jean Colliard, 11 rue August-Comte, 69 Lyon, France—*beaux livres anciens.*
Maxime Cottet-Dumoulin, 3 rue Séguier, 75006 Paris, France—*étitions originales.*
C. Coulet & A. Faure, 5 rue Drouot, 75006 Paris, France—*éditions originales.*
Mme Couturier, 7 rue de Duras, 75008 Paris, France—*livres anciens.*
Damms Antikvariat, Tollbodgatan 25, Oslo 1, Norge—*old and rare.*
Mme Veuve Ronald Davis, 12 avenue Franklin-Roosevelt, 75008 Paris, France—*éditions originales.*
Max-Philippe Delatte, 133 rue de la Pompe, 75116 Paris, France—*éditions originales.*
Jean Deschamps, 22 rue Visconti, 75006 Paris, France—*éditions originales.*
"Docett", Via A. Righi 9/A, 40126 Bologna, Italia —*old and rare.*
Helmuth Domizlaff, Martiusstrasse 5/II, 8 München, Deutschland—*Drucke des 15 und 16 Jahrhunderts.*
F. Dörling, Neuer Wall, 2 Hamburg 36, Deutschland—*alte und seltene Bücher.*
Librairie Dubouchet, 2 rue Général Foy, 42 St.-Etienne, France—*livres anciens.*
Paul Eppe, 49 rue de Provence, 75009 Paris, France—*éditions originales.*
Erasmus Antiquariaat, Spui 2, Amsterdam, Nederland—*16th century books.*
Michel Fauron, 10 bis rue de Chateaudun, 75009 Paris, France—*éditions originales.*
Librairie Flammarion, 4 rue Casimir Delavigne, 75006 Paris, France—*éditions originales.*
Christian Galantaris, 11 rue de Vaugirard, 75006 Paris, France—*éditions originales, reliures.*
Gallimard, 15 boulevard Raspail, 75007 Paris, France—*éditions originales.*
A. L. Van Gendt & Co., Keizersgracht 610, Amsterdam, Nederland—*incunabula.*
Gilhofer Buchantiquariat, Bognergasse 2, 1010 Wien, Österreich—*alte und seltene Bücher.*
Gilhofer & Ranschburg, Haldenstrasse 9, 6006 Luzern, Schweiz—*Inkunabeln, 16 Jahrhunderts.*
Paul Gothier, Rue Bonne Fortune 3, Liège, Belgique—*old and rare, 15th and 16th centuries.*
De Graaf, Zuidende 40, Nieuwkoop, Nederland—*books printed 1500-1700.*
Antoine Grandmaison, 8 rue de Castiglione, 75001 Paris, France—*reliures.*
Mas Günther, Charlottenbrunnerstrasse 5-a, 1 Berlin 33, Deutschland—*Seltenheiten, Sammlerstücke.*
Else Haas, Dollstrasse 7, 807 Ingolstadt 21, Deutschland—*alte Drucke vor 1750.*
Karl M. Halosar, Margaretenstrasse 35, 1040 Wien, Österreich—*Erstausgaben.*
Jean-Jacques Hankard, 25 rue de la Paix, 1050 Bruxelles, Belgique—*fine editions.*

Hauswedell & Nolte, Pöseldorferweg 1, 2 Hamburg 23, Deutschland—*Erstausgaben.*

Georges Heilbrun, 3 rue Gît-le-Coeur, 75006 Paris, France—*beaux livres anciens et rares.*

Menno Hertzberger, Eemnesserweg 81, Baarn, Nederland—*incunabula.*

Hesperia, Plaza Los Antonio 10, Zaragoza, España—*old and rare Hispanica.*

Hans Höchterberger, Elsenheimerstrasse 18, 8 München 21, Deutschland—*Erstausgaben Deutsches Literatur.*

Ernst Hoffmann, Weissadlergasse 3, 6 Frankfurt-am-Main, Deutschland—*Inkunabeln, alte Drucke.*

H. Hugendubel, Salvatorplatz 2, 8 München, Deutschland—*alte Drucke.*

Jean Hugues, 1 rue de Furstenberg, 75006 Paris, France—*reliures.*

B. M. Israel, N.Z.Voorburgwal 264, Ansterdam, Nederland—*old and rare.*

N. Israel, Keizersgracht 526, Amsterdam, Nederland—*rare books.*

Paul Jammes, 3 rue Gozlin, 75006 Paris, France—*livres anciens.*

Gunnar Johanson-Thor, Hallsfarm, 24100 Eslöv, Sverige—*old Swedish books.*

Boris Kaplanski, 8 rue du Loing, 75014 Paris, France—*éditions anciennes.*

Karl & Faber, Karolinenplatz 5-A, 8 München 2, Deutschland—*alte Bücher.*

René Kieffer, 46 rue St.-André-des-Arts, 75006 Paris, France—*éditions originales, reliures.*

Erwin & Rolf Kistner, Breite Gasse 52, 85 Nürnberg, Deutschland—*seltene und vertvolle Bücher.*

Hans Horst Koch, Hauptstrasse 7, 1 Berlin 62, Deutschland—*alte und schöne Bücher.*

Wilhelm Kuhdt, Paulusstrasse 28, 48 Bielefeld, Deutschland—*Erstausgaben*

C. F. Labarre, 22 rue Dauphine, 75006 Paris, France—*livres anciens.*

Jeanne Lafitte, 106 boulevard Longchamp, 13001 Marseille, France—*éditions originales.*

Lardanchet, 10 rue Président Carnot, 69002 Lyon, France—*beaux livres.*

Günther Leisten, In der Höhle 6, 5 Köln, Deutschland—*schöne und seltene Bücher.*

Richard Levin, Dannebrogade 1/IV, 1660 København-V, Danmark—*old and rare.*

Librairie des Galeries, Galerie du Roi 2, 1000 Bruxelles, Belgique—*antiquarian.*

Libris Antikvariatet, Kommendörsgatan 14, 10243 Stockholm, Sverige—*old and rare, bindings.*

Dr. Konrad Liebmann, Lürman-Strasse 47, 45 Osnabrück, Deutschland—*Erstausgaben, Einbände.*

Claus Lincke, Königsallee 96, Düsseldorf, Deutschland—*alte und seltene Bücher, Erstausgaben.*

Edouard Loewy, 184 boulevard Haussmann, 75008 Paris, France—*éditions originales.*

Bernard Loliée, 72 rue de Seine, 75006 Paris, France—*éditions originales.*

Marc Loliée, rue des Saints-Pères, 75007 Paris, France—*éditions originales, livres anciens.*

G. Casella di Lo Schiavo, Piazza Municipio 84, Napoli, Italia—*rare books.*

Löwendahls Antikvariat, P.O. Box 2101, 75002 Uppsala 2, Sverige—*old and rare.*

A. Lunge Larsen, Øygardveien 16-E, Bekkestua, Norge—*old and rare.*

Lynge & Son, Løvstraede 8, 1152 København-K, Danmark—*rare books.*

Jean-Jacques Magis, 12 rue Guenégaud, 75006 Paris, France—*livres anciens.*

Yves Margotat, 8 rue de l'Odéon, 75006 Paris, France—*livres rares.*

Paul-Robert Marin, 18 boulevard Haussmann, 75009 Paris, France—*reliures.*

Martelli, Via Santo Stefano 43, 40125 Bologna, Italia—*incunabula, first editions.*

Jacques Matarasso, 2 rue Longchamp, 06 Nice, France—*éditions originales.*
H. Mellgrens Antikvariat, Centrumhuset Östra Larmgatan 17, 41107 Göteborg, Sverige—*old and rare.*
Konrad Meuschel, Kaiserplatz 5, 53 Bonn, Deutschland—*alte und seltene Bücher.*
Daniel Morcrette, 4 avenue Joffre, 95270 Luzarches, France—*livres rares.*
Gia Nardecchia, Piazza Cavour 25, 00193 Roma, Italia—*old Italian books.*
Nicaise, S.A., 145 boulevard St.-Germain, 75005 Paris, France—*éditions originales.*
Günther Nobis, Forststrasse 12, 62 Wiesbaden, Deutschland—*Erstausgaben, alte und wertvolle Bücher.*
Palmaverde, Via Castiglione 35, 40124 Bologna, Italia—*modern first editions.*
Pierre Petitot, 234 boulevard St.-Germain, 75007 Paris, France—*beaux livres.*
Pierre Picard, 60 boulevard Malesherbes, 75008 Paris, France—*reliures.*
L. & J. H. Pinault, 36 rue Bonaparte, 75006 Paris, France—*livres en petit format.*
Pinkus Genossenschaft, Froschaugasse 7, 8001 Zürich, Schweiz—*Erstausgaben, alte Drucke.*
Pregliasco, Via Accademia 3 bis, 10123 Torino, Italia—*old and rare.*
Dr. Karl H. Pressler, Herzogstrasse 58, 8 München 40, Deutschland—*schöne und seltene Bücher.*
Puzin, 30 rue de la Paroisse, 78 Versailles, France—*livres anciens.*
Radaeli, Via A. Manzoni 39, 20121 Milano, Italia—*miniatures, incunabula, Italian XV–XVIII century books.*
Bjørn Ringstrøms Antikvariat, Ullevalsveien 1, Oslo, Norge—*Norwegian first editions.*
Ludwig Rohrscheid, Am Hof 28, 53 Bonn, Deutschland—*Erstausgaben.*
Rosenkilde og Bagger, 3 Kron-Prinsens-Gade, 1114 København, Danmark—*old and rare.*
Jacques Rosenthal, Frühlingstrasse 12, 8051 Eching, Deutschland—*alte Drucke.*
Ludwig Rosenthal's Antiquariaat, Bussumergrintweg 4, Hilversum, Nederland—*incunabula.*
Emile Rossignol, 8 rue Bonaparte, 75006 Paris, France—*editions anciennes, incunables.*
Eugéne Rossignol, 4 rue de l'Odéon, 75006 Paris, France—*16, 17, 18 siecles, livres rares.*
Maurice Rouam, 29 rue Mazarine, 75006 Paris, France—*éditions originales.*
Umberto Saba, Via San Nicolo 30, 34121 Trieste, Italia—*old and rare, incunabula.*
Jean-Louis Sainte-Marie, 43 boulevard Alsace-Lorraine, 82200 Moissac, France —*livres anciens.*

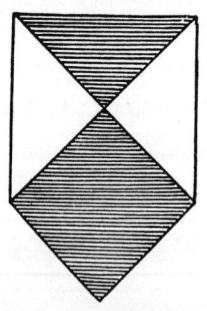

Libreria Vinciana, Via Monte Napoleone 23, 20121 Milano, Italia—*old and rare.*
Roger Wastiau, Rue de l'Industrie, 1040 Bruxelles, Belgique—*first editions, bindings.*
Bernhard Wendt, 8081 Buch-am-Ammersee-Oberbayern über München, Deutschland—*Inkunabeln, alte Drucke.*
H. Th. Wenner, Grosse Strasse 69, 45 Osnabrück, Deutschland—*alte Drucke.*
Angelos Zambakis, 84 Solonis, Athens, Ellas—*old and rare.*

9. JUVENILE: LIVRES D'ENFANTS: KINDERBÜCHE

Antiquariat Amelang, Cranachstrasse 45, 2 Hamburg 52, Deutschland—*alte Kinderbücher.*
Denyse Chertin, 14 rue de Richelieu, 75001 Paris, France.
H. Dirckinck-Holmfeld, Aabenraa 29, 1124 København-K, Danmark.
Frankfurter Bücherstube, Börsenstrasse 2, Frankfurt-am-Main, Deutschland—*alte Kinderbücher.*
Le Grenier du Collectionneur, Avenue Orban 238, 1150 Bruxelles, Belgique—*children's books, toys.*
Karl M. Halosar, Margaretenstrasse 35, 1040 Wien, Österreich—*alte Kinderbücher.*
Antiquariat Klaussner, Professor-Kurt-Huber-Strasse 19, 8032 Gräfeling (München), Deutschland—*ältere Jugendbücher.*
Loose, Papestraat 3, 's-Gravenhage, Nederland.
Klaus Lux, Im Hausgarten 33, 7800 Freiburg, Deutschland.
Paul-Robert Marin, 18 boulevard Haussmann, 75009 Paris, France.
Thulin & Ohlson, Kungsgatan 9-B, 41119 Göteborg, Sverige—*old Swedish children's books.*

10. HISTORY: HISTOIRE: GESCHICHTE

Robert Alder, Junkerngasse 41, Bern, Schweiz.
Librairie d'Argences, 38 rue St.-Sulpice, 75006 Paris, France.
Armarium Antiquariat, Stresemannstrasse 4, 4 Düsseldorf, Deutschland.
Paul Bataille, 14 rue Châteauredon, 13 Marseille, France.
Biblarte Ltda., Rua de Sao Pedro de Alcantara 71, Lisboa, Portugal.
Hieronymus Bosch, Spuistraat 125, Amsterdam, Nederland—*Dutch history before 1800.*
Bouma's Boekhuis, Turfsingel 3, Groningen, Nederland.
Le Bouquiniste, Via Principe Amedeo 29, 10123 Torino, Italia.
Bourcy & Paulusch, Wipplingerstrasse 5, 1010 Wien, Österreich—*Genealogie.*
Robert Bourdon, 184 bis route de Châteaudun, 45190 Beaugency, France.
Walther Breinersdorf, Ebitzweg 7, 7 Stuttgart-Bad Cannstadt, Deutschland.
Daniel Brun, 6 rue Clodion, 75015 Paris, France.
Castro e Silva, Rua da Rosa 31, Lisboa, Portugal.
Charavay, 3 rue de Furstenberg, 75006 Paris, France—*documents historiques.*
Librairie du Chariot d'Or, 38 rue des Remparts d'Ainay, 69002 Lyon, France.
Carl F. Chrispeels, Combahnstrasse 15, 53 Bonn-Beuel 1, Deutschland—*Geschichte bis 15 Jahrhunderts.*
Raymond Clavreuil, 37 rue St.-André-des-Arts, 75006 Paris, France.
Pierre Clerc, 13 rue Alexandre-Cabanel, 34000 Montpellier, France.
Francis Dasté, 16 rue de Tournon, 75006 Paris, France—*histoire de Paris.*
André Deruelle, 30 rue des Saints-Pères, 75007 Paris, France—*héraldique.*

Lucien Dorbon, 156 boulevard St.-Germain, 75006 Paris, France.
Librairie Dorbon-Ainé, 19 boulevard Haussmann, 75009 Paris, France.
Galerie Durance, 5 allée d'Orléans, 44000 Nantes, France.
Alice Elchepp, Schillerstrasse 14, 3360 Osterode a. Harz, Deutschland.
Elwert Universitätsbuchhandlung, Reitgasse 7, 355 Marburg, Deutschland.
Librairie Encyclopedique, rue du Luxembourg, 1040 Bruxelles, Belgique.
Librairie de l'Europe, 1 Val des Roses, 1000 Bruxelles, Belgique—*Genealogie, histoire contemporain.*
Roberte Fricke, Hardenbergplatz 13, 1 Berlin 12, Deutschland.
H. G. Gerritsen, Van Welderenstraat 88, Nijmegen, Nederland.
Karl Gess, Kanzleistrasse 5, 7750 Konstanz, Deutschland.
H. Geyer, Hofmühlgasse 14, Wien 6, Österreich.
Heinrich Gilsing, Kaiserstrasse 3, 8205 Kiefersfelden, Deutschland.
Pierre Girard, 17 rue de Chateaudun, 75009 Paris, France.
Hans von Goetz, Wörthstrasse 28, 62 Wiesbaden, Deutschland.
Gerhard Goldau, Gasteigweg 4, 8022 Grünwald, Deutschland.
Dr. Hans Eberhard Goldschmidt, Döblinger Haupstrasse 61, Wien 19, Österreich.
René Gonot, 99 boulevard Haussmann, 75008 Paris, France.
Librairie Gonot, 22 rue de Miromesnil, 75008 Paris, France.
Fernand Gothier, place du 20 Août 11, 4000 Liège, Belgique.
Oreste di Pietro Chellini Gozzini, Via Ricasoli 49, 50122 Firenze, Italia.
De Graaf, Zuidende 40, Nieuwkoop, Nederland—*Reformation.*
Antoine Grandmaison, 8 rue de Castiglione, 75001 Paris, France.
J. Grubb's Antikvariat, Nørregade 47, København-K, Danmark.
Goolliuo'ooho Antiquariat, Hertastrasse 16, 1 Berlin 37, Deutschland.
Michel Guillaume & Cie, 98 rue St.-Pierre, 14 Caen, France.
Dr. Annemarie Guyer-Halter, Auf der Mauer 1, 8000 Zürich, Schweiz.
Gysbers en Van Loon, Bakkerstraat 7-a, Arnhem, Nederland—*Dutch history.*
Hachette, 58 rue Jean-Bleuzen, 92170 Vanves, France.
Adolf M. Hakkert, Spuistraat 90/A, Amsterdam, Nederland—*ancient history.*
George C. Hamel, Brandenburgerstrasse 74, 1 Berlin 31, Deutschland.
Victor Hankard, 27 rue de la Madeleine, Bruxelles 1, Belgique.
A. L. Hasbach, Wollzeile 9, Wien 1, Österreich.
J. J. Heckenhauer, Holzmarkt 5, 74 Tübingen, Deutschland.
Heckenhauer-Sonnewald, Waldhof 1, 7947 Mengen, Deutschland.
Andr. Fred Høst & Søn, Bredgade 35, 1260 København-K, Danmark.
Hiving & Zn., Kleine Houtstraat 50, Haarlem, Nederland.
l'Intermédiaire du Livre, 88 rue Bonaparte, 75006 Paris, France.
Xavier Jehanno, 4 place de l'Église, 78 Louveciennes, France.
Gunnar Johanson-Thor, Hallsfarm, 24100 Eslöv, Sverige.
Boris Kaplanski, 8 rue du Loing, 75014 Paris, France.
Albert Kohls, Winterfeldstrasse 44, 1 Berlin 30, Deutschland.
Walter Krieg, Kärtnerstrasse 4, 1010 Wien, Österreich.
Günther Kubiak, Martin-Luther-Strasse 127, 1 Berlin 62, Deutschland.
Herbert Lang & Cie, Munzgraben 2, 3000 Bern, Schweiz.
Lestringant, 123 rue Général-Leclerc, 76000 Rouen, France.
Jacques Levy, 46 rue d'Alésia, 75014 Paris, France.
Jules Lorieul, 3 rue de Poterie, 50 Valognes, France.
Klaus Lux, Im Hausgarten 33, 7800 Frieburg, Deutschland.
Christian Macoir, Val des Roses 1, Bruxelles, Belgique—*history, genealogy.*
Sté Many, 12 rue Delambre. 75014, Paris, France.
Yves Margotat, 8 rue de l'Odéon, 75006 Paris, France.

Martelli, Via Santo Stefano 43, 40125 Bologna, Italia.
F. & A. Mehren, Mauritzstrasse 3, 44 Münster, Deutschland.
Müller & Gräff, Calwerstrasse 54, 7 Stuttgart 1, Deutschland.
S. & P. Neser, Kreuzlingerstrasse 11, 775 Konstanz, Deutschland.
Buchantiquariat Neues Schloss, Stockerstrasse 17, 8027 Zürich, Schweiz.
Félix Nicolas, Leliestraat 61, Hove, Belgie.
Günther Nobis. Forststrasse 12, 62 Wiesbaden, Deutschland.
Nordiska Antikvariska Bokhandeln, Norra Magasingatan 6, Helsingfors, Suomi.
Leo S. Olschki, 52046 Lucignano (Arezzo), Italia.
H. K. Overdiep, Korte Gasthuisstraat 45, 2000 Antwerpen, Belge.
J. P. Parrot, 59 rue de Rennes, 75006 Paris, France.
Jean Peysson, 7 rue du Plat, 69 Lyon, France—*héraldique*.
A. & J. Picard, 82 rue Bonaparte, 75006 Paris, France.
F. Pinczower, 83 Sokolow Street, Tel Aviv, Israel—*contemporary history*.
Librairie Poursin, 21 rue St.-Sulpice, 75006 Paris, France.
Dr. Karl H. Pressler, Herzogstrasse 58, 8 München 40, Deutschland.
Wilhelm Puskas, Weiburggasse 16, 1010 Wien, Österreich.
Librarie Puzin, 30 rue de la Paroisse, 78 Versailles, France.
Librairie Raoust, 11 rue Neuve, 59000 Lille, France.
A. Remy, 25 rue Stainislas, 54000 Nancy, France.
Günther Richter, Breite Strasse 29, 1 Berlin 33, Deutschland.
Bjørn Ringstrøms Antikvariat, Ullevalsveien 1, Oslo 1, Norge.
Ludwig Rohrscheid, Am Hof 28, 53 Bonn, Deutschland.
A. Rombaut, Lievestraat 14, 9000 Gent, Belgie—*genealogy*.
Saffroy, 3 quai Malaquais, 75006 Paris, France—*documents historiques*.
Gaston Saffroy, 4 rue Clément, 75006 Paris, France—*généalogie, héraldique*.
Jean-Louis Saint-Marie, 43 boulevard Alsace-Lorraine, 82200 Moissac, France.
Ferdinand Schöningh, Domhof 4-c, 45 Osnabrück, Deutschland.
Pierre Sieur, 3 rue de la Université, 75007 Paris, France—*documents historiques*.
Lib. Ant. Soave, Via Po 48, 10123 Torino, Italia.
J. A. Stargadt, Universitätsstrasse 27, 355 Marburg, Deutschland—*Genealogie, Heraldrik*.
Th. Stenderhoff & Co., Alter Firschmarkt 21, 44 Münster, Deutschland.
Edmond Tamiz, 30 rue Madame, 75006 Paris, France.
Marcel Thourel, 61 rue du Taur, 31 Toulouse, France.
Francine Van der Perre, 23 rue de la Madeleine, 1000 Bruxelles, Belgique—*genealogy, heraldry*.
Galerie Vauquelin, 4 rue Vauquelin, 76200 Dieppe, France.
J. Vrin, 6 place de la Sorbonne, 75005 Paris, France.
Roger Wastiau, Rue de l'Industrie, 1040 Bruxelles, Belgique.
Elisabeth Wellnitz, Sachsenstrasse 35, 61 Darmstadt, Deutschland.

11. LANGUAGEṢ: LANGUES: SPRACHE

Antiquariaat Antiqua, Herengracht 159, Amsterdam, Nederland—*philology*.
Librairie d'Argences, 38 rue St.-Sulpice, 75006 Paris, France—*philologie*.
Aristeucos, Paseo de la Bonanova 14 G, Barcelona, España—*Spanish, Catalan, Latin language books*.
Björck & Börjesson, Kungsgatan 5/II, Stockholm-C, Sverige—*philology*.
Bouma's Boekhuis, Turfsingel 3, Groningen, Nederland—*philology*.
Walther Breinersdorf, Ebitzweg 7, 7 Stuttgart-Bad Cannstadt, Deutschland—*philologie*.

Claude Buffet, 7 rue St.-Sulpice, 75006 Paris, France—*littérature francaise et traductions.*
Castro e Silva, Rua da Rosa 31, Lisboa, Portugal.
F. Deuticke, Helferstorferstrasse 4, 1010 Wien, Österreich—*Philologie.*
Librairie Encyclopedique, 40 rue du Luxembourg, 1040 Bruxelles, Belgique—*philology.*
Gerold & Co., Graben 31, 1011 Wien, Österreich—*Philologie.*
Paul Geuthner, 12 rue Vavin, 75006 Paris, France—*linguistique.*
J. Grubb's Antikvariat, Nørregade 47, København-K, Danmark—*philology.*
B. R. Grüner, Nieuwe Herengracht 31, Amsterdam-C, Nederland—*linguistics.*
Adolf M. Hakkert, Spuistraat 90/A, Amsterdam, Nederland—*classical philology.*
Victor Hankard, 27 rue de la Madeleine, Bruxelles 1, Belgique—*philology.*
A. L. Hasbach, Wollzeile 9, Wien 1, Österreich—*Sprachwissenschaft.*
Sté Hébraica Judaica, 12 rue des Hospitalières St.-Gervais, 75004 Paris, France—*Judaica et Hebraica en toutes langues.*
Iberia, Hirschengraben 6, Bern, Schweiz—*littérature espagnole.*
J. Kitzinger, Schellingstrasse 25, 8 München 13, Deutschland—*Altphilologie.*
Kniha, Malé Námesti No. 11, Praha 1, Ceskoslovensko—*foreign literature.*
Lynge & Son, Løvstraede 8, 1152 København, Danmark—*linguistics.*
H. K. Overdiep, Korte Gasthuisstraat 45, 2000 Antwerpen, Belge—*languages.*
Palmaverde, Via Castiglione 35, 40124 Bologna, Italia—*philology.*
Panayiotis Georgiou & Co., P.O. Box 622, Athens, Ellas—*dictionairies.*
Prandi, Viale Timavo 75, Reggio Emilia, Italia—*philology.*
Hans Rohr, Oberdorferstrasse 5, 8024 Zürich, Schweiz—*Altphilologie.*
Schuhmacher, Gelderschekade 107, Amsterdam, Nederland—*language.*
Wolfgang Symanczyk, Hubertusweg 32, 404 Neuss, Deutschland—*Klassiche Philologie.*
Thanh-Long, 34 Rue Dekens, 1040 Bruxelles, Belgique—*books in Vietnamese language.*

12. LAW AND CRIMINOLOGY: DROIT ET CRIMOLOGIE: RECHT

Bonfanti, Via Macedonio Melloni, 20129 Milano, Italia.
Chauny & Quinsac, 18 rue Soufflot, 75005 Paris, France.
Duchemin, 18 rue Soufflot, 75005 Paris, France.
Librairie Encyclopedique, 40 rue du Luxembourg, 1040 Bruxelles, Belgique.
Bottega d'Erasmo, Via Gaudenzio Ferrari 9, 10124 Torino, Italia.
Heinrich Gilsing, Kaiserstrasse 3, 8205 Kiefersfelden, Deutschland.

Oreste di Pietro Chellini Gozzini, Via Ricasoli 49, 50122 Firenze, Italia.
B. R. Grüner, Nieuwe Herengracht 31, Amsterdam-C, Nederland.
Michel Guillaume & Cie, 98 rue St.-Pierre, 14 Caen, France.
Juridisch Antiquariaat, Laan van Meerdervoort 45, 's-Gravenhage, Nederland.
Ferdinand Kiep, Hainerweg 46, 6 Frankfurt-am-Main, Deutschland.
Kuppitsch, Schottenring 8, Wien, Österreich.
Herbert Lang & Cie, Munzgraben 2, 3000 Bern, Schweiz.
Pasquale Lombardi, Via San Eufemia 11, 00187 Roma, Italia.
Jean-Jacques Magis, 12 rue Guenéguad, 75006 Paris, France.
Hans Raunhardt, Kirchgasse 17, 8000 Zürich, Schweiz.
J. Schweizer Sortiment, Marsstrasse 4, 8 München 2, Deutschland.
Dr. Karl Stropek, Währingerstrasse 122, 1181 Wien, Österreich.

13. MEDICINE: MÉDICINE: MEDIZIN

L'Ane d'Or, Boite Postale 6, 95450 Vigny, France.
Antiquariaat Antiqua, Herengracht 159, Amsterdam, Nederland—*history of medicine*.
Bertocchi, Strada Maggiore 70, 40125 Bologna, Italia.
Félix Bloch, 10 route de Rolle, 1162 Saint-Prex, Suisse—*histoire de médecine*.
Paul Boulinier, 20 boulevard St.-Michel, 75006 Paris, France.
Bourcy & Paulusch, Wipplingerstrasse 5, 1010 Wien, Österreich.
Alain Brieux, 48 rue Jacob, 75006 Paris, France.
Brighenti, Via Guido Reni 4, 40125 Bologna, Italia—*early medicine*
Pierre Brun, 68 rue Carnot, 13 Pelissanne, France.
François Chamonal, 40 rue le Peletier, 75009 Paris, France.
Cosmos Antiquarian Books, Kastanjelaan 3, 6570 Lochem, Nederland—*history of medicine*.
Chez Durtal, 12 rue Jacob, 75006 Paris, France.
A. L. Van Gendt & Co., Keizersgracht 610, Amsterdam, Nederland.
Gilhofer & Ranschburg, Haldenstrasse 9, 6006 Luzern, Schweiz—*geschichte der Medizin*.
O. A. Hagelin, Tegnergatan 14, 11358 Stockholm, Sverige—*history of medicine*.
Menno Hertzberger, Eemnesserweg 81, Baarn, Nederland.
B. M. Israel, Voorburgwaal 264, Amsterdam, Nederland.
Carl-Ernst Kohlhauer, Graser Weg 2, 8805 Feuchtwangen, Deutschland—*alte Medizin*.
Lange & Springer, Heidelbergerplatz 3, 1 Berlin 33, Deutschland.
W. Maudrich, Alserstrasse 19, 1080 Wien, Österreich.
Jean Michel de Floesser, 28 rue des Remparts, 33 Bordeaux, France—*médecine ancienne*.
Leo S. Olschki, 52046 Lucignano (Arezzo), Italia.
Herbert Preidel, Bismarckstrasse 20, 3011 Gehrden, Deutschland—*medizin, geschichte der medizin*.
C. E. Rappaport, Via Sistina 23, Roma, Italia.
Hans Raunhardt, Kirchgasse 17, 8000 Zürich, Schweiz.
Oscar Rothacker, Hardenbergstrasse 11, 1 Berlin 12, Deutschland.
Oscar Rothacker, Pettenkoferstrasse 18, 8 München 15, Deutschland.
W. N. Schors, Reguliersgracht 52, Amsterdam-C, Nederland.
Hans Ferdinand Schulz, Friedrichring 13, 78 Freiburg, Deutschland.
Thomas-Scheler, 19 rue de Tournon, 75006 Paris, France.
Dr. Helmut Vester, Friedrichstrasse 7, 4 Düsseldorf, Deutschland.

"Veille France", 65 boulevard Général-Leclerc, 33120 Arcachon, France.
Robert Vivien, 41 rue Mazarine, 75006 Paris, France.
J. Vrin, 6 place de la Sorbonne, 75005 Paris, France.
Wötzel, Paul-Ehrlich-Strasse 24, 6 Frankfurt-am-Main, Deutschland.
J. Wristers, Minrebroederstraat 13, Utrecht, Nederland.

14. MUSIC: MUSIQUE: MUSIK UND NOTEN

S. Agostino, Via S. Agostino 17/A, Roma, Italia.
Les Amis de la Musique, 58 rue Dautzenberg, 1050 Bruxelles, Belgique.
Antiquariaat Antiqua, Herengracht 159, Amsterdam, Nederland.
Garnier Arnoul, 39 rue de Seine, 75006 Paris, France.
Bog-Messen, Gammel Kongevej 19, 1610 København-V, Danmark.
Das Bücherkabinett, Poststrasse 14, 2 Hamburg 36, Deutschland.
Candide, 7 rue Montault, 49000 Angers, France.
Creyghton: Musicology-Musica Antiqua, Lassuslaan 45, Bilthoven, Nederland.
Ludwig Doblinger, Dorotheergasse 10, 1010 Wien, Österreich.
Gertrude Drewsen, Fredensgade 16, 2200 København-N, Danmark.
Gérard Ferhadian, 36 rue Montholon, 75009 Paris, France.
Natale Gallini, Via Del Conservatorio 17, 20122 Milano, Italia.
Pierre Girard, 17 rue de Chateaudun, 75009 Paris, France.
Dr. Emil Katzbichler, 8210 Giebing Post Prien, Deutschland.
Robert Legouix, 4 rue Chaveau-Lagarde, 75008 Paris, France.
G. de Lucenay, 15 rue Petite-Fusterie, 84000 Avignon, France.
Ricordi, Negozio di Via Berchet 2, 20121 Milano, Italia.
A. Rombaut, Lievestraat 14, 9000 Gent, Belgie.
Hans Schneider, Mozartweg 1, 8132 Tutzing über München, Deutschland.
Société Livres & Musique, 6 rue Lamartine, 75009 Paris, France.
J. Voerster, Relenbergstrasse 33, 7 Stuttgart, Deutschland.
Mme S. Zlatin, 46 rue Madame, 75006 Paris, France.

15. NATURAL HISTORY: SCIENCES NATURELLES: NATURWISSENSCHAFT

J. Berger, Kohlmarkt 3, 1010 Wien, Österreich—*Archäologie*.
La Bibliofila, Corso Porta Nuova, 20121 Milano, Italia—*geography*.
A. Blanchard, 9 rue de Médicis, 76006 Paris, France—*sciences naturelles*.
E. J. Brill, Oude Rijn 33-A, Leiden, Nederland—*ethnography*.
F. A. Brockhaus, Räpplenstrasse 20, 7000 Stuttgart, Deutschland—*Geographie, Ethnologie, Naturwissenschaften*.
Broekema, 28 Titiaanstraat, Amsterdam, Nederland—*geography*.
Friedrich Burchard, Sonnbornerstrasse 144, 56 Wuppertal-Sonnborn, Deutschland.
Giocondo Cassini, San Marco 2424, 30124 Venezia, Italia—*geography*.
François Chamonal, 40 rue le Peletier, 75009 Paris, France—*géographie*.
Georges Chauvin, 78 rue Mazarine, 75006 Paris, France—*géographie*.
Van Coevorden, Varenstraat 41, Soest, Nederland—*archaeology*.
Gaston Colas, 84 boulevard Raspail, 75006 Paris, France—*archéologie*.
Cosmos Antiquarian Books, Kastanjelaan 3, 6570 Lochem, Nederland.
André Deruelle, 30 rue des Saints-Pères, 75007 Paris, France—*archéologie*.
F. Deuticke, Helferstorferstrasse 4, 1010 Wien, Österreich.

Harri Deutsch, Graefstrasse 47, 6 Frankfurt-am-Main 3, Deutschland.
N. G. Elwert, Reitgasse 7, 355 Marburg, Deutschland—*Geographie*.
Librairie de la Faculté des Sciences, 12 rue Pierre et Marie Curie, 75005 Paris, France—*périodiques de sciences naturelles*.
Erwin Fluhrer, Weisensteigerstrasse 17, 7340 Geislingen/Steige, Deutschland.
R. Friedländer & Sohn, Nonnendammallee 92-f, 1 Berlin 13, Deutschland.
François Girand, 75 rue de Seine, 75006 Paris, France—*géographie*.
Goecke & Evers, Dürerstrasse 13, 415 Krefeld, Deutschland—*Biologie, Zoologie, Botanik, Geologie*.
Gsellius'sche Antiquariat, Hertastrasse 16, 1 Berlin 37, Deutschland—*alte Naturwissenschaften*.
Dr. Rudolf Habelt, Am Buchenhang 1, 53 Bonn 5, Deutschland—*Archäologie*.
O. A. Hagelin, Tegnergatan 14, 11358 Stockholm, Sverige.
Bruno Hessling, Rankestrasse 31, 1 Berlin 30, Deutschland—*Archäologie*.
Andr. Fred. Høst & Søn, Bredgade 35, 1260 København-K, Danmark—*zoology, botany*.
M. L. Huizenga, O.Z.Achterburgwaal 156, Amsterdam, Nederland—*anthropology*.
Antiquariaat Junk, Walderstraat 10, Lochem, Nederland—*natural history, anthropology*.
Kiepert, K.G., Hardenbergstrasse 4, 1 Berlin 12, Deutschland.
Erwin & Rolf Kistner, Briete Gasse 52, 85 Nürnberg, Deutschland.
Rainer Köbelin, Amalianstrasse 53, 8 München 40, Deutschland—*alte Naturwissenschaft*.
Otto Koeltz, Herrnwaldstrasse 6, 624 Königstein-Taunus, Deutschland—*Botanik, Zoologie, Paleontologie, Geologie*.
Carl-Ernst Kohlhauer, Graser Weg 2, 8805 Feuchtwagen, Deutschland—*alte Naturwissenschaften*.
C. Koolemans, Willemsparkweg 164, Amsterdam, Nederland—*ethnography, natural history*.
M. Krebser & Co., Bälliz/Bahnhofbrücke, 3600 Thun, Schweiz.
Detlev Kurth, Am Markt 24, 2202 Barmstedt, Deutschland—*Zoologie, Botanik, Ethnologie, Archäologie*.
Lange & Springer, Heidelbergerplatz 3, 1 Berlin 33, Deutschland.
Louis Leconte, 73 rue des Saints-Pères, 75006 Paris, France.
Löwendahls Antikvariat, P.O. Box 2101, 75002 Uppsala 2, Sverige.
Klaus Lux, Im Hausgarten 33, 7800 Frieburg, Deutschland—*Geographie*.
Lynge & Son, Løvstraede 8, 1152 København-K, Danmark.
Achim Makrocki, Quellenstrasse 14, 35 Kassel, Deutschland—*Geographie*.
Ludwig Mayer, Ltd., Shlomzion Hamalka 4, Jerusalem, Israel—*natural history, archaeology*.
Minerva Antiquariaat, Zeestraat 48, 's-Gravenhage, Nederland—*geography*.
Annie Muriset, 4 place du Molard, 1200 Genève, Suisse—*géographie*.
H. D. Pfann, Rokin 122, N.Z.Voorburgwal 127, Amsterdam, Nederland—*geography*.
A. & J. Picard, 82 rue Bonaparte, 75006 Paris, France—*archéologie*.
Klaus Renner, Konrad-Celtis-Strasse 33, 8 München 25, Deutschland—*Ethnologie, Anthropologie, Archäologie*.
Heinrich Rimanek, Kaiserstrasse 6, 1070 Wien, Österreich.
Renzo Rizzi, Via Cernaia 4, 20121 Milano, Italia—*palaeography*.
Oscar Rothacker, Hardenbergstrasse 11, 1 Berlin 12, Deutschland.
Oscar Rothacker, Pettenkoferstrasse 18, 8 München 15, Deutschland.
Jean Rousseau-Girard, 7 rue de la Bourse, 75002 Paris, France.

SPECIALITÉS SPEZIALITÄTEN

Dr. Martin Sändig, Nelkenstrasse 2, 6226 Walluf 1, Deutschland.
Karl Schmetz, Kleinmrschierstrasse 5, 51 Aachen, Deutschland.
Bücher-Schmidt Antiquariat, Torgasse 4, 8000 Zürich, Schweiz—*Zoologie, Botanik.*
Librairie Scientifique Ancienne, 20 rue des Fossés, 75005 Paris, France—*geologie, paleontologie, prehistoire, speleologie.*
René Simmermacher, Talstrasse 5, 7800 Freiburg, Deutschland—*illustrierte Naturwissenschaft.*
Technisches Antiquariat, Lauteschlagerstrasse 4, 61 Darmstadt, Deutschland.
Wladimir Tiraspolsky, 69 avenue Victor-Cresson, 92 Issy-les-Moulineaux, France.
The Universitas-Booksellers, 9 Shlomzion Hamalka, Jerusalem, Israel—*archaeology.*
Dr. Helmut Vester, Friedrichstrasse 7, 4 Düsseldorf, Deutschland.
La Vie Rustique, 40 avenue Winston Churchill 40, 1180 Bruxelles, Belgique—*natural history, geology.*
V.R.I.L.L.E., 3 rue St.-Philippe-du-Roule, 75008 Paris, France—*archéologie.*
Wasmuth Antiquariat, Hardenbergstrasse 9-a, 1 Berlin 12, Deutschland—*Archäologie.*
Robert Wölfle, Amalienstrasse 65, 8 München 13, Deutschland.
Wötzel, Paul-Ehrlich-Strasse 24, 6 Frankfurt-am-Main, Deutschland.

16. PERIODICALS: PERIODIQUES: ZEITSCHRIFTEN

John Benjamins, Amsteldijk 44, Amsterdam, Nederland—*liberal arts and social science periodicals.*
Bertocchi, Strada Maggiore 70, 40125 Bologna, Italia.
Biblarte Limitada, Rua de Sao Pedro de Alcantara 71, Lisboa, Portugal.
Björck & Börjesson, Kungsgatan 5/II, Stockholm-C, Sverige—*scientific.*
Dawson-France, S.A., Zone Industrielle "La Prairie", 91121 Villebon-sur-Yvette, France.
Europeriodiques, S.A., 31 avenue de Versailles, 78170 La Celle Saint-Cloud, France.
Librairie de la Faculté des Sciences, 12 rue Pierre et Marie Curie, 75005 Paris, France—*sciences naturelles.*
Gérard Ferhadian, 36 rue Montholon, 75009 Paris, France.
Frederiksberg Antikvariat, Gammel Kongevej 120, 1850 København-K, Danmark.
Paul Geuthner, 12 rue Vavin, 75006 Paris, France.
H. Geyer, Hofmühlgasse 14, Wien 6, Österreich.
Heinrich Gilsing, Kaiserstrasse 3, 8205 Kiefersfelden, Deutschland.
George C. Hamel, Brandenburgerstrasse 74, 1 Berlin 31, Deutschland.
Frédéric Van Hoeter, 61 rue St.-Quentin, Bruxelles 4, Belgique.
J. Joly, 6 rue Victor-Cousin, 75005 Paris, France—*périodiques juridiques.*
"Journal Franz" Arnulf Liebing, Werner von Siemans-strasse 5, 87 Würzburg 2, Deutschland.
J. B. Lafitte, 13 rue de Budi, 75006 Paris, France.
Herbert Lang & Cie, Munzgraben 2, 3000 Bern, Schweiz.
Lange & Springer, Heidelbergerplatz, 1 Berlin 33, Deutschland.
Achim Makrocki, Quellenstrasse 14, 35 Kassel, Deutschland.
Louis Moorthamers, 124 rue Lesbroussart, 1050 Bruxelles, Belgique.
Gia Nardecchia, Piazza Cavour 25, 00193 Roma, Italia.

SPECIALITIES

L. M. C. Nierynck, Verdilaan 85, Vlissingen, Nederland—*early newspapers from 16th to 19th century*.
Martinus Nijhoff, Lange Voorhout 9, 's-Gravenhage, Nederland.
Nordiska Antikvariska Bokhandeln, Norra Magasingatan 6, Helsingfors, Suomi.
Rudolf Patzer, Mainzer Berg 23, 6731 Weidenthal, Deutschland.
Presses Académiques Européenes. 98 Chaussée de Charleroi, Bruxelles, Belgique —*scientific*.
Rönnells Antikvariat, Birger Jarlsgatan 32, 11429 Stockholm, Sverige—*scientific*.
Oscar Rothacker, Pettenkoferstrasse 18, 8 München 15, Deutschland.
M. Slatikine et Fils, 15 Cours de Rive, 1200 Genève, Suisse.
Swets & Zeitlinger, Heereweg 347-B, Lisse, Nederland.
E. Von den Velden, Neureuther Strasse 1, 8 München 13, Deutschland.
D. Weil, 1 rue du Dragon, 75006 Paris, France—*périodiques anciens et modernes, littéraires et scientifiques*.

17. PICTORIAL ART: BEAUX-ARTS: KUNST UND GRAPHIK

Theodore Ackermann, Promedadeplatz 11, 8 München, Deutschland.
S. Agostino, Via S. Agostino 17/A, Roma, Italia.
A. Degli Albizi, Piazza Duomo 22-r, Firenze, Italia.
Robert Adler, Junkerngasse 41, Bern, Schweiz.
Aux Amateurs de Livres, 62 avenue de Suffren, 75015 Paris, France.
Bottega Ambrosiana, Via Vitruvio 47, 20124 Milano, Italia.
Amelang, Cranachstrasse 45, 2 Hamburg 52, Deutschland.
Les Amis du Livre, 9 Valaoritis Street, Athens 134, Ellas.
L'Art Ancien, Signaüstrasse 6, 8008 Zürich, Schweiz—*Graphik und Zeichungen grosser Meister*.
Adolf Auer, Volgersweg 43/1, 3 Hannover-C, Deutschland—*alte Graphik*.
Peter Babendererde, Danziger Strasse 49, 24 Lübeck, Deutschland—*dekorative Graphik*.
Paul Bataille, 14 rue Châteauredon, 13 Marseille, France.
Angel Batlle y Tejedor, Calle de la Paja 23, Barcelona 2, España—*engravings, popular art*.
Maurice Baudon, 27 rue de Seine, 75006 Paris, France—*gravures*.
Fernand Beaufils, avenue Victor-Hugo 169, 75016 Paris, France.
A. von der Becke & Sohn, Widenmayerstrasse 43, 8 München 22, Deutschland.
J. L. Beijers, Achter Sint Pieter 14, Utrecht, Nederland—*emblem and other illustrated books, art nouveau*.
A. Bellanger, 5 place du Bon Pasteur, 44 Nantes, France—*gravures*.
Van Berg Antiquariaat, Oude Schans 8, Amsterdam, Nederland.
Gertrud Iris Berger, Finkenau 30, 2 Hamburg 76, Deutschland—*alte und moderne Graphik*.
J. Berger, Kohlmarkt 3, 1010 Wien, Österreich.
Paul Bezzina, 114 St. Lawrence Street, Vittoriosa, Malta—*Maltese engravings*.
Biblarte Ltda, Rua de Sao Pedro de Alcantara 71, Lisboa, Portugal.
Das Bibliographikon, Carmerstrasse 19, 1 Berlin-Charlottenberg 2, Deutschland —*alte Graphik, Farbstiche*.
August Blaizot, 164 faubourg St.-Honoré, 75008 Paris, France.
Bla Tornet, Drottninggatan 85, Stockholm, Sverige.
Bøckmann's Antikvariat, Rosensgade 11, 8000 Aarhus-C, Danmark.
Pierre H. Le Bodo, 31 rue de Bordeaux, 37 Tours, France—*gravures*.

C. G. Boerner, Kasernenstrasse 14, 4 Düsseldorf, Deutschland—*alte Graphik, alte Handzeichnungen.*
Boghallens Antikvariat, Raadhuspladsen 37, 1585 København-V, Danmark.
Bog Messen, Gammel Kongevej 19, 1610 København-V, Danmark.
Helmut Bolenz, Türkenstrasse 48, 8 München, Deutschland.
Hieronymus Bosch, Spuistraat 125, Amsterdam, Nederland—*Dutch art before 1800.*
Paul Boulinier, 20 boulevard St.-Michel, 75006 Paris, France.
Bice Bourlot, Piazza Castello 9, Torino, Italia—*costumes.*
Branners Bibliofile Antikvariat, Bredgade 10, 1260 København-K, Danmark—*illustrated, decorative prints.*
Librairie Bretonne, 1 fue des Fossés, 35000 Rennes, France—*gravures anciennes.*
Louis Broder, 187 boulevard St.-Germain, 75006 Paris, France.
Siegried Brumme, Braubachstrasse 34, 6 Frankfurt-am-Main, Deutschland—*alte Graphik.*
Das Bücherkabinett, Poststrasse 14, 2 Hamburg 36, Deutschland.
Arnold Busck, Fiolstraede 24, 1171 København-K, Danmark—*art, architecture.*
G. Buzzanca, Piazzetta Pedrocchi 4, 35100 Padova, Italia.
Fernand Caffin, 80 rue St.-Lazare, 75009 Paris, France.
Marie & Reine Caillon, 10 rue Montault, 49 Angers, France.
Candide, 7 rue Montault, 49 Angers, France.
Castro e Silva, Rua da Rosa 31, Lisboa, Portugal.
Henri Cazer, 49 rue de Seine, 75006 Paris, France.
Carlo Alberto Chiesa, Via Bigli 11, 20121 Milano, Italia—*illustrated books 15–18 centuries.*
Carl F. Chrispeels, Combahnstrasse 15, 53 Bonn-Beuel 1, Deutschland—*Kunst bis 15 Jahrhunderts.*
Van Coevorden, Varenstraat 41, 75006 Paris, France.
Gaston Colas, 84 boulevard Raspail, 75006 Paris, France—*architecture.*
Maxime Cottet-Dumoulin, 3 rue Séguier, 75006 Paris, France.
Jean Coulet, 1 rue Dauphine, 75006 Paris, France.
Coulet & Faure, 5 rue Drouot, 75006 Paris, France.
Max-Philippe Delatte, 133 rue de la Pompe, 75016 Paris, France.
Mme Delplace, 23 boulevard de Waterloo, Bruxelles 1, Belgique—*prints, drawings, paintings.*
F. Deuticke, Helferstorferstrasse 4, 1010 Wien, Österreich.
Diepenbroick-Grüter, Haus Mark, 4542 Tecklenburg, Deutschland—*Porträts.*
Lucien Dorbon, 156 boulevard St.-Germain, 75006 Paris, France.
F. Dörling, Neuer Wall, 2 Hamburg 36, Deutschland—*Graphik.*
Dresdener Antiquariat, Bautzner Strasse 27, 806 Dresden, D.D.R.—*Kunstwissenschaft.*
Dubouchet, 2 rue Général Foy, 42 St.-Etienne, France.
Maurice Dussarp, 36 rue du Mont Thabor, 75001 Paris, France—*gravures.*
Fritz Eggert, Felix Dahn Strasse 53, 7 Stuttgart, Deutschland.
Alice Elchlepp, Schillerstrasse 14, 3360 Osterode a. Harz, Deutschland—*alte Graphik.*
Meijer Elte, Korte Poten, 13, 's-Gravenhage, Nederland—*fine arts, illustrated books 15–19 century.*
S. Emmering, N.Z.Voorburgwal 304, Amsterdam, Nederland—*Old Master prints.*
Librairie Encyclopedique, rue du Luxembourg 40, 1040 Bruxelles, Belgique.
Galerie Engelberts, 11 Grand Rue, 1204 Gèneve, Suisse—*art contemporain, gravures, livres illustrés par les peintures.*

197

Erasmus Antiquariaat, Spui 2, Amsterdam, Nederland—*history of art*.
Kunstgalerie Esslingen, Grünerweg 17, 73 Esslingen, Deutschland—*illustrierte Bücher des 20 Jahrhunderts, Karikaturen*.
Joseph Fach, Krögerstrasse 2, 6 Frankfurt-am-Main, Deutschland—*Graphik, Handzeichnungen, illustrierte Bücher*.
Michel Fauron, 10 bis rue de Chateaudun, 75009 Paris, France—*livres modernes illustrés*.
Luigi Finzi, Foro Buonaparte 12, 20121 Milano, Italia.
Jean Fournier & Cie, 22 rue du Bac, 75007 Paris, France.
Klaus von Francheville, Marktstrasse 45, 3 Hannover, Deutschland—*dekorative Graphik*.
Frankfurter Bücherstube, Börsenstrasse 2, 6 Frankfurt-am-Main, Deutschland.
Frankfurter Kunstkabinett, Börsenplatz 13, 6 Frankfurt-am-Main, Deutschland.
Günter Fuchs, Cranachplatz 1, 4 Düsseldorf, Deutschland—*Kunst 1880–1975*.
Christian Galantaris, 11 rue de Vaugirard, 75006 Paris, France.
Gallimard, 15 boulevard Raspail, 75007 Paris, France.
Garisenda, Strada Maggiore 14/A, 40125 Bologna, Italia.
Gibert Jeune, 23 quai St.-Michel, 75005 Paris, France.
Hans von Goetz, Wörthstrasse 28, 62 Wiesbaden, Deutschland—*Kunstgeschichte*.
Dr. Hans Eberhard Goldschmidt, Döblinger Hauptstrasse 61, Wien 19, Österreich.
Gonnelli & Figli, Via Ricasoli 14, Firenze, Italia—*old and modern prints*.
Antikvariat Gordin, Nylandsgatan 11, 00120 Helsingfors 12, Suomi.
Robert Goumy, 6 bis rue de Chateaudun, 75009 Paris, France.
Oreste di Pietro Chellini Gozzini, Via Ricasoli 49, 50122 Firenze, Italia.
Antoine Grandmaison, 8 rue de Castiglione, 75001 Paris, France.
Ernst Grosser, Rebbachstrasse 11, 7987 Weingarten, Deutschland—*dekorative Graphik*.
J. Grubb's Antikvariat, Nørregade 47, København-K, Danmark.
Gysbers en Van Loon, Bakkerstraat 7-a, Arnhem, Nederland.
Else Haas, Dollstrasse 7, 807 Ingolstadt 21, Deutschland.
Hachette, 58 rue Jean-Bleuzen, 92170 Vanves, France.
Karl M. Halosar, Margaretenstrasse 35, 1040 Wien, Österreich.
Jean-Jacques Hankard, 25 rue de la Paix, 1050 Bruxelles, Belgique.
A. L. Hasbach, Wollzeile 9, Wien 1, Österreich.
August Hase, Im Trutz 2, Frankfurt-am-Main, Deutschland—*Graphik*.
Elsa Hauser, Schellingstrasse 17, 8 München 13, Deutschland—*alte und moderne Graphik*.

Hauswedell & Nolte, Pöseldorferweg 1, 2 Hamburg 23, Deutschland—*Kunstwissenschaft, Graphik, Handzeichnungen.*
Rudolf Heger, Wollzeile 2, 1010 Wien, Österreich.
Leopold Heidrich, Plankengasse 7, Wien 1, Österreich.
Menno Hertzberger, Eemnesserweg 81, Baarn, Nederland.
Bruno Hessling, Rankestrasse 31, 1 Berlin 30, Deutschland.
Werner Heybutzki, Pfeilstrasse 8, 5 Köln, Deutschland.
Hans Höchterberger, Elsenheimerstrasse 18, 8 München 21, Deutschland—*illustrierte Bücher, Kunstwissenschaft.*
Ernst Hoffmann, Weissadlergasse 3, 6 Frankfurt-am-Main, Deutschland—*Holzschnittbücher, dekorative Graphik.*
Jurgen Holstein, Gerichtsstrasse 7-a, 6240 Königstein, Deutschland.
Karl Hölzl, Seilergasse 3, 1010 Wien, Österreich.
Andr. Fred Høst & Søn, Bredgade 35, 1260 København-K, Danmark.
Bernard Houthakker, Rokin 98, Amsterdam, Nederland—*Rembrandt etchings.*
C. Hovingh & Zn., Kleine Houtstraat 50, Haarlem, Nederland.
Interlibrum Establishment, Schloss-Strasse 6, 9490 Vaduz, Liechenstein.
Gunnar Johanson-Thor, Hallsfarm, 24100 Eslöv, Sverige—*old prints.*
Kaabers Antikvariat, Skindergade 34, 1159 Köbenhavn-K, Danmark.
Karl & Faber, Karolinenplatz 5-A, 8 München 2, Deutschland.
Kauffmann, 28 Stadium Street, Athens 132, Ellas—*engravings.*
René Kieffer, 46 rue St.-André des Arts, 75006 Paris, France—*illustrés modernes.*
Erwin & Rolf Kistner, Breite Gasse 52, 85 Nürnberg, Deutschland—*alte und dekorative Graphik.*

Galerie Klihm, Franz-Joseph-Strasse 9, 8 München 13, Deutschland—*Expressionistische Graphik und Bilder*.

Rainer Köbelin, Amalienstrasse 53, 8 München 40, Deutschland—*dekorative Graphik*.

Jean Lafitte, 106 boulevard Longchamp, 13001 Marseille, France.

Leonce Laget, 75 rue de Rennes, 75006 Paris, France—*beaux-arts, architecture*.

Leonardo Lapiccirella, Lungarno Vespucci 18, 50123 Firenze, Italia—*woodcut books*.

Lardanchet, 10 rue Président Carnot, 69002 Lyon, France—*gravures*.

August Laube & Sohn, Trittligasse 19, 8001 Zürich, Schweiz.

Marcel Lecomte, 17 rue de Seine, 75006 Paris, France—*livres illustrés, beaux-arts, éstampes originales*.

Librairie Legueltel, 17 rue Drouot, 75009 Paris, France.

Günther Leisten, In der Höhle 6, 5 Köln, Deutschland—*Graphik*.

Arnold Levilliers, 118 route de Chartres, 91400 Gometz-le-Chatel, France—*gravures, dessins, beaux-arts*.

Librairie des Galeries, Galerie du Roi 2, 1000 Bruxelles, Belgique—*art, architecture*.

Claus Lincke, Königsallee 96, Düsseldorf, Deutschland.

Louis Loeb-Larocque, 36 rue le Peletier, 75009 Paris, France—*éstampes*.

Margot Loercher, Heubergstrasse 42, 7000 Stuttgart, Deutschland—*Japanische Farbholzschnitte*.

Alexandre Loewe, 85 rue de Seine, 75006 Paris, France.

Bernard Loliée, 72 rue de Seine, 75006 Paris, France—*surrealisme, livres illustrés*.

Marc Loliée, 40 rue des Saints-Pères, 75007 Paris, France.

Madsen-Linds Antikvariat, Klosterstraede 24, 1157 København-K, Danmark.

Sté Many, 12 rue Delambre, 75014 Paris, France.

Hans Marcus, Grabenstrasse 11-A, 4 Düsseldorf, Deutschland—*alte illustrierte Bücher, Graphik*.

Martelli, Via Santo Stefano 43, 40125 Bologna, Italia.

Jacques Matarasso, 2 rue Longchamp, 06 Nice, France—*livres illustrés, beaux-arts, éstampes modernes*.

Galerie Matthiesen, Meinekestrasse 11, 1 Berlin 15, Deutschland—*Graphik, Gemälde, Skulpturen*.

Alain Mazo, 15 rue Guénégaud, 75006 Paris, France.

Mediolanum, Via Montebello 30, 20121 Milano, Italia—*engravings*.

H. Mellgrens, Centrumhuset Östra Larmgatan 17, 41107 Göteborg, Sverige.

Minerva, Zeestraat 48, 's-Granvenhage, Nederland.

Mirto, Ruiz de Alarcon 27, Madrid, España.

Müller & Gräff, Calwerstrasse 54, 7 Stuttgart 1, Deutschland—*Architektur*.

Annie Muriset, 4 place du Molard, 1200 Genève, Suisse—*gravures anciennes*.

Karlheinz Murr, Karolinenstrasse 4, 86 Bamberg, Deutschland—*alte Graphik*.

Fritz Neidhart, Relenbergstrasse 20, 7 Stuttgart, Deutschland—*schöne illustrierte Bücher, Graphik*.

Buchantiquariat Neues Schloss, Stockerstrasse 17, 8027 Zürich, Schweiz.

Horst Nibbe, Auf dem Berlich 9, 5 Köln, Deutschland—*Expressionismus, Kunst, illustrierte Bücher*.

Nicaise, 145 boulevard St.-Germain, 75005 Paris, France—*éditions illustrés, surrealisme, gravures modernes*.

Nierendorf, Hardenbergstrasse 19, 1 Berlin 12, Deutschland—*Kunst, Gemälde, Skulptur, Graphik Deutsche Expressionisten*.

Günther Nobis, Forststrasse 12, 62 Wiesbaden, Deutschland—*illustrierte Bücher*.

Nordiska Antikvariska Bokhandeln, Norra Magasingatan 5, Helsingfors, Suomi —*prints*.

P. C. Notebaart, Postbox 7289, Amsterdam, Nederland—*surrealisme*.

Leo S. Olschki, 52046 Lucignano, Italia—*art, architecture*.

J. P. Parrot, 59 rue de Rennes, 75006 Paris, France.

C. P. J. Van der Peet, 33 Nieuwe Spiegelstraat, Amsterdam, Nederland—*decorative arts, old prints*.

Henri Petiet, 8 rue de Tournon, 75006 Paris, France—*livres illustrés, gravures*.

H. D. Pfann, Rokin 112, Amsterdam, Nederland.

Annemarie Pfister, Petersgraben 18, 4051 Basel, Schweiz.

Libreria Piazza S. Babila, Corso Monforte 2, 20122 Milano, Italia—*old and modern prints*.

Pinkus Genossenschaft, Froschaugasse 7, 8001 Zürich, Schweiz—*illustrierte Bücher*.

La Porte Etroite, 10 rue Bonaparte, 75006 Paris, France—*beaux-arts, tous les écrits sur les arts plastiques*.

Poursin, 21 rue St.-Sulpice, 75006 Paris, France.

Prandi, Viale Timavo 75, Reggio Emelia, Italia—*fine arts, modern prints*.

Arturo Pregliasco, Via Accademia 3 bis, 10123 Torino, Italia—*fine arts, old prints*.

La Proue, 6 rue des Eperonniers, 1000 Bruxelles, Belgique—*modern art, surrealism*.

Guy Prouté, 15 rue du 18-Juin, 92210 Saint-Cloud, France—*éstampes*.

Librairie Quartre Chemins-Editart, 3 place St.-Sulpice, 75006 Paris, France.

C. E. Rappaport, Via Sistina 23, Roma, Italia.

De Renaissance van het Boek, Walpoortstraat 7, 9000 Gent, Belgie—*prints*.

Rivarès, 3 rue Rivarès, 64000 Pau, France—*lithogravures*.

Ludwig Rohrscheid, Am Hof 28, 53 Bonn, Deutschland—*Graphik*.

A. Rombaut, Lievestraat 14, 9000 Gent, Belgie.

Librairie Saint-Louis, 21 rue Servandoni, 75006 Paris, France.

G. & V. Salimbeni, Via Matteo Palmieri 10, 50122 Firenze, Italia.

Bernhard Schäfer, Conradistrasse 2, 3522 Karlshafen, Deutschland—*Graphik*.

Ferdinand Schöningh, Dom Hof 4-c, 45 Osnabrück, Deutschland.

Hanno Schreyer, Euskirchenerstrasse 57, 53 Bonn 1, Deutschland—*alte dekorative Graphik, illustrierte Bücher 15 bis 20 Jahrhundert*.

René Simmermacher, Turnseestrasse 4-a, 6 Frankfurt-am-Main, Deutschland.

René Simmermacher, Talstrasse 5, 7800 Freiburg, Deutschland.

Soave, Via Po 48, 10123 Torino, Italia—*old prints and engravings*.

Galerie Stangl, Briennerstrasse 11, 8 München, Deutschland.

M. A. Steinbach, Hirschenweg 36, 8011 Eglharting, Deutschland—*Kunst, illustrierte Bücher des 20 Jahrhunderts*.

Librairie Stendahl, 4 rue de Sault, 38000 Grenoble, France—*éstampes*.

Antikvariat Sten Ryö, Arsenalsgatan 4, 11147 Stockholm, Sverige—*art, illustrated books, old and modern prints*.

Horst Stobbe, Ottostrasse 11, 8 München 2, Deutschland.

Thornams Antikvariat, Kompagniestrade 16, 1208 København-K, Danmark.

Matthäus Truppe, Stubenberggasse 7, 8011 Graz, Österreich—*Graphik*.

Paul Van der Perre, 21 rue de la Régence, 1000 Bruxelles, Belgique.

A. Van Loock, 51 rue St.-Jean, 1000 Bruxelles, Belgique—*old engravings*.

Galerie Vauquelin, 4 rue Vauquelin, 76200 Dieppe, France.

Venator, Apernstrasse 56, 5 Köln, Deutschland—*dekorative Graphik*.

Jean Viardot, 13 rue de l'Echaudé, 75005 Paris, France.

René Vigneron, 74 rue de Seine, 75006 Paris, France.

Vincent, Freal & Cie, 4 rue des Beaux-Arts, 75006 Paris, France.

H. A. Vloemans, Anna Paulownstraat 10, 's-Gravenhage, Nederland—*modern arts and architecture.*

Galerie Vömel, Königsallee 30, 4 Düsseldorf, Deutschland—*Gemälde, Handzeichnungen, Skulpturen, Graphik.*

Karl Vonderbank, Goethestrasse 11, 6 Frankfurt-am-Main, Deutschland.

V.R.I.L.L.E., 3 rue St.-Philippe-du-Roule, 75008 Paris, France.

Ed. Walz, Lerchenfeldstrasse 4, 8 München 22, Deutschland—*Graphik.*

Wasmuth Antiquariat, Hardenbergstrasse 9-a, 1 Berlin 12, Deutschland—*Kunst, Architektur.*

Lucie & Pierre-André Weill, 6 rue Bonaparte, 75006 Paris, France.

Galerie Welz Salzburg, Sigmund-Haffnergasse 16, Salzburg, Österreich—*Graphik.*

Wiener Antiquariat, Seilergasse 16, Wien, Österreich.

Elfriede Wirnitzer, Ludwig-Wilhelmstrasse 17-a, 757 Baden-Baden, Deutschland —*Graphik.*

Kunstverlag Wolfrum, Augustinerstrasse 10, 1010 Wien, Österreich.

Zentralantiquariat der D.D.R., Talstrasse 1080, Leipzig, D.D.R.

18. RELIGION AND PHILOSOPHY (I): RELIGIONS ET PHILOSOPHIE (I): THEOLOGIE UND PHILOSOPHIE (I)

Theodore Ackermann, Promenadeplatz 11, 8 München, Deutschland—*Geisteswissenschaften.*

Robert Alder, Junkerngasse 41, Bern, Schweiz—*Geisteswissenschaften.*

Alfa Antiquarian Booksellers, P.O. Box 1116, Nijmegen, Nederland—*comparative religion.*

Bottega Ambrosiana, Via Vitruvio 47, 20124 Milano, Italia.

Antiquariat Antiqua, Herengracht 159, Amsterdam, Nederland.

Librairie d'Argences, 38 rue St.-Sulpice, 75006 Paris, France.

Leo Bisterbosch, St. Luciensteeg 22, Amsterdam-C, Nederland—*Catholic books.*

E. J. Bonset, Patrijzenstraat 8, Zandvoort, Nederland—*psychology.*

Bouma's Boekhuis, Turfsingel 3, Groningen, Nederland.

Bourdon, 75 rue de Rennes, 75006 Paris, France—*histoire religieuse.*

Robert Bourdon, 184 bis route de Chateaudun, 45190 Beaugency, France—*religion.*

Bouvier, Am Hof 32, 53 Bonn, Deutschland—*Geisteswissenschaften.*

W. Breinersdorf, Ebitzweg 7, 7 Stuttgart, Deutschland—*Theologie.*

F. A. Brockhaus, Räpplenstrasse 20, 7 Stuttgart, Deutschland—*Geisteswissenschaften.*

Daniel Brun, 6 rue Clodion, 75015 Paris, France.

Georges Chauvin, 78 rue Mazarine, 75006 Paris, France.

H. Coebergh, Gedempte Oude Gracht 74, Haarlem, Nederland.

"De Tille", Wirdumerdijk 24, Leeuwarden, Nederland.

F. Deuticke, Helferstorferstrasse 4, 1010 Wien, Österreich.

N. G. Elwert, Reitgasse 7, 355 Marburg, Deutschland.

S. Emmering, N.Z. Voorburgwal 304, Amsterdam, Nederland—*Judaica.*

Librairie Encyclopedique, 40 rue du Luxembourg, 1040 Bruxelles, Belgique.

Bottega d'Erasmo, Via Gaudenzio Ferrari 9, 10124 Torino, Italia.

Erasmus Antiquariaat, Spui 2, Amsterdam, Nederland—*Judaica.*

Roberte Fricke, Hardenbergplatz 13, 1 Berlin 12, Deutschland.

Gerold & Co., Graben 31, 1011 Wien, Österreich.

Karl Gess, Kanzleistrasse 5, 7750 Konstanz, Deutschland.

Paul Geuthner, 12 rue Vavin, 75006 Paris, France—*Islam, religion.*

De Graaf, Zuideinde 40, Nieuwkoop, Nederland—*Reformation.*
J. Grubb's Antikvariat, Nørregade 47, København-K, Danmark.
Gsellius'sche Antiquariat, Hertastrasse 16, 1 Berlin 37, Deutschland—*Geisteswissenschaften, Philosophie.*
Dr. Annemarie Guyer-Halter, Auf der Mauer 1, 8000 Zürich, Schweiz.
Horst Hamecher, Goethestrasse 74, 35 Kassel, Deutschland—*Geisteswissenschaften.*
Jean-Jacques Hankard, 25 rue de la Paix, 1050 Bruxelles, Belgique.
Sté Hébraica Judaica, 12 rue des Hospitalières St.-Gervais, 75004 Paris, France—*Judaica et Hébraica en toutes langues.*
J. J. Heckenhauer, Holzmarkt 5, 74 Tübingen, Deutschland.
Heckenhauer-Sonnewald, Waldhof 1, 7947 Mengen, Deutschland.
Historica e Utlramarina, Travessa da Queimada 28, Lisboa 2, Portugal—*Judaica.*
Ernst Hoffmann, Weissadlergasse 3, 6 Frankfurt-am-Main, Deutschland—*Reformation.*
M. L. Huizenga, O.Z.Achterburgwal 156, Amsterdam, Nederland.
Iberia, Hirschengraben 6, Bern, Schweiz.
L'Intermédiaire du Livre, 88 rue Bonaparte, 75006 Paris, France.
Adolf Kapp, Bahnhofstrasse 17, 7407 Rottenburg, Deutschland—*Katholische Theologie.*
Jos. A. Kienreich, Sackstrasse 6, 8011 Graz, Österreich.
J. Kitzinger, Schellingstrasse 25, 8 München 13, Deutschland—*Geisteswissenschaften.*
Friedrich Kohlhoff, Holzweg 14/I, 637 Oberursel, Deutschland.
Kuppitsche, Schottenring 8, Wien, Österreich.
Herbert Lang & Cie, Munzgraben 2, 3000 Bern, Schweiz.
Pierre Lemallier, 4 rue des Orfèvres, 67 Strasbourg, France—*Judäisme.*
Richard Levin, Dannebrogsgade 1/IV, 1660 København-V, Danmark—*Judaica.*
Jacques Levy, 46 rue d'Alésia, 75014 Paris, France—*Judaica, Hebraica.*
Dr. Konrad Liebmann, Lürman-Strasse 47, 45 Osnabrück, Deutschland.
Pasquale Lombardi, Via San Eufemia 11, 00187 Roma, Italia.
Librairie "Le Lotus", 53 rue Malibran, 1050 Bruxelles, Belgique—*psychology.*
Alfred Mader, 67 rue St.-Jacques, 75005 Paris, France.
Clemens Müller, Kapellenweg 59, 56 Wuppertal, Deutschland.
Müller & Gräff, Calwerstrasse 54, 7 Stuttgart 1, Deutschland.
Félix Nicolas, Leliestraat 61, Hove, Belgie.
P. C. Notebaart, Postbox 7289, Amsterdam, Nederland.
Leo S. Olschki, 52046 Lucignano, Italia.
Annemarie Pfister, Petersgraben 18, 4051 Basel, Schweiz—*Geisteswissenschaften.*
A. & J. Picard, 82 rue Bonaparte, 75006 Paris, France.
Pinkus Genossenschaft, Froschaugasse 7, 8001 Zürich, Schweiz.
Joachim Reinhardt, Burgrreiheit 8, 48 Bielefeld, Deutschland—*Judaica.*
Hans Rohr, Oberdorferstrasse 5, 8024 Zürich, Schweiz—*Philosophie, Psychologie.*
Ludwig Rosenthal's Antiquariat, Bussumergrintweg 4, Hilversum, Nederland—*Reformation, Protestant and Catholic theology.*
Ludwig H. Schiller, Birkenrain 28, 7811 St. Peter-Schwarzald, Deutschland.
Karl Schmetz, Kleinmrschierstrasse 5, 51 Aachen, Deutschland—*Geisteswissenschaften.*
W. N. Schors, Reguliersgracht 52, Amsterdam-C, Nederland—*comparative religion, psychology.*
Th. Stenderhoff & Co., Alter Firschmarkt 21, 44 Münster, Deutschland.
Jean Tassy, 20 rue de Bresis, 30 Ales, France.

J. Vrin, 6 place de la Sorbonne, 75005 Paris, France.
Carl Wegner, Martin-Luther-Strasse 113, 1 Berlin 62, Deutschland.
Bernhard Wendt, 8081 Buch-am-Ammersee, Oberbayern über München, Deutschland—*Reformation und Gegen-Reformation, Theologie vor 1850, Geisteswissenschaften.*
Wötzel, Paul-Ehrlich-Strasse 24, 6 Frankfurt-am-Main, Deutschland—*Psychologie.*
J. Wristers, Minreoderstraat 13, Utrecht, Nederland.
Zohar, 3 Nahalat Benjamin, Tel Aviv, Israel—*Hebraica, Judaica.*

19. RELIGION AND PHILOSOPHY (II): RELIGIONS ET PHILOSOPHIE (II): THEOLOGIE UND PHILOSOPHIE (II)

Libreria Alessandria, Via Alessandria 216/A, Roma, Italia—*occult.*
B.M.C.F. Antiquariat, Langer Weg 35, 7901 Ulm-Gögglingen, Deutschland—*Bibliotheca magica.*
Librairie Dorbon-Ainé, 19 boulevard Haussmann, 75009 Paris, France—*occultisme.*
Rudolf Ebbel, Schüttingstrasse 7, 29 Oldenburg, Deutschland—*Freimauererei, Mystik.*
Das Gute Buch, Rosengasse 10, 8001 Zürich, Schweiz—*Okkulta.*
Jean-Jacques Hankard, 25 rue de la Paix, 1050 Bruxelles, Belgique—*occult.*
Høst & Søn, Bredgade 35, 1260 København-K, Danmark—*Freemasonry.*
Libraire "Le Lotus", 53 rue Malibran, 1050 Bruxelles, Belgique *occult.*
Alfred Mader, 67 rue St.-Jacques, 75005 Paris, France—*occultisme.*
Joachim Reinhardt, Burgfreiheit 8, 48 Bielefeld, Deutschland—*Occulta, Masonica.*
W. N. Schors, Reguliersgracht 52, Amsterdam-C, Nederland—*alchemy, Freemasonry, occult.*
Robert Vivien, 41 rue Mazarine, 75006 Paris, France—*occultisme.*

20. SOCIOLOGY: SOCIOLOGIE: SOZIOLOGIE

Arno Adler, Hüxstrasse 55, 24 Lübeck, Deutschland—*Wirtschafts-und Sozialwissenschaften.*
L'Ane d'Or, Boite Postale 6, 95450 Vigny, France—*sciences humaines.*
Athenaeum Antiquarian Booksellers, Keizersgracht 6008, 1002 Amsterdam, Nederland—*political science.*
J. L. Beijers, Achter Sint Pieter 14, Utrecht, Nederland—*political economy.*
John Bemjamins, Amsteldijk 44, Amsterdam, Nederland—*social science periodicals.*
Josef Beyer, Ahornweg 15, 5070 Bergisch Gladbach, Deutschland—*Kriegspropagandazettel, Psychologischer Krieg.*
B.M.C.F. Antiquariat, Langer Weg 35, 7901 Ulm-Gögglingen, Deutschland—*Folkloristica.*
Libreria Bonfanti, Via Macedonio Melloni 19, 20129 Milano, Italia—*political science.*
E. J. Bonset, Patrijzenstraat 8, Znadvoort, Nederland—*social sciences.*
Walther Breinersdorf, Ebitzweg 7, Stuttgart-Bad Cannstadt, Deutschland—*Volkskunde.*
Librairie Bretonne, 1 rue des Fossés, 35 Rennes, France—*folklore.*
Brighenti, Via Guido Reni 4, 40125 Bologna, Italia—*economics.*

Pierre Brun, 68 rue Carnot, 13 Pelissanne, France—*économie politique.*
Chauny & Quinsac, 18 rue Soufflot, 75005 Paris, France—*économie politique.*
F. Deuticke, Helferstorferstrasse 4, 1010 Wien, Österreich—*folklore.*
S. Emmering, N.Z.Voorburgwal 304, Amsterdam, Nederland—*political science.*
Librairie Encyclopedique, 40 rue du Luxembourg, 1040 Bruxelles, Belgique—*economics, sociology.*
Roberte Fricke, Hardenbergplatz 13, 1 Berlin 12, Deutschland—*Politik.*
H. Geyer, Hofmühlgasse 14, Wien 6, Österreich.
Antikvariat Gordin, Nylandsgatan 11, 00120 Helsingfors 12, Suomi—*folklore.*
La Guilde, 18 rue de Turbigo, 75002 Paris, France—*sciences humaines.*
Gysbers en Van Loon, Bakkerstraat 7-a, Arnhem, Nederland—*folklore.*
George C. Hamel, Brandenburgerstrasse 74, 1 Berlin 31, Deutschland—*Politik.*
Rudolf Heger, Wollezeile 2, 1010 Wien, Österreich—*Folklore.*
Xavier Jehanno, 12 place Budapest, 75009 Paris, France—*politique.*
Xavier Jehanno, 4 place de l'Eglise, 78 Louveciennes, France—*politique.*
Juridisch Antiquariaat, Laan van Meerdervoort 45, 's-Gravenhage, Nederland—*economics.*
Ferdinand Keip, Hainerweg 46, 6 Frankfurt-am-Main, Deutschland—*Wirtschaft und Gesellschaft.*
Jean Lafitte, 106 boulevard Longchamp, 13001 Marseille, France—*folklore.*
Herbert Lang & Cie, Munzgraben 2, 3000 Bern, Schweiz—*Wirtschaft-und Sozialwissenschaften.*
Livres et Revues de France, 38 rue Desbordes-Valmore, 75016 Paris, France—*sciences humaines.*
Christian Macoir, 1 Val des Roses, Bruxelles, Belgique—*folklore.*
Jean-Jacques Magis, 12 rue Guenégaud, 75006 Paris, France—*sciences économiques, politiques.*
Martelli, Via Santo Stegano 43, 40125 Bologna, Italia—*folklore.*
S. & P. Neser, Kreuzlingerstrasse 11, 775 Konstanz-Bodensee, Deutschland—*Politik.*
H. K. Overdiep, Korte Gasthuesstraat 45, 2000 Antwerpen, Belge—*folklore.*
Dott. Ada Peyrot, Via Consolata, 8, 10122 Torino, Italia—*economics.*
Pinkus Genossenschaft, Froschaugasse 7, 8001 Zürich, Schweiz—*Politik, Socialismus, Arbeiterliteratur.*
Prandi, Viale Timavo 75, Reggio Emilia, Italia—*folklore.*
Wiöhelm Puskas, Weiburggasse 16, 1010 Wien, Österreich—*folklore.*
Günther Richter, Breite Strasse 29, 1 Berlin 33, Deutschland—*Politik.*
Hugo Streisand, Eislebener Strasse 4, 1 Berlin 30, Deutschland—*Politik, Staatswissenschaften, Sozologie.*
J. Vrin, 6 place de la Sorbonne, 75005 Paris, France—*économie politique.*
Carl Wegner, Martin-Luther-Strasse 113, 1 Berlin 62, Deutschland—*Sozialwissenschaften.*
Elisabeth Wellnitz, Sachsenstrasse 35, 61 Darmstadt-Eberstadt, Deutschland—*Politik.*

21. SPORTS, GAMES AND PASTIMES: SPORTS ET JEUX: SPORT UND SPIELE

Libreria Alpina, Via Savioli 39/2, 40137 Bologna, Italia—*mountaineering.*
Bourcy & Paulusch, Wipplingerstrasse 5, 1010 Wien, Österreich—*Alpinismus.*
Bice Bourlot, Piazza Castello 9, Torino, Italia—*sports and pastimes.*
Dias & Andrade, Rua do Carmo 70, Lisboa 2, Portugal—*sports.*

C. F. Labarre, 22 rue Dauphine, 75006 Paris, France—*imagerie, jeux*.
August Müller, Maximiliansplatz 20, 8 München 2, Deutschland—*Englische Sportblätter, Pferde*.
Librairie Scientifique Ancienne, 20 rue des Fossés, 75005 Paris, France—*speleologie*.
Skakhuset, 24 Studiesstraede, 1455 København-K, Danmark—*chess*.
Librairie Stendhal, 4 rue de Sault, 38 Grenoble, France—*alpinisme*.
A. Tavares de Carvalho, Avenida da Republica 46–3, Lisboa, Portugal—*chess*.
La Vie Rustique, 40 avenue Winston Churchill, 1180 Bruxelles, Belgique—*hunting*.
H. de Vries, Gedempte Oude Gracht 27, Haarlem, Nederland—*sports, physical education*.
Wagner'sche Universitäts Buchhandlung, Museumstrasse 4, 6021 Innsbruck, Österreich—*Alpinismus*.
Mme Adré Wahl, 6 rue de Seine, 75006 Paris, France—*alpinisme, speleologie*.

22. TECHNICAL AND EDUCATIONAL: TECHNIQUE ET ERUDITION: TECHNIK

Aux Amateurs de Livres, 62 avenue de Suffren, 75015 Paris, France—*aéronautique, érudition*.
Ernest Artigue, 6 rue du Lorgues, 83 Toulon, France—*marine*.
Arts et Lettres, Le Vieux Chateau, 83 Le Castellet, France—*érudition*.
J. L. Beijers, Achter Sint Pieter 14, Utrecht, Nederland—*history of learning*.
Dorsums Forlag og Antikvarlat, Fr. Nansens-plass 2, Oslo 1, Norge—*marine*.
André Bottin, 2 rue Défly, 06 Nice, France—*érudition*.
Paul Boulinier, 20 boulevard St.-Michel, 75006 Paris, France—*technique*.
Bretonne, 1 rue des Fossés, 35 Rennes, France—*marine*.
Daniel Brun, 6 rue Clodion, 75015 Paris, France—*érudition*.
François Chamonal, 40 rue le Peletier, 75009 Paris, France—*marine*.
Jean Coulet, 1 rue Dauphine, 75006 Paris, France—*art militaire*.
Georges A. Deny, 5 rue du Chêne, 1 Bruxelles, Belgique—*early technology*.
Dias & Andrade, Rua do Carmo 70, Lisboa 2, Portugal—*technical*.
W. C. Van Dijk, Burgwal, 75, Kampen, Nederland—*textbooks*.
Chez Durtal, 12 rue Jacob, 75006 Paris, France—*horologie*.
Alice Elchepp, Schillerstrasse 14, 3360 Osterode a. Harz, Deutschland—*Militaria*.
Gerhard Goldau, Gasteigweg 4, 8022 Grünwald, Deutschland—*Militaria*.
August Hase, Im Trutz 2, 6 Frankfurt-am-Main, Deutschland—*Postgeschichte*.
H. Hugendubel, Salvatorplatz 2, 8 München, Deutschland—*Militaria*.
Kiepert, KG., Hardenbergstrasse 4, 1 Berlin 12, Deutschland—*Technik*.
Rainer Köbelin, Amalienstrasse 53, 8 München 40, Deutschland—*Militaria*.
R. Krey, Braben 13, 1010 Wien, Österreich—*Militaria*.
Lange & Springer, Heidelbergerplatz 3, 1 Berlin 33, Deutschland—*Technik*.
Bouquinerie du Languedoc, 12 rue de l'Université, 34 Montpellier, France—*livres universitaires*.
Les Meilleurs Livres, 18 boulevard St.-Michel, 75006 Paris, France—*érudition*.
Panayiotis Georgiou & Co., P.O. Box 622, Athens, Ellas—*encyclopedias*.
Pierre Petitot, 234 boulevard St.-Germain, 75007 Paris, France—*art militaire*.
L. & J.-H. Pinault, 36 rue Bonaparte, 75006 Paris, France—*marine*.
F. Pinczower, 83 Sokolow Street, Tel Aviv, Israel—*military*.
Jean Polak, 8 rue de l'Échaudé, 75006 Paris, France—*marine*.
Nissen Preminger Ltd., 9 Montefiore Street, Tel Aviv, Israel—*horology*.

Quartier Latin, 21 rue Albert-ler, 17 La Rochelle, France—*enseignement*.
Günther Richter, Breite Strasse 29, 1 Berlin 33, Deutschland—*Militaria*.
Oscar Rothacker, Hardenbergstrasse 11, 1 Berlin 12, Deutschland—*Technik*.
Dr. Martin Sandig, Nelkenstrasse 2, 6226 Walluf 1, Deutschland—*Technik*.
Helmut Gerhard Schulz, Friedrichring 13, 78 Freiburg, Deutschland—*Militaria*.
Heinz Tattermusch, Bergiusstrasse 10, 41 Duisburg-Ruhrort, Deutschland—*Rheinschiffahrt*.
Technisches Antiquariat, Lauteschlagerstrasse 4, 61 Darmstadt, Deutschland—*Technik*.
J. A. Telles da Sylva, Travessa do Marquês de Sá da Bandeira 19-3,Lisboa1, Portugal—*navigation*.
Elisabeth Wellnitz, Sachsenstrasse 35, 61 Darmstadt, Deutschland—*Wehrwesen*.

23. SCIENCE: SCIENCES: WISSENSCHAFTEN

Libreria Alessandria, Via Alessandria 216/A, Roma, Italia—*science*.
Bottega Anbrosiana, Via Vitruvio 47, 20124 Milano, Italia—*science*.
Antiquariaat Antique, Herengracht 159, Amsterdam, Nederland—*history of science*.
Paul Bataille, 14 rue Châteauredon, 13 Marseille, France—*sciences*.
Björck & Börjesson, Kungsgatan 5/II, Stockholm-C, Sverige—*science*.
A. Blanchard, 9 rue de Médicis, 75006 Paris, France—*mathematique, physique, chemie*.
Félix Bloch, 10 route de Rolle, 1162 Saint-Prex, Suisse—*histoire de science*.
Bourlot, Piazza San Carlo 183, 10123 Torino, Italia—*old science*.
Alain Brieux, 48 rue Jacob, 75006 Paris, France—*sciences*.
Brighenti, Via Guido Reni 4, 40125 Bologna, Italia—*early science*.
Pierre Brun, 68 rue Carnot, 13 Pelissane, France—*sciences*.
François Chamonal, 40 rue le Peletier, 75009 Paris, France—*sciences*.
Denyse Chertin, 14 rue de Richelieu, 75001 Paris, France—*sciences anciennes*.
Cosmos Antiquarian Books, Kastenjelaan 3, 6570 Lochem, Nederland—*history of physics, chemistry, astronomy*.
Georges A. Deny, 5 rue de Chêne, 1 Bruxelles, Belgique—*early science*.
Libreria Dotti, Via Della Scrofa 58, 00186 Roma, Italia—*sciences*.
Chez Durtal, 12 rue Jacob, 75006 Paris, France—*sciences*.
Librairie Encyclopedique, 40 rue du Luxembourg, 1040 Bruxelles, Belgique—*science*.
Fritsch, Postfach 1830, 79 Ulm/Donau, Deutschland—*Geschichte der Wissenschaften*.
A. L. Van Gendt & Co., Keizersgracht 610, Amsterdam, Nederland—*old science*.
Gilhofer Antiquariat, Bognergasse 2, 1010 Wien, Österreich—*Wissenschaften*.
Gilhofer & Ranschburg, Haldenstrasse 9, 6005 Luzern, Schweiz—*Geschichte der Wissenschaften*.
Michel Guillaume & Cie, 98 rue St.-Pierre, 14 Caen, France—*sciences*.
Dr. Annemarie Guyer-Halter, Auf der Mauer 1, 8000 Zürich, Schweiz—*Wissenschaften*.
Dr. Rudolf Habelt, Am Buchenhang 1, 53 Bonn 5, Deutschland—*Altertumwissenschaft*.
O. A. Hagelin, Tegnergatan 14, 11358 Stockholm, Sverige—*history of science*.
Menno Hertzberger, Eemnesserweg 81, Baarn, Nederland—*sciences*.
Bruno Hesssling, Rankestrasse 31, 1 Berlin 30, Deutschland—*Altertumwissenschaft*.

Frédéric van Hoeter, 61 rue St.-Quentin, Bruxelles 4, Belgique—*science.*
M. L. Huizenga, O.Z.Achterburgwal 156, Amsterdam, Nederland—*science.*
Interlibrum Establishment, Schloss-Strasse 6, 9490 Vaduz, Liechtenstein—*history of science.*
B. M. Israel, N.Z.Voorburgwal 264, Amsterdam, Nederland—*sciences.*
Gunnar Johanson-Thor, Hallsfarm, 24100 Eslöv, Sverige—*old science.*
Richard Levin, Dannebrogsgade 1/IV, 1660 Købehnavn-V, Danmark—*early science.*
Dr. Konrad Liebmann, Lürman-Strasse 47, 45 Osnabrück, Deutschland— *Wissenschaft.*
Ludwig Mayer, Ltd., Shlomzion Hamalka 4, Jerusalem, Israel—*mathematics.*
Leo S. Olschki, 52046 Lucignano, Italia—*science.*
C. E. Rappaport, Via Sistina 23, Roma, Italia—*science.*
Gerh. Renner, Hechingerstrasse 34, 747 Albstadt 2, Deutschland—*alte Wissenschaft, Mathematik.*
Rönnells Antikvariat, Birger Jarlsgatan 32, 11429 Stockholm, Sverige—*science.*
Jean Rossea-Girard, 7 rue de la Bourse, 75002 Paris, France—*sciences exactes.*
Francis Roux-Devillas, 12 rue Bonaparte, 75006 Paris, France—*sciences anciennes.*
Dr. Martin Sändig, Nelkenstrasse 2, 6226 Walluf 1, Deutschland—*Mathematik, Geschichte der Wissenschaften.*
Santo Vanasia, Via M. Macchi 58, 20124 Milano, Italia—*mathematics, physics, chemistry.*
Jörg Schafer, Hottingerstrasse 5, 8032 Zürich, Schweiz—*Geschichte der Wissenschaften.*

Hans Ferdinand Schulz, Ost-West-Strasse 47, 2 Hamburg 11, Deutschland—*Wissenschaft*.
J. Schweitzer Sortiment, Marstrasse 4, 8 München 2, Deutschland—*Wissenschaft*.
Sibrium Libri, Via Bigli 21, Milano, Italia—*science*.
Soave, Via Po 48, 10123 Torino, Italia—*old books on sciences*.
Sonnewald Heckenhauer, 7947 Mengen, Deutschland—*klassiche Wissenschaft*.
Wolfgang Symanczyk, Hubertusweg 32, 404 Neuss, Deutschland—*Geschichte der Wissenschaften*.
A. Tavares de Carvalho, Avenida da Republica 46–3, Lisboa, Portugal—*sciences*.
Technisches Antiquariat, Lauteschlagerstrasse 4, 61 Darmstadt, Deutschland—*Mathematik*.
Librairie Thomas-Scheler, 19 rue de Tournon, 75006 Paris, France—*sciences*.
Thulins Antikvariat, 57060 Österbymo, Sverige—*old science*.
Matthäus Truppe, Stubenberggasse 7, 8011 Graz, Österreich—*Wissenschaftliche*.
A. Van Loock, 41 rue St.-Jean, 1 Bruxelles, Belgique—*science*.
Jean Viardot, 13 rue de l'Echaudé, 75005 Paris, France—*sciences*.
La Vie Rustique, 40 avenue Winston Churchill, 1180 Bruxelles, Belgique—*exact sciences*.
Wagner'sche Universitäts Buchhandlung, Museumstrasse 4, 6021 Innsbrück, Österreich—*Wissenschaften*.
Wiener Bücherstube, Eschersheimer Landstrasse 18, 6 Frankfurt-am-Main, Deutschland—*Wissenschaften*.
Zentralantiquariat der DDR, Talstrasse 1080, 701 Leipzig, D.D.R—*Wissenschaften*.

24. TOPOGRAPHY AND TRAVEL: REGIONALISME ET VOYAGES: TOPOGRAPHIE UND REISEN

Robert Alder, Junkerngasse 41, Bern, Schweiz—*Helvetica*.
Les Amis du Livres, 9 Valaoritis Street, Athens 134, Ellas.
Aristeucos, Paseo de la Bonanova 14-G, Barcelona, España—*Catalonia*.
Ernest Artigue, 6 rue du Lorgues, 83 Toulon, France.
Peter Babendererde, Danziger Strasse 49, 24 Lübeck, Deutschland—*Städteansichten und Landkarten*.
Alexandre Baer, 2, rue Livingstone, 75018 Paris, France—*livres très rares concernant les Ameriques*.
Paul Bataille, 14 rue Châteauredon, 13 Marseille, France—*voyages*.
A. Bellanger, 5 place du Bon Pasteur, 44 Nantes, France—*voyages, régionalisme*.
Van Berg Antiquariaat, Oude Schans 8–10, Amsterdam, Nederland—*topography*.
Libreria Berruto, Via San Francesco da Paola 10 bis, 10123 Torino, Italia—*topography (Italy, Piedmont)*.
Paul Bezzina, 114 St. Lawrence Street, Vittoriosa, Malta—*Malta—books and maps*.
La Bibliofila, Corso Porta Nuova 2, 20121 Milano, Italia—*Americana, geography*.
Das Bibliographikon, Carmerstrasse 19, 1 Berlin-Charlottenberg 2, Deutschland—*Städteansichten*.
Paul Bisey, 35 plade de la Réunion, 68100 Mulhouse, France—*régionalisme*.
Le Bouquiniste, Via Principe Amedeo 29, 10123 Torino, Italia—*Italian topography*.
Bourcy & Paulusche, Wipplingerstrasse 5, 1010 Wien, & Österreich—*Alpinismus, Austriaca*.
Bice Bourlot, Piazza Castello 9, Torino, Italia—*atlases, maps*.

Bourlot, Piazza San Carlo 183, 10123 Torino, Italia—*geography, Italian topography.*
Branners Bibliofile Antikvariat, Bredgade 10, 1260 København-K, Danmark—*maps, views.*
E. J. Brill, Oude Rijn 33-A, Leiden, Nederland—*Orientalia, Slavica.*
Broekema Antiquariaat, 28 Titianstraat, Amsterdam, Nederland—*geography, cartography, travel.*
Siegfried Brumme, Braubachstrasse 34, 6 Frankfurt-am-Main, Deutschland—*Landkarte, Topographie.*
Herman E. Bub, Kürschner hof 7, 87 Würzburg 2, Deutschland—*alte Städteansichten und Landkarten.*
Das Bücherkabinett, Poststrasse 14, 2 Hamburg 36, Deutschland—*alte Städteansichten und Landkarten.*
Burgersdijk & Niermans, Niermans, Nieuwsteeg 1, Leiden, Nederland—*regional.*
Arnold Busck, Fiolstraede 24, 1171 København-K, Danmark—*topography.*
G. Buzzanca, Piazzatte Pedrocchi 4, 35100 Padova, Italia—*maps.*
Marie & Reine Caillon, 10 rue Montault, 49 Angers, France—*régionalisme.*
Candide, 7 rue Montault, 49 Angers, France—*régionalisme.*
J. W. Cappelens, Kirkegatan 15, Oslo 1, Norge—*old and rare maps and views relating to Scandinavia, Iceland and Greenland, travel and topography.*
Giocondo Cassini, San Marco 2424, 30124 Venezia, Italia—*geography, Italian topography.*
François Chamonal, 40 rue le Peletier, 75009 Paris, France—*géographie, voyages, marine.*
Chariot d'Or, 38 rue des Remparts d'Ainay, 69002 Lyon, France—*régionalisme.*
I. Chmeljuk, 1 rue de Fleurus, 75006 Paris, France—*Slavisme, Europe de l'est.*
Cité des Vieux Livres, 139 Grand Rue, 25 Besançon, France—*histoire locale.*
Pierre Clerc, 13 rue Alexendre-Cabanel, 34 Montpellier, France—*régionalisme.*
Bouquinerie Comtoise, 9 rue Morand, 25 Besançon, France—*régionalisme.*
José Corradini, 18 rue Vineuse, 75016 Paris, France—*Americana.*
Maxime Cottet-Dumoulin, 3 rue Séguier, 75006 Paris, France—*régionalisme.*
Eugen Crusius, Karl-Marx-Strasse 15, 675 Kaiserslautern, Deutschland—*Pfalzliteratur.*
Damms Antikvariat, Tollbodgatan 25, Oslo 1, Norge—*atlases and maps, topography.*
Henri Danigo, 17 rue Marc-Sangnier, 29 Quimper, France—*Bretagne.*
Ernest Dargent, 11 rue Alain-Blanchard, 76 Rouen, France—*Normandie.*
Francis Dasté, 16 rue de Tournon, 75006 Paris, France—*topographie de Paris.*
Madame Delplace, 23 boulevard de Waterloo, Bruxelles 1, Belgique—*topography.*
F. Dörling, Neuer Wall, 2 Hamburg 36, Deutschland—*Städteansichten.*
Dubouchet, 2 rue Général Foy, 42 St.-Etienne, France—*régionalisme.*
Durance, 5 allée d'Orleans, 44 Nantes, France—*régionalisme, voyages.*
Edi Centre J. P. Krippler-Muller, 17 rue Gibraltar, Luxembourg—*Luxembourg.*
N. G. Elwert, Reitgasse 7, 355 Marburg, Deutschland—*Deutsche Orts- und Landeskunde, Geographie.*
S. Emmering, N.Z.Voorburgwal 304, Amsterdam, Nederland—*Americana (West-Indies).*
Librairie de l'Europe, 1 Val des Roses, 1 Bruxelles, Belgique—*topographie.*
Europeriodiques, 31 avenue de Versailles, 78170 La Celle St.-Cloud, France—*régionalisme, extrême Orient, Japan.*
Louis Fillet, 13 rue de Boigne, 73 Chambéry, France—*régionalisme.*
Luigi Finzi, Foro Buonarte 12, 20121 Milano, Italia—*Italian topography.*

M. Fiol, Olmos 119-A, Palma de Mallorca, España—*rare books on Majorca.*
Erwin Fluhrer, Weisensteigerstrasse 17, 7340 Geislingen/Steige, Deutschland—*Länder und Ortsbände von Westdeutschland.*
Klaus von Francheville, Marktstrasse 45, 3 Hannover, Deutschland—*Ansichten Topographie.*
Louis Gangloff, 20 place de la Cathédrale, 67 Strasbourg, France—*régionalisme, Alsace.*
Gangloff, 13 avenue Auguste-Wicky, 68100 Mulhouse, France—*régionalisme, Alsace.*
Garisenda Libri, Strada Maggiore 14/A, 40125 Bologna, Italia—*geography.*
Paul Geuthner, 12 rue Vavin, 75006 Paris, France—*Afrique, Egypte, Extrême Orient.*
Gilhofer Buchantiquariat, Bognergasse 2, 1010 Wien, Österreich—*Austriaca, Bohemia.*
François Girand, 76 rue de Seine, 75006 Paris, France—*géographie, régionalisme —livres et gravures.*
Gordin, Nylandsgatan 11, 00120 Helsingfors 12, Suomi—*Finnish books, prints and maps, travels, Baltic, Russia, Scandinavia.*
Paul Gothier, 3 rue Bonne Fortune, Liège, Belgique—*Belgicana.*
B. R. Grüner, Neiuwe Herengracht 31, Amsterdam-C, Nederland—*Orienatlia.*
Gsellius'sche Antiquariat, Hertastrasse 16, 1 Berlin 37, Deutschland—*alte Städteansichten und Landkarten.*
Librairie Guénégard, 10 rue de l'Odéon, 75006 Paris, France—*régionalisme.*
Max Günther, Charlottenbrunnerstrasse 5-a, 1 Berlin 33, Deutschland—*Baedeker.*
Gysbers en Van Loon, Bakkerstraat 7-a, Arnhem, Nederland—*Dutch topography.*
Else Haas, Dollstrasse 7, 807 Ingolstadt 21, Deutschland—*Bavarica, Bayerische, Städtegraphik.*
Dr. Rudolf Habelt, Am Buchenhang 1, 53 Bonn 5, Deutschland—*Ostasien.*
O. A. Hagelin, Tegnergatan 14, 11358 Stockholm, Sverige—*travels.*
Halbert, Wahle & Cie, 11 rue des Carmes, 4000 Liège, Belgique—*local history, topography.*
Hamburgensien-Meyer, Poststrasse 2, 2 Hamburg 36, Deutschland—*Topographie.*
Harrassowitz, Taunusstrasse 5, 62 Wiesbaden, Deutschland—*Orientalistik.*
Hans Hartinger, Xantener Strasse 14, 1 Berlin 15, Deutschland—*Slavica, Orientalia.*
V. A. Heck, Kärntner Ring 12, 1010 Wien, Österreich—*Austriaca, alte Landkarten.*
J. J. Heckenhauer, Holzmarkt 5, 74 Tübingen, Deutschland—*Slavischen Lander.*
Heckenhauer-Sonnewald, Waldhof 1, 7947 Mengen, Deutschland—*Slavischen Lander.*
Leopold Heidrich, Plankengasse 7, Wien 1, Österreich,—*Austriaca, Viennennsia.*
Libreria Hesperia, Plaza Lose Antonio 10, Zaragoza, España—*old and rare Hispanica, Americana.*
Historia e Ultramarina, Travessa da Queimada 28k Lisboa 2, Portugal—*Africana, maps.*
Frédérick van Hoeter, 61 rue St.-Quentin, Bruxelles 4, Belgique—*topography.*
Wilhelm Hofmann, Bismarckstrasse 98, 67 Ludwigshafen, Deutschland—*Landkarten, Pfalz und Rhein.*
Eduard Höllrigl, Sigmund-Haffner-Gasse 10, 5020 Salzburg, Österreich—*Austriaca.*
Karl Hölzl, Seilergasse 3, 1010 Wien, Österreich—*alte Landkarten.*
L.Homme de Fer, 32 rue des Dominicans, 54 Nancy, France—*Lorraine, Alsace.*

H. Hugendubel, Salvatorplatz 2, 8 München, Deutschland—*Bavarica*.

Interlibrum Establishment, Schloss-Strasse 6, 9490 Vaduz, Liechtenstein—*Helvetica*.

L'Invitation au Voyage, 15 quai St.-Michel, 75005 Paris, France—*voyages*.

B. M. Israel, N.Z.Voorburgwal 264, Amsterdam, Nederland—*travel*.

N. Israel, Keizersgracht 526, Amsterdam, Nederland—*cartography, travel, voyages*.

Xavier Jehanno, 12 place Budapest, 75009 Paris, France—*voyages*.

Boris Kaplanski, 8 rue du Loing, 75014 Paris, France—*Rossica*.

Kauffmann, 28 Stadium Street, Athens 132, Ellas—*Greece, Turkey, maps*.

Heinrich Kerler, Platzgasse 26, 7900 Ulm, Deutschland—*Landeskund, Baden-Württemberg*.

Jos. A. Kienrich, Sackstrasse 6, 8011 Graz, Österreich—*Austriaca*.

Frank Kirkop, 106 Blanche Street, Sliema, Malta—*Malta*.

Klaussner, Prof.-Kurt-Huber-Strasse 19, 8032 Gräfelfing, Deutschland—*Bavarica*.

Kniha, Malé Námesti No. 11, Praha 1, Ceskoslovensko—*topography*.

C. Koolemans, Willemsparkweg 164, Amsterdam, Nederland—*Africa, Australia*.

Bouquinerie du Languedoc, 12 rue de l'Université, 34 Montpellier, France—*régionalisme*.

Lengerts Antikvariat, Adelgatan 19, Malmö-C, Sverige—*topography*.

Lestringant, 123 rue Général-Leclerc, 76 Rouen, France—*Normandie*.

Franz Leuwer, Am Wall 171, 28 Bremen, Deutschland—*Bremen, Norddeutschland*.

Libri, 6 rue du Pont, 71 Macon, France—*régionalisme*.

Louis Loeb-Larocque, 36 rue le Peletier, 75009 Paris, France—*atlas, voyages*.

Logos Bookshop, 38 Ben Yehuda Street, Tel Aviv, Israel—*Palestine—books, maps, engravings*.

Loose, Papestraat 3, 's-Gravenhage, Nederland—*topography*.

Jules Lorieul, 3 rue de Poterie, 50 Valognes, France—*régionalisme*.

Librairie "Le Lotus", 53 rue Malibran, 1050 Bruxelles, Belgique—*Orientalia*.

Löwendahls Antikvariat, P.O. Box 2101, 75002 Uppsala 2, Sverige—*travels, Scandinavia*.

G. de Lucenay, 15 rue Petite-Fusterie, 84 Avignon, France—*Provence*.

A. Lunge Larsen, Øygardveien 16-E, Bekkestua, Norge—*Scandinavia*.

Lynge & Son, Løvstraede 8, 1152 København-K, Danmark—*Greenland*.

Adrien Maisonneuve, 11 rue St.-Sulpice, 75006 Paris, France—*l'Orient et l'Orientales*.

MAM, 192 Ledra Street (Flat 4), Nicosia, Cyprus—*Cyprus*.

Ludwig Mayer Limited, Shlomzion Hamalka, 4, Jerusalem, Israel—*Orientalia*.

Mellgrens Antikvariat, Centrumhuset Östra Larmgatan 17, 41107 Göteborg, Sverige—*Old maps*.

Metais, 12 rue Jean Prieur, 27340 Pont de l'Arche, France—*Régionalisme Normand*.

Morvran, 16 bis rue René-Madec, 29000 Quimper, France—*Bretagne et pays celtiques*.

August Müller, Maximiliansplatz 20, 8 München 2, Deutschland—*Städteansichten, Landkarten*.

Clemens Müller, Kapellenweg 59, 56 Wuppertal-Barmen, Deutschland—*Topographie*.

Rudolf Muller, P.O. Box 9016, Amsterdam, Nederland—*Geography, geology, cartography*.

Karlheinz Murr, Karolinen-Strasse 4, 86 Bamberg, Deutschland—*Städteansichten und Landkarten*.

Ge. Nabrink & Zoon, Korte Korsjespoortstraat 8, Amsterdam-C, Nederland—*Orientalia.*

Buchantiquariat Neues Schloss, Stockerstrasse 17, 8027 Zürich, Schweiz—*Helvetica.*

Gustav Neuwirth, Frankfurterstrasse 16/I, 71 Heilbronn, Deutschland—*Alte Stiche (Städteansichten) Deutschland und Osteuropa.*

Nordiska Antikvariska Bokhandeln, Norra Magasingatan 6, Helsingfors, Suomi —*Maps, Scandinavia.*

H. K. Overdiep, Korte Gasthuesstraat 45, 2000 Antwerpen, Belge—*Belgium.*

C. P. J. can der Peet, Jansweg 39, Haarlem, Nederland—*Orientalia.*

C. P. J. van der Peet, 33–35 Nieuwe Spiegelstraat, Amstersdam, Nederland—*Old maps and prints. Oriental, Asiatic, African etc.*

Ada Peyrot, Via Consolata 8. 10122 Torino, Italia—*Topography.*

Jean Peysson, 7 rue du Plat, 69 Lyon, France—*Régionalisme.*

A. & J. Picard, 82 rue Bonaparte, 75006 Paris, France—*Régionalisme.*

F. Pinczower, 83 Sokolow Street, Tel Aviv, Israel—*Middle East.*

Jean Polak, 8 rue de l'Échaudé, 75006 Paris, France—*Voyages.*

Quartier Latin, 21 rue Albert-Ier, 17000 La Rochelle, France—*Régionalisme.*

G. Raffy, 85 rue des Rosiers, 93400 Saint-Ouen, France—*Topographie.*

Librairie Raoust, 11 rue Neuve, 59000 Lille, France—*Régionalisme, Flandre-Artois.*

Joachim Reinhardt, Burgfreiheit 8, 48 Bielefeld, Deutschland—*Westphalica.*

A. Remy, 25 rue Stanislas, 54000 Nancy, France—*Régionalisme.*

De Renaissance van het Boek, Walpoortstraat 7, 9000 Gent, Belgie—*Old maps.*

Ringstøms Antikvariat, Ullevalsveien 1, Oslo 1, Norge—*Topographie.*

Librairie Rivarès, 3 rue Rivarès, 64000 Pau, France—*Régionalisme, Pyrénées.*

Hans Rohr, Oberdorferstrasse 5, 8024 Zürich, Schweiz—*Helvetica.*

A. Rombaut, Lievestraat 14, 9000 Gent, Belgie—*Topographie.*

Rönnells Antikvariat, Birger Jarlsgatan 32, 11429 Stockholm, Sverige—*Old Swedish maps and views.*

R. B. Rosenthal, Rua do Alecrim 47–4. (Salas D) Lisboa, Portugal—*Africa.*

Francis Roux-Devillas, 12 rue Bonaparte, 75006 Paris, France—*Americana.*

Gaston Saffroy, 4 rue Clément, 75006 Paris, France—*Histoire régionale.*

H. Samuelian, 51 rue Monsieur le Prince, 75006 Paris, France—*Orientalisme, Arabie, Arménie, Extrême Orient.*

Sartoni et Cerveau, 101 rue de Seine, 75006 Paris, France—*Cartes, Atlases.*

Ludwig H. Schiller, Birkenrian 28, 7811 St. Peter-Schwarzwald, Deutschland—*Baden, Elsass.*

Hanno Schreyer, Euskirchenerstrasse 57–59, 53 Bonn 1, Deutschland—*Alte Landkarten.*

M. Slatkine et fils, 15 Cours de Rive, 1200 Genève, Suisse—*Romanica, Helvetica.*

Sonnewald-Heckenhauer, 7947 Mengen, Deutschland—*Ost Europa.*

Wolfgang Staschen, Bülowstrasse 11, 1 Berlin 50, Deutschland—*Stahlstich Ansichten.*

Librairie Stendhal, 4 rue de Sault, 38000 Grenoble, France—*Voyages.*

Hartwig Strück, Bäringerstrasse 4, 338 Goslar, Deutschland—*Harz.*

Edmund Tamiz, 30 rue Madame, 75006 Paris, France—*Voyages.*

A. Tavares de Carvalho, Avenida da Republica 46–3, Lisboa, Portugal.—*early and rare books on Brazil.*

J. A. Telles da Sylva, Travessa do Marquès de Sá da Bandeira 19–3, Lisboa 1, Portugal—*Portuguese and Spanish explorations.*

Editions Thanh-Long, 34 rue Dekens, 1040 Bruxelles, Belgie—*Far East.*

Gérard Thomas, 1 rue des Fossés, Rennes, France—*Régionalisme*.
Librairie Thomas-Scheler, 19 rue de Tournon, 75006 Paris, France—*Voyages*.
Michéle Trochon, 76 rue du Cherch-Midi, 75006 Paris, France—*tiers monde francophone*.
Universitas Booksellers, 9 Shlomzion Hamalka, Jerusalem, Israel—*Cartography*.
Van Benthem en Jutting, Lange Delft 64, Middelburg, Nederland—*Topography*.
Francine van der Perre, rue de la Madeleine 23, 1000 Bruxelles, Belgique—*Topographie*.
A. W. Vandevelde, Dweerstraat 6, Bruges, Belgique—*Flandrica, Far East*.
A. van Loock, rue Saint-Jean 51, 1000 Bruxelles, Belgique—*Travel*.
Librairie Vasiliu, 67 rue des Martyrs, 75009 Paris, France—*Tourisme*.
Galerie Vauquelin, 4 rue Vauquelin, 76200 Dieppe, France—*Régionalisme*.
Jean Viardot, 13 rue de l'Echaudé, 75005 Paris, France—*Voyages*.
La Vie Rustique, Avenue Winston Churchill 40, 1180 Bruxelles, Belgique—*Travels*.
Louis Vuille, Maison Rouge 5, 1400 Yverdon Suisse.—*Gravures de vues; voyages*.
Ed. Walz, Lerchenfeldstrasse 4, 8 München 22, Deutschland—*Städteansichten*.
Carl Wegner, Martin-Luther-Strasse 113, 1 Berlin 62, Deutschland—*Berlinensia; Städteansichten*.
Wolfgang Weidlich, Savignystrasse 61, 6 Frankfurt am Main, Deutschland—*Ost- und Mitt-el Deutschland*.
Julius Weise, Königstrasse 17, 7 Stuttgart, Deutschland—*Württembergica*.
Galerie Widmer, Neugasse 35, 9000 St. Galen, Schweiz—*Helvetica, Reisewerke, Atlanten*.
Angelos Zambakis, 04 Solonis, Athens, Ellas—*Maps*.
Zohar, 3 Nahalat Benyamin, Tel Aviv, Israel—*Orientalia*.

LIST OF ADVERTISERS

LISTE DES ANNONCES
VERZEICHNIS DER INSERATEN

Garnier Arnoul, Paris, France   59

Josef Beyer, Bergisch Gladbach,
   Deutschland   27
The Bookdealer, London,
   England   xxviii
Hieronymus Bosch,
   Amsterdam, Nederland   108
Henry Bristow of Ringwood,
   England   xxx

Cat Book Center, New Rochelle,
   N.Y., U.S.A.   185
Stanley Crowe, London,
   England   186
Cultural Interchange Service,
   London, England   xiv

Peter Eaton, London and Ayles-
   bury, England   160

Manuel Ferreira, Porto, Portugal   129
Günther Fuchs, Düsseldorf,
   Deutschland   29

Thomas C. Godfrey, York,
   England   148
Le Grenier du Collectionneur,
   Bruxelles, Belgique   3

Else Haas, Ingolstadt,
   Deutschland   45
Hachette, Vanves, France   78
Horst Hamecher, Kassel,
   Deutschland   23
Richard Hatchwell,
   Chippenham, England   167
Dr. Ernest Hauswedell & Co.,
   Hamburg, Deutschland   24

Nico Israel, Amsterdam,
   Nederland   110

Antiquariaat Junk, Lochem,
   Nederland   116

Frank Kirkop, Sliema, Malta   106

Henri Laffitte, Paris, France   63
Dr. Liebmann, Osnabrück,
   Deutschland   30
Livres et Revues de France,
   Paris, France   76
Pasquale Lombardi, Roma,
   Italia   90
John Lyle, Sidmouth, England   167

La Maison du Livre, Angoulême,
   France   77
Achim Makrocki, Kassel,
   Deutschland   25
May and May, London, England   199
Konrad Meuschel, Bonn,
   Deutschland   31

L.M.C. Nierynck, Vlissingen,
   Nederland   117

Leo S. Olschki, Lucignano, Italia   98

Albert J. Phiebig, White Plains,
   N.Y., U.S.A.   189
Piccadilly Rare Books, London,
   England   191

P. J. Radford, Sheffield Park,
   Sussex, England   xx
P. R. Rainsford, St. Ives,
   Cornwall, England   198
Rinhart Galleries, Litchfield,
   Conn. U.S.A.   208
Rossignol, Cannes et Les Arcs,
   France   86

Sawyers, London, England   xii

LIST OF ADVERTISERS